VICTORS IN BLUE

MODERN WAR STUDIES

VICTORS IN BLUE

How Union Generals Fought the
Confederates, Battled Each Other, and
Won the Civil War

Albert Castel with Brooks D. Simpson

Maps by George Skoch

University Press of Kansas

Published by the University Press of Kansas (Lawrence, Kansas 66045),
which was organized by the Kansas Board of Regents and is operated
and funded by Emporia State University, Fort Hays State University,
Kansas State University, Pittsburg State University, the University of
Kansas, and Wichita State University

Library of Congress Cataloging-in-Publication Data

Castel, Albert E.
Victors in blue : how Union generals fought the Confederates,
battled each other, and won the Civil
War / Albert Castel with Brooks D. Simpson.
p.   cm. — (Modern war studies)
Includes bibliographical references and index.
ISBN 978-0-7006-1793-7 (cloth : alk. paper) 1. United States—
History—Civil War, 1861–1865—Campaigns. 2. Generals—United States—
History—19th century. 3. Command of troops—History—19th
century. 4. United States. Army—History—Civil War, 1861–1865.
I. Simpson, Brooks D. II. Title.
E470.C25 2011
973.7'3—dc23
2011029923

British Library Cataloguing-in-Publication Data is available.
Printed in the United States of America

10 9 8 7 6 5 4 3 2 1

The paper used in this publication is recycled and contains 30 percent
postconsumer waste. It is acid free and meets the minimum requirements
of the American National Standard for Permanence of Paper for Printed
Library Materials Z39.48-1992.

TO GEORGE ANN CASTEL . . . MY POOCHIE
1933–2010

A long war produces upon a democratic army the same effects that a revolution produces upon a people; it breaks through regulations, and allows extraordinary men to rise above the common level. Those officers whose bodies and minds have grown old in peace, are removed, or superannuated, or they die. In their stead, a host of young men are pressing on. . . . They are bent on advancement at all hazards, and perpetual advancement.
—Alexis de Tocqueville, *Democracy in America,* 1840

I have only just now found out what military jealousy is.
—Abraham Lincoln, September 5, 1862

CONTENTS

MAPS AND ILLUSTRATIONS

PREFACE

This book's purpose is threefold. First, it describes succinctly the battles and/or campaigns that contributed decisively to Union victory in the Civil War and explains how they did so. Second, it examines the performances of the generals who achieved these victories—the "victors in blue"—with a view to judging the quality of their generalship. And third, when pertinent, it takes note of what might be termed the war within a war that occurred among the top Union generals and how it affected their conduct of military operations.

With the exception of the very first, all of the campaigns and consequent battles discussed herein have been the subject of many books—in some instances perhaps too many. Hence, what follows usually offers little new by way of facts, and if some of the analyses seem somewhat original, even heretical, as a rule they merely restate views expressed long ago but which have become buried beneath the ever-accumulating historical silt deposited by subsequent chroniclers of the "American Iliad." All I have endeavored to do, when deemed appropriate, is excavate and present these views in a more objective fashion supported by greater documentation—an exercise, if you will, in interpretative archeology.

The closest this book comes to exploring some hitherto uncharted historical terrain is when it deals with the aspirations of the generals who comprise its main cast of characters and how they endeavored to attain them. All of them possessed superior personal qualities, albeit of different kinds and degrees, and all were West Pointers who found in the Civil War a once-in-a-lifetime opportunity to ascend the ladder of military rank, power, and glory, thereby realizing ambitions far transcending their prewar professional expectations—supposing they still retained any. They also recognized, once hostilities began and they achieved some measure of success on the battlefield, that extremely few of them would be able to reach the top rungs of that ladder. Only one of them would become commander of the whole army and from there rise to the only place higher still. Such being the case, intense and sometimes vicious rivalries were bound to occur among them, and so they did—rivalries complicated by the presence in the army of high-ranking non–West Pointers with political wagons attached to the stars on their shoulders. This competition had profound consequences for both their careers and the course of the war, as shall be demonstrated in ensuing pages.

To repeat in order to emphasize, none of the interpretations contained in this book is truly original. Yet some are likely to be found novel, even outrageous. I, of course, hope for agreement, the more the merrier, but I am prepared for disagreement, mayhap vehement. Indeed, I shall welcome it: passionate dissent is preferable to passive indifference.

The first thirteen chapters reflect my views on the subject matter therein discussed. For the final five chapters, I have had some assistance from a once-young historian, Brooks D. Simpson, who is not above having opinions of his own. Occasionally, Simpson persuaded me that I should reconsider some of my own views, and at other times we found ourselves in agreement, perhaps to the surprise of one or both of us. However, when we have disagreed, the views expressed in the book remain mine. Simpson can write his own book to clear his name.

Prologue

On Judging Civil War Generals

THE NORTH'S IMMENSE ADVANTAGE IN MANPOWER, manufacturing, material, and money made its victory in the Civil War possible but not inevitable. Factors other than sheer strength determine the outcomes of wars. Chief among them is quality of military leadership. Sufficient superiority in the skill of its army commanders would have more than compensated for the Confederacy's inferiority in everything else except the courage of its soldiers. "It was not the legions," spake Napoleon, "which crossed the Rubicon, but Caesar."[1]

The Confederates could have realized command superiority in two ways, one positive, the other negative. The positive way would have been for their top generals to have been so outstanding that their Union counterparts, even if competent, still would have lost more battles than they won, especially the decisive ones. Unfortunately for them, they produced only one such general—Robert E. Lee. Thanks mainly to him they did have three opportunities, potential at least, to win the war and their independence: (1) In the early fall of 1862, when Lee, following his victories near Richmond and at Second Manassas, invaded Maryland; (2) in the summer of 1863 when Lee, having defeated a Federal army twice the size of his own at Chancellorsville, marched into Pennsylvania; and (3) as autumn approached in 1864, with Lee having fought Grant to a standstill in Virginia, inflicting such heavy losses on his army that Northern morale plummeted and Lincoln despaired of victory both in the upcoming presidential election and in the war.

But the South failed to produce another great commander, one able to do for it in the West what Lee did for it in the East. Conceivably, Albert Sidney Johnston might have been that commander had he not lost his life while seemingly winning the Battle of Shiloh on April 6, 1862. What is known beyond reasonable doubt is that none of Johnston's successors in the West—P.G.T. Beauregard, Braxton Bragg, Joseph E. Johnston, and John Bell Hood—displayed an extraordinary talent for generalship. The most that can be said for any one of them is that he might have been able to defeat a Federal force of equal or lesser size, as did Bragg at Chickamauga; but even that victory was the product of luck rather than skill, and it turned out to be pyrrhic (see chapters 12 and 13). As for Joseph Johnston, commonly deemed the ablest of them, only three times during four years of more-or-less active service did he attempt to defeat an enemy army by attacking it.

Each time he applied the same basic method, and not once did he succeed. He was the Southern equivalent of his good prewar friend George B. McClellan in that he was so afraid of losing that he was incapable of winning except when the foe was obliging enough to assault him in an impregnable position (Kennesaw Mountain). That the end of the war found him commanding what by then passed for the Confederacy's only major army other than Lee's is a testimony to the South's shortage of generals competent to head more than a corps or its equivalent.[2]

The negative way in which the South could have enjoyed a decisive edge in military leadership was for all of the Federal commanders to have been so inept that even mediocre ability on the part of the Confederate generals would have provided war-winning superiority. This, obviously, did not happen. The Union developed some top generals who were, or became, highly capable—in some instances more than that—and thus able to apply the North's greater power in a fashion that achieved total Union victory.

What follows are accounts of the decisive applications of that power and the reasons they were decisive. At the same time judgments will be offered about the quality of generalship displayed by the Union commanders who did the applying—the "victors in blue." That being the case, a statement of the criteria by which their performance is assessed should be, and therefore will be, given. First, though, let us examine how Civil War commanders went about their job of commanding and why.

During the Civil War the means for commanding in battle a major army—defined here as consisting by 1862 of at least 25,000 men but usually many more—still were emerging from what the Israeli military historian Martin Van Creveld aptly terms the "stone age of command."[3] For all practical purposes the leader of such an army could personally supervise and direct no greater areas of a battlefield than did Alexander the Great, Hannibal, Julius Caesar, Belisarius, Charlemagne, Gustavus Adolphus, or, for that matter, Frederick the Great and Napoleon. Indeed, his ability to control what went on actually was less than that of those mighty warriors. Two reasons explain why. First, thanks to the steamboat and, above all, the railroad, which were first used on a large scale in the Civil War, both the North and the South put into the field and maintained far bigger armies and more of them than had normally been the case in the Western world prior to the nineteenth century.[4] Second, infantry firepower vastly increased as rifles superseded smoothbores, breechloaders, and muzzleloaders, and repeaters began replacing singleshooters. The enhanced range and accuracy of artillery made it necessary, as well as possible, to employ less compact troop formations, with the result that the Civil War's larger armies occupied far broader fronts than their European predecessors. Thus, to provide a comparison derived from the two most written about, at least in English, battles in all history, on the third day of Gettysburg (July 3, 1863), Robert E. Lee's army, by then reduced by casualties to no more than 60,000 troops of all arms, was deployed along a five-mile line; whereas at Waterloo on June 18, 1815, Napoleon massed his 72,000 infantry, cavalry, and cannoneers on a two-and-a-half-mile front, which enabled him, unlike Lee at Gettysburg, to view the entire battlefield through a small telescope and react quickly to what happened on it as it happened.[5]

Rarely, if ever, did Civil War commanders enjoy the same advantage to the same degree. Not only were their troops spread out over too great a distance, but combat tended to take place in densely forested country, where it was impossible for them to see most of their own army, much less the enemy's. Furthermore, although technology had increased the size of armies and of the battleground, the main means by which commanders received information from and sent instructions to their generals remained essentially what they had been when Hannibal crossed the Alps into Italy and Napoleon did the same twenty centuries later: verbal or written messages carried by a man on horseback who might be killed, captured, or become lost on the way, or, if he reached his destination, he would arrive so late that acting on those messages might make matters worse rather than better. The telegraph, to be sure, enabled commanders in the field to be in unprecedentedly rapid and frequent contact with their superiors, including the heads of the government, but this was not necessarily an advantage. In any event, Samuel Morse's invention proved to be of small practical use during combat, except in siege or siege-like operations, as also was the case with signal flags and lights. In sum, the more troops Civil War commanders had, the less able they were to control them effectively, especially when attacking. This paradox helps explain why Grant and Lee, generally deemed the ablest generals of the Civil War, waged their least successful campaigns when conducting operations with the strongest armies they ever headed: Grant with about 120,000 men during May–June 1864 in Virginia; Lee in the Seven Days Battles (June 25–July 1, 1862), which he began with about 85,000 troops, and at Gettysburg (July 1–3, 1863), where from first to last he threw approximately 75,000 soldiers into the fray, losing nearly one-third of them and the battle.[6] Another and more fundamental reason why Grant and Lee failed in these encounters is that they fought on the tactical offensive in a war dominated to an unprecedented degree by the tactical defensive owing to the aforementioned improvements in weaponry, improvements enhanced by both sides as the war progressed, resorting ever more to to and receive from their corps and division commanders communications with all practicable rapidity. As a rule, only in moments of crisis would they ride toward or along the firing line, as did Grant at Shiloh, William S. Rosecrans at Stones River, and Lee during the Battle of the Wilderness, where his attempt to lead a counterattack caused his troops to refuse to advance until he reluctantly complied with their shouts of "Lee to the rear! Lee to the rear!"

A staff assisted the Civil War commander to command. By modern standards it was very, one might say, quaintly small. Thus Lee's numbered at most fourteen and Grant's never more than twenty officers—fewer by far than today's division commanders. These officers consisted of two types, although their roles could overlap: (1) personal staff, headed by a chief of staff or, more commonly, an assistant adjutant general and comprising aides de camp; and (2) general staff, made up of chiefs of engineers, ordnance, artillery, and commissary, plus a quartermaster, medical director, judge advocate, and perhaps a topographer (or topographical bureau) charged with preparing maps. The commander selected all or most of the former, who dined (messed) with him and accompanied him should he be reassigned. They owed their posts primarily to his perception of their personal qualities, as witnessed the head of Grant's staff, John A. Rawlins, a young lawyer from Galena, Illinois. Totally without military experience prior to the summer of 1861, Rawlins's fellow townsman Grant became a general and asked him to help out with the paperwork. Officers of the general staff, on the other hand, usually were assigned to an army by the war department in Washington or Richmond, not by its commander per se, and they tended to be West Pointers with regular army experience—although there were many exceptions, most famously Jedediah Hotchkiss, Stonewall Jackson's mapmaker in the Shenandoah Valley.

The basic tasks of the general staff had to do with administration, supervision, inspection, and, in the case of the engineers, the construction of fortifications, bridges, and roads. Also the chief of artillery might perform a combat role, depending on what the commander wished and circumstances. The personal staff, for its part, drafted orders as dictated or instructed by the commander, delivered and when necessary explained them, reported on their implementation, provided assessments of the situation on sectors the commander could neither see nor visit, guided units to their designated positions, and did all else the commander might desire or require, such as assistance in trying to rally fleeing troops.

What Civil War staff officers of both types, including those bearing the title of chief of staff, did not do was prepare and present to the commander detailed plans ("recommendations") for the conduct of a campaign or battle, as became the standard practice in European and eventually the U.S. armed forces following the spectacular success of the Germans, with their *Generalstab des Herres,* in the Franco-Prussian War of 1870–1871.[9] All, or at least nearly all, of the top Union and Confederate generals made their own plans, strategical, operational, and tactical, and then issued the orders embodying them verbally, in written form, or a combination of the two. They might discuss affairs informally with staff officers, seek or receive advice from one or more of their generals, and hold "councils of war" attended by most if not all of their corps and sometimes division commanders—something Lee and Grant rarely did. Yet regardless of how much or little advice they obtained from others, it was they who decided, both before and during battle, what was to be done; when, where, how, and by whom; and to what purpose. It was also they who garnered the glory of victory or bore the blame of defeat. Sometimes they deserved neither, but that is the way it was because, fair or not, it was the way it had to be and still is.

To achieve victory against a potent enemy under difficult circumstances a Civil War commander required, like all successful military leaders past, present, and future, a strong but not necessarily brilliant intellect, self-confidence, and the ability to inspire confidence in others, enormous energy and endurance, moral courage, coolness and presence of mind in times of crisis, and, above all, a knack for war and good luck in waging it—an attribute Napoleon considered more important in a general than skill. All but one of the Union commanders deemed "victors" in the ensuing pages possessed these qualities, albeit in varying degrees and proportions (Halleck's contributions being of a different order).[10] None, though, began the war qualified through training and experience to head a large body of troops in active operations, much less battle. At West Point they learned how to drill an infantry platoon, load and aim a cannon, and ride a horse while waving a saber, but their sole exposure to anything that had to do with the "art of war" came from a few lectures on the subject by Professor Dennis Hart Mahan and whatever they chanced to read on their own about matters military, which in the cases of Grant and Philip Sheridan evidently was little or nothing.[11] Moreover, only three of them—Grant, George Thomas, and George Meade—had any previous experience in the Mexican War of combat against regular troops, and all except Thomas, Meade, and Sheridan had left the army long before 1861 to pursue civilian careers with indifferent success and without expectation of returning to it.[12] Therefore, the "victors in blue" were fortunate in that all of them, save one, had an opportunity to develop the military know-how needed to command successfully a

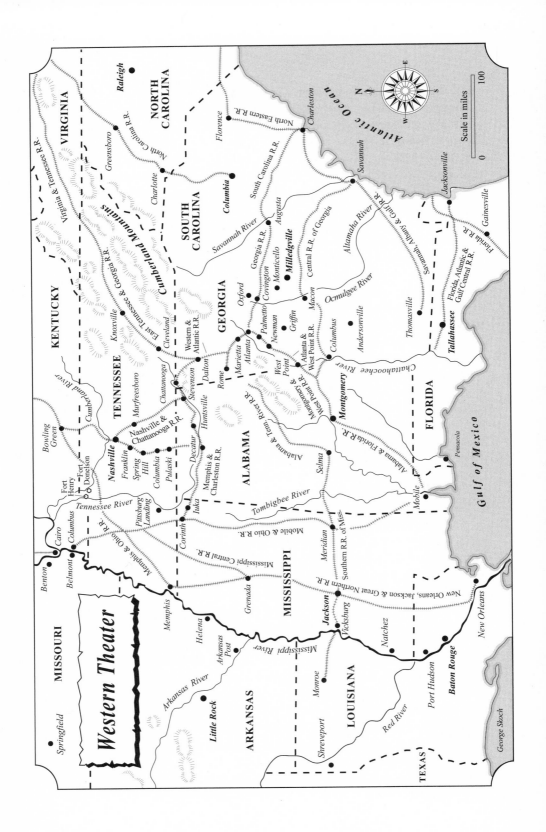

major army by first heading regiments or brigades, then divisions, corps, or small armies. Even the exception—William Tecumseh Sherman, who failed miserably on being placed, much against his desire, in charge of Federal forces in Kentucky during the fall of 1861—had an opportunity to redeem himself in less demanding roles while acquiring the confidence and competence, despite several more miserable performances, to become what he eventually became—second only to Grant in rank and prestige.

By the same token, and again with one exception, the West Pointers who began the war with high rank and command, or obtained them early on—Irvin McDowell, Don Carlos Buell, John Pope, and most notoriously McClellan—ended up by the fall of 1862 either on the military shelf or in the military boondocks.[13] The exception was Henry Wager Halleck. He not only began high, albeit not as high as he would have had he not been in California when the war began, but soared still higher until he became in July 1862 the highest of all as general in chief of the U.S. Army. Halleck held this post until he was superseded by Grant in March 1864, whereupon he continued doing most of what he did before as Grant's chief of staff. Like George C. Marshall in World War II, he never waged, much less won, a battle, decisive or otherwise. Nor did he always perform well as either de facto or de jure chief of staff, suffering particularly in the latter role under Grant, who came to find him more hindrance than help. Nevertheless, as shall be seen in the forthcoming pages, he made important, indeed essential, contributions to Northern victory, and he did so from behind a desk rather than astride a horse, thereby pioneering the role performed by Marshall during World War II.[14]

Success, of course, is the hallmark of proficiency in a commander. Yet it is not an absolute one. If so, then Wellington would have to be considered superior to Napoleon, and Montgomery to Rommel. Since this is (or should be) an obvious absurdity when it comes to judging a general's generalship, other, more sophisticated questions must be asked and answered than merely whether he won or lost. The following are the main ones:

1. If victorious in a battle and/or campaign, did he contribute decisively to the victory and how so?
2. Why did he win? Through superior skill on his part? The far greater strength of his army? A brilliant feat of arms by one or more of his generals? Enemy blunders? Sheer chance? Or a combination of some or all of these factors?
3. What were his objectives and how did he set about realizing them?
4. Did he accomplish as much as could be reasonably expected under the circumstances? More? Less?

5. If less, what could, and therefore should, he have done on the basis of information available to him at the time to achieve more, and why did he not do it?

The first question contains the standards for selecting the generals who won the war for the Union. The following four queries present the criteria by which these generals will be examined and judged. Readers, of course, will decide how well or ill this has been done. All I ask of them is to be prepared for some surprises—even, mayhap, some shocks.

I

Rosecrans in West Virginia: A Tale of a Goose, a Dog, and a Fox

(June–November 1861)

"I HAVE NOT A BRIG GENL WORTH HIS SALT—Morris is a timid old woman—Rosecranz a silly fussy goose—Schleich knows nothing." So wrote Major General George Brinton McClellan to his wife, Nelly, on July 3, 1861.[1] A high degree of conceit prompted his low opinion of his brigadiers, yet that conceit was understandable. Born in Philadelphia on December 3, 1826, he entered West Point when not quite sixteen; graduated second in the class of 1846, which included a gawky Virginian named Thomas J. Jackson and twenty others destined to become Civil War generals; served capably as one of Winfield Scott's engineer officers in the Mexican War; traveled across the Atlantic with two much older officers to observe the Crimean War and report on the European armies; and even designed a saddle that would bear his name and be standard in the American army until the combustion engine rendered horses obsolete nearly ninety years later.

In 1857 McClellan found himself still only a captain despite his outstanding record, which also included conducting explorations in the Far West. He resigned his commission and within four years became president of the eastern division of the Ohio & Mississippi Railroad headquartered in Cincinnati, where he resided with his beautiful young bride, Ellen "Nelly" Marcy, who in accepting his suit rejected that of another West Pointer (class of 1847) named Ambrose Powell Hill.

The advent of civil war in April 1861 saw McClellan's career skyrocket faster, higher, and brighter than any of the shells fired from Confederate cannons at Fort Sumter. As soon as President Abraham Lincoln called for 75,000 three-month volunteers to suppress the Southern insurrection, Ohio Governor William Dennison placed the young railway executive, who had promptly proffered his military know-how, in charge of organizing and training the Buckeye State's contribution to that number, which soon far exceeded its quota. Highly impressed by the efficiency of his former staff officer, whom he long had deemed suited for high rank in the event of a major war, Winfield Scott urged the president to appoint McClellan a major general in the regular army and assign him command of "The Department of the Ohio." This Lincoln did, having formed a favorable opinion of his intelligence on meeting him in Illinois in 1858. Thus it was that McClellan, a mere four years after resigning his captain's commission, became at age thirty-four second in rank only to Scott. And since "Old Fuss and Feathers" at seventy-five had become so infirm physically that he could not mount, much less ride, a horse, McClellan stood in line to replace him as commanding general. All he needed to do next was demonstrate that his talent for waging war matched his ability at preparing for it.[2]

Soon he had the opportunity. Late in May 1861 Scott instructed him, at Lincoln's behest, to occupy western Virginia. Although historically part of the Old Dominion, the Alleghenies separated this region geographically, economically, and politically from the eastern portion, with the result that most of its inhabitants, few of whom owned slaves, remained loyal to the Union. Helping them to secede from secession would take the first long stride toward restoring the United States to states united, Lincoln's prime goal and at this stage of the war his sole professed one.[3]

McClellan responded to Scott's directive by assembling several regiments under Brigadier General Thomas Morris of the Indiana militia at Grafton. From there Morris advanced and drove a much smaller Confederate force southward in the "Phillipi Races," thereby securing control of the Baltimore & Ohio Railroad, the main land link between Washington, D.C., and the Midwest. In turn the Confederates sent reinforcements westward over the mountains to regain what had been lost, whereupon McClellan proceeded by rail to Parkersburg in western Virginia with 7,000 Ohio and Indiana volunteers. This gave him a field army of around 11,000, including Morris's brigade but excluding 9,000 troops assigned to guarding the Baltimore & Ohio and a brigade of three-year recruits being readied at Camp Dennison near Cincinnati for an expedition up the Great Kanawha River to the south.[4]

Never before had McClellan commanded so much—or so little—as a squad in combat. Yet he had no doubt he would succeed. Why should he? Throughout his short life he had gone from success to success. He had done so by taking care never to fail. This he would continue doing. "I shall be," he assured Scott on arriving at Parkersburg, "cautious in my movements."[5]

The main obstacles to success, as he saw it, were his generals and his soldiers. The latter consisted almost entirely of three-monthers and militia, so ill-trained and undisciplined that anything or nothing at all might cause them to flee in wild panic on encountering the enemy. As for the former, we already know his opinion: none was "worth his salt." And in truth all of them, with one exception, were nonprofessionals who owed their rank to political connections rather than tactical know-how, with the prime example being Brigadier General Jacob D. Cox, commander of the troops slated for the Kanawha River expedition. A thirty-one-year-old lawyer-politician totally devoid of previous military training or experience, Cox's sole apparent qualification for his position was being a close friend of Governor Dennison.[6]

The lone exception was that "silly fussy goose" Rosecranz—or, to give his full and correctly spelled name, William Starke Rosecrans. A tall, lean, forty-one-year-old native of Ohio, he was a West Point graduate, class of 1842, wherein he ranked fifth. He had served in the elite Corps of Engineers until 1854, when, like McClellan, he resigned from the army to seek a more rewarding career in business. By 1861 he, along with two partners, operated a kerosene factory in Cincinnati and upon the outbreak of war again donned a uniform, one soon adorned with the bright silver star of a brigadier general in the regular army.

He wanted the two stars of a major general and command of an army. Serving with McClellan in western Virginia provided a chance to obtain them. In fact, he had no practicable alternative to doing so. As June gave way to July in 1861, the only other place where an imminent prospect of significant military action existed was in northern Virginia. There the head of the main Federal force, Irvin McDowell, who was about to launch an "on to Richmond" thrust, was a brigadier general too and had no openings for another one.

Besides, McClellan possessed an attribute that Rosecrans so far in his career, both military and civilian, had lacked: abundant luck. Despite his 1842 graduation from West Point, Rosecrans saw no action in Mexico, whereas McClellan of the class of 1846 went there to serve on Scott's staff and gain his favor and favoritism. Then, after leaving the army to enter business, Rosecrans lived comfortably but fell far short of McClellan's financial success. He also suffered the misfortune of having an experiment with a kerosene "safety lamp" he had invented literally blow up in his face, inflicting a permanent burn scar on his right cheek. Finally, and most irksome of all, it was McClellan who received the credit for Ohio's rapid mobilization and with it the major generalship, even though it was Rosecrans, as "Chief Engineer," who did much of the actual, practical work of quartering, provisioning, and arming the eager Buckeye volunteers. Small wonder, therefore, that when on the eve of the western Virginia campaign a journalist told him that he intended "to join my fortunes in this war to yours," Rosecrans replied, "I shall connect my fortune with McClellan," adding, "You had better join Mac's to yours—Mac is a lucky dog."[7]

The "lucky dog" disliked Rosecrans—disliked him because he distrusted him. What he wanted in subordinates were men who lacked either the desire or the ability, or both, to be other than subordinates and therefore content to remain such while advancing his own aspirations by doing what he ordered them to do—this and nothing more nor less. His characterization of him as a "silly fussy goose" notwithstanding, McClellan realized that Rosecrans was not that kind of man. Manifestly, he possessed a keen mind, high professional credentials, great energy and enterprise, and strong ambition—qualities quite likely to cause him to disregard orders if he thought it necessary or, worse, act without any orders whatsoever. This, from McClellan's standpoint, made him dangerous, even potentially calamitous, for he believed, so he wrote Nellie, that "everything"—by which he meant becoming what he hoped to become—"requires success in my first operations" as a commander.[8] When on June 27 his army began moving east toward Buckhannon, near where the Confederates reportedly were concentrating, he resolved to seize on the first occasion available to teach Rosecrans a lesson in subordination.

It came on the evening of the very next day. Learning that Rosecrans had camped his brigade beyond the point instructed, McClellan sent him a sharp reprimand, asserting that he had thereby exposed the advance to enemy detection. Rosecrans replied on the twenty-ninth, explaining that there had been insufficient space for a camp at the place designated and that in any case he had ascertained that there were no Confederates at Buckhannon, which one of his regiments would occupy before nightfall.[9] He then declared:

> No one, my dear general, among your general friends, has more disinterested and earnest wishes for the success of your efforts than the writer of this letter. None under your command are more loyally, cheerfully ready to conform to the duties of a subordinate position, and I even flatter myself I understand the position as well as most of your brigadiers. Review, if you please, that letter which you have put on record, and say whether, after you receive this, both private feelings and public interest are likely to be the better for it.

The sentiment expressed in the first sentence merely signifies that Rosecrans knew, as we have seen, that he could not hope to succeed should McClellan's campaign fail; the second sentence reeks of sarcasm; and the third is a thinly veiled warning that unless McClellan withdrew the reprimand from the record Rosecrans would make it both a personal and official issue. Either McClellan was deceiving himself or his wife, Nelly, when he wrote to her on July 2 that Rosecrans "is very meek now after a very severe rapping I gave him a few days since."[10] The record offers a different tale: McClellan's reprimand does not appear in the *Official Records*, only Rosecrans's letter, suggesting the original letter had been withdrawn by McClellan. He had learned what others holding official authority over the scar-faced Ohioan would discover during the next two years: attempts to intimidate him tended to result in the reverse.

By early July the Confederate contingent in northwestern Virginia numbered approximately 5,000 troops under the command of Brigadier General Robert S. Garnett and was deployed atop Laurel Hill to the north and Rich Mountain to the south of the Staunton-Parkersburg Pike, the principal road connecting this area to the rest of Virginia. Garnett hoped to hold these heights until he received sufficient reinforcements to launch a counter-offensive. McClellan planned to drive him back across the Alleghenies or, better still, trap and destroy him west of them. At the same time Cox was to cross his four regiments by means of steamboats from Gallipolis to Point Pleasant, then advance up the Kanawha River Valley, thereby bringing all of western Virginia under Union control.[11]

Both Laurel Hill (actually a small mountain) and Rich Mountain were strong positions; a frontal attack against either would almost certainly fail, or if it somehow succeeded, then at inordinate cost. Realizing this, on July 5 McClellan telegraphed Scott's adjutant, Colonel E. D. Townsend, that he intended to move against the enemy on Rich Mountain, where "I shall, if possible, turn the position to the south. . . . If possible I will repeat the maneuver of Cerro Gordo."[12] It was at Cerro Gordo in 1847 that Scott, finding his army confronted by an impregnable enemy front, sent a column circling around its southern flank to rout the Mexican forces and open the way for the eventual capture of Mexico City—the "Halls of Montezuma."

McClellan's version of the maneuver called for Morris's brigade to "amuse" Garnett's main body atop Laurel Hill while his other three brigades seized Rich Mountain, which he calculated could be accomplished without excessive casualties because, according to his estimate, the defenders numbered about 3,000 whereas he had 7,500 troops, giving him a more than two-to-one advantage. Then he would occupy Beverly, a small town located a mile east of the mountain on the Parkersburg-Staunton Turnpike, thus cutting Garnett's supply line and forcing him to abandon Laurel Hill in an attempt to escape back across the Alleghenies into the Shenandoah

Valley of Virginia. No "prospect of a brilliant victory," he assured Scott through Townsend in his July 5 telegram, "shall induce me to depart from my intention of gaining success by maneuvering rather than fighting. I will not throw these raw men of mine into the teeth of artillery and entrenchments if it is possible to avoid it."[13]

Two days later McClellan's column set out for Rich Mountain and on July 9 arrived two miles from it at Roaring Creek. Although not particularly high, the mountain proved to be rugged, covered with dense underbrush, and very steep. Worse, a "reconnaissance in force" conducted the next day ascertained that the entrance to the pass over it was lined with fortifications on each side of the road leading to Beverly—fortifications bolstered by four cannons and, according to a couple of prisoners that had been taken, manned by eight or nine thousand Rebels! As an Ohio colonel put it, a frontal assault would be like "marching to a butcher shop rather than a battle."[14]

Was there an alternative? According to McClellan's official report, dated July 14, 1861, he "at once determined . . . to make an effort to turn" the enemy flank and so "ordered General Rosecrans to move at 4 o'clock in the morning" of September 11 with four regiments and a cavalry detachment to the "lofty summit of Rich Mountain" by a route leading through "almost impenetrable thickets of brush." He was to report "the progress of his march" to "me every hour," and "attack the [enemy] intrenchments in rear," whereupon the "remainder of this command" would "assault in front as soon as Rosecrans's musketry would indicate that he was immediately" in the rear of the Confederates defending the pass.[15]

All of these statements are true, yet actually their effect is false because they omit two key facts: (1) Around 10 o'clock on the night of July 10 Rosecrans came to McClellan and informed him that he had learned from a young local Unionist named David Hart that there was a cattle path along the south slope of Rich Mountain leading to his family's farm (which doubled as a tavern) on the road to Beverly at the top of the mountain about two miles behind the enemy defenses; and (2) that Rosecrans proposed to take his brigade and, guided by Hart, proceed by the path and strike the Confederates by surprise in the rear, whereupon the rest of the army would assail them in front. Furthermore, McClellan adopted this plan with reluctance—after all, it cast Rosecrans in a starring role—and only after his father-in-law and his de facto chief of staff, Major Randolph Marcy, urged him to do so.[16] Without doubt McClellan deliberately designed his report to make it seem that he alone conceived the plan, which was a virtual clone of Scott's Cerro Gordo stratagem, and (as shall be seen) set the stage for blaming Rosecrans for the failure of the plan to be executed exactly as envisioned.

Rosecrans set out for the Hart farm at daybreak on July 11 with four infantry regiments, all three-month outfits, and a small cavalry detachment, the whole totaling 1,917 men. Fearful that the Confederates had been alerted to his presence on the south slope of the mountain when the bugler of one of the regiments blew reveille, he took a longer route to reach the cattle path than planned. Then, once on it, the going proved hard and soon became harder still owing to rain, resultant mud, and finally the departure of guide Hart, who, in Rosecrans's words, became "too much scared to be with us longer." Furthermore, Rosecrans found it impracticable to report the "progress of his march" to McClellan "every hour"; how could he do so when he did not know where he was himself? Not until about 11 A.M., by which time the rain had ceased, did he send word to McClellan that he was in sight of the mountaintop.

Approximately three more hours passed before he reached it—only to encounter a sizable Confederate force supported by a cannon and behind log-piles and boulders at the Hart farm! He assumed that the enemy, thanks to the early-morning bugle call, had detected his flanking march and reacted accordingly. Not so. The Rebels, some 310 strong under ex-regular army Captain Julius de Lagnel, were there because McClellan, worried by the absence of "progress" reports from Rosecrans, had dispatched a courier by way of a trail that curved around the north half of Rich Mountain to ascertain his whereabouts, and the courier, disregarding a warning from the Union pickets that enemy soldiers were up ahead, had been captured by the Confederates, with the result that their commander, Lieutenant Colonel John Pegram, sent De Lagnel's detachment and the cannon to the Hart farm, where it joined some pickets already stationed there. Thus it was that, because of McClellan's anxiety and the courier's asininity, Rosecrans found himself facing not a few foes who could be easily brushed aside, but enough of them to offer stiff resistance—and who did.[17]

Like McClellan, Rosecrans never before had experienced combat; indeed, unlike that "lucky dog," he had not so much as witnessed a battle, having been assigned to duty in the United States during the Mexican War. Even so, he subsequently wrote to his wife, "I was as collected under the enemy's fire and as little sensible of danger as at any time in doing ordinary business"— a self-description confirmed by the accounts of others present. Reacting rapidly, he deployed his troops as fast as they came up, then attacked. For awhile nothing went right and much went wrong, causing the assault to fail and the enemy to cheer in triumph. Then he charged on horseback at the

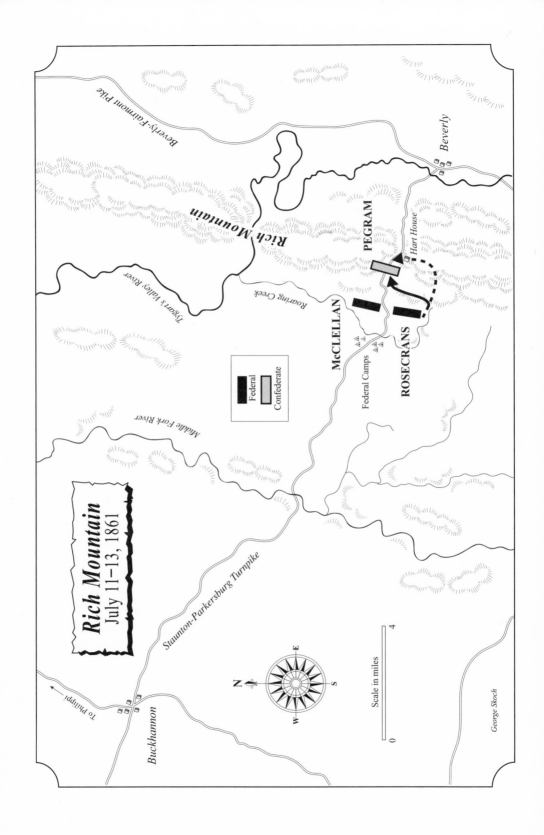

Rich Mountain
July 11–13, 1861

Buckhannon

To Philippi

Staunton-Parkersburg Turnpike

Middle Fork River

Scale in miles

0   4

N E S W

George Skoch

Beverly-Fairmon Pike

Rich Mountain

Tygart's Valley River

Roaring Creek

Beverly

Hart House

PEGRAM

McCLELLAN

ROSECRANS

Federal Camps

Federal
Confederate

head of one of his regiments while another delivered two devastating volleys into the Rebel ranks. All of the Confederates still able fled, leaving behind a wounded De Lagnel and their cannon, plus a second one that was being wheeled into position. The Federals occupied the Hart farm and the road to Beverly, but did not pursue. More hills and valleys lay ahead, mayhap more foes, and it was becoming dark, a darkness increased by more showers. Where, wondered Rosecrans, was McClellan? Why had he not attacked the enemy's front as soon as he heard, as he must have heard, the din of battle in the enemy's rear? What was he doing?[18]

McClellan was trying to decide what to do. Throughout the morning and the early afternoon he had remained in his headquarters tent on the west bank of Roaring Creek anxiously awaiting "progress" reports from Rosecrans and then, after one finally arrived, listening for the sound of "musketry" behind the Confederates guarding the entrance to Rich Mountain pass. At long, long last he heard the fighting at the Hart farm. Minutes later he galloped up to where his troops, determination overcoming trepidation, eagerly awaited the order to storm the enemy entrenchments. No such order came. According to the diary-journal of Ohio colonel John Beatty, who was present, "The general halted a few paces from our line and sat on his horse listening to the guns, apparently in doubt as to what to do; and as he sat there with indecision stamped on every line of his countenance, the battle grew fiercer in the enemy's rear."[19]

Late in the afternoon the firing ascended to a crescendo, then sputtered into silence. McClellan concluded that Rosecrans had been either repulsed or destroyed—a conclusion soon confirmed in his mind when he saw an officer ride among the Confederates, appear to deliver a speech, and then heard a cheer. Hence he withdrew his troops, except pickets, to their camp on Roaring Creek, putting it between them and the Rebels should they attack, which he considered so likely and dangerous that he had father-in-law Marcy distribute firearms among the teamsters. But should they remain in their entrenchments, then come morning he would drive them from the pass with an artillery bombardment, his chief of engineers having informed him that he had discovered a hill from where cannons could enfilade the enemy position, turning it into a death trap tenable only by the dead. This, McClellan believed, was the correct way to wage war; it was the way the British and French had taken the Russian fortress of Sebastopol in the Crimea; and it also was the sure and safe way—sure to succeed and thus safe for the reputation and ambition of the commander who employed it.[20]

Night passed, morning came. Most of the Union troops remained in camp while others cut a road and dug emplacements for the dozen cannon that were to blast the Rebels from the pass. Meanwhile, Rosecrans, having ascertained from a captive that the enemy was "disorganized and probably dispersing," advanced along the Beverly road until he reached the Confederate camp and nearby entrenchments. The latter contained only two spiked brass six-pounders, the former sixty-nine Southerners waiting to surrender. From them he learned that their now former commander, Pegram, had set out late yesterday afternoon with three hundred men to reinforce De Lagnel but, arriving far too late and after dark, had returned to the camp where a council of war decided to abandon the mountain and attempt to join Garnett on Laurel Hill. The prisoners also revealed that their entire force had numbered a mere 1,200 soldiers capable of fighting—which meant that when Rosecrans encountered De Lagnel's detachment at the Hart farm McClellan's 5,000 troops faced only 900 opponents, and that when McClellan withdrew to his Roaring Creek camp just 600 defended the pass. It is conceivable that had he attacked with two of his regiments, which averaged some 700 men each, he might have broken through.

At about 7 A.M. McClellan received a message from Rosecrans informing him that the Confederates had abandoned Rich Mountain. He thereupon ordered the occupation of Beverly and instructed Morris to press "closely" the main enemy force under Garnett when it withdrew from Laurel Hill— which it already had done. Then, after telegraphing Scott, "Our success complete and almost bloodless," he set out for Beverly himself. There, the following day, Pegram and close to six hundred of his troops surrendered, having found themselves trapped and faced with starvation. That same day Morris's advance guard overtook Garnett's rearguard at Corrick's Ford on the Cheat River, killing him and capturing his wagon train. What remained of his little army managed to make its way back across the Alleghenies into the Shenandoah Valley, but so demoralized and depleted that McClellan exaggerated but slightly when he telegraphed Scott on July 14 that "we have annihilated the enemy in Western Virginia."[21]

Later that day he composed his aforementioned report on Rich Mountain—a long one covering three-plus pages of the *Official Records*. In it, after (as we have seen) taking credit for conceiving the Cerro Gordo–like flanking maneuver against the Confederates, he praised Rosecrans for "conducting his command up the very precipitous sides of the mountains" and for the "very handsome manner in which he planned and directed his attack upon the rebels at Hart's farm." At the same time, though, he said nothing about having heard sustained gunfire from that vicinity throughout the late afternoon of July 11. He gave as the reasons for his non-assault on the Confederate front a failure by Rosecrans to carry out "the order . . . to attack the rear of the enemy's lower intrenchments" and not having received any "communication from General Rosecrans" other than his 11 A.M. dispatch stating that "he was still distant about a mile and a half from Hart's farm." Finally, instead of reporting that Rosecrans's capture of the Hart farm led to Pegram's withdrawal from Rich Mountain and that he did not learn of the withdrawal until after Rosecrans occupied the enemy camp and informed him of it, McClellan asserted obscurely that Rosecrans's troops "encamped on the battle-field [at Hart's farm] at about 2 P.M., and remained there until the following morning," when "intelligence was received that the enemy had evacuated their works and fled over the mountains."[22]

The manifest purpose of McClellan's report was to make it seem that he was the sole architect of a brilliant victory in which, at the cost of only "killed, 12, wounded, 59," his forces had dislodged a Confederate army, found to have totaled 10,000 troops, from virtually impregnable mountain fortresses while inflicting on it at least a thousand casualties in killed, wounded, and captured, with the "really important results" being the "complete rout and annihilation of the rebel forces," the "capture of one and the death of the other of their leaders," and the rendering of "this portion of Western Virginia . . . entirely freed from their presence."[23]

This purpose he achieved. Taken to Washington by Marcy along with some captured Confederate banners, the report heightened Lincoln's and Scott's already high opinion of McClellan, an opinion shared by the House of Representatives, which adopted a resolution thanking him for his victory in what was the first engagement of the war that accurately could be called a battle. At the same time, McClellan became the popular hero of the North, where the press hailed him as the "Young Napoleon," a sobriquet enhanced by his issuing to his troops on July 16 a proclamation inspired by the style of the old Napoleon's addresses to his "soldats":

> *Soldiers of the Army of the West!*
> I am more than satisfied with you.
> You have annihilated two armies, commanded by educated and experienced soldiers and intrenched in mountain fortresses fortified at their leisure. . . .
> Soldiers! I have confidence in you, and I trust you have learned to confide in me.[24]

Rosecrans's report on Rich Mountain is dated July 19, 1861. In it, although he briefly related having proposed "a plan for turning the enemy's position" to McClellan on the night of July 10, he made no reference to

McClellan's failure to assail the Confederates on hearing the sound of the fight at the Hart farm. The reason is obvious: a subordinate does not criticize his commander in an official report submitted, as it must be under army regulations, to that commander. What he could and did do was voice complaints about McClellan's conduct to members of his staff, other officers, and (probably) newspaper correspondents. We do not know the precise wording of what one of those journalists, Whitelaw Reid of the *Cincinnati Gazette,* subsequently termed these "casual hints," but in all likelihood their essence appears in Rosecrans's 1865 statement to the Congressional Committee on the Conduct of the War: McClellan "was bound, as a military man, to have made the attack in his front, for the purpose of preventing the enemy from falling on me with too heavy a force."[25]

Almost surely McClellan soon knew of Rosecrans's aspersions; when it comes to tale-bearing, nothing surpasses an army. If so, then no doubt he intensely resented them, for throughout his entire life he rarely admitted to making a mistake and always blamed failures to achieve greater success on the incompetency or malignancy of others. Yet he took no action against Rosecrans, not even another "rapping." Either he decided to wait until the completion of the operations in western Virginia, or else the course of events overtook him before he found an appropriate opportunity to retaliate. On July 21 McDowell's Union army in eastern Virginia met, fought, and was routed by the Confederates at Bull Run; instead of advancing triumphantly to Richmond, it fled in disarray back to Washington.

The following day McClellan received a telegram from Scott: "Circumstances make your presence here [Washington] necessary. Charge Rosecrans or some other general with your present department and come hither without delay."[26] This meant, it could only mean, that he was to replace McDowell at the head of what the North regarded then and to the end of the war as its most important army—the one that would put down the rebellion and restore the South to the Union. The general who led it to the victories achieving these goals not only would rise to the very top militarily but also politically—to wit, become the next president. McClellan intended—indeed, expected—to be that general. He deemed it his destiny.

McClellan set out for Washington by train from Grafton on July 24. Behind he left Rosecrans in command. Regardless of his personal feelings toward him, the "goose" was the sole readily available general possessing sufficient rank and professional credentials for the post. Besides, what difference could it make? Despite its impressive geographic dimension, the "Department of the Ohio" in essence consisted solely of western Virginia, most of which the Rebels already had been driven from. Since Cox now was occupying the Great Kanawha River Valley, the rest also soon would be under Union domination. Leaving Rosecrans in charge, therefore, was tantamount to placing him in a military limbo where anything he might do, good or bad, would signify little or nothing.

Rosecrans accompanied McClellan to Grafton. He could not have felt sorrow, sweet or otherwise, on parting from him. Thanks to that "lucky dog's" latest stroke of luck—luck that he had made possible for him at Rich Mountain—he now at last commanded an army. Moreover, he expected soon to lead it into battle, for he did not share McClellan's view that the routing of Garnett's army had eliminated any serious Rebel threat to western Virginia. As he wrote his wife on July 25, he feared that McDowell's debacle at Bull Run "would increase the enemy's activity and enterprise in our direction."[27]

This fear proved justified. Faced with no immediate danger in eastern Virginia and lacking the means to take the offensive there themselves, the Confederates turned their attention to making another and this time much stronger attempt to establish control over the recalcitrant mountaineers in the trans-Allegheny counties of the Old Dominion. To be precise, they began assembling forces eventually totaling 17,000 men for a counteroffensive under the direction of Robert E. Lee.

Lee was not yet known as the "Gray Fox." In fact, apart from a very recently donned Confederate brigadier general's uniform, there was nothing gray about him at all. At fifty-four his hair and mustache—as yet he had no beard—remained predominantly black. Had he told a stranger that he was forty-something, he would have been believed. But he had a reputation for being one of the ablest, perhaps *the* ablest, of all the officers in the "old army," a reputation acquired and earned by his exploits during the Mexican War in finding ways to circumvent otherwise impregnable enemy defenses (Cerro Gordo derived from his enterprise and courage). So highly did Winfield Scott appreciate his services, without which it is unlikely he would have reached, much less captured, Mexico City, that following the outbreak of civil war in April 1861 he urged Lincoln to place Lee in field command of the entire Union army. After Lincoln agreed, he offered that post to him. Had Lee been capable of waging war against his native Virginia and of placing ambition ahead of what he deemed honor, he, instead of McClellan, would have become the second highest-ranking general in the U.S. Army and the heir-apparent to Scott.

As it was, he drew his sword to defend Virginia, which in turn placed him in charge of its defense, a task he retained upon the state formally joining the Confederacy, which thereupon transferred its capital to Richmond, thus making that small city the North's main target and the place that the South felt it must hold above all else. Pierre Gustave Toutant Beauregard and Joseph Eggleston Johnston won the Southern public's plaudits for parrying at Bull Run the first Yankee attempt to take it, but Lee deserved at least an equal share of the credit by having provided the means for their victory and recommending that they concentrate their forces behind Bull Run. This fact was recognized by Confederate President Jefferson Davis, who soon would name him third among the Confederacy's five full generals, with Johnston (who never forgave him) fourth and Beauregard (whom Davis came to detest almost as much as he did Johnston) fifth. Lee, though, longed to exchange his chair behind a desk for a saddle on a horse at the head of an army; hence, he was delighted when, late in July, Davis assigned him the mission of redeeming Garnett's defeat. At last, at long last, he had an opportunity to demonstrate that he was not only an adept administrator and adviser, but an able warrior as well.[28]

Soon Rosecrans knew that "Lee is coming." What did he do? At first, nothing other than to take measures designed to suppress pro-Confederate guerrillas. His reason? There was nothing else he could do. Most of the three-month volunteers, the bulk of his army, were going home. Not until early September did he accumulate enough of the new three-year troops to launch a campaign to counter Lee.

He based his plans on the geography of western Virginia, where he had traveled prior to the war as a businessman but viewed what he saw with the eyes of a professional soldier. The strategic keys to it were the Tygart River Valley in the north and the Kanawha River Valley to the south. Should the Confederates penetrate both, they would be able to cut off the Federals from Ohio the river and Ohio the state. It soon became apparent that such was Lee's design. His main body, personally led by him, threatened to advance into the Tygart River Valley by way of the Staunton-Parkersburg Pike, and late in August several Rebel regiments headed by Brigadier General John B. Floyd crossed over to the west side of the Gauley River at Carnifex Ferry, where they then could outflank Cox's brigade at nearby Gauley Bridge on the north bank of the Kanawha.[29]

Rosecrans assessed the situation and decided to check Lee with Brigadier General John J. Reynolds's brigade at Cheat Mountain Pass, the sole logistically practical route by which Lee could reach the Tygart River Valley. Some 3,500 feet high, narrow, and fortified, the pass proved an ideal defensive position for a small force to check the advance of a far larger one. As for Floyd, on September 3, Rosecrans set out from Clarksburg to strike and destroy him with 4,500 Ohio troops, none of whom had seen previous action. Seven days later and late in the afternoon he approached Carnifex Ferry, whereupon he instructed his lead brigade under Brigadier General Henry Benham to reconnoiter the Confederate defense line, which was located atop a densely wooded cliff overlooking the Gauley River.

Instead, Benham, filled with whisky-inspired ardor, attacked headlong. Floyd's 2,500 Virginians, posted behind log barricades, responded with a withering fire. Only the advent of darkness and an order from Rosecrans to suspend operations until daylight prevented heavy Union loss. During the night, however, Floyd, who had strong personal reasons for avoiding capture (he faced accusation that as James Buchanan's secretary of war he had filled southern armories with weapons in anticipation of secession and war), crossed his force to the other side of the river by means of a footbridge and flatboat, which he then destroyed, preventing pursuit by Rosecrans on discovering the enemy's departure in the morning.[30]

The following day, September 12, Lee attempted but failed to breach Cheat Mountain Pass by yet another Cerro Gordo–style maneuver, one that probably would have succeeded had it been carried out by Rosecrans but which Lee, the gentleman in him prevailing over the general, entrusted to the young, totally inexperienced colonel who proposed it and then became paralyzed by the responsibility of executing a plan that he himself had conceived. Realizing that the Federals had now been alerted to the pass's vulnerability to a flanking move, and barely able to feed his soldiers owing to rain that transformed the mountains into lofty swamps, Lee abandoned his effort to reach the Tygart River Valley and withdrew to Staunton, where he could be supplied via the Virginia Central Railroad and be in position to counter a Federal thrust toward the Shenandoah Valley or East Tennessee.[31]

Rosecrans now possessed the initiative. Two weeks passed, though, before he could bridge the Gauley and accumulate sufficient men and means to exploit it. He then headed for Lewisburg, about thirty miles distant, with 5,200 troops in hopes of being able to seize it before Lee could reinforce Floyd's brigade and another small Confederate contingent, at present its sole defenders. If he did, he next intended to move southward into East Tennessee and occupy Wytheville, Tennessee, on the Virginia & Tennessee Railroad, the sole rail link between the states that gave it that name. This, he believed with good cause, would ignite an uprising in predominantly Unionist East Tennessee that would lead to that region becoming another western Virginia—an outcome he knew was dear to Lincoln's heart and which surely would gain him the president's gratitude and a major general-ship and command of a major army. He realized that he was playing for high stakes with low cards, yet it was worth a try.[32]

On September 26 he reached Big Sewell Mountain, about fifteen miles west of Lewisburg. Here he halted and began fortifying along a high ridge. Facing him a mile distant across a virtual gorge and atop another ridge was Lee with an army that soon increased to a nominal strength of 15,000, but in fact numbered little more than half that total in combat effectives owing to measles, pneumonia, and exhaustion. Realizing that to assault would be suicidal, Rosecrans and Lee each hoped the other would assail him. Day after day and night after night passed, accompanied by almost constant rain. Then on the night of October 5 Confederate pickets heard creaking wheels behind the Federal lines. Were the Yankees moving up their artillery preparatory to an assault? Lee, who reluctantly had decided to attempt a turning movement, eagerly awaited the answer, wishing it to be yes. Morning revealed it to be no. The Yankees were gone, headed back north.

Rosecrans's supply line stretched from the Kanawha to Big Sewell Mountain along sixty miles of dirt roads that incessant and torrential rains had turned into streams of mud and in some places totally obliterated. By October he had three choices: attack and be slaughtered, stay until starvation forced him to surrender, or withdraw to where he could obtain provisions and shelter for his wet and shivering soldiers. For obvious reasons he chose the third, retreating to the area around Gauley Bridge, where he could draw supplies from Charleston, which was at the head of steamboat navigation on the Kanawha. Lee did not follow, owing to the rain, mud, and the tracks of the Virginia Central terminating eleven miles east of Lewisburg. His logistical situation was little better than Rosecrans's, resulting in his soldiers and horses being literally weak from hunger.[33]

At the end of October, rightly concluding that neither he nor Rosecrans could mount a serious offensive thrust, Lee returned to Richmond. His first campaign as a field commander had proved a failure when it came to reuniting the two Virginias, and Southern newspapers so pronounced it. Almost nine months passed before he began performing the feats that caused him to be dubbed the "Gray Fox." Meanwhile, some scorned him as "Granny Lee"—a sneer inspired not only by his lack of success in western Virginia but also by his change of appearance. While at Cheat Mountain he let his beard grow. It came out gray, verging toward white, and his hair and mustache turned the same color. He who early in 1861 could pass for a man much younger than his years now looked much older.[34] Yet he also was much wiser, having learned that even a good plan would not succeed unless executed by a good lieutenant. What he did not know was that such a lieutenant was available, that rather ironically he was a native of western Virginia, and that he already had become somewhat famous for the defeat-preventing stand his brigade had made at Bull Run—a stand that gained for him a nickname that, unlike "Granny Lee," would stick with him forever: "Stonewall."

Winter brought an end to significant military activities in western Virginia in 1861. In fact, from a strategic standpoint none occurred there throughout the rest of the war. None could. The rugged terrain, wretched roads, and total absence of railways and navigable rivers outside the northwest corner rendered it logistically impossible for Federals and Confederates alike to advance beyond where they already were with sufficient strength to achieve decisive results. Consequently, the region became a military backwater and has so remained in Civil War history.[35]

Yet its occupation and retention by Federal forces in the summer of 1861 was a decisive accomplishment for the North—perhaps, indeed, the most decisive one, in a positive sense, of the initial year of the war. To Lincoln and the vast majority of Northerners, the main purpose, if not sole purpose, of the war was to restore the seceded states to the Union. Depriving the most populous and powerful of those states, Virginia, of a sizable portion of its territory constituted a mighty stride toward the attainment of that goal. It also demonstrated that the Confederacy was vulnerable, and that sooner or later all of it would be forced to acknowledge the supremacy of the Stars and Stripes—if God so willed, which most Northerners believed he did, as proclaimed in Julia Ward Howe's "Battle Hymn of the Republic":

Mine eyes have seen the glory of the coming of the Lord;
He is trampling out the vintage where the grapes of wrath are stored;
He hath loosed the fateful lightning of His terrible swift sword;
His truth is marching on.

On October 24, 1861, less than six weeks after Floyd's flight from Carnifex Ferry and Lee's repulse at Cheat Mountain, the voters of western Virginia overwhelmingly approved a proposal to establish what in 1863 became the state of West Virginia, thereby formally completing their secession from secession.

As we have seen, McClellan garnered the credit for this outcome, and with it the reward. As we also have seen, Rosecrans deserved it for what he did and for what he prevented Lee from doing (he was the only Union general ever to best Lee without the advantage of superior numbers). In the process he displayed, unlike the "Young Napoleon," a high degree of energy and enterprise, decisiveness and determination, and a willingness to take risks in hope of obtaining through daring what could not be gained by sheer strength. In sum, he possessed the qualities needed to win more and greater victories if given the opportunity, the means, capable lieutenants, and either enough good luck or else not too much bad luck.

First, though, he required a higher rank and command. Yet, although he had by the close of 1861 amply earned both, neither was likely to be forthcoming in the foreseeable future. The reason was simple and, for the time being, insurmountable. On November 1 McClellan had become general in chief, replacing Scott, who had resigned in protest against his former junior staff officer having shown his gratitude to him by acting as if he already held that post. Now he did hold it, and Rosecrans would have had to have been a "silly goose," indeed, to have expected any favors, in particular promotion, from the "lucky dog."

He did not. Instead, he waited—waited for the wheel of fortune to turn, confident that it would, and prepared to give it a nudge in his direction when he could.

2

Grant in Missouri and Tennessee

A Tale of How a Nobody Became
a Somebody

(July 1861–February 1862)

WHEN SPRING AND WAR CAME IN 1861, no one among America's tiny military community, where everybody knew (or knew of) everybody, expected much, if anything of Ulysses "Sam" Grant. Why should they? To be sure, he was an 1843 graduate of West Point, but the sole exceptional military talent he had displayed there was equestrian, and that had not prevented him from being assigned to the infantry rather than the cavalry.[1] Likewise, although he had proved himself a diligent quartermaster during the war in Mexico and won the brevet (honorary) rank of captain by blasting the enemy from a hitherto impregnable position with a cannon mounted in a church tower, his postwar career not only had been less than distinguished, it was also tainted with disgrace, rumor having it that he had been forced to resign from the army in order to escape being cashiered for chronic drunkenness. Nor did it help that he did nothing afterward to redeem his reputation. At the outset of 1861 he was little more than a clerk in a leather goods store owned by his father and managed by a younger brother in Galena, Illinois, where he resided with his wife, Julia, and their four children. By then little short of thirty-nine—he became so on April 27, 1861—he was regarded, if not precisely a failure, certainly not a success, either as a soldier or a civilian.

Yet undeniably he was a West Pointer and an ex-regular army officer who had fought in actual battles. So when the men of Galena, responding to Lincoln's call for volunteers to suppress the Southern insurrection, gathered on April 18 to raise a company of troops, the town's leading politician, Republican Congressman Elihu Washburne, arranged for Grant to preside at the meeting. This he did, and afterward he took charge of organizing and drilling the recruits. They in turn asked him to be their captain, but he declined, believing he was qualified to command a regiment. With that goal in mind, he went to Springfield to solicit a colonel's commission from Illinois

29

governor Richard Yates. Yates first ignored him, then put him to work preparing forms and mustering regiments—regiments headed by ambitious politicians eager to advance their ambitions by exploits on the battlefield.

By late May no more regiments remained to be mustered, whereupon Grant traveled to his native state of Ohio in hope of obtaining a colonelcy from George McClellan, with whom he had become acquainted in Mexico and met again in 1853 at Fort Vancouver when that brilliant young officer came there while on a railway survey expedition through the Far West. Surely McClellan would remember him.

McClellan did remember him—remembered him being drunk one evening at Fort Vancouver. Perhaps, too, he recalled him as the quartermaster who seemed to enjoy fighting and even once put a cannon up in a church tower, something that not even the Turks, allies of the British and French in the Crimean War, had done. In any case, he was not the sort of person he wanted serving under him, despite his desire for "educated officers." For two days Grant sat in the anteroom of McClellan's Cincinnati headquarters without so much as seeing the general. The third day he headed back to Galena, from where he wrote his father, who now resided in Covington, Kentucky, across the Ohio River from Cincinnati, that "I am perfectly sickened at the political wire-pulling for all these commissions." It appeared that the war, which he expected, along with the vast majority of Northerners, to be short, would be waged and won without him.

Then his luck changed. Or, to employ the terminology customarily used in writing about persons who otherwise would not be written about, he began to fulfill his destiny. The officers of the Twenty-first Illinois Infantry Regiment, encamped at Springfield, having come to realize that their politician-colonel was an oaf, asked Governor Yates to replace him "preferably with Captain Grant," whose quiet efficiency had impressed them back in May, when he had mustered the regiment at Mattoon, Illinois. Yates, ever sensitive to the desires of his constituents, agreed. On June 15—the same day that McClellan, in his capacity as commander of the Department of the Ohio, inspected the Twenty-first Illinois and pronounced it fit for service under its present commander—he appointed Grant its new colonel.

Three days later Grant took charge of the regiment. Attired in an old, out-at-the-elbows civilian coat and looking shorter than his five feet eight inches because he walked with his head bent forward as if he intended to ram into something, he scarcely cut a dashing figure, but when some of his soldiers audibly expressed that opinion, a single glance from him silenced them. At once he set about transforming the Twenty-first from being little more than an armed mob into a military unit. Also he induced nearly all of its men to reenlist for three years—an outcome abetted by patriotic speeches delivered to them by Illinois congressmen John A. Logan and John A. McClernand, both of whom would play significant roles in Grant's career, albeit in very different ways.

On June 28 Grant received an order to take the regiment to Quincy, Illinois. From there, on July 12–13, it crossed the Mississippi over to northeastern Missouri, its mission to suppress pro-Confederate partisans. Before long Grant learned that a large band of them commanded by Colonel Thomas Harris was camped twenty-five miles to the south near a village called Florida, which happened to be the birthplace of one of its members, a newly unemployed Mississippi River steamboat pilot named Samuel Clemens (who many years afterward also would enter Grant's life, by which time he had become, like Grant, world famous by a name he had adopted from his steamboat days: Mark Twain). On July 17 Grant set out with the Twenty-first to attack the rebels. Since his march toward them proved to be a key, perhaps *the* key, experience in the formation of his character as a commander, let his own subsequent, splendidly written account of it now be read:

> As we approached [on the morning of July 18] the brow of the hill from which it was expected we could see Harris' camp, and possibly find his men ready formed to meet us, my heart kept getting higher and higher until it felt to me as though it was in my throat. I would have given anything then to have been back in Illinois, but I had not the moral courage to halt and consider what to do; I kept right on. When we reached a point from which the valley below was in full view I halted. The place where Harris had been encamped a few days before was still there and the marks of a recent encampment were plainly visible, but the troops were gone.
>
> My heart resumed its place. It occurred to me at once that Harris had been as much afraid of me as I had been of him. This was a view of the question I had never taken before; but it was one I never forgot afterwards. From that event to the close of the war, I never experienced trepidation upon confronting an enemy, though I always felt more or less anxiety. I never forgot that he had as much reason to fear my forces as I had his. The lesson was valuable.[2]

It indeed was a valuable lesson and Grant learned it well—perhaps, as we shall shortly see, too well.

He and the Twenty-first passed the remainder of July and early August in

Mexico, Missouri, where, to his astonishment, he read in a St. Louis newspaper that he had been promoted to brigadier general of volunteers, to date from May 17! He owed his sudden jump in rank to Congressman Washburne, who had met with other Illinois congressmen to parcel out the state's allotment of four brigadierships, the other three going to McClernand, Benjamin Prentiss, and Stephen A. Hurlbut. Moreover, again thanks to Washburne, Grant's name headed the list, making him senior in rank. He who less than two months before doubted that he had a future in the war now had a very promising one—provided he was in the right place at the right time and did the right things (or got away with doing the wrong ones).

Throughout the rest of August, Grant served in southeast Missouri on orders from the commander of the Union Department of the West, Major General John C. Frémont, whose explorations in the Far West during the 1840s had made him famous as "The Pathfinder" and in 1856 the new-born Republican Party's first (but unsuccessful) presidential candidate. Now heading several regiments, the equivalent of a brigade, Grant found the need for a staff and so appointed one consisting of three officers. The most important among them was the adjutant general, Captain John A. Rawlins, a thirty-year-old Galena lawyer totally without military training or experience of any kind. Grant selected him for the job because he liked and trusted him, admired his keen intellect, and knew that he was a good friend of Washburne. Later some would say that his main function was to keep Grant sober, and that were he to be fatally shot it would be the equivalent of blowing out Grant's brains. The first assertion is extravagant, the second ignorant. He remained with Grant until the war's end, rising to major general, and when Grant became president he became his secretary of war for five months before dying of tuberculosis. Obviously, Grant found him indispensable; Rawlins in turn ended up literally dedicating his life to Grant.

On September 1 Grant arrived at Cape Girardeau, Missouri, with his brigade and instructions from Frémont to drive a band of Confederate irregulars under Colonel M. Jeff "Swamp Fox" Thompson out of southeast Missouri preparatory to crossing the Mississippi over into Kentucky, a state so sharply divided between Unionists and secessionists that its government had declared it to be neutral—as if it were a sovereign nation! For this purpose Grant was to command also the brigade of Benjamin Prentiss, one of the Illinoisans who obtained his general's commission at the same time as Grant. Prentiss, however, refused to take orders from Grant, contumaciously contending that he was senior in rank. Disgusted, Grant thereupon moved via steamboats with his own brigade alone to Cairo, Illinois, at the confluence of the Ohio and Mississippi—a highly strategic point. The very same day he landed there, September 3, a Confederate force sent from Tennessee by Major General Leonidas Polk occupied the Mississippi River town of Columbus, Kentucky. Polk, a West Pointer by education but an Episcopal bishop by vocation, acted on his own initiative, asserting that he merely forestalled the Yankees from doing it. He was not necessarily wrong, as indicated by Frémont's instructions to Grant regarding crossing over into Kentucky. Even so, he committed an egregious blunder in that he caused the Confederacy to be the first to violate the Bluegrass State's legally specious but emotionally precious neutrality, thereby swinging public sentiment there toward the Union.

Worse, he provided the Federals with a legitimate reason to enter the state themselves. Grant immediately recognized this. On September 5 he wired Frémont in St. Louis that unless otherwise directed he would seize Paducah, Kentucky, where the Tennessee River empties into the Ohio. Frémont responded by authorizing Grant to do so—but in a telegram couched, presumably for security reasons, in Magyar! Not having, like Frémont, Hungarian staff officers, the telegram was Greek to Grant. Concluding that if Frémont did not want him to go to Paducah he would have said so in English, he decided to head for there at once. Shortly before midnight he set out for the town with two regiments aboard as many steamers, reached and occupied it early in the morning, and the following day sent a detachment to do the same at Smithfield, Kentucky, near the mouth of the Cumberland River. As a result, he prevented a Confederate force, marching overland, from taking both.[3]

He also set the stage for the North achieving a major strategic success. Although the Cumberland and Tennessee flow northward into the Ohio, they offered what anybody capable of reading a map could see: liquid avenues southward through Kentucky and the western half of the state of Tennessee, and thence into Mississippi, Alabama, and Georgia—the very heartland of the Confederacy, the loss of which would mean the loss of the war for the South, barring total military calamity for the North in the East. The Federals possessed, or soon would possess, sufficient strength in soldiers, ships, and supplies to achieve this outcome—provided that they also had commanders with the talent and tenacity to employ their strength effectively.

Frémont was not such a commander. A man of many qualities, he suffered from a fatal flaw: high ambitions combined with low abilities for realizing them. He demonstrated this in the political sphere by issuing, on August 30, and without authorization from Lincoln but with a view to succeeding him as president, a proclamation in the form of a military order declaring that the slaves of Missourians guilty of supporting secession henceforth would be free. This attempt to institute at least partial emancipation, while applauded by Northern abolitionists, threatened disaster for the Union cause not only in Missouri but all of the slaveholding border states, in particular Kentucky. Kentucky-born Lincoln, well aware of this, asked Frémont to withdraw the order. When Frémont refused, Lincoln canceled it himself, at the same time reaffirming that the purpose of the war was to preserve the Union and not to extirpate slavery, a stance that all Northerners, save abolitionists, supported—although a growing number of them believed, as did Grant, that sooner or later slavery would and should cease to exist.

Next Frémont added military fumbling to political folly. In mid-September Major General Sterling Price, commander of the pro-secessionist Missouri State Guard, having in conjunction with Confederate forces out of Arkansas defeated Brigadier General Nathaniel Lyon's Federal army near Springfield, Missouri, on August 10, advanced all the way to Lexington on the Missouri River, where he besieged and on September 20 captured its 3,500-man garrison. Then, when Frémont moved against Price, he did so too slowly either to intercept or overtake him as he fell back first to Springfield and next almost into northwest Arkansas. Frémont planned to follow him there and, no doubt, would have had not Lincoln, exasperated by his shortage of competence and surplus of conceit, relieved him of command on November 2.[4]

Meanwhile, Grant had been growing restive. Downriver from Cairo the Confederates were transforming Columbus into a "Gibraltar of the West." Also across the Mississippi from Columbus on the Missouri shore they had established a troop camp at Belmont. Increasingly it seemed to Grant that the prospect of a successful Union offensive southward by way of the Mississippi was decreasing. Therefore, he reasoned, the sooner he attacked, the better. Unfortunately, his instructions from Frémont forbade this; instead, they called for him to carry out "demonstrations" against Jeff "Swamp Fox" Thompson in southeast Missouri so as to prevent him from reinforcing Price in the southwest part of the state—something in fact about as likely to occur as Thompson's motley irregulars rowing up the Mississippi in canoes to land at and take St. Louis.

Then came word of the "Pathfinder's" removal from command. This meant that Grant now was free of Frémont and of his instructions, especially one which expressly prohibited "attacking the enemy" while making "demonstrations." He decided to take advantage of this freedom. On the evening of November 6 he loaded five infantry regiments, two cavalry companies, and a six-gun battery aboard six steamboats and accompanied by two gunboats headed for Belmont, his objective the Rebel camp. Capturing it would be the best way to prevent Thompson or any other Confederate force from going to Price. Better still, it could open the way for taking or bypassing Columbus, then advancing southward via the Mississippi.

Grant felt confident of success. He would have the advantage of surprise. This in turn should have enabled him to defeat whatever foe he found at Belmont before Polk could send aid to it from Columbus, an eventuality he sought to further forestall by directing Brigadier General Charles F. Smith, commander of Union troops at Paducah, to threaten the "Gibraltar of the West" from its landside. But, above all, he believed that by attacking he would compel the enemy to react to his actions, giving him both the tactical and psychological advantage. This was the way Winfield Scott and Zachary Taylor, under whom he also had served, had fought and won in Mexico; it now was the way he intended to fight and win in the South. Besides, only by fighting could a general succeed in war, and, having experienced more than enough failure, he was determined to succeed if given the chance, even if he had to do what he was doing now—create that chance.

Early on the morning of November 7 Grant's 3,114 troops landed near Belmont (all three buildings of it) and, apart from five companies left behind to guard the transports, began marching toward the Rebel camp. At first only a few hundred Mississippians and Arkansans were there to oppose them. Soon, though, four Tennessee regiments headed by Brigadier General Gideon J. Pillow joined them, having been sent across the river in steamboats by Polk. Now slightly superior in numbers to the Federals engaged, the Confederates held Grant in check until, short of ammunition and their left flank giving way, all of them still able—Pillow among them—fled down to the riverbank. Assuming that the battle was over and they had won it, instead of pursuing the fleeing Rebels, Union soldiers began ransacking the enemy camp or gathered to listen to various officers, notably former congressman Brigadier General John McClernand, deliver victory speeches. But while the Yankees plundered and celebrated, several thousand additional Confederates began landing on the Missouri shore. Before long it was the Southern soldiers who were pressing forward, driving back the Northern ones until they reached the transports and scrambled aboard. The last to do so was Grant, who guided his horse up a gangplank onto the deck of a boat just as it pulled away to follow the others steaming back to Cairo. Going to the captain's cabin, he lay down on a couch to catch his breath and gather his thoughts, then got up to go outside and check, as a general should, on the overall situation. When he returned to the cabin, he saw a still-warm bullet hole in the couch exactly where his head had been.

Both Grant and Polk claimed victory at Belmont. Assessing the engagement as such, Polk was right and Grant wrong. Obviously Grant failed to seize and hold Belmont, and far from destroying the Confederate force, he was fortunate to escape with his own still intact after suffering approximately 600 casualties, slightly less than Polk's. Apart from his rookie soldiers thinking that they had won before the fighting ended, three reasons explain his defeat. First, Smith did not, because he could not on such short notice and with the small number of troops at his disposal, mount a sufficient threat to Columbus on land to deter Polk from eventually sending more than five thousand men over to Belmont; indeed, the closest Smith's main column got to Columbus was twelve miles, and that not until the evening of November 7! Second, Grant lacked the foresight, probably because he did not foresee the need, to arrange beforehand with Commander Henry Walke, in charge of the two gunboats accompanying the expedition, to block any attempt by Polk to ship reinforcements across the river to Belmont. Moreover, Walke lacked the pugnacity to at least attempt to do this on his own initiative, for although his gunboats were "woodclads," they carried eight-inch cannons, a single projectile from which, striking one of the densely packed Confederate steamships, would have been so devastating that in all likelihood it would have caused the others to turn back. Third, and the most fundamental reason because the others derived from it, Grant conceived and conducted the Belmont sortie on the premise that Polk, taken by surprise and fearful of a land attack on Columbus, would stay on the passive defensive; having learned in July that an enemy was equally afraid, he now needed to learn that an enemy can also be equally brave.[5]

Although a present defeat, Belmont helped prepare the way for future Federal victory. It provided Grant with his first experience in conducting a battle and the troops with him their initial exposure to fighting one, with the result that the next time they engaged in large-scale combat, they both would know better what to expect and how to act. And, much more important, it strengthened the already strong belief of the Confederates that the principal perils to their defense line in Kentucky lay in the central part of the state at Bowling Green and on its western flank at Columbus. Consequently, they, in particular Polk, tended to discount, even disregard, the region between and with it the Tennessee and Cumberland rivers.[6] It would prove to be a fatal mistake—perhaps the most fatal strategic misjudgment of the entire Civil War.

On November 19 both Missouri and Grant received a new commander: Major General Henry Wager Halleck. His appointment to that post surprised nobody and pleased almost everybody, Grant included. Forty-six and a native of New York state, Halleck enjoyed the reputation of being the smartest man in America possessing a professional military pedigree. He had finished third in the West Point class of 1839, been assigned to the Corps of Engineers, gone to France to report on its fortifications, played a key role in the military government of California during the Mexican War, and, most impressive of all, published several books, notably one on the *Elements of Military Art and Science,* an accomplishment that caused him to be dubbed in army circles as "Old Brains," an appellation made all the more apt by his enormous, bulbous cranium. Although he totally lacked combat experience and had resigned from the army in 1854 to become a wealthy San Francisco lawyer, had he not been in far-off California at the outbreak of the war, probably he instead of McClellan would have become the number one major general. As it was, he ranked in seniority only behind McClellan and now out-of-favor Frémont with a command in the West surpassed in prestige and importance solely by McClellan's in the East. Should the "Young Napoleon" falter in his perceived mission of winning the war by taking Richmond, then he, Halleck, translator from the French of Henri Jomini's mammoth biography of the old Napoleon, possessed the best prospect of superseding him as the North's premier commander, provided, of course, that he practiced the elements of military art with the same skill he wrote about them.[7] He intended and expected to do so. The problem, as he saw it, was that at present he lacked the requisite means.

"Affairs here," he telegraphed McClellan on November 27, "in complete chaos. Troops unpaid, want clothing and arms . . . some utterly demoralized. Hospitals overflowing with sick." Reports from southwest Missouri stated that Price, with 15,000 or perhaps 23,000 men, was again advancing northward. Although armored gunboats were under construction at St. Louis and Mound City, Illinois, none yet were ready for service.[8] But the worst deficiency, in Halleck's eyes, lay in his generals. With three exceptions none possessed professional backgrounds or any true military experience; instead, like McClernand and Prentiss, they merely were ambitious politicians with a silver star on each shoulder. As for the triad of exceptions, only two could be deemed reliable. One was Smith at Paducah. Fifty-four and an 1825 graduate of West Point, where he later served as commandant of cadets (including Grant), he had performed superbly in Mexico and by 1854 risen to lieutenant colonel. Unfortunately, though, he had not become a brigadier general until August and therefore was junior in rank to all other brigadiers.

The other was John Pope, a thirty-nine-year-old West Pointer (class of 1842) who also happened to be the nephew of a U.S. senator from his native Kentucky, related by marriage to Mary Todd Lincoln, the president's wife, and the son of a judge before whom Lincoln had tried cases. These connections, along with an excellent record in Mexico and as an engineer officer, had led to his being commissioned a brigadier general as of May 17, making him at least equal in seniority to all of the other brigadiers in Missouri. Yet he too could not be used at present to supersede any of them because he now headed the forces opposing Price, Frémont's temporary successor, Major General David Hunter, having been given command of the newly established Department of Kansas. For several weeks in November, Halleck hoped to make Pope available for a more important assignment by replacing him with Brigadier General William Tecumseh Sherman. He had known "Cump," as family and close friends called Sherman, long and well. Together they had traveled in 1846–47 aboard a ship sailing from New York around the tip of South America to California. Subsequently, in the 1850s, after each resigned from the army, both had gone into business in San Francisco, where Halleck succeeded and Sherman did not. Even so, "Old Brains" deemed Sherman one of the few worthy to belong in his own rarefied intellectual class. Moreover, thanks to a politically influential father-in-law and a younger brother who was a powerful Republican senator from Ohio, Sherman ranked seventh among all Union brigadiers, despite not having buckled on his sword again until two months after Fort Sumter, and thus was senior to Pope. But Halleck's hope soon turned into disappointment. Sent to southwestern Missouri to inspect the military situation there, all Sherman did was to complete the nervous breakdown that had caused him to be relieved, at his request, from command in Kentucky and so had to be put on sick leave in order to recuperate at his wife's family home in Lancaster, Ohio.

The third exception—or, to be precise, the exception to the exceptions—was, of course, Grant. Halleck viewed him with disdain and distrust. Disdain because he had heard of his chronic drunkenness while stationed out on the West Coast, distrust because he believed his rash dash to Belmont had achieved nothing while barely escaping disaster. For now Halleck had no alternative to leaving Grant in command in Cairo—indeed, he soon created a separate "District of Cairo"—but at the same time he resolved to keep a close watch and a short rein on Grant, ready to jerk the latter hard should the occasion occur. He hoped it would—and the sooner the better.[9]

Having thus found his means inadequate, Halleck decided to do nothing until able to decide everything: when, where, and with what to secure Missouri and open up the Mississippi by driving the Confederates down it. It was a sound decision; it also was an easy and safe one to make, for he was under no pressure from Washington to launch any immediate offensive operation. The reason was the president. Lincoln wished to achieve in predominantly East Tennessee what had been accomplished in Unionist-dominated West Virginia. Hence, soon after McClellan replaced Scott as commanding general on November 2 he had asked him to send an expedition by way of Cumberland Gap into that region, thereby touching off a popular uprising that would liberate it from Rebel control.

The "Young Napoleon" was quite willing to oblige—in his fashion—the "original gorilla," as he dubbed Lincoln in letters to his wife, Ellen. An attempted invasion of eastern Tennessee would relieve him of mounting public and Republican pressure to strike for Richmond in eastern Virginia, something he had no intention of doing until he could do it without any risk of a defeat that could be attributed to him. And an attempted invasion almost surely would be what it would be since the force that made it would have to march and be supplied by a single wretched road stretching some two hundred miles through largely barren country from the main Union base, Camp Dick Robinson, in central Kentucky to Knoxville, the principal town of East Tennessee. But even should it by some near miracle succeed, it would make no difference as far as the course of the war and the trajectory of his career were concerned. Once he took Richmond, the war would be won, and he would be acclaimed its winner and, quite likely, the next president of the United States. The Southern states would be restored to the Union with their constitutional rights, among them the right of slavery, guaranteed, thereby preventing Lincoln and the Republicans from turning the conflict into a crusade to abolish slavery, something that he as a staunch Democrat strongly opposed, believing that this would render a true reunification of the nation impossible.

So, when on November 7, and again five days later, McClellan wrote letters of instruction to Brigadier General Don Carlos Buell, who was about to take over from Sherman in Kentucky, he stated that while a move via Cumberland Gap into East Tennessee was desirable, he left it up to him to decide if it would be practicable. In doing this McClellan felt confident that Buell, a forty-three-year-old West Pointer who shared his views on how the war should be fought and for what, would find it to be the latter. His confidence proved well placed. Less than two weeks after assuming command in Kentucky on November 15, Buell informed his "Dear Friend" McClellan that seizing Nashville promised superior strategic results to occupying Knoxville, for which he lacked sufficient strength in any case. This message delighted McClellan, who telegraphed in response, "Your letter received. I fully approve of your course and agree in your views," and then added: "I now feel sure that I have a 'lieutenant' in whom I can fully rely."[10]

He certainly could.

The remainder of November, all of December, and most of January passed without any significant military activity in the West on the part of Halleck and Buell for the Federals or by General Albert Sidney Johnston, commander of all Confederate forces west of the Appalachians. Meanwhile, at Cairo and Paducah, Grant's strength in manpower and materiel steadily grew. As February drew nigh, he possessed nearly 25,000 soldiers, ample field artillery, enough steamships to carry them, plus needed supplies, and the potential support of eleven gunboats, seven of them newly launched armored ones mounting monstrous cannons capable of propelling giant shells several miles with destructive accuracy. His desire to use this power also grew. He had never read Halleck's translation of Jomini's book about Napoleon or, probably, any book on generalship; but even so, he realized that with rare exceptions it is necessary to fight battles in order to win wars. Besides, since the Confederates showed no sign of attacking, that could only mean they were weak, in which case why not attack them now that the Federals were strong? Yet the only instructions he received from Halleck were the same as sent by Frémont: conduct "demonstrations" while taking care to avoid bringing on a battle. Writing to a friend on January 17, he complained that "sloshing about in mud, rain, sleet and snow" merely to worry the enemy "is not war."[11]

Specifically, Grant wanted (as did Halleck) to take Columbus, and he believed that this could be done—indeed, only could be done—by attacking it from the landside, it truly being a "Gibraltar of the West" on the waterside. Reconnaissances undertaken late January by him and Smith revealed that the roads in the Columbus area were virtually impassible owing to mud, whereas Confederate Fort Henry, guarding the Tennessee River just south of the Kentucky-Tennessee border, was very vulnerable to land and river assault. Eager to exploit this weakness before the enemy corrected it, Grant traveled to St. Louis, where on January 20 he proposed to Halleck, in their first meeting ever, that he take a large portion of his forces up the Tennessee in transports and, in conjunction with Flag Officer Andrew Hull Foote's gunboats, capture the fort. Halleck, though, barely bothered to listen to him before curtly rejecting such a venture. He simply did not trust Grant as a commander or a man.

Toward the end of January two events occurred that changed Halleck's mind. First, Lincoln, frustrated by the passivity of his armies, especially

McClellan's Army of the Potomac in Virginia, decreed that all of them were to advance southward on Washington's birthday! Next, Halleck received an order from McClellan to do something in western Kentucky to reduce the enemy threat to Buell's army in central Kentucky—a threat about to be increased, according to McClellan's intelligence service, by the transfer there from Virginia of Confederate General Pierre Gustave Toutant Beauregard, the "hero" of Fort Sumter and Bull Run, along with fifteen regiments. (Actually, although Beauregard went to Kentucky, no troops accompanied him.) Deciding now that he had no choice except to make a decision, Halleck on January 28 authorized Grant to execute a plan he had submitted for taking Fort Henry. Should this expedition succeed, then fine. He could claim the credit. On the other hand, if it resulted in another Belmont-type near debacle, then he could not be rightly blamed, having been denied competent field commanders and thus obliged to employ the likes of Grant.[12]

On February 3 Grant set out from Cairo up the Ohio to Paducah and then up the Tennessee toward Fort Henry.[13] His ground force numbered 15,000 formed into two divisions, one under Smith, the other headed by McClernand, who had performed well in combat at Belmont and been praised accordingly by Grant. Seven gunboats, four of them the new ironclads, accompanied the transports, their commander Flag Officer Foote, a white-bearded veteran of forty years of service afloat that began at age sixteen. Also with Grant was a larger, more professional staff, headed by Colonel Joseph D. Webster, a highly competent former regular army officer, and including as chief engineer Lieutenant Colonel James B. McPherson, a handsome, thirty-three-year-old graduate of West Point, where he graduated number one in the class of 1853. Both would serve Grant well, and he in turn would serve them well, in particular McPherson, who like himself was a native of rural Ohio and from an even humbler background. Rawlins, though, remained the adjutant general and, on the personal level, much more than that—increasingly more.

Late the following day the Union river armada anchored six miles north of Fort Henry, which was located on the east bank of the Tennessee at a point where it bulged off to the west. Prior to departing Cairo, Grant believed its garrison totaled a mere 3,000; subsequent information caused him to double this estimate. Nevertheless, as he wrote his wife, Julia, that evening, he retained "a confidant [*his spelling*] feeling of success."[14]

He had better reasons than he realized for such confidence. Fort Henry's garrison, in fact, numbered a mere 2,700 raw troops, most armed with hunting rifles, shotguns, or flintlocks dating from the War in 1812, and its nine riverfront cannons were positioned so that they could fire only downstream.

Worse, the fort itself would soon become untenable. Built during the spring of 1861, it was situated on ground so low that the river, which was rapidly rising while incessant rain poured down, soon would inundate it! Recognizing that it had been poorly sited, Albert Sidney Johnston, upon assuming command of Confederate western forces in September, had ordered the construction of a new fort atop a lofty height across the way on the left bank of the Tennessee. Since then, some work had been done on the new bastion, but not nearly enough. "Bishop General" Polk, believing as devoutly as he believed in the Episcopal Book of Common Prayer that the Yankees intended to move first and only against Columbus, continued to devote himself to strengthening its already strong fortifications. At the same time, Johnston, preoccupied by Buell's nonexistent threat in central Kentucky, neglected to prod his chief engineer to complete the uncompleted fort, a task for which that individual felt no sense of urgency, as he too assumed that the Federals intended to strike by way of the Mississippi, and they would not do so until spring. Consequently, when the Union flotilla approached Fort Henry, what had been dubbed Fort Heiman consisted merely of ramparts behind which were neither cannons nor soldiers.[15]

Grant's plan for taking Fort Henry envisioned Smith's division occupying Fort Heiman, then bombarding Henry with artillery while McClernand's division assailed it on land from the east and Foote's gunboats pounded it from the north. Rain and mud, though, bogged down Smith's and Mc-Clernand's troops so badly after they landed on February 5 that nightfall found them still far from their respective objectives. Aware that the rising river alone rendered Henry untenable, its commander, Brigadier General Lloyd Tilghman, thereupon sent all but fifty-five of its garrison to reinforce Fort Donelson on the Cumberland River, a dozen miles to the east and presumably the next Federal objective. He himself remained at Henry, his sole intention to defend it long enough to satisfy military honor, then evacuate the place before he and his men drowned.

In the morning Smith and McClernand resumed their creeping march while Foote's gunboats, the four ironclads in the van, steamed forward to engage the Confederate battery. Shortly before noon they opened fire and, once they got the range, their projectiles began ripping through the fort's earthen parapets as if they were pine boards. Even so, Tilghman's little band of cannoneers responded vigorously and accurately, with some of their shot scattering and sometimes penetrating the iron plates that gave the ironclads their name; these craft, it became evident to their crews, were far from being invulnerable. For two hours the duel between ship and shore raged. Then, with his usable cannons reduced to four and having held out twice as long as he had hoped, Tilghman lowered the fort's flag. A boatload of Union naval officers sent by Foote to receive formal surrender paddled into it by way of the sally port.[16]

Thus Grant gained his first indisputable victory, but he gave Foote the credit. Actually it belonged to the rain, which had caused the Tennessee to rise thirty feet above its normal level. Had the Union expedition set out from Cairo two or three days later than it did, Henry would have been semi-submerged in water, its garrison gone and cannons destroyed, and Foote would not have fired a shot, having nothing to fire one at.

Yet it was Grant's initiative and energy that brought about the seizure of the fort and with it the first penetration of the Confederate defense line in the West. This he knew, and the knowledge inspired him to do the same at Donelson on the Cumberland. "I shall," he concluded a February 6 telegram to Halleck announcing that day's triumph, "take and destroy Fort Donelson on the 8th and return to Fort Henry."[17] News of the fall of Henry relieved Halleck's apprehension of a debacle. Grant's intention next and so soon to go after Donelson, something he hitherto had not so much as hinted doing, revived it. But he decided to allow this new venture to proceed in hope that it succeeded—or, should it fail, provide him at last with a good reason to get rid of this independent-minded, almost insubordinate ex-captain and, according to tales being circulated by some, still drunkard.

Grant's time schedule for capturing Donelson proved overly optimistic, Foote's gunboats having to return to Mound City, Illinois, for repairs before heading to and then up the Cumberland.[18] Not until February 12 did Grant start marching toward Donelson. Despite the delay, he continued to anticipate a quick, easy victory, even though intelligence reports indicated that this fort was far more formidable than Henry and defended by a much larger garrison. Two factors prompted his optimism.

First, the commander at Donelson was Pillow, whom he viewed with contempt, as did other West Pointers who had served in Mexico, where Pillow had been a high-ranking general thanks solely to his close political and personal relationship with President James K. Polk. Second, Grant again would have the support of Foote's armored gunboats, which, he assumed, again would demonstrate that cannons protected by iron outmatched cannons bulwarked by dirt.

The march from Fort Henry to Donelson occurred in springlike weather, causing the Union soldiers to discard overcoats and even blankets—an act they soon regretted when night brought a return of winter in the form of snow and frigid cold. On February 13 Grant deployed Smith's division to the left and McClernand's to the right. On the following day, he inserted a newly arrived third division, headed by Brigadier General Lew Wallace of Indiana, between Smith and McClernand, giving him altogether about 25,000 field troops, with more on the way aboard steamboats. Opposite him lay Donelson's landside fortifications, a semicircular line of rifle pits (as trenches were called during the Civil War) fronted by various types of obstructions and running, as did the Cumberland at this point, from east to northwest. He had no intention of assaulting them; there would be no need to. Once Foote's big guns smashed the Rebel river defenses, even a poltroon like Pillow would realize that he had no choice other than capitulation. It would be that easy.

It was not that easy. Donelson's garrison now numbered 20,000, having been reinforced by the troops from Fort Henry and by units sent by Johnston, who belatedly realized that should the Federals capture it, they then could steam up the Cumberland all the way southward to Nashville, Tennessee's capital and his chief supply base—a realization that had caused him to order his forces at Bowling Green in Kentucky to withdraw to that city. Furthermore, among Donelson's reinforcements was a Virginia contingent under John B. Floyd, the very same man who had opposed Rosecrans in West Virginia. Being senior in rank to Pillow, he now commanded the fort; furthermore, as noted in his behavior at Carnifex Ferry, he was not one to allow himself to be captured if he could avoid it. He was very much aware that Northerners believed, wrongly but strongly, that while secretary of war in Buchanan's cabinet he had transferred government weapons southward for the treasonous purpose of abetting rebellion, and that should he fall into Federal hands a prison, perhaps even the gallows, awaited him.

But the prime reason Donelson would prove much harder to take lay in its shore batteries. They numbered two, located one above the other on a high bluff overlooking the river and containing twelve large caliber cannons. Unlike Henry's batteries, they could fire down upon attacking ships, which for their part would have to fire up at them. When engaging Donelson, Foote and his crews might need to have the god of the sea, Neptune, intervene on their behalf against the god of war, Mars.

If Neptune did, Mars paid him no heed. At 3 P.M. on February 14, four ironclads advanced toward the fort, their unarmored upper decks covered with chains, lumber, and bags of coal to ward off plunging shot. Little more than an hour later they staggered back, two of them so badly damaged as to be unmanageable, a third out of action, and the fourth badly riddled and its gundeck slippery with blood. Casualties totaled eleven killed, several by having their heads literally obliterated, and forty-three wounded, among them Foote himself. As for the Confederates, only a few were slightly injured, their fortifications were barely damaged, and just two cannons were disabled, one by an accident. The gunboats' fire, subsequently reported a Rebel artillery officer, would have been much more potent from two miles, at which range the fort's cannons could not even reach them, than it was at 200 yards because "they over-fired us from that distance."[19]

Foote's unexpected repulse disappointed but did not dismay Grant. Unable to capture Donelson from its waterside and unwilling to assault its rifle pits on the landside with "my raw troops," he decided to starve it into submission. This would require a siege, and a siege could last weeks, perhaps many of them. "The taking of Fort Donelson," he wrote that night to Julia, "bids fair to be a long job."[20]

Even as Grant penned this pessimistic prediction three Confederate generals began making it unravel. One was Floyd. Sometime during the day he had received a telegram from Johnston: "If you lose the fort, bring your troops to Nashville if possible." Despite the defeat of Foote's ironclads, Floyd, who thought Grant had twice as many men as he did, feared that he soon would lose the fort—and with it his freedom. On the other hand, he believed that it might be possible to bring his troops (and himself) to Nashville. According to scouting reports the Federal right wing (McClernand's division) was "in the air"—that is, exposed to an attack in flank and rear. Hence, at a nighttime meeting with Pillow and Brigadier General Simon Bolivar Buckner of Kentucky and West Point, he proposed concentrating most of their troops on the left, then at daybreak launch an attack designed to drive the Yankees from the Forge and Wynn's Ferry roads, both of which led to Nashville. Pillow and Buckner agreed, the latter with misgivings, for he distrusted Floyd and in common with other military professionals disdained Pillow, attitudes he did little to conceal.

During the still-dark hours of early morning on February 15 nearly all of Buckner's division, which held the Confederate right opposite Smith, joined Brigadier General Bushrod Johnson's division and Colonel Nathan Bedford Forrest's cavalry contingent southeast of Donelson. Then, as a murky dawn broke, first Forrest, then Johnson, and finally Buckner, all under the field command of Pillow, struck the Union right and struck it hard. By noon they had seized the Forge Road and threatened to secure the Wynn's Ferry Road, having bent back McClernand's division until it was almost at a right angle to its original position. Elated, Pillow dashed off a message to be telegraphed to Johnston: "On the honor of a soldier, the day is ours."

Grant knew naught of this. Out of a desire to facilitate communication with Foote, he had established his headquarters in a log farmhouse behind the Union left and near a river landing. Then, on receiving early in the morning a note from Foote asking him to come to his flagship—his wound prevented him from leaving it—he had hastened to the craft after instructing his staff to order Wallace and McClernand not to bring on a battle and without informing Smith of his departure. As at Belmont, his mind was so focused on what he would do to the enemy that he gave no thought to what the enemy might do to him.

That is why he had planned to confer with Foote in any event, for he wished to ascertain the condition of the ironclads in hope they could at least bombard the fort while he tightened his investment of it. Hence on meeting with the old sea dog he was disappointed to hear that only two of the vessels remained capable of action, that the other two needed to return to Mound City for repairs, and that nothing decisive could be achieved from the river until the arrival of boats carrying mortars able to loft huge shells down onto Donelson's deadly batteries. During their conference Grant heard the rumble of gunfire off to the east but assumed that it was merely skirmishing.

Not until noon, when he stepped ashore at the landing from a rowboat, did he learn from a white-faced staff officer who had just arrived there of the desperate situation on the right. He rode at once to headquarters, where Rawlins and chief of staff Webster provided further information, and then set out for the right accompanied by the latter, pausing only to order Smith to dispatch one of his three brigades to reinforce McClernand.

On arrival, he found that counterattacks by two of Wallace's brigades, who on his own initiative had gone to McClernand's assistance, had dammed the Confederate torrent. Good. Bad, though, was the sight of large bodies of McClernand's troops standing about rather than fighting. He asked them why; no ammunition they answered. The reason? Many of their company, regimental, and even brigade commanders simply did not realize the need to keep soldiers engaged in combat constantly supplied with it, this being unmentioned in the drill manuals. Finally, and best of all, he learned that captured Confederates carried food-filled haversacks. This could only mean that they were endeavoring to escape from Donelson!

Turning to Webster, Grant said: "Some of our men are pretty badly demoralized, but the enemy must be more so, for he has attempted to force his way out, but has fallen back; the one who attacks first now will be victorious and the enemy will have to be in a hurry if he gets ahead of me." Then Webster and he rode among McClernand's men, shouting at them to refill their cartridge boxes—"tons" of ammunition were close by—and to reform their ranks, for "the enemy is trying to escape and he must not be permitted to." These words "acted like a charm." Soon all except one of

McClernand's three brigades were back in action, along with Wallace's division and the brigade sent by Smith, assailing the Confederates, who continued to fight defensively and in some sectors withdraw.

Satisfied that all now was well on the right, Grant next rode back to the left, where he ordered Smith to "take Fort Donelson." This, he explained, could be done with relative ease and without excessive loss, for in order to make such a heavy attack on their left the Rebels must have stripped their right of most of its defenders.[21] "I will do it," Smith replied. And do it he did. First he feinted a charge with the smallest of his brigades. Then he delivered the actual assault with the largest one, riding at its head with an uplifted sword, his hat on its tip—an assault spearheaded by the Second Iowa, which he had instructed to uncap muskets and fix bayonets. As Grant foresaw, a mere beadlike line of Confederates, wretchedly armed with shotguns, attempted to stem the oncoming Yankee swarms to no avail. Scrambling through brush piles and over spiked abatis stakes, Smith's men soon reached the rifle pits, driving from them all foes other than those who were dead, badly wounded, or threw up their hands in surrender.

Stimulated by the elixir of victory, Smith reformed his regiments, brought up artillery, and then resumed the attack, his target a high ridge from which, once taken, he could bombard Fort Donelson per se into submission. This time, though, his troops encountered opposition, opposition that grew so strong that they fell back to the already-seized trenches, where they remained, exchanging fire with the enemy until the advent of night, along with more snow and cold, brought fighting to an end.

Obviously, a far larger Rebel force now faced Smith than before. To be precise, it numbered approximately 4,000 and consisted of the main portion of Buckner's division, which had begun returning to the Confederate right just as Smith delivered his first assault. Had it arrived a bit sooner, or had Smith attacked a little later, in all likelihood Donelson's outer defense line would have remained intact. But as it was, it had been breached, and in Grant's estimation this meant the fort and its garrison were as good as taken. Come tomorrow, he doubted not, they would be.

Unknown to Grant because unknowable, the person most responsible for what he perceived to be his forthcoming triumph, other than himself, was Gideon J. Pillow. At noon, it will be recalled, Pillow thought that "the day is ours." Soon thereafter he changed his mind. Why? Some say that he decided that the Confederate success had been so great that there was no need to evacuate the fort, at least not yet. Others contend that he suddenly realized that while a way out of Donelson now was open via the Forge Road, his troops (other than Buckner's) were without haversacks, knapsacks, or even blankets; that no arrangements had been made to supply them during the retreat to Nashville, seventy-five miles distant; that nothing had been done to remove the mobile artillery and the rest of the garrison; and that many of his units were scattered and their men (as Grant had sensed) demoralized. Whatever the reasons, at about 1:30 P.M. Pillow, without so much as informing Floyd, much less requesting his approval, directed Buckner to return to his sector, and when Buckner objected, pointing out that one of his regiments in conjunction with Forrest's had just captured the last Yankee battery barring the Wynn's Ferry Road, Pillow went to Floyd and prevailed on him to repeat the order to Buckner. Then, and again without Floyd's prior consent but with his passive acquiescence, Pillow began pulling back Bushrod Johnson's division and Forrest's cavalry. Their withdrawal made it easier, if not possible, for Wallace and McClernand to regain by evening what they had lost in the morning. In effect, after opening a door out of Donelson, Pillow reclosed it.

Around midnight, Floyd, Pillow, and Buckner, their mood matching the somber sky, met to decide what to do next. Finally they agreed to attempt another breakout, and Floyd issued orders for it. Then scouts brought word that campfires indicated the Federals had resumed their former positions astride the Forge and Wynn's Ferry Roads. This information, which should not have been surprising, suggested that a second attack on the Union right would be more difficult and less successful than the first, which in turn meant that the only potential escape route left was the River Road, so called because it ran eastward along the river bank before turning southward to the town of Charlotte (which caused it to be called also the Charlotte Road). But was it a practicable route? More scouts went out, then came back. Some reported that it was, others that it was not owing to knee-deep mud on the road and the need to wade a creek chest-high with icy water and a hundred yards wide from melting snow. Pillow thereupon announced that he still favored cutting their way out. Buckner countered by declaring that "I cannot hold my position half an hour after an attack," and when Pillow asked him why not, he replied that Grant, whom he credited with possessing 40,000 troops, could bring "any given number" against his exhausted, shivering, half-famished 4,000. On hearing this, Pillow reverted to a modified version of his previous view. The fort, he argued, could be held at least another day, during which reinforcements might arrive from Johnston or, failing that, the garrison could escape by crossing to the other side of the river aboard steamboats. Back and forth the debate went. Finally, Floyd ended it. Buckner, he stated, was right—the sole alternative to a slaughter of the garrison was its surrender.

But, he continued, not by him. Risking his life on the battlefield was one thing, risking it in a Yankee courtroom another. Therefore, he did de jure what yesterday he had done de facto—relinquish command to Pillow. Pillow, who also had compelling (at least to him) personal reasons for not becoming a Union prisoner, in turn passed it on to Buckner, who accepted it in accordance with what in later years became the West Point motto of "Duty, Honor, Country." Forrest, who was present, then announced that he, too, would not surrender because he deemed it unnecessary. Having personally reconnoitered the River Road and found it both open and passable, he intended to take his cavalry and anybody else who wished to go with them out of Donelson by that route.

Toward dawn, as Grant sought to secure some sleep in his log house headquarters, Smith informed him that a Confederate courier carrying a white flag was outside, then handed him a note from Buckner. It asked for an armistice and terms of surrender.

"What answer shall I send him, General?" Grant asked Smith.

"No terms to the damned rebels," replied the white-haired veteran.

Grant thereupon drafted a reply. After being recopied by him, it read:

Sir:

Yours of this date proposing Armistice and appointment of Commissioners to settle terms of Capitulation is just received. No terms except unconditional and immediate surrender can be accepted.

I propose to move immediately upon your works.[22]

Grant's response offended Buckner. Like many professional soldiers of the period, he viewed war as a sort of knightly tournament. Besides, back in 1854, when Grant showed up in New York City at the end of his voyage from California following his resignation from the army, Buckner, who happened to be present, lent him money and provided lodging.[23] To be sure, Grant promptly repaid the loan and, of course, they now were official enemies, yet his demand for unconditional surrender backed up by a threat of immediate onslaught if it was refused showed no trace of friendship, much less a respect for the customs of civilized warfare (so called). Hence in reply Buckner stated stiffly that only "the overwhelming forces under your command" compelled him to "accept the ungenerous and unchivalrous terms which you propose."

In the morning upward of 16,000 Rebel soldiers became prisoners of war.[24] Floyd and Pillow were not among them. Floyd escaped by fleeing to Nashville with most of his Virginians in a steamboat, thereby preserving his freedom but destroying his reputation so thoroughly that Confederate President Jefferson Davis relieved him of duty. Pillow, by crossing over to the other side of the Cumberland in a scow, likewise eluded captivity and after months of suspension returned to service, but never again commanded more than a brigade and that, as we shall have occasion to note, with more ill-fortune.[25] As for Forrest, he began his ascent to high rank and even higher fame by marching out of Donelson via the River-Charlotte Road to Nashville with five hundred cavalry and approximately two hundred sundry artillerists and infantry who chose to accompany him. Encountering no opposition, nor seeing any Yankees in the vicinity, he opined in his official report that "two-thirds of our army" could have done the same. Possibly, but probably not; certainly it would have been much more difficult for thousands of foot soldiers to do in daylight what a much smaller number of predominantly mounted men did at night without the Federals detecting them and reacting accordingly.[26]

Grant's seizure of Forts Henry and Donelson, while putting out of action, either as casualties or captives, at least 18,000 Rebel troops at the cost of less than 3,000 of his own men provided the North with its first major victory of the war.[27] In fact, it constituted by far the greatest triumph gained by either side so far. Rosecrans's success in establishing Union dominance in West Virginia was, to repeat, paramountly a psychological one, with geography making that region a strategical dead end; and although the rout of McDowell's army at Bull Run humiliated Northerners and exalted Southerners, it left the basic military situation in the East unchanged, the Confederates lacking the means to follow it up with an offensive of their own and so remaining on the defensive. Grant's conquests, in contrast, not only thrilled the North and shocked the South, they also had an enormous impact on the course of the war both in the West and as a whole. They left Sidney Johnston with no rational choice, if he were to avoid total disaster, other than to do what he started doing as soon as Henry fell—withdraw the main part of his army from Bowling Green in central Kentucky to Nashville: now he had to abandon that as well because he could not hold the Tennessee capital with his available force. In sum, thanks to Grant, by mid-February 1862 the Federals controlled all of Kentucky and stood poised to occupy western Tennessee, invade the upper part of the Lower South, and advance by land and water down the Mississippi, thereby bisecting, symbolically if not physically, the Confederacy. Even should McClellan somehow fail to take Richmond in the East, it now had become possible for the Union to defeat the Confederacy in the West.

Grant did not originate the concept of piercing the Southern heartland via the Tennessee and Cumberland; this, as has been noted, was apparent to anyone able to understand a map. But it was he who acted upon it—first, by securing control of the mouths of those rivers along the Ohio, and, next, by seizing the forts that the Confederates had built along Tennessee's northern border in their miserably executed effort to prevent such a penetration. Of course, possession of the means to employ naval power on land against a foe who lacked it made his success possible, yet again it was he who made use of this advantage and in the process displayed initiative, great determination, and, above all, coolness and resourcefulness when faced, as it seemed to be at Donelson on February 15, with calamitous failure. The Northern press and people accorded him the credit for the victory in western Tennessee and, unlike McClellan for his putative accomplishments in western Virginia, he truly deserved it.

Henry and Donelson also made Grant a popular hero in the North. There his terse, stern demand for Buckner's unconditional surrender struck the public fancy and, in conjunction with his initials, caused him to be hailed as "Unconditional Surrender Grant." At the same time, newspaper accounts of Donelson in which he was described as riding about the battlefield with a cigar rather than a sword in his hand led to admirers sending him so many cigars that he soon discarded the pipe he hitherto had smoked in favor of stogies, and in so doing enhanced the image he already had begun to acquire of being a victorious commander who nevertheless was a plain, direct, no-nonsense man, a man of the people with whom people could identify.[28] Only three previous American generals ever had achieved such a status: Andrew Jackson, William Henry Harrison, and Zachary Taylor. All of them had become presidents.

For all of these reasons, Grant's capture of Forts Henry and Donelson represented a turning point in his career as well as the war—and he sensed it. On the very day Donelson surrendered, he wrote Julia: "My impression is that I shall have one hard battle more to fight and will find easy sailing after that."[29] His forecast proved accurate as regards fighting another hard battle. He failed, though, to foresee that he would not have easy sailing after it or, for that matter, before it. In front of him stood Albert Sidney Johnston, resolved to restore his once brilliant, now badly tarnished, military reputation—even if he died in the attempt. And behind him sat, at his desk, Henry Wager Halleck, who remained determined, despite Grant's victories, or perhaps because of them, to find a way to replace this reckless, probably alcoholic, upstart from Illinois with someone more reliable and less dangerous, especially when it came to his own aspirations.

During the next four months Grant would discover all of these things and learn lessons from the discovery, with the most important one being that to be a successful commander, in the sense of continuing to rise upward, you must be on guard against not only generals on the other side but also generals on your own side.

Like the lesson he learned outside of Florida, Missouri, in July 1861, it was a lesson he learned well—and learning it well would serve him well.

3

Grant, Halleck, and a Failure to Communicate

(February–March 1862)

ON THE EVENING OF FEBRUARY 16, 1862, recently installed Secretary of War Edwin M. Stanton went to the White House and handed Lincoln a document naming Grant a major general of volunteers. Lincoln signed it, commenting as he did so: "If the Southerners think that man for man they are better than our Illinois men, or Western men generally, they will discover themselves in a grievous mistake." Three days later the Senate confirmed the appointment and Congressman Elihu Washburne, Grant's Illinois political patron, telegraphed him the good news.[1]

The promotion pleased Grant. It provided professional gratification and personal vindication. "Is father afraid yet," he wrote his wife, Julia, who now was staying at Jesse Grant's Covington, Kentucky, home, "that I will not be able to sustain myself? He expressed apprehension on that point when I was made a Brigadier."[2] No one, above all his father, henceforth could deem him a failure.

He had no desire, though, to bask in the success achieved at Donelson. The Confederates in Tennessee were on the run and should be kept that way. "I can have," he wired Halleck's chief of staff, Brigadier General George W. Cullum, on February 19, "Nashville on Saturday week."[3]

Halleck, too, wanted to take Nashville—but not by Grant alone. Instead, he planned to have him do it in conjunction with Buell. That accomplished, then both of their armies were to switch over from the Cumberland to the Tennessee River and move by steamboats south on it until they reached a point near the Mississippi line, whereupon he would assume personal command of their forces, advance into the Mississippi, crush Johnston should he resist, and thus open the way for total Northern victory in the West and perhaps in the war as a whole—a victory designed and achieved by himself.[4]

This vision, and the ambition that inspired it, explains why, on learning of Donelson's fall, Halleck on February 17 telegraphed McClellan: "Make Buell, Grant, and John Pope major generals of volunteers and give me

command of the West. I ask this in return for Forts Henry and Donelson."
They also explain why the next day he ordered Grant not to "let gunboats
go higher up than Clarksville": he wished to forestall that overly aggressive
and insufficiently subordinate general from steaming up the Cumberland
to Nashville without prior authorization in the same fashion he had gone
after Belmont and Donelson.[5] Finally, in all likelihood they account for Halleck making no immediate response to Grant's February 19 message that he
could "have Nashville on Saturday week." He was waiting to obtain what
he desired far more than the speedy occupation of Tennessee's capital—to
wit, a positive response from McClellan to his request for command of the
West, by which he meant the entire Mississippi Valley.

It did not come. McClellan possessed sufficient intelligence to recognize
that placing the West under a single commander would provide the North
with the same advantages the South enjoyed there, albeit so far to little
actual avail, in Sidney Johnston—a top general able to formulate strategy
for and direct operations in all of that vast region. But he also was smart
enough to realize the danger that Halleck would pose to his own position
and aspirations should he receive such a post. Already Halleck stood second
solely to him among Union major generals with regular army rank, not
counting the now-commandless Frémont. Should he obtain the power to
gain a decisive, perhaps war-winning, victory in the West before his own
Army of the Potomac could win the war in the East by capturing Richmond, then he would supplant him as the North's number one general and
hero.

McClellan resolved to prevent even the possibility of this happening.
Hence he replied to Halleck's February 17 behest for command of the West
by not replying and remained silent after receiving a second one two days
later. Then, on February 20, a third arrived. It went beyond asking to almost
demanding: "I must have command of the armies of the West. Hesitation
and delay are losing us the golden opportunity. Lay this before the President
and Secretary of War. May I assume command? Answer quickly."[6]

McClellan did answer quickly (February 21) and his answer was negative: "Buell at Bowling Green knows more about the state of affairs [with
regard to Nashville] than you at St. Louis. Until I hear from him I cannot
see necessity of giving you entire command."[7]

Probably this response did not surprise Halleck; certainly it should not
have. Less than two weeks before he had asked McClellan to place him at
the head of a "Western Division," only to be told that this was impossible
because David Hunter, who now commanded the Department of Kansas,
was senior to him in rank as a major general of volunteers![8] Halleck knew

better and he knew that McClellan knew better, for it had been established during the Mexican War that a regular army commission trumped a volunteer army commission for the same rank regardless of date. Obviously, McClellan did not want him to command the West. So be it. Blocked in his attempt to go through normal official channels, he now felt free to appeal directly to a higher authority. On the same day he received McClellan's rejection he telegraphed the following to Secretary of War Stanton:

> One whole week has been lost already by hesitation and delay. There was, and I think there still is, a golden opportunity to strike a fatal blow, but I can't do it unless I can control Buell's army . . . I have explained everything to General McClellan and Assistant Secretary of War [Thomas A.] Scott. There is not a moment to be lost. Give me authority, and I will be responsible for results.[9]

Stanton answered the next day:

> Your telegram of yesterday, together with Mr. Scott's reports [from Louisville on the military situation in the West], have this morning been submitted to the President, who, after full consideration of the subject, does not think any change in the organization of the Army or the military departments at present advisable. He desires and expects you and General Buell to cooperate fully and zealously with each other, and would be glad to know whether there has been any failure of cooperation in any particular.[10]

Halleck must have read these words with pleasure. They meant that although he was not to have immediate command of the West, he now could hope to secure it in the near future, especially since he also had received a telegram from Stanton stating that "Your plan of organization [of the West into a single department] has been transmitted to me by Mr. Scott and strikes me very favorably."[11] He had, it seemed, the backing of the Secretary of War, an official second in power when it came to military matters only to the president.

February 24 brought more good news: a confirmed report that the Confederates had evacuated Nashville. From this Halleck concluded that Buell, who at long last had set out overland from Bowling Green with most of his army, should be able to reach the place that very day. This in turn would free Grant to return to the Tennessee at Fort Henry, from where his forces could then be transported up that river down toward Mississippi. Most annoyingly, though, a hitch had developed that threatened to delay the execution of this movement. Without first clearing it with him, chief of staff George Cullum had provided one of Buell's divisions, that of Brigadier General William Nelson, with the steamboats that Halleck had intended for Grant's army on the Tennessee, so that it could travel to Nashville via the Cumberland! This, he wired Cullum, "disconcerted my plans. You should not have done it without my orders. If you can stop them by telegraph, do so, and order them to rendezvous at Paducah."[12]

It proved too late—much too late. Most of the ships carrying Nelson's division reached Donelson during the night of February 23, and in the morning Nelson asked Grant, as commander of the newly designated District of West Tennessee, for instructions. Grant, having received no word from Cullum or any orders to the contrary from Halleck, told him to proceed to Nashville, the Confederate evacuation of which he too had learned.[13]

The rest of February 24 and the ensuing day passed still without any communications, much less instructions, from Halleck or Cullum. What, Grant wondered, were Halleck's plans now that Nashville had fallen and what role did he have in them? Finally he decided to go to Nashville to confer with Buell, who reportedly had reached there, and (he wrote Julia) "learn what I can of the movements of the enemy." He also sent Cullum a letter—he had no direct telegraphic connection with Cairo—informing him of his intention to go to Nashville "immediately after the arrival of the next mail, should there be no orders to prevent it."[14]

The mail arrived, and it contained no orders for him at all; hence, February 26 found him aboard a steamboat headed for Nashville. On the way he stopped off at Clarksville, which had been occupied by 2,000 troops under Smith. Buell, Smith informed him, had just sent an order to come at once with his force to Nashville—an order that was "nonsense." Grant agreed but said it should be obeyed. He then continued on to Nashville, more eager than before to talk with Buell.

He landed there early the next morning. In the city, which lay on the south bank of the Cumberland, he found Nelson with his division but not Buell. Where was he? He would arrive soon, Nelson answered. Several hours passed but no Buell. Finally, unable to wait longer, Grant addressed a letter to him stating that Smith was on the way to Nashville with "probably 2,000 men" but adding that "should you deem them unnecessary to your security, I request that they be ordered back" to Clarksville. He then signed the letter "U. S. Grant, Maj. Gen. Com'd'g"—his first-ever use of this title and no doubt designed to impress on Buell that he outranked him.[15]

Returning to the steamboat landing he by chance met Buell, who had just disembarked after crossing over from the other side of the river, where most of his troops remained. Before him stood a man identical to him in height (five foot eight), yet standing much more erect and with a waist so small and a chest so full as to rival even McClellan in these respects. He also beheld a stern face and cold eyes, with an unsmiling mouth framed by a graying mustache and short beard. Forty-three and an 1841 graduate of West Point, Buell neither possessed nor claimed intellectual distinction, but during the Mexican War he had displayed uncommon courage in Scott's army, where such was common among West Pointers, and by 1861 had attained the rank of major and a post on Winfield Scott's staff. As previously noted, he owed his present rank and command to McClellan, with whom he had developed a close friendship while they served together in Texas during the early 1850s. Like him he believed the war should be fought strictly to restore the Union and not free slaves, a number of whom he owned.[16] He shared McClellan's view that the best way to assure victory in military operations was to reduce the risk of defeat to the lowest possible minimum by not taking risks—an attitude that stood in stark contrast to the lesson that Grant derived from his July 1861 discovery in Missouri that the enemy, too, was afraid.

Their different approaches to waging war manifested themselves during a brief conversation on the Nashville wharf. Grant stated that according to his information Johnston's troops were "retreating as fast as possible" toward Chattanooga, about 150 miles to the southwest of Nashville. No, countered Buell, in all likelihood Johnston soon would return and attack him with 40,000 men, whereas at present he had only 15,000, including Nelson's division, which unfortunately had made itself vulnerable by occupying Nashville and thus putting itself south instead of north of the Cumberland. In the absence of positive word to the contrary, responded Grant, he believed his information to be correct. He knew, replied Buell, that he was right. "Well," said Grant, "I do not know." Then, after telling Buell that Smith's force was on the way from Clarksville, he boarded his steamboat and headed back to Donelson. Evidently Buell failed to realize that it would have been rather peculiar for Johnston to have abandoned the capital of Tennessee and a major Confederate supply source in the West merely to return a few days later in an attempt to retake it. In fact, Johnston evacuated Nashville because his "army" was only 14,000 "strong," and although he was not retreating all the way to Chattanooga, at present he had no more intention than he had the means to launch an offensive. For the time being, at least, Buell was as safe from an enemy attack in Nashville as he would have been if still in Louisville.[17]

On February 28 Grant returned to Donelson, where he found that still no instructions or intelligence of any kind had arrived from Halleck or Cullum. What did this long silence mean? Then, on March 2, a telegraphic message from Halleck, dated March 1, finally arrived. It notified him that transports would be sent to him "as soon as possible to move your column up the Tennessee River," with the object of breaking the Memphis & Charleston Railroad at four designated places, the sole continuous rail link in the entire South between the Mississippi and the Atlantic, plus cutting at two of those places the main north-south rail lines in West Tennessee. Grant recognized this to be the excellent strategy it was. On the other hand, Halleck's instructions were addressed to him at "Fort Henry," to which he had received no orders to take troops. Well, so be it. On March 4 he marched with two brigades, enough for what basically would be a raid, from Donelson to Henry.

There, the following day, he received another telegram from Halleck. Dated March 4, it read: "You will place Major Genl C. F. Smith in command of expedition, and remain yourself at Fort Henry. Why do you not obey my orders to report strength and position of your command?"[18] These words surprised and perplexed Grant. When had Smith become a major general?—not that he objected, for he deemed Smith most worthy of the rank and found it embarrassing to exercise command over his former commandant at West Point. And why did Halleck accuse him of disobeying orders to report on the strength and location of his troops when he had done so often and without orders? Something was wrong, something that needed to be made right. At once he wrote Halleck a letter wherein, after saying that the instructions regarding Smith and the Tennessee River expedition would be executed, he stated in essence that any failure by him to implement Halleck's orders and of Halleck to obtain reports from him had been caused not by disobedience on his part, but by his not receiving the orders and by his reports not reaching Halleck. With the letter he sent a statement of the number and position of his command.[19]

Grant correctly surmised that there had been a breakdown of communication between Halleck and him. Not until Grant returned to Fort Henry on March 4 did he have telegraphic contact, via Paducah and Cairo, with St. Louis, and even this had not existed until toward the end of February, when a line finally had been laid from Paducah to Henry. During late February and early March the already overworked Cullum in Cairo was very ill, with the quite possible result that (as Grant implied in the above letter to Halleck) he failed to convey promptly or fully to St. Louis dispatches from Grant. Also the final week of February saw violent storms in northwestern

Kentucky, storms that brought down telegraph wires or caused them to malfunction between Cairo and Paducah. And, as if all of this were not enough, it eventually turned out that the Union telegraph operator at Fort Henry was a Confederate adherent who at first refrained from forwarding messages to Grant at Donelson and then decamped, taking them with him![20]

Other than the presence of a traitorous telegraph operator at Henry, Halleck was well aware of the problems plaguing communications in the area where Grant was operating.[21] So why, instead of accusing Grant of disobeying orders, did he not ask him if he had received those orders or have some officer visit him with a view to finding out what the problem might be? And why, too, did he instruct Grant to place Smith in charge of the Tennessee expedition while at the same time casually informing him that Smith was major general, date of rank unstated?

The answer is simple and should come as no surprise: Halleck, despite the victories at Henry and Donelson, still distrusted Grant both as a man and a commander and wished to supersede him with Smith—indeed, if at all possible, to get rid of him altogether. Thus on February 19, when all he knew about the details of the fighting at Donelson was what he might have read in newspapers, Halleck on his own initiative informed McClellan that it was Smith who, "by his coolness and bravery at Fort Donelson when the battle was against us, turned the tide and carried the enemy outworks. Make him a major general. You can't get a better one."[22]

Next, on March 2, presumably aware that come tomorrow Lincoln would be submitting to the Senate a list of generals to be promoted that included Smith, Halleck telegraphed McClellan as follows:

> I have had no communication with General Grant for more than a week. He left his command without my authority and went to Nashville. His army seems to be as much demoralized by the victory of Fort Donelson as was that of the Potomac by the defeat of Bull Run. It is hard to censure a successful general immediately after a victory, but I think he richly deserves it. I can get no returns, no reports, no information of any kind from him. Satisfied with his victory, he sits down and enjoys it without any regard to the future. I am worn-out and tired with this neglect and inefficiency. C. F. Smith is almost the only officer equal to the emergency.[23]

Since Halleck surely knew that McClellan shared his low opinion of Grant's moral and mental character, just as surely he expected a favorable response to his complaints about him. This he got, and soon. "Your dispatch of last evening received," telegraphed McClellan at 6 P.M. March 3. "The future success of our cause demands that proceedings such as Grant's should at once be checked. . . . Do not hesitate to arrest him at once . . . and place C. F. Smith in command." And making perfect the already excellent, McClellan's message bore an endorsement from Stanton: "Approved."[24]

When on March 4 Halleck read McClellan's answer and Stanton's sanction, quite likely he smiled, at least inwardly, for he now possessed the power not only to replace Grant with Smith but also to put him under arrest as well. Moreover, he also now possessed another and, in its way, even stronger reason for doing these things, a reason he promptly communicated to McClellan: "A rumor had just reached me that since the taking of Fort Donelson General Grant has resumed his former bad habits. If so, it will account for his neglect of my often-repeated orders."[25]

Yet Halleck's next telegram to Grant, sent March 6, confined itself to again chastising him for "neglect of repeated orders to report the strength of your command" and declaring that this and his "going to Nashville without authority" were matters of "very serious complaint in Washington, so much so that I was advised to arrest you."[26] These words, of course, were deceptive, being designed to create the impression that he, Halleck, was shielding Grant from the anger of the Washington authorities at his misconduct and so conceal the fact that it was he who had initiated it, but they fell far short of the drastic action McClellan and Stanton had authorized.

Halleck had good reasons for caution in dealing with Grant. Along with making him a popular hero in the North, his triumph at Donelson also had gained him Lincoln's gratitude, as witness his swift promotion to major general. Therefore, to remove and arrest him without proof positive of serious misconduct on his part would raise an outcry in the press and offend the president, which in turn almost certainly would prevent Halleck from obtaining what he desired far more than getting rid of Grant—command of the entire West. So, for the time being he refrained from taking any action against Grant until sure he could do so safely.

Grant received Halleck's March 6 telegram on March 7. After reading it he wired a two-paragraph reply. In the first paragraph he stated: "I did all I could to get you returns of the strength of my command. . . . I have averaged writing more than once a day since leaving Cairo to keep you informed of my position, and it is no fault of mine if you have not received my letters. My going to Nashville was strictly intended for the good of the service, and not to gratify any desire of my own." The second paragraph consisted of one sentence: "Believing sincerely that I must have enemies between you and myself, who are trying to impair my usefulness, I respectfully ask to be relieved from further duty in the department."[27]

This telegram reached Halleck on March 8. Upon perusing it, he could congratulate himself on holding back from removing or arresting Grant, for he worried that Grant possessed the means to demonstrate, via his Washington political patrons and the press, that a failure in communications rather than a failure by him to obey orders accounted for the nonarrival of his reports, and that he could justify his trip to Nashville as well. As for the request "to be relieved from further duty in the department," Halleck realized that fulfilling such a request would be highly imprudent, especially in view of another telegram he received on March 8. From Stanton, it stated: "Please send to me the limits of a military department that would place all the Western operations you deem expedient under your command."[28]

This could only mean that Lincoln had decided, or at least was about to decide, to give him what he desired and thought he deserved—control of all Union forces in the West. It also meant that there was no immediate need to remove Grant in order to replace him with Smith, even if that could be done with impunity, which clearly was not the case. What was needed instead was to continue giving Grant the impression that his displeasure with him originated in pressure from Washington to provide information that he could not provide owing to the nonreceipt of the pertinent communications from Grant. To this end, he replied as follows to Grant's March 7 telegram, with its assertion that "I must have enemies between you and myself":

You are mistaken. There is no enemy between you and me. There is no letter of yours stating the number and position of your command since the capture of Fort Donelson. General McClellan has asked for it repeatedly with reference to ulterior movements, but I could not give him the information. He is out of all patience waiting for it.[29]

The next day, March 9, Grant's March 5 letter giving the strength of his army and explaining why previous reports probably had failed to reach Halleck finally arrived at headquarters in St. Louis. This provided Halleck with the information he had falsely claimed McClellan was "repeatedly" demanding—McClellan at this time had other matters on this mind—and also made it still more evident that Grant could cause serious trouble were he to be relieved. Then, early on March 10 word came that a Federal army under Brigadier General Samuel Ryan Curtis had routed a Rebel force containing Price's Missourians on March 6–7 at Pea Ridge in northwestern Arkansas. This victory, along with Polk's March 2 evacuation of his "Gibraltar

of the West" at Columbus, which had become untenable with the collapse
of Johnston's front in Kentucky, ended any serious enemy threat to Union
control of Missouri, where the Confederates retained only one foothold,
New Madrid, and Pope's army and Foote's gunboats now were besieging
it.[30] It also added to the list of successes achieved by armies operating under
Halleck's overall command—a list that stood in stark contrast to the record
so far compiled by McClellan's huge Army of the Potomac: not a single
full-fledged battle so much as fought, much less won, while suffering several
humiliating fiascoes.

Later in the day Halleck received another telegram. It came from Adjutant
General Lorenzo Thomas of the War Department and contained both good
news and potentially bad news. The former consisted of the title by which
Thomas addressed him: "Commanding Department of the Mississippi."[31]
Now there could be no doubt that Lincoln had decided definitely to give him
what McClellan had denied him—command of the West—and thus render
him operationally independent of McClellan while placing him in control of
Buell and of Hunter's forces in Kansas. At long last he could do as he wanted
and be sure of sufficient strength to do it successfully. Also, he now could
have the pleasure of frankly telling the "Young Napoleon" what he thought
of his generalship and his conduct toward him. This he proceeded to do, albeit without revealing the change in his military status, in a 7 P.M. telegram:

> Reserves intended to support General Curtis [whose victory Halleck
> had reported to McClellan] will be drawn in as rapidly as possible and
> sent to the Tennessee. . . . That is now the great strategic line of the
> Western campaign, and I am surprised that General Buell should hesi-
> tate to re-enforce me. He was too late at Fort Donelson, as Hunter has
> been in Arkansas. I am obliged to make my calculations independent of
> both. Believe me, general, you make a serious mistake in having three
> independent commands in the West. There never will and never can be
> any co-operation at the critical moment; all military history proves it.
> You will regret your decision against me on this point. Your friendship
> for individuals [i.e., Buell] has influenced your judgment. Be it so. I shall
> soon fight a great battle on the Tennessee unsupported, as it seems, but
> if successful it will settle the campaign in the West.[32]

The potentially bad news in Adjutant General Thomas's telegram appeared in a single long sentence that in essence stated that Stanton, per
instructions from the president, desired Halleck to supply proof of his allegations against Grant. Again there could be no doubt in Halleck's mind

as to what this indicated—namely, that Grant's Washington political patron Washburne had paid a visit to the White House armed with evidence supplied by their protégé that the North's new hero was innocent of insubordination. Yet, as he mulled the matter over, Halleck concluded that Lincoln did not believe him guilty of deliberately slandering Grant with false charges; otherwise, Thomas would not have addressed him as "Commanding Department of the Mississippi." The danger, therefore, now lay in someone, possibly Grant himself, informing the newspapers of Grant's request to be relieved and the reason for it. To forestall that, and to do it without seeming to do it, Halleck wired Grant a short message informing him that Curtis's victory "relieves the reserves intended for his support," that "they will be sent to you immediately," and that he was to "be ready yourself to take the general command" of his army as it advanced up the Tennessee.[33] This, hoped Halleck, should satisfy Grant.

It did. After reading it on March 11 Grant wrote Julia that soon more troops would be joining him at Fort Henry, after which "I will go in command of the whole" Tennessee expedition. "What you are to look out for," he continued, "I cannot tell you but you may rely upon it that your husband will never disgrace you nor leave a defeated field. We all volunteered to be killed, if needs be, and whilst any of us are living there should be no feeling other than we are so far successful" in defeating the enemy. "We have," he added, "such an inside track of the enemy that by following up our success we can go anywhere."[34] In short, with his restoration to command, Grant felt vindicated, and in so feeling was himself again: expecting the best, yet ready for the worst.

Unlike Grant, McClellan did not receive his March 10 message from Halleck the following day; instead, it reached him at the earliest on March 12.[35] Also unlike Grant, he read it with the reverse of pleasure. It was insulting; more than that, insubordinate. But there was nothing he could do about it—nothing. Lincoln had issued a "President's War Order" on March 11 relieving him of command of all military departments, except that of the Potomac, and putting Halleck in charge of a "Department of the Mississippi," which embraced all of the vast region west of the Appalachians, save West Virginia and the eastern part of East Tennessee, which became the "Mountain Department" under Frémont. The order was a concession to the Radical Republicans, so called because they wished to make the abolition of slavery a Northern war aim, along with restoration of the Union.[36]

Lincoln justified the order on the grounds that McClellan, "having personally taken the field at the head of the Army of the Potomac," could not exercise effective control over more than it. This was true and in fact had been true for a long time, in spite of McClellan's boast on supplanting Winfield Scott that "I can do it all." But the decisive reason Lincoln reduced the "Young Napoleon" to command of the Army of the Potomac lay in frustration with his continued failure to take any offensive action. His frustration climaxed on March 10 when word reached Washington that General Joseph E. Johnston's Confederate army at Manassas Junction, Virginia, only twenty-five miles from the capital, had slipped away to the south toward the Rappahannock River. The Confederate withdrawal negated McClellan's long and much-cherished grand plan to outflank it by transporting his forces by ship down the Potomac into Chesapeake Bay and landing them near the mouth of the Rappahannock, in Johnston's rear and within easy striking distance of Richmond, which they then would take without a battle and so win the war in one brilliant, bloodless stroke.[37] As commander of the North's main army, McClellan still possessed both the mission and the means to accomplish this feat, but until he did he would be unable to respond to Halleck's lecture with one of his own, for now Halleck answered only to Lincoln and need only satisfy him.

This Halleck felt confident he would do, especially since he no longer had to endeavor, so far in vain, to cajole Buell into cooperating with the advance up the Tennessee and instead could order him to join it. The general who remained a problem was Grant—a problem and also a danger. Early in March, Judge David Davis of Illinois, a close friend of Lincoln who was in St. Louis as president of a commission investigating military corruption in the West, had provided Halleck with an unsigned letter from a "man of integrity and perfectly reliable" containing a detailed account of how certain officers at Forts Henry and Donelson were selling captured Confederate supplies and even weapons for private gain. Seeing in this another instrument that could be used to replace him with Smith, Halleck in March sent a copy of the letter to Grant accompanied by a threat.

> The want and order of discipline and the numerous irregularities in your command since the capture of Fort Donelson are matters of general notoriety, and have attracted the serious attention of the authorities at Washington. Unless these things are immediately corrected I am directed to relieve you of your command.[38]

Because they wended their way to Henry by boat, the threat and accompanying letter-copy took until March 13 to reach Grant. Although the March 6 date of the former made it evident that Halleck wrote it before Grant's March 5 explanation of the probable reasons for the breakdown of communications between them could have reached him, Grant saw in it a new accusation against him, one as unwarranted as the old one of disobeying orders. This, he decided, was the last straw, and he proceeded in effect to say so in the reply he immediately telegraphed to Halleck:

> Yours of the 6th instant, inclosing an anonymous letter to Hon. David Davis, speaking of frauds committed against Government, is just received. I refer you to my orders to suppress marauding as the only reply necessary. There is such a disposition to find fault with me that I again ask to be relieved from further duty until I can be placed right in the estimation of those higher in authority.[39]

The final sentence clearly implied that if Grant had not already provided Lincoln, through an intermediary, with proof that he had endeavored to keep Halleck posted on the strength and location of his troops, he now intended to do so: with the removal of McClellan as commander of the whole Union army, the only person "higher in authority" in relationship to Grant than Halleck, or for that matter even Stanton, was the president. When, some hours later, Halleck read the sentence, he realized the danger and at once telegraphed Grant:

> You cannot be relieved of your command. There is no good reason for it. I am certain that all which the authorities in Washington ask is that you enforce discipline. . . . The power is in your hands; use it, and you will be sustained by all above you. Instead of relieving you, I wish you as soon as your new army is in the field to assume immediate command and lead it on to new victories.[40]

This message achieved its purpose. After he received it on March 14 Grant wired back: "Your telegram of yesterday . . . places such a different phase upon my position that I will again assume command, and give every effort to the success of our cause. Under the worst circumstances I would do the same."[41]

As soon as he read these words on March 15, Halleck knew that he no longer need fear Grant causing trouble in Washington, whereupon he notified Adjutant General Thomas, which was the same as informing Stanton and Lincoln, that "General Grant has made the proper explanations" regarding his visit to Nashville, that the "irregularities" committed by some of his officers were "in violation of the orders issued" by him, and that there "never has been any want of military subordination on the part of General

Grant," that "his failure to make returns of his forces has been explained as resulting partly from the failure of colonels of regiments to report to him . . . and partly from an interruption of telegraphic communications," and that "all these irregularities have now been remedied."

In addition, Halleck sent a copy of this statement to Grant so that he could see that in him he had a protector, not a persecutor.[42] Grant so saw it. Not until after the war would he learn that Halleck had caused McClellan and Stanton to authorize his removal and even arrest. As it was, he now believed that Halleck, whom he continued to deem highly, if not uniquely, qualified for his high post, had on discovering the truth about the false allegations against him, informed "Washington" of his innocence while at the same time expressing his restored confidence in him by restoring him to the command of his army.[43]

So believing, Grant's overriding desire became to join that army and, in Halleck's words, "lead it on to new victories." This he set out to do by boarding on March 16 a steamboat headed for Savannah on the east bank of the Tennessee, the place where Smith had landed his troops. Before embarking he found time to dash off two brief letters to Julia. In the first he informed her that "I now have orders to proceed up the river in command of the whole force on the Ten. What you may look for is hard to say, possibly a big fight." The second contained these words: "You will probably hear from me again soon, either that or I or some one els [*sic*] is whipped."[44] Both predictions would come true—but neither in a manner Grant could have foreseen.

4

Grant at Shiloh

How to Win by Not Losing

(March–April 1862)

On the evening of March 17, Grant came ashore at Savannah, Tennessee, a hamlet located on the east bank of the Tennessee River, then went with his staff to a hilltop mansion where Smith had established his headquarters. There he found Smith painfully lurching about by holding onto chairs, the consequence of having scraped his left shin down to the bone five days ago while jumping from the riverbank into a rowboat. Also he learned that he had five divisions at his disposal, with three of them being old ones—McClernand's, Smith's, and Lew Wallace's—and two new ones headed by Brigadier Generals William T. Sherman and Stephen A. Hurlbut, both presently disembarking at Pittsburg Landing, seven miles south of Savannah, on the west side of the river.[1]

This information presented Grant with the need to make the first of a succession of key decisions he would render during the next three weeks: How many, if any, troops should he station on the west bank? There they would be exposed to enemy attack, whereas on the east bank they would be invulnerable. Then a dispatch arrived from Sherman that provided an answer. In it Sherman recommended, on the basis of a survey he had conducted along with McPherson, that the entire army be deployed around Pittsburg Landing, a large, mainly flat area that "admits of easy defense by a small command and yet affords admirable camping ground for a hundred thousand men." Grant liked this proposal, and on learning that Smith had approved an earlier version of it by directing Sherman to stay at Pittsburg Landing "for the present making such fortifications as may be necessary for temporary defence . . . and frequent and extended reconnaissances," he adopted it—but with two amendments: McClernand's division would remain at Savannah and Wallace's at Crump's Landing, on the west bank about two miles upriver from Savannah, where Smith had posted it to guard the rapidly growing number of supply ships anchored there. Both McClernand and Wallace had been promoted to major general at the same time as Smith, which meant that they outranked Sherman. And with Smith incapacitated, Grant wanted his only other West Point–trained general to be in charge at Pittsburg Landing. That general was Sherman, whom he had known slightly at the academy and who had gained his gratitude during the Donelson operation by his zeal in funneling reinforcements from Paducah and even offering to take orders from him despite his then being junior in rank. Also Grant was aware that Sherman's brother John was a powerful Republican senator from Ohio and that Sherman possessed Halleck's friendship and favor. He could be useful in other than strictly military ways.[2]

Being on the west side of the Tennessee exposed to enemy attack bothered Grant not at all—nor, for that matter, Smith and Sherman. They realized that Johnston was gathering strength—according to some reports a great deal of strength—at Corinth; but they assumed that before he undertook any offensive action, something they deemed unlikely because of the advantage he would derive from fighting on the defensive, plus his past lack of aggressiveness, Buell's army would arrive and then, with Halleck in command, the Federal forces would strike and crush him. "The great mass of the rank and file of the rebel troops," Grant assured Halleck on March 21, "are heartily tired" of the war, hence "there is but little doubt . . . that Corinth will fall much more easily than Donelson did, when we move." And on March 29 he predicted to Julia that "a big fight may be looked for someplace before a great while which it appears to me will be the last in the West."[3]

Halleck shared Grant's, Smith's, and Sherman's optimism. His chief concern was that an overly aggressive Grant might make a premature attack on the Confederates. To forestall this he instructed him to remain at Pittsburg Landing and fortify his position. Grant did the first—incessant rain that turned the roads to Corinth into muddy streams made it impossible to do otherwise—but not the second. He believed the troops, especially those in the new regiments, needed drilling more than entrenchments, a view endorsed by Smith and supported by McPherson, who following a survey reported that the sole feasible location for a fortified line would require the army to concentrate atop the bluffs overlooking the landing, which would leave it without sufficient space for drill fields.[4] Therefore, it stayed where it was, scattered about in camps located, to quote a young soldier from Indiana, amidst "thickly wooded country seamed with ravines and bayous, rising nobody knows where and running into the river under sylvan arches draped with Spanish moss," while learning how to march and deploy according to the approved military gospel of the time.[5]

Grant also decided to establish his headquarters in the Savannah mansion occupied by Smith, as this would put him in telegraphic communication with Halleck and in position to meet Buell on his arrival. Doing this, though, created a problem. Starting March 20 McClernand's division joined the other Union forces at Pittsburg Landing. With it, of course, went McClernand, who outranked Sherman. So how to prevent him from exercising his undeniable right to assume command there? Grant's solution was to have him encamp his troops behind Sherman's and then designate Smith "the senior officer of the forces at Pittsburg . . . to command that post." Since the still-ailing Smith remained at Savannah, Grant thus placed McClernand in a subordinate position, which in turn enabled Sherman to continue as de facto field commander.

Or so he thought. For March 27 brought a letter from McClernand protesting an order from Smith to provide a work detail from his division. Grant alone, McClernand declared, had the right to order him. Not only had he been senior to Smith as a brigadier general, he too had been, according to "rumor," promoted to major general and therefore would not recognize Smith as superior to him in that rank until so notified officially. In addition, McClernand proposed that "the various camps here should be formed upon some general and connected plan," because such "a precaution might be necessary to avoid confusion and self destruction in case of a possible night attack."[6]

Grant ignored the proposal but could not do the same regarding the relative seniority of Smith and McClernand. He asked Smith about it, only to have him reply that McClernand might be right, that he too lacked official confirmation of his promotion in the form of a commission. This left Grant no alternative other than to request Halleck to ask the War Department to report the status of all recently appointed major generals in the West. Meanwhile, he would issue all orders to McClernand and also spend more time at Pittsburg Landing while still maintaining his headquarters at Savannah awaiting Buell's arrival.[7]

Where, he wondered, was Buell? Why had he not come? He should have by now.

Grant was correct. Halleck, on becoming head of the Department of the Mississippi, had experienced the pleasure of ordering rather than urging Buell to join Grant for an advance on Corinth. Despite still believing that the Confederate posed a dangerous threat to Nashville, Buell could only obey, but in so doing asked permission to march overland instead of traveling by river, as stipulated by Halleck. Perhaps assuming that a less reluctant Buell would be more willing, Halleck agreed. On March 15 the first of what eventually would be five divisions totaling 35,000 men set out from Nashville for Savannah, about 130 miles by road. At the same time, Buell sent a sixth division under Brigadier General Ormsby Mitchel south to protect his left flank, and with it Nashville, and, should it prove feasible, sever the Memphis & Charleston Railroad in northern Alabama, thereby cutting off Corinth from the east and opening the way to Chattanooga.

Buell's initial objective was Columbia, Tennessee, forty-two miles from Nashville and situated on the south bank of Duck River. To this end, he sent a cavalry regiment galloping ahead to Columbia with orders to seize the bridge spanning the Duck before Rebel horsemen burned it. The regiment reached the north bank on March 16, only to find the bridge aflame and the river uncrossable except by swimming over on horseback. Two days later Buell's lead division began constructing a new bridge, work necessitated by Buell having shipped his pontoon train by way of the Ohio and Tennessee to Savannah so that it would not slow his march. His troops, he assured Halleck by telegraph from Nashville, would complete the new bridge in four or five days.

They did not. Heavy rains transformed the Duck into a roaring torrent forty feet deep. This Buell saw for himself when he finally joined his army on March 26. Then, the following day, he discovered something that Grant already had told him by messengers but which had failed to register in his mind, perhaps because it was so alien to his way of waging war: Grant had stationed his army on the west side of the Tennessee, where it could be assailed and crushed by the Confederates! Why had he not remained safe on the east bank? Appalled by such recklessness, Buell ordered the laying of a "boat bridge" across the Duck. He also telegraphed Halleck that his army would cross the Duck on March 31 and gave Nelson permission to try to wade his division across the river. This it accomplished on the morning of March 29, the water now being only waist deep. Then on the thirty-first the rest of Buell's army began passing over both the new and the "boat" bridge. After taking, in effect, two weeks to move a mere forty-two miles, Buell was on the way to Savannah, ninety miles distant.[8]

That same day two mounted couriers sent ahead by Nelson reached Savannah, where they informed Grant that Buell was on the way—welcome news confirmed on April 3 by the arrival of some advance units from Nelson's column. "Soon," Grant wrote Julia, "I hope to be permitted to move from here and when I do there will probably be the greatest battle fought of the war. I do not feel that there is the slightest doubt about the result."[9]

Grant intended, come the morrow, to review at Pittsburg Landing the recently arrived division of Illinois political general Benjamin Prentiss, who had refused to serve under him at Cairo, claiming to be the senior brigadier.

Torrential showers, however, forced a cancellation of the review. After a short stay at the landing, Grant returned to Savannah, where he passed the rest of the day tending to routine business, the sole exception being to instruct Sherman and now-Brigadier General W.H.L. Wallace to be ready to assist Lew Wallace should he be attacked by a Confederate force reportedly hovering to the west of Crump's Landing.

In contrast, April 4 proved an active, indeed hectic, day for Sherman. Starting in the morning and persisting throughout the afternoon he received message after message from various brigade, regimental, and even company commanders that their troops had seen, and in some cases exchanged shots with, Rebel cavalry and infantry. Far from alarming him, these reports exasperated him. They had to be false because they could not be true. Not until one of his brigades came under artillery fire did he move out with two regiments and a battery to investigate. But on arriving he found no sign of the enemy, and when the brigade commander showed him a dozen prisoners taken from an Alabama cavalry regiment, he scolded him for precipitating a battle! Likewise, after two of his colonels suggested preparing to meet an attack, he replied: "Oh! tut, tut. You militia officers get scared too easily."

No one had better cause than Sherman to know how dangerous it could be to scare too easily. The reason lay in his past.[10] He was born in Lancaster, Ohio, in 1820, and his father died nine years later, leaving behind many children and little money. Thomas Ewing, a wealthy neighbor who soon became a U.S. senator, took him in, raised him as one of his own sons, and secured his appointment to West Point, where he graduated in 1840. Tall, slender, and called "Cump" by family and friends because of his middle, originally first, name of Tecumseh, he possessed a sparkling intellect, enormous energy, and seemed destined for great success, something he himself expected, as did his foster father, Ewing, who in 1849 became secretary of the interior in the cabinet of Whig President Zachary Taylor.

Instead, he succeeded only at failure. First, in 1853, still just a captain with no prospect of promotion and unable to provide for his wife, Ellen, Ewing's daughter, in the fashion to which she was accustomed, he resigned from the army to become head of the San Francisco branch of a St. Louis bank. For awhile all went well; then came a panic and bankruptcy, leaving him heavily in debt. Next he tried his hand at being a lawyer and speculator in Kansas, only to lose all of his few cases and most of the money Ewing and Ellen had invested in his schemes. "I look upon myself," he wrote Ellen, "as a dead cock in the pit." Soon, though, he regained financial independence and social status as superintendent of a newly established military academy in Louisiana, but when early in 1861 that state joined the rest of the Lower South in secession, he quit the post and again became, as he put it, "a vagabond."

Then came war and with it a colonel's commission in the regular army. At First Bull Run he headed a brigade and performed well for someone who never before had experienced combat—or at least well enough to receive promotion to brigadier general and assignment as second in command to Brigadier General Robert Anderson, a position he preferred to commander, for so pessimistic did he feel about the North defeating the more zealous South that, so he wrote Ellen, "Not until I see daylight ahead do I want to lead."

A month after arriving in Louisville, he found himself having to lead when Anderson left for reasons of health. Soon his own health, physical and mental, faltered. Fearing he was about to be overwhelmed by what he imagined to be Johnston's vastly superior Rebel army at Bowling Green, he told Secretary of War Simon Cameron that he needed 60,000 troops for defense and 200,000 for offense in Kentucky. Astounded by these impossible figures, Cameron let it be known to the press that he thought Sherman "unbalanced." Sherman thereupon requested to be replaced, and he was—by Buell. Halleck, with whom he had formed a close friendship while in California, then brought him to Missouri, where in November Sherman investigated the military situation in the central part of the state. His reports of enemy hordes marching on Jefferson City and St. Louis proved to be so fantastic that Halleck, concluding that Sherman's "physical and mental system is so completely broken by labor and care as to render him for the present entirely unfit for duty," had Ellen escort him home to Ohio to recuperate. Proclaimed "insane" by the *Cincinnati Commercial,* the state's largest circulation newspaper, only consideration for his children prevented him from committing suicide.

During the winter of 1861–1862, Halleck gradually eased Sherman back into service, first in organizing new regiments, next as commandant at Paducah, and finally at the head of a division in Grant's army. Sherman, for his part, recognized that this would be his final chance to command troops in the field. Should he fail, he never would succeed. And this meant, above all, not again exaggerating the threat posed by the enemy. Besides, if Grant and Smith believed a Confederate attack unlikely, almost inconceivable, why should he think otherwise?

He must not. He would not. He did not.

He did, though, on returning to his headquarters tent located near a small log church called Shiloh, send Grant a dispatch to the effect that his outposts had been engaged by the enemy "apparently in considerable force." Grant, on reading the message, immediately set out for Pittsburg Landing aboard a small steamer named *Tigress*. By the time he reached the landing, it was so dark and the rain so intense that he had to let his horse find the way on the road that led to Sherman's tent. But before going far he met McPherson and W.H.L. Wallace, who informed him that they had just seen Sherman and been assured by him that the Confederates merely had made a reconnaissance in force. Satisfied that all was well, he turned back. Then, as the horse descended the steep hill above the landing, it slipped, tripped, and fell on its side. Mud softened the impact, saving Grant from a broken leg or worse, but he suffered a sprained ankle, which obliged him to use crutches for the next several days in order to walk.[11]

Around noon on April 5, a Saturday, the main body of Nelson's division began arriving at Savannah. Nelson reported to Grant and proposed to continue on to the east bank of the Tennessee across from Pittsburg Landing, there to be ferried to the landing. Grant answered that swamps made the road to there from Savannah impassable. He would have boats take Nelson's troops to the landing on "Monday or Tuesday or some time early in the week." On receiving this same day a message from Buell stating, "I shall be in Savannah myself tomorrow with one perhaps two divisions," Grant replied, "I will be here to meet you tomorrow." He then added: "Pontoon bridge arrived today."

Clearly Grant felt no urgency with regard to Buell's forces joining him. He believed, as he told Nelson, that there would be "no fight at Pittsburg Landing, we will have to go to Corinth. . . . If they [the Confederates] come to attack us we can whip them, as I have more than twice the troops as I had at Fort Donelson." And, possibly an equal if not stronger reason, he had decided to post Buell's army at Hamburg, a village on the west bank of the river four miles south of Pittsburg. There it would not only be on a road leading directly to Corinth but also remain under Buell's immediate control. Although Halleck had instructed him, as the senior major general, to assume command over Buell once he reached Savannah, he realized from his encounter with him in Nashville that Buell might balk at taking orders from him—a justified concern, for as Buell would admit years later, "I did not look upon him [Grant] as my commander."[12]

As to Sherman, he spent April 5 much the way he had the previous day—rejecting, often scornfully, reports of Confederates being sighted or even engaged. Thus when a messenger from Colonel Jesse Appler of the Fifty-third Ohio informed him that butternut-clad soldiers were lurking in the woods near his regiment, Sherman told him: "Take your damn regiment to Ohio!

There is no enemy nearer than Corinth!" On receiving a written query from Grant about hostile activity, Sherman replied: "I have no doubt that nothing will occur today more than some picket firing. The enemy is saucy, but got the worst of it yesterday. . . . I will not be drawn out far unless with certainty of advantage, and I do not apprehend anything like an attack on our position."[13]

His conviction that the bulk of the Confederate army remained, and would remain, at Corinth, confirmed by Sherman, Grant closed out the day by posting a letter to Halleck informing him of Buell's imminent arrival and stating, in words virtually identical to Sherman's, that "I have scarcely the faintest idea of an attack (general one) being made upon us but will be prepared should such a thing take place."[14] This done, he paid an evening visit to Pittsburg Landing aboard the *Tigress*, conferred with McPherson, and then returned to Savannah, where he remained on the steamer until around midnight before going to his mansion headquarters. He was unaware that Buell had reached Savannah, but on learning that Grant had gone to Pittsburg, Buell dined and then went to sleep in Nelson's tent without notifying Grant's headquarters of his arrival.

Sherman also probably did not go to bed until midnight or later; indeed, some wondered when, if ever, he slept. In any case, he was up and breakfasting at 6:30 A.M. on Sunday, April 6, when a crackle of musketry came from the southwest where Prentiss's two-brigade division was camped to the left of Sherman's division, one of whose four brigades, Colonel David Stuart's, covered Prentiss's left—an arrangement that can only be described as absurd. Sherman again dismissed this gunfire as merely a scuffle between pickets. On being informed by a staff officer sent by Colonel Appler, whom yesterday he had told to take his "damn regiment" back to Ohio, that a large Rebel force was advancing on this regiment, he commented sarcastically: "You must be badly scared over there." But after the passage of another hour or so, during which the sound of firing off to the left grew in volume, Sherman decided to check on the matter himself.

Arriving, accompanied by his staff, at the front, he first saw that Appler's troops had fallen back and formed a battle line facing south. He thereupon rode, his staff still following him, beyond the line, halted, and pulled out a spyglass to observe a large body of troops moving a half mile off to the left. As he did so, a line of gray-uniformed infantry emerged from some woods only fifty yards to his right. "General," one of Appler's officers yelled at him, "look to your right!" Sherman did, exclaimed, "My God, we are attacked!" and dropped the spyglass from his upraised right hand. Perhaps before it hit the ground a buckshot pellet ripped through the palm of that hand and at the same time a .69 caliber bullet struck and killed his orderly—a bullet, Sherman knew, intended for him.

Yes, the Confederates were attacking, 40,000 of them headed by Albert Sidney Johnston. Following the Donelson debacle and his retreat from Kentucky and Middle Tennessee, Johnston had been subjected to bitter denunciation, accompanied by demands for his removal, in the Southern press. He reacted stoically. "The test of merit in my profession with the people is success," he wrote a friend. "It is a hard rule but I think it right." Only through success could he redeem failure, and this he resolved to do. So, too, did his fellow West Pointer and devoted friend, Jefferson Davis. Declaring that if Johnston "is no general, we had better give up the war, for we have no generals," he provided him with what he should have provided long before—thousands of troops from the Gulf Coast and other areas where they were accomplishing nothing because there was nothing they could accomplish. At the same time, Beauregard, who indeed had come West, but only with a tiny personal staff and not with fifteen regiments from Virginia, pried Polk out of his "Gibraltar" at Columbus and brought his troops to Corinth, where they joined Major General Braxton Bragg's troops from the Gulf Coast, Johnston's former Bowling Green contingent under Major General William J. Hardee, and new levies from Alabama and Mississippi. For the first time, Johnston, who took personal command at Corinth on March 24, possessed sufficient concentrated strength to stand a reasonable chance of defeating either Grant or Buell.

But not both together. Hence, when on April 2 word arrived from cavalry scouts that Buell was marching west from Columbia to link up with Grant and soon would, Johnston adopted a proposal from Beauregard to attack Grant at once, crush him, and then do the same to Buell. Early the next day the Confederates set out for Pittsburg Landing, their army organized into three corps headed by Hardee, Bragg, and Polk, plus a reserve under Brigadier General John C. Breckinridge of Kentucky, presidential candidate of the Southern Democrats in 1860 and former Vice President of the United States.

Since the landing was only about twenty miles distant, they could and should have arrived within striking distance no later than the evening of April 4, despite rain that turned the roads into mud slush, but inexperience and sheer incompetence resulted in only a few mounted units approaching close enough to clash with Union outposts that day. On April 5 most of the rest managed to come up, yet further encounters with the enemy and soldiers firing their rain-drenched muskets into the air to make sure they would shoot caused Beauregard to conclude that any chance of defeating

Grant, much less surprising him, had been lost. He therefore urged Johnston to return to Corinth. The Federals, he asserted, would be waiting for
them "intrenched to their eyes." Johnston pondered the matter, then declared they would attack come morning. To go back to Corinth without
fighting, he believed, would be more demoralizing to his troops, keyed up
as they were for battle, than defeat. It also would leave him with no choice
other than to resign his command in utter disgrace.[15]

Grant was eating breakfast in his room when an orderly entered and reported a rumble of cannon fire coming from Pittsburg Landing. He hobbled
outside on his crutches, heard "heavy firing" from that quarter, summoned
his staff, and hastened to the *Tigress*. As it fired up its engine, he had Rawlins write an order to Nelson to "move your entire command to the river
opposite Pittsburg" while he scrawled a message to Buell, informing him
"that an attack has been made upon our most advanced positions," that
it "necessitates my joining the forces up the river instead of meeting you
today," and that "I have directed Gen. Nelson to move up the river with his
Division." He still did not know that Buell was at Savannah, since Buell had
still not gone to his headquarters nor sent a messenger there to announce his
presence—another indication that he was in no rush to meet with Grant.[16]

He then set out for Pittsburg Landing. On the way he stopped briefly at
Crump's Landing, where he found Lew Wallace aboard a docked steamer
and ordered him to be ready to march his division in any direction—an
order inspired by fear that the Confederates might attempt to capture or
destroy the numerous supply boats stationed there. He then continued on
to Pittsburg Landing, arriving at about 9 A.M. and riding his horse down a
plank onto the shore.

At once any doubt he still may have harbored that a full-fledged battle
was under way disappeared. Swarms of panic-stricken Federal troops, their
number rapidly increasing, cowered along the river bank. Inland, dense
clouds of bluish-white powder smoke hovered above the trees, whence
came a steady din of mingled musket and cannon fire. Thousands, tens of
thousands, of men were doing their best to kill each other.

Throughout the morning and on into the afternoon, the Confederates
attacked fiercely, relentlessly, and on the whole successfully. Along with superior numbers, which enabled them to overpower or outflank their hastily
deployed, if deployed at all, foes, they enjoyed the psychological advantage
of knowing that they were about to go into battle, whereas Grant's troops
suddenly found themselves plunged into it. Yet they too suffered heavy losses
while advancing. Then they encountered a sunken road held by Prentiss's
raw troops supported by W.H.L. Wallace's and Hurlbut's divisions, and they

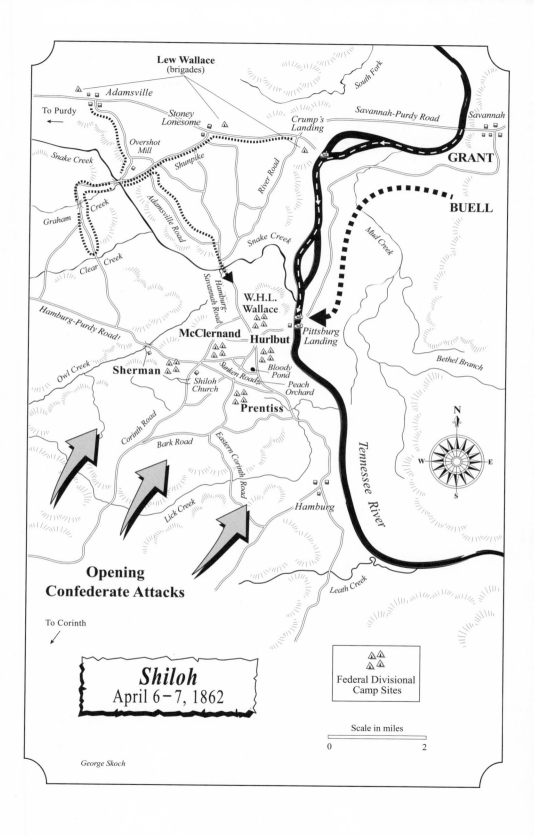

Shiloh
April 6–7, 1862

Lew Wallace
(brigades)

Adamsville

To Purdy

Stoney
Lonesome

Overshot
Mill

Snake Creek

Graham

Clear Creek

Hamburg-Purdy Road

Owl Creek

Sherman

McClernand

Shiloh
Church

Corinth Road

Bark Road

Lick Creek

Opening
Confederate Attacks

To Corinth

Shunpike

Adamsville Road

Hamburg-Savannah Road

Sanken Road

Prentiss

Eastern Corinth Road

Snake Creek

W.H.L.
Wallace

Hurlbut

Bloody
Pond

Peach
Orchard

Hamburg

Crump's
Landing

River Road

South Fork

Savannah-Purdy Road

Savannah

GRANT

BUELL

Mud Creek

Pittsburg
Landing

Bethel Branch

Tennessee River

Leath Creek

N

W E

S

Federal Divisional
Camp Sites

Scale in miles

0   2

George Skoch

ceased to advance. Again and again they charged, and again and again they had to fall back, leaving behind hundreds of dead and wounded. Urging them on, Johnston suddenly swayed in his saddle, a bullet having punctured an artery in his left leg. Staff members carried him to a sheltered place, but before they could discover the wound and apply a tourniquet he bled to death. Not until late afternoon did the Confederates succeed—by blasting it with sixty-two cannons while simultaneously flanking it—in driving the Federals from the "Hornet's Nest," in the process mortally wounding Wallace and capturing Prentiss along with 2,000-some other Yankees.

Meanwhile, Grant endeavored to secure reinforcements. It now being clear that the enemy target was Pittsburg Landing, not Crump's Landing, he first sent a staff officer via the *Tigress* to the latter place with a pencil-inscribed note written by Rawlins ordering (as best as anyone afterward could recollect) Lew Wallace to "come up and take position on the right of the army." Grant took it for granted that Wallace would come by way of the River Road, a mere five-mile march due south from Crump's Landing. Not so. Assuming that "right of the army" meant the right of Sherman's division, Wallace headed for it by a road leading to the vicinity of Shiloh Church, eight miles distant. Next, presuming that Nelson's division was on the way to Pittsburg, but unsure whether Nelson or Buell headed it, Grant dispatched another officer over to the east side of the river with a message addressed to "Cmdg. Officer of Advanced Forces Near Pittsburg, Ten." In it he urged whomever that might be to hasten his march and stated that his coming "would possibly save the day to us" against "Rebel forces . . . estimated at over 100,000 men." The officer, however, failed to find Nelson's column, and for a very good reason: Nelson still was at Savannah, searching for someone to guide him through the "impassable" swamps on the road to the riverbank opposite Pittsburg Landing.

When not engaged in these futile efforts to obtain much-wanted because much-needed reinforcements, Grant rode along the Union front, going from division to division to see for himself what was happening. Like Johnston, he frequently exposed himself to hostile fire; unlike him, he went unscathed, the only bullet to hit him striking his scabbard just below the sword hilt, breaking off the blade. Luck? Destiny? In any case, had the bullet been a little higher or a bit to either side of the scabbard, perhaps Grant's life, or at least his military career, would have ended along the west bank of the Tennessee River on April 6, 1862.

By early evening the Union line had been pushed back to the high ground above the landing and consisted of, from its right to its left, the remnants of Sherman's, McClernand's, W.H.L. Wallace's, and Hurlbut's divisions, plus some survivors of Prentiss's. Altogether they numbered at most 15,000, probably less, deployed along a front that faced west along the road from Crump's Landing and then curved off to the east, where, as it neared the river, it overlooked a deep, steep ravine created by a tributary of the Tennessee. Correctly assuming that the main enemy attack would be, as it had been all day, directed against his left, Grant had bolstered it with ten batteries supplemented by 24-pounder and 30-pounder siege guns. In addition, two gunboats lay offshore, lobbing huge shells among the Confederates.

Grant knew full well that he was making a last stand. Should the new line fail to hold, the battle would be lost and with it most, if not all, of his army. Where was Nelson? Even more frustrating, where was Lew Wallace? He should have come long ago. To ascertain why not and hasten him, he had sent staff officers, among them McPherson and Rawlins, to look for him. They had found him heading toward what now was the enemy rear. After they persuaded him that if he continued in that direction his division would be cut off and captured, he turned around, reached the River Road, and set out on it for Pittsburg Landing, but so belatedly that there was no chance of his joining the rest of the army before dark. As the sun began to set, Grant realized this and placed a mental question mark after Wallace's name.[17]

On the other hand, he knew that Nelson was on the way. Word of that had been brought by Buell, who had showed up at Pittsburg Landing in a steamboat at 1 P.M. Four hours later, the head of Nelson's division finally did arrive on the east bank of the river. Its march from Savannah had been first delayed by an inability to find a guide, leaving them to come by a road (if such it could be called) that often disappeared beneath swamps through which his troops had to wade knee deep in muddy water and without their artillery. Soon two small steamers, all that were presently available, carried Nelson and eight companies of the Thirty-sixth Indiana to the landing, where they pushed their way past the throng of fugitives huddled there and went into support of one of the batteries nearest the river.

Then the Confederates attacked, their objective the extreme Union left, which if they could penetrate, drive back, or flank would enable them to cut off Grant's entire army from the landing, leaving it with two choices: surrender or slaughter. Their assailing force, though, consisted of just two brigades backed by one battery; furthermore, one of the brigades lacked ammunition, and the other was exhausted both in body and spirit by almost constant combat throughout the day. Small wonder, therefore, that when they started to descend the ravine and the massed Union cannons opened up, they faltered, halted, and then fell back. After a bit they came on again, only to retreat beneath another storm of shell and canister.[18]

And that was that. As the sun sank beneath the all-encompassing forest, the Confederates withdrew, many on their own accord, most on orders from Beauregard, who had taken command following Johnston's death. He believed that he could and so would finish off Grant's army come morning. Not only had it been fatally mauled, but word had come from Confederates in Alabama that Buell, instead of moving west to join Grant, was heading south. To be sure, the captured Yankee general Prentiss claimed that Buell was close at hand, maybe even present, but if that were so, then why would he reveal such information? He must be merely bluffing. Therefore, Beauregard, sitting at a desk in what had been Sherman's but now was his headquarters tent, penned a message to the Confederate War Department and handed it to a courier to take to Corinth, from there it would be telegraphed to Richmond. It read: "We this morning attacked the enemy at Pittsburg, and after a severe battle . . . gained a complete victory."

During the night the rest of Nelson's division joined Grant, as did two others from Buell's army, with both coming from Savannah aboard steamers. Also Lew Wallace's peripatetic troops finally showed up, going into line on Sherman's right. Altogether they added about 25,000 men to the Federal forces, giving Grant close to a two-to-one advantage over the Confederates, who in addition to their huge casualties suffered from large-scale straggling by men seeking plunder, food, or escape—for, like so many of their Northern counterparts, they had found that "seeing the elephant," Civil War slang for first experiencing battle, was like being plunged into Hell.

Night also brought more rain. Grant, unable to sleep in his log cabin headquarters because it had been turned into a hospital filled with starving and screaming wounded, passed most of it beneath a tree, propped up by his crutches, holding a lantern, and puffing a cigar. Here Sherman found him. Yes, Grant agreed, it had been a rough day. Then he paused. "Lick 'em tomorrow, though."

The rain ceased, the sun rose, and the Federals attacked. Now it became the Confederates' turn to be surprised—they had expected to finish off the Yankees come morning—and then to try to fend off what not only seemed like superior numbers but actually were such. Even so, they put up a stout fight, enough of one to cause eighteen-year-old Ambrose Bierce of the Ninth Indiana to realize the "paramount importance of numbers" in stand-up combat: whichever side could continue replacing its losses after exchanges of fire would in the end prevail no matter how brave the foe.[19]

Since the Federals possessed this advantage, they slowly but steadily pressed forward. By early afternoon they had pushed the Confederates almost back to where they started their onslaught the day before. Beauregard, perceiving that further resistance would lead only to further losses, ordered retreat. Late afternoon found his troops, except a rearguard, trudging back to Corinth, their ranks depleted by close to 11,000 killed, wounded, and missing, more than one-fourth their original strength. Many of them were famished, all of them weary, and, according to a message Bragg sent to Beauregard, most of them were "utterly disorganized and demoralized," having seen dazzling victory turn into dismal defeat.

Grant did not pursue or ask Buell, whom he continued to refrain from ordering, to do so. Neither his army, which had suffered nearly 11,000 casualties, nor Buell's, which had lost slightly over 2,000, were in physical or psychological condition to make an effective pursuit.[20] Furthermore, Grant feared that the Confederates, whom he thought still numbered more than 100,000, might be preparing to attack again. To find out, on April 8 he sent Sherman forward with a mixed body of cavalry and infantry to reconnoiter. About five miles out, Forrest sprang an ambush, routed the cavalry, missed a chance to kill Sherman, and almost was killed himself but lived to frustrate Sherman again—and again and yet again. Nevertheless, Sherman ascertained that most of the enemy were on the way back to Corinth and so informed Grant, who thereupon decided to remain at Pittsburg Landing while awaiting Halleck's arrival and burying the dead.

There were many of them to bury—upwards of 3,000 Yankees and Rebels—for Shiloh was one of the bloodiest battles of the Civil War. Also it was a decisive battle in its effect on the course and conduct, if not the outcome, of the war. But not in the way many Southerners then and some historians since have contended. According to them, had Johnston not died or Beauregard not suspended attacking in the false belief that victory was assured, then Grant's army would have been smashed or forced to surrender on April 6, whereupon the Confederates would have gone on to retrieve Middle Tennessee and reenter Kentucky, thus reversing the tide of the war in the West and as a whole. By failing to do so, they lost a battle the "South had to win" in order to succeed in its struggle for independence.[21]

Perhaps this is true. But almost surely it is not for these reasons: (1) Grant's army, without significant assistance from Buell's, easily repulsed the final enemy thrust, and there is no reason to believe that a still-alive Johnston or further assaults by a still-aggressive Beauregard would have made any difference. (2) Even had the Confederates been able to defeat and capture most of Grant's army, they still would have had to cross the Tennessee in the face of the Union gunboats, Buell's 35,000 troops, and probably substantial remnants of Grant's army, among them, quite possibly, Lew Wallace's division. Since their effective force had been reduced by the evening of April 6 to no more than 25,000, and probably less, the only way they could have managed to do this would have been for Buell to have displayed extraordinary timidity and/or ineptitude. (3) Buell soon would have been joined, as in fact he was, by 20,000 troops under Pope, who on April 8 captured Island No. 10 along with about 4,000 of its defenders, and then during the next two weeks by 50,000 more soldiers. In contrast, the sole large reinforcement Beauregard received during the same period was Van Dorn's 14,000-man army, which Johnston had belatedly summoned from Arkansas and which did not begin reaching Memphis until April 15.[22]

In sum, the Confederates came close to smashing Grant's army on the first day at Shiloh but failed to do it because they lacked the strength. Of course, had they somehow done it, no doubt their victory would have sent Southern morale soaring and Northern spirits plummeting, plus it would have enabled them to acquire great quantities of cannon, rifles, munitions, and other spoils. But then, confronted on the east side of the Tennessee by a much-superior Federal force that was growing ever more superior and that, thanks to its gunboats and transports, could land troops on the west side at any point or points it chose, they would have had no rational choice except to do what they started doing on the afternoon of April 7: withdraw to Corinth in hope of there defeating the Yankees when they, in their turn, became the assailant.

So how was Shiloh decisive? Before answering this question, let us observe the obvious. At Shiloh, as at Donelson, Grant's focus on attacking the enemy blinded him to the possibility that the enemy might attack him, with the result that he again was caught off-guard and faced with disaster. Yet, like also at Donelson, he reacted quickly, resolutely, and effectively to the unexpected, thereby making it possible for his troops, thanks to the courage and tenacity of most of them, to stave off the Confederates until the coming of Buell's divisions enabled him to transform a defensive victory into an offensive one, a victory that maintained the strategic initiative for the North in the West, inflicted on the South a defeat all the more depressing because it came on the heels of Beauregard's premature proclamation of triumph, and—perhaps most important of all in its bearing on the subsequent conduct and course of the war—prevented his removal from command and, in all likelihood, the permanent termination of his military career.

This almost occurred anyway. Why it did, and why it did not, shall be recounted in the next chapter. Suffice to say for now that on April 9 Grant wrote a report on Shiloh, and the following day Sherman did the same.

5

Grant Advances by Staying Put

(April–July 1862)

ON THE EVENING OF APRIL 11, Halleck came ashore at Pittsburg Landing from the steamboat aboard which he had spent the past two and a half days traveling from St. Louis. He wore a new uniform, appropriate attire for a general who never before had commanded an army, or for that matter more than a platoon, in the field. Now he would have an opportunity to put his profound knowledge of military theory into military practice.

First, though, he wanted to find out more about the recent battle now most often being referred to as Shiloh. So far all he knew about it, officially at least, came from a telegram sent by Grant on the night of April 7 and read by him prior to leaving St. Louis on the morning of April 8. In it Grant reported that his army had been attacked the day before by "rebels" in "overwhelming force," that it had been driven from its "advanced position to near" Pittsburg Landing, and that upon the arrival of three of Buell's divisions he had "ordered an attack, which resulted in a fight which continued until late that afternoon, with severe loss on both sides, but a complete repulse of the enemy."[1]

What Halleck learned informally upon arriving at Pittsburg is unknowable, but it is safe to assume that he discovered that the Confederate attack had been a surprise to almost all of Grant's army, Grant included; that many of the Union troops had fled in panic; that Grant had not fortified his position as instructed; that his forces had come close to destruction; and that the casualties for both sides had been more than "severe"— they had been enormous, as one could tell from the sickening stench of hundreds of still unburied corpses. In sum, it was evident that because of his carelessness and recklessness Grant again, as at Donelson, had barely escaped a calamitous defeat and that this time his eventual victory had resulted from the just-in-time arrival of Buell's divisions.[2]

So Halleck now possessed an opportunity to remove, or at least suspend, Grant from his command, giving as the reason a need to investigate what happened and why at Shiloh. Yet Halleck chose not to do this and, if need be, even lie to keep him in command—for the time being, at least. Apart from the fact that Grant, after all, had won the battle and possessed in

83

Washburne an influential political patron, two considerations prompted this decision.

One pertained to McClernand. On April 6 Halleck received from the War Department a reply to his query about the relative seniority of Smith and McClernand. To his dismay and disgust he found that the latter was senior to the former thanks to *M* preceding *S* in the alphabet![3] This meant that if Grant should be relieved, McClernand would replace him. Better, therefore, to retain Grant. Despite his faults, he was a West Pointer and not an ambitious politician posing as general.

The other consideration involved Sherman. Should Grant be blamed for his army being surprised on April 6, then it would be impossible to prevent the same fate befalling Sherman, who as the de facto commander at Pittsburg Landing bore the primary responsibility for the surprise. This Halleck resolved to forestall. Not only was "Cump" his personal friend and a professional protégé to whom he had given a second chance to redeem his Kentucky collapse, he also desired to add another West Point–trained major general to Grant's army—all the more so because it was becoming increasingly evident that Smith's condition was worsening rather than improving.

How to protect Grant and promote Sherman? That was the question. Grant's report on Shiloh, which Halleck surely read soon after arriving at Pittsburg Landing, provided the answer. It made no reference to a surprise. Instead, it asserted that when the Union pickets were "driven in by the enemy" on the morning of April 6, all five of the divisions at Pittsburg "were drawn up in line of battle, ready to meet them," and then toward the end made "special mention" of the "gallant and able officer, Brig. Gen. W. T. Sherman," who "not only was with his command during the entire two day's action, but displayed great judgment and skill in the management of his men," despite being wounded twice and having "three horses killed under him." No doubt, too, Halleck saw a copy of a dispatch Grant had sent him on April 9 stating that the "attack on Sunday was made, according to the best evidence I have, by one hundred and sixty-two regiments"—twice the number of regiments the Confederates actually possessed.[4]

If not on April 11, then almost certainly on the twelfth, Grant also showed Sherman's report to Halleck. Sherman admitted in it that it was not until 8 A.M. on April 6, when he saw "heavy masses of [Confederate] infantry" in the woods "to our left front," that he became "satisfied for the first time that the enemy designed a determined attack on our camp." He declared that by then "all of the regiments of my command were then in line of battle at their proper posts." Together with McClernand, he continued, he held this line until the collapse of the Union left forced both of them to withdraw first to the Hamburg-Purdy Road and finally to the River Road so as to avoid being outflanked. In the last position, he stated, the right of his division covered the "bridge [across Snake Creek] by which General [Lew] Wallace had to approach," thereby enabling him to join the rest of the army and participate, along with him, in the April 7 counterattack.[5]

Thus informed—or, to be more accurate, armed—by Grant and Sherman, on April 13 Halleck wrote the following to Stanton:

> It is the unanimous opinion here that Brig. Gen. W. T. Sherman saved the fortune of the day on the 6th instant, and contributed largely to the glorious victory on the 7th. He was in the thickest of the fight on both days, having three horses killed under him and being wounded twice. I respectfully request that he be made a major general of volunteers, to date from the 6th instant.[6]

During April 6 Sherman did display, as he always would once involved in actual combat, a remarkable blend of fiery courage and icy coolness. But it was not the "unanimous opinion" of Grant's army that he "saved the fortune of the day." The reason is that it was untrue, and most of the army knew it. Had the main Confederate thrust been directed against the Union right instead of left, Sherman's and McClernand's divisions would have suffered the same fate as Prentiss's, W.H.L. Wallace's, and, to a lesser extent, Hurlbut's. Likewise, Sherman, after he fell back to the River Road, did not guard the bridge over Snake Creek; instead, his extreme right was a mile and a half from the bridge, and had even a single Confederate brigade, either by intent or chance, penetrated this gap, it could have blocked Wallace's approach, struck Sherman in flank and rear, or both. Last, albeit least, Sherman's division contributed little to the Federal victory on April 7 because too few of its men remained in action to contribute more—nor did Lew Wallace's division do much better, its 5,000 troops suffering a mere 296 causalities, by far the lowest total of any Union division engaged at Shiloh.[7]

Grant showed Sherman his report, and Halleck gave him a copy of his letter to Stanton. Both delighted him, especially the second, which he enclosed in an April 14 letter to his wife, Ellen, wherein he chortled, "so at last I Stand redeemed from the vile slanders of that Cincinati paper"—a reference to the *Cincinnati Commercial* having branded him "insane" back in November.[8] But, ironically, on that very same day another Cincinnati newspaper, the *Gazette*, carried an eyewitness account of Shiloh by Whitelaw Reid, its correspondent with Grant's army. According to Reid, the Rebel

April 6 onslaught came as a total surprise, produced horrendous Northern losses, and would have resulted in a complete calamity had it not been for the coming of Buell's troops. Since this was the first detailed description of the battle to appear in print and vividly written, many other newspapers, especially in the Midwest, also published it, often along with editorials denouncing Grant and Sherman and calling for their removal. Perturbed, Lincoln had Stanton telegraph Halleck on April 23 that the "President desires to know why you have made no official report . . . regarding the late battle at Pittsburg Landing, and whether any neglect or misconduct by General Grant or any other officer contributed to the sad casualties that befell our forces on Sunday."[9]

Obviously, this portended trouble—serious trouble—for Grant and Sherman. How, then, to defend them? Drawing on his lawyer skills, Halleck decided to play for time so that a counterattack could be mounted to prevent Grant's removal and secure Sherman's promotion, both now all the more imperative because Charles Smith was dying. Hence, on April 25, on which day Smith did die, Halleck replied to Stanton with what in essence was a nonreply:

> The sad casualties of Sunday, the 6th, were due in part to the bad conduct of officers who were utterly unfit for their places, and in part to the numbers and bravery of the enemy. I prefer to express no opinion in regard to misconduct of individuals till I receive the reports of commanders of divisions. A great battle cannot be fought or a victory gained without many casualties. In this instance the enemy suffered more than we did.[10]

Halleck showed Stanton's telegram to Sherman and gave him a copy of his in response. The first could only have intensified the anger and fear Sherman felt on reading Reid's account, similar ones by other reporters, and the consequent denunciations of him by various politicians, among them the lieutenant governor of Ohio. Was he again to be disgraced personally and ruined professionally, this time irredeemably, by one of the "most contemptible of the race of men that exist"—a journalist?[11]

The answer soon came. It was no. Thanks to the many efforts of brother John the senator, foster father/father-in-law Thomas Ewing Sr., and wife Ellen, who visited Washington in behalf of her husband, Lincoln nominated Sherman for promotion to major general, and on May 1 the Senate approved it. The next day, his goal of elevating Sherman now achieved, Halleck sent a definitive reply to Stanton's April 24 query: "Reports [by division commanders] of the battle of the 6th and 7th are received, and copies forwarded [to War Department] as rapidly as possible. The newspaper accounts that our divisions were surprised are utterly false. Every division had notice of the enemy's approach hours before the battle commenced."[12]

None of this was totally true. In fact, most if it was totally false, and Halleck knew it. He had to know it. Well before April 24 all of Grant's division commanders, including the successors to Prentiss and W.H.L. Wallace, had submitted their reports. Not even Sherman, as has been seen, stated that he had expected a full-fledged enemy attack or had been prepared to meet one "hours before the battle commenced," as implied by Halleck. Instead, every one of them, save Sherman, described the experience of his division in basically the same fashion employed by Colonel James Tuttle, who as senior brigade commander in W.H.L. Wallace's division had taken charge of it upon Wallace being mortally wounded: "We had been in line but a few moments when the enemy made their appearance and attacked."[13]

Halleck, though, felt confident that he could lie to Stanton, and through him to Lincoln, with impunity, even should the former bother to read the copies of the division commanders' reports being forwarded to him. Not only had he obtained Sherman's promotion, he also was about to advance on Corinth, there to defeat and, he hoped, destroy Beauregard's army. Should he succeed—and he intended to make sure he did—then his victory, coming in the wake of Shiloh, Pope's capture of Island No. 10, and the April 25 seizure by Rear Admiral David G. Farragut's fleet of New Orleans, the South's largest city and main seaport, would give the North domination of the entire upper Mississippi Valley and open the way for the conquest of the rest. Given this prospect, not even Stanton would dare question the truth of what he stated about what had occurred at Shiloh.

For the Corinth campaign Halleck had assembled between 100,000 and 110,000 troops organized into three armies, each with a newly designated official name. One, Pope's Army of the Mississippi, consisted of five divisions, four infantry and one cavalry, and constituted the left wing. Another, Buell's Army of the Ohio, formed the center but retained only three of its five divisions. And the third, the Army of the Tennessee, comprised the right wing and numbered five divisions, four of which, including Sherman's, were from Grant's army, and the fifth from Buell's. Grant, however, did not command it, nor did it include McClernand's and Lew Wallace's divisions. The latter two now belonged, along with the other division taken from Buell, to a Reserve Corps headed by McClernand. As for Grant, he now was second in command to Halleck, so named by "Old Brains," as he was beginning to be called, and leading his former army was Major General George H. Thomas.[14]

Forty-five, tall, and massively built, Thomas was an 1840 graduate of West Point and thus a classmate of Sherman, with whom he had shared a room. Like Sherman, he had been assigned to the artillery; unlike him, he saw combat in Mexico, notably at Buena Vista (February 22–23, 1847), where by his skill and bravery he had gained promotion to captain. Again unlike Sherman, he had remained in the army following the war and in 1859 had become a major in the newly formed Second U.S. Cavalry, a regiment whose colonel was Albert Sidney Johnston, its lieutenant colonel Robert E. Lee, and its other major William J. Hardee, whose corps had spearheaded Johnston's attack at Shiloh. A Virginian, had he chose, as they did, to support secession, he surely would have joined them in rapidly securing high rank in the Confederate army. Instead, he sided with the Union, a decision that caused his kinfolk to disown him and which some attributed to his wife being a New Yorker. More likely, he believed that the United States should stay united, and that it was his duty as one of its soldiers to help it do so. And this he would do, more so than all but a very few.

Following service during the summer of 1861 in the East, where as a colonel he headed a cavalry regiment, he received promotion to brigadier general and a transfer to Kentucky, where under Sherman and then Buell he took on the task of trying to realize Lincoln's pet project of "liberating" predominantly Unionist East Tennessee. This eventually led, after a panicky Sherman aborted an initial attempt, to his gaining the first Federal battle victory in the West by defeating at Mill Springs, Kentucky, on January 17, 1862, a larger Confederate army that had attacked him. He wanted to exploit this success by entering East Tennessee, but Buell, deeming it impracticable, forbade him. Next he participated in Buell's two-stage march to join Grant's army, but since his division brought up the rear, it reached Savannah too late to participate in the fighting. Soon afterward, though, he received a badly belated promotion to major general, with rank dating from April 25.[15]

Which explains why Halleck made him commander of the Army of the Tennessee, Grant second in command, and McClernand head of a "Reserve Corps" composed of his, Lew Wallace's, and one of Buell's divisions. By so doing, he did what he long had desired to do—in effect place Grant, McClernand, and Wallace on the military shelf while at the same time punishing Buell for his past failures to cooperate by reducing his army to the equivalent of a corps. Yet, in fairness, there can be no doubt that he acted in the sincere belief that Thomas was more capable and reliable than Grant, and that it was an insult to all professional soldiers to have amateurs such as McClernand and Wallace be senior in rank to Thomas—and also Sherman. Oh! How fortunate Confederate West Pointers were to have for their president Jefferson Davis, himself a West Point graduate, rather than a backwoods politician who obviously thought that being able to win elections qualified one to win battles.

Understandably, Buell resented the diminution of his army and quickly let Halleck know it. "You must excuse me," he wrote him on April 30, "for saying that, as it seems to me, you have saved the feelings of others very much to my injury."[16] Grant, on the other hand, expressed, and evidently felt, no grievance whatsoever about his new assignment. Given the mammoth size of the Union host now assembled along the west bank of the Tennessee and the nature of the country where it would be operating, it made sense for Halleck to have a deputy commander who could oversee the execution of his orders or, if need be, issue orders of his own. Also he expected that soon, so he wrote Julia on April 30, there would be "another battle, and I think the last big one," which would be "the last in the Mississippi Valley" and end the war in the West, whereupon he hoped that Julia could join him or he could return home, "then go either to Texas or on the coast somewhere."[17]

On May 3 Halleck telegraphed Stanton: "I leave here tomorrow morning, and our army will be before Corinth tomorrow night."[18] It took longer than that. More rain, more roads of mud, and more bogged down wagons, cannons, and caissons saw to that. So, too, did Halleck. Crediting Beauregard with numbers equal, if not superior, to his own, he feared a repeat of April 6. To prevent it, he halted his army each day to entrench. Result of such weather and prudence: an average daily advance of less than a mile.

Far quicker, Grant realized that being second-in-command meant in practice commanding nothing, not even McClernand's Reserve Corps, to which Halleck issued orders directly. Also he found that although he now accompanied Halleck's headquarters, Halleck never assigned him a mission, informed him of plans and operations, or consulted him. But most of all he resented not leading his own army in what he expected to be the final, decisive battle in the West and having it instead headed by Thomas, a general who only recently had been elevated to two-star rank, who had not shared in its travails and triumphs, and who had been brought over from Buell's army, which bragged of saving the day on April 6 and then winning the battle on the seventh in fighting he considered "mere child's play" compared to what his troops underwent the day before.[19] So feeling, Grant on May 11 sent Halleck a letter, the key passage of which read:

> I believe it is generally understood through this army that my position [as second in command] differs but little from that of one in arrest, and as this opinion may be much strengthened from the fact that orders to the *Right Wing* and the *Reserve,* both nominally under my command, are transmitted direct from General Head Quarters, without going through me, I deem it due to myself to ask either full restoration to duty, according to my rank, or to be relieved entirely from further duty.
>
> I cannot, do not, believe that there is any disposition on the part of yourself to do me any injustice, but my suspicions have been aroused that you may be acting under instructions, from higher authority, that I know nothing of.[20]

Halleck answered the next day:

> I am very much surprised, general, that you should find any cause of complaint in the recent assignment of commands. You have precisely the position to which your rank entitles you. Had I given you the right wing or reserve only it would have been a reduction rather than increase of command, and I could not give you both without placing you in the position you now occupy.
>
> You certainly will not suspect me of any intention to injure your feelings or reputation or to do you any injustice; if so, you will eventually change your mind on this subject. For the past three months I have done everything in my power to ward off the attacks which were made upon you. If you believe me your friend you will not require explanations; if not, explanations on my part would be of little avail.[21]

It would be surprising if Halleck's reply surprised Grant; after all, Halleck had told him the same back in March about being his friend and protector. To be sure, Halleck had supported his claim that in spite of the April 6 attack coming sooner and in greater strength than expected his army had been ready to meet it, but surely he knew that Halleck had done this more for Sherman's sake than his. Hence, Halleck's response merely intensified his desire, announced in a May 11 letter to Julia, to go "home, and [then] to Washington, as soon as the present impending fight or footrace is decided." His purpose in visiting Washington, he explained to Julia two days later after receiving Halleck's letter, would be to obtain a command in "some other field," not to defend himself against the "attacks" of the press. Although these, as he put it in a May 14 letter to Washburne thanking him for his support, had "distressed" him, "for I have a father, mother, wife & children who read them and are distressed by them," even so "I would scorn being my own defender against such attacks except through the record which has been kept of all my official acts and which can be examined at Washington at any time."[22]

Unlike Grant, Sherman wished to remain with Halleck for obvious reasons. Also unlike Grant, he did not refrain from responding to criticisms in the press and penning letter after letter, many long and repetitious, to brother John, Thomas Ewing Sr., Ellen, and brothers-in-law Charles and Phil denouncing the "slanders" of the "dirty newspaper scribblers" while giving his version of what happened at Shiloh, particularly on April 6. Some of what he wrote was valid—thus, for example, not a single Union soldier was bayoneted in his tent as reported by Reid—but much more consisted of exaggerations, equivocations, and fabrications.[23] Among the worst of the last was a claim, to quote from a May 12 twelve-page epistle to brother John, that "in times of danger and trouble all [of the other division commanders] lean on me," that during the afternoon of April 6 "McClernand leaned on me all the time," that "my staff officers heard him despair and despond," and that "I actually gave orders to his troops."[24]

Presumably, Sherman's family believed these assertions. There is no reason for a historian to do the same. Not only do the reports of the other division commanders contradict them, so too does Sherman's own report and even his *Memoirs*. Furthermore, except for McClernand, the other division commanders and, in the cases of Prentiss and W.H.L. Wallace, their successors were too far distant from Sherman to "lean" on him in the sense of seeking his instructions, supposing they had wanted to and had not been fully occupied directing their own troops. As for McClernand, his biographer, Richard L. Kiper, correctly states that "regimental and brigade reports of the fighting [on April 6] are replete with references to McClernand at the front issuing orders to form line of battle, pull out of line to obtain ammunition, support artillery batteries, and, eventually, retreat to form a new line," an "extremely difficult maneuver even with experienced soldiers and officers" when "under enemy pressure." And if McClernand had given way to "despair and despond," why then did Grant, scarcely an admirer, direct him on the evening of April 6 to "assume command of all detached and fragmentary corps [units]" in the vicinity of his line? Whatever his faults, McClernand was no coward, and, although a political general, he possessed far more battle experience than Sherman.[25]

Was Sherman so sensitive to criticism that he felt compelled to claim he had done nothing wrong while accusing others of things they did not do and could not have done? Or did he truly believe to be true the falsehoods he told his family? Let us postpone an attempt to answer these questions until later. There will be ample future opportunities, and by then Sherman will have taken center stage in our historical tragicomedy and not be, as he is now, merely a member of the supporting cast, albeit a prominent one.

Meanwhile, Halleck continued creeping toward Corinth. Beauregard, whose battle-worthy troop strength had been reduced to little more than half of Halleck's, tried to stop him by concentrating for a strike against one or the other of the Union wings. Each time, though, he found the Yankees ready and literally "intrenched to their eyes." Finally, on May 26, with enemy cannons now in range of Corinth's main fortifications and in danger of having his rail supply line severed, he ordered an evacuation that was completed during the night of May 29–30. Not until morning did the Federals discover he had gone, leaving behind only some logs fixed to look like cannons and a few hundred deserters.

Thus, Halleck gained Corinth and with it his first and, so it turned out, his last success as a field commander. He made no serious attempt to pursue the Confederates, who withdrew down the Mobile & Ohio Railroad to Tupelo, Mississippi, fifty miles due south. His troops too were suffering from disease and exposure—23,000 of them had been stricken—and with good cause he feared their number would increase as spring gave way to Deep South summer. Also any further advance would have to be supplied by rail rather than river, the Tennessee no longer being navigable beyond Eastport in the extreme northeast corner of Mississippi. Before that could be done, long stretches of ripped-up track would have to be re-laid, dozens of burnt bridges replaced, and sufficient rolling stock acquired. Besides, he now had accomplished all he had set out to accomplish upon arriving in St. Louis six months ago. Since then, armies acting under his direction (more or less) had driven the Confederates from Missouri and Kentucky, penetrated deep into Arkansas, occupied Nashville and most of the western half of Tennessee, entered Alabama and Mississippi, and opened the way for the seizure of Memphis, where on June 6 two Federal regiments, backed by gunboats, landed and ran up the U.S. flag over the defenseless city. Understandably, he felt satisfied.[26]

So did Sherman. On May 26 he finally had received his major general's commission. Even though he wrote Ellen that "it gives me far less Emotion than my old commission as 1st Lieut. of artillery," because "the latter I knew I merited, this I doubt"—which he had reason to do—it meant for him that he could make good on the words he had written his father-in-law after reading Halleck's April 24 telegram to Stanton that neither Grant nor he were responsible for the "sad casualties" at Shiloh, thereby clearing the way for his promotion: "I know I can take what position I choose among my Peers."[27]

Grant, on the other hand, remained disgruntled—indeed, more so than before, having found being second in command to Halleck not merely meaningless but demeaning. Hence, he decided that unless there was "an early move" against the Rebels, most of whom he believed had "heartily tired of the war," and he received an "important command," he would take a "short leave," visit Julia and the children, who were staying with his father in Covington, Kentucky, across the Ohio from Cincinnati, and then perhaps go to Washington, there to seek assignment to "some other field" than the West.[28]

Discovering his intent, Sherman and some other generals of the Army of the Tennessee went to him and urged him to stay. He refused, and Sherman assumed he would leave. Then Halleck asked him to remain—a request that revived his hope, expressed in letters to Julia, that he might be placed in charge of West Tennessee with headquarters in Memphis, where she and the children could join him, and so decided to stay on at Corinth. Learning of this change of mind from a note sent him by Grant, on June 6 a delighted Sherman, whose division was at Chewalla, Tennessee, wrote him that "you could not be quiet at home for a week, when armies were moving, and rest could not relieve your mind of the gnawing sensation that injustice has been done you." They were true words and sincere words, words which heightened Grant's already high regard for "Cump," as expressed in a May 4 letter to Julia: "In Gen. Sherman the country has an able and gallant defender and your husband a true friend."[29]

Next, on June 10, Halleck abolished the wings, center, and reserve organization and restored Grant, Buell, and Pope to "the command of their respective army corps." At the same time, he directed that Thomas would return, along with his division, to the Army of the Ohio. Prompting these changes was a decision by Halleck, reflecting his belief that all had been done along the east bank of the Mississippi that presently could be done, to place Grant's and Pope's armies on the defensive while Buell's army satisfied Lincoln's desire to free East Tennessee from Confederate dominance by advancing via the Memphis & Charleston Railroad to take Chattanooga, for which purpose it needed to be restored to its full strength.[30]

Pleased to have his army back, Grant on June 12 wrote Julia that he hoped to go soon to Memphis and wanted her to join him there.[31] Not until June

23 did he and his staff reach the city, on the way escaping a Confederate attempt to capture or kill him. The delay, almost certainly, was occasioned by a June 15 summons from Washington for Pope to come there immediately to combine and command three separate Union armies operating in northern Virginia under McDowell, Frémont, and Nathaniel P. Banks, all of them recent victims of a single Rebel army headed by Thomas J. "Stonewall" Jackson, whose dazzling campaign in the Shenandoah Valley had made him the South's number one hero and gained the mixed fear and admiration of the North. Both Halleck and Pope had protested the assignment, but to no avail. Pope's string of virtually bloodless victories down the Mississippi had caused Lincoln and Stanton to deem him the Western general best suited to bring east and put an end to Jackson's exploits. As a result, on June 15, Pope's Army of the Mississippi acquired a new commander: William S. Rosecrans. How and why this came about will be related in due course. Suffice for now to observe that although still a brigadier, at long last Rosecrans headed a large army, one that included a cavalry regiment led by a thirty-one-year-old colonel named Philip H. Sheridan, concerning whom more also will be said later.[32]

In Memphis, Grant enjoyed the presence of Julia and his children, who joined him there on July 1, but not having to deal with Rebel sympathizers inside the city and Rebel cavalry and guerrillas outside it. Also, he had a couple more spats with Halleck, with the second one being another accusation from "Old Brains" that he had done what he had not done or not done what he had done, producing an ominous July 11 telegram from Halleck: "You will immediately repair to this place [Corinth] and report to these headquarters." What, wondered Grant, did this mean? Did Halleck intend to give him another lecture on proper military conduct? Or a new assignment? Or even relieve him? So he telegraphed back: "Am I to repair alone or take my staff?" The answer quickly came: "This place will be your Head Quarters. You can judge for yourself."

Grant now knew that he was to command at Corinth—what and why he would find out on meeting with Halleck. This he did on July 15 after traveling to Corinth with his family and staff by steamboat and train. Halleck, he learned, had been summoned by Lincoln to Washington, there to be general in chief of all Union armies. As a consequence, he, Grant, henceforth would again head the Army of the Tennessee plus the Army of the Mississippi in the District of West Tennessee, but not Buell's Army of the Ohio as it moved out of that district in an endeavor to take Chattanooga. No doubt, he thanked Halleck. No doubt, too, his thanks was sincere. Although he resented Halleck's hectoring and being shelved by him during the Corinth campaign, he regarded him, so he wrote Washburne on July 22, as "a man of gigantic intellect" who was "well studied in the profession of arms" and who would make an excellent commanding general—indeed, "a better selection could not be made." "He and I," he added, "have had several little spats but I like and respect him nevertheless."[33]

What Grant did not know, and would not know until years later, was that Halleck, upon being notified that he now was the top Northern general, had met with Colonel Robert Allen, chief quartermaster for the Department of the Mississippi, and offered to have him elevated to major general with a seniority surpassing that of all the other Union generals of that rank in the West, something he said he could easily arrange—and this despite Allen, a fifty-one-year-old West Pointer, never before having commanded troops in the field, much less in combat!

Since he could not have had any other motive, obviously Halleck wanted Allen to replace him as head of the Department of the Mississippi, a post for which, just as obviously, he deemed Grant unfit. Allen, though, declined the offer, stating that he already had all he could do, if not more, in his present position. He made the right decision. While a superb quartermaster, in temperament and experience he was ill-equipped to plan and conduct campaigns by large armies operating in a vast region. Furthermore, the ascension to command in the West of a mere colonel would have outraged the generals in that theater, men who had gained their stars on the battlefield (or so they liked to think), and led to many, perhaps all of them, tendering their resignations, Grant among them. As it was, Allen enabled Grant to advance to the front of all the North's Western generals by staying put with Halleck after being shunted by him literally to the rear.[34]

Both Halleck and Grant deserved to be what they had become, Halleck for organizing and directing the Union sweep down both sides of the Mississippi deep into the South, Grant for rendering the sweep possible by his aggressiveness, determination, and ability to react rapidly, vigorously, and perceptively to unforeseen enemy onslaughts—onslaughts unforeseen because of his sometimes displaying too much of the first attribute. Yet, ironically, both Halleck and Grant also owed their new status to a man who despised them both: George Brinton McClellan. This, of course, was not intentional on the "Young Napoleon's" part—far from it. Even so, he did it, did it by not doing what he said he would do, could have done, and should have done during the spring and summer of 1862.

6

Nobody at Antietam

WHILE HALLECK PRESIDED OVER NORTHERN success in the West, McClellan endeavored to achieve the same in the East. Not, though, in the same manner. Instead of commanding from afar, he took the field with his army, the army he had created, the Army of the Potomac. Also, he wished to accomplish far more than merely occupying enemy forts, towns, and territory. He intended to win the war in one mighty stroke, a stroke so crushing that the rebel states, realizing the futility of further resistance, would return voluntarily to the Union if guaranteed that the slavery issue would be settled by constitutional means rather than by cannon. The purpose of the war, he believed, was peace, for only through peace could the divided nation be truly restored in union based on consent, not conquest. This secured, he not only hoped but also expected to receive the appropriate reward: president of the newly reunited United States.

Hence, Richmond remained his target. Northern public opinion demanded it be; so, too, did proper strategy. Although not a large city, Richmond was a major rail hub with six lines connecting it directly or indirectly to every portion of the Confederacy east of the Mississippi, and it contained numerous factories devoted to war production, chief among them the Tredegar Iron Works, the sole plant in the entire South presently capable of forging heavy ordnance. But, most of all, as the capital of the Confederate States of America, it was both the symbol and the incarnation of the South's claim to sovereign independence. Should it fall to Federal arms, then surely (so reasoned McClellan) the Southern people would seek peace in preference to continuing a war they could not win against the superior power of the North concentrated in one place—Virginia—and wielded by one general—himself.

His plan to take Richmond by landing his army near the mouth of the Rappahannock having been thwarted by Joseph Johnston's withdrawal of his forces from Manassas to the south side of that river, McClellan thereupon decided to strike at the city by way of the Virginia Peninsula, a neck of land jutting out into Chesapeake Bay between the York and James Rivers.[1] To this end, starting in mid-March, he rapidly transported 108,000 troops aboard hundreds of ships of all kinds to Fort Monroe, a Union-held bastion at the tip of the Peninsula. This move, which strategically outflanked Johnston, was described by a contemporary British military writer as "the stride of a giant." But instead of brushing aside the scant 11,000 Rebels who initially stood between him and Richmond, he next made what the same author called "the step of a midget" by advancing early in April against Yorktown with the object of securing control of the York River and a railroad leading from it to Richmond, thus providing Johnston ample time to shift his army to the Peninsula. Moreover, rather than seize Yorktown by assault, which he easily could have done, he chose to besiege it. "No one but McClellan could have hesitated to attack," commented Johnston, a close prewar friend.

For nearly a month sweating Yankees dragged huge cannons through sweltering swamps in preparation for the bombardment of Yorktown's fortifications—fortifications that barely existed prior to the siege. By May 3, McClellan's big guns were ready to open up, and that night the Rebels evacuated Yorktown. McClellan sent a portion of his army in pursuit. The next day Johnston, whose strength totaled 55,000, checked it at Williamsburg, then resumed retreating. McClellan, who believed that Johnston possessed at least 120,000 and maybe as many as 200,000 troops, slowly followed. Not until late May did he reach the far outskirts of Richmond, with rain, mud, and most of all caution, slowing his advance to a crawl.

There he halted to await the arrival from northern Virginia of the 35,000-man corps of Major General Irvin McDowell, the loser at Bull Run back in July 1861. This reinforcement, he insisted, was essential to taking Richmond. Also, he urged that it be sent to him by ship, for if it did not come soon, then Johnston might overwhelm him with his vastly superior numbers.

Lincoln refused to do this. For him, safeguarding Washington was an absolute necessity. Should the Rebels seize it, even briefly in a raid, many Northerners, especially Democrats, would despair of saving the Union by war and so call for restoring it by peace. Worse, such a calamity might cause Britain and France to recognize Confederate independence on the grounds that since the U.S. government had proved incapable of either taking Richmond or protecting its own capital, it no longer exercised actual sovereignty over the seceded states. That in turn would leave no option except to declare war against Britain and France—a war which would make it more difficult, if not impossible, to achieve victory over a South now backed by the world's dominant sea power (Britain) and the world's strongest land power (France).

So believing, Lincoln instructed McDowell to join McClellan by marching overland, thus keeping his force between the enemy and Washington. McClellan thereupon extended the right wing of his army to the north of Richmond across the Chickahominy, a swamp-lined stream that flowed southeastward through the Peninsula into the James River, so as to link up with McDowell when he arrived.

McDowell, however, never arrived. Stonewall Jackson saw to that. Acting on a plan conceived by Lee, who had become Jefferson Davis's military adviser, he swept north down the Shenandoah Valley late in May, routed Major General Nathaniel Banks's troops, and (at least in the eyes of some observers) put himself in position to strike at Washington from the west. Alarmed, yet seeing a chance to cut off and destroy Jackson, Lincoln sent McDowell, with 20,000 of his troops, and Frémont, now commanding in western Virginia, to trap him. This they attempted to do but failed. Jackson eluded them with hard marching and hard fighting as he withdrew southward up the Valley—an outcome that led to Pope being placed at the head of McDowell's, Banks's, and Frémont's forces, which in turn caused the last to resign in protest against being subordinated to a general who only a few months before in Missouri had been his very junior subordinate.[2]

Meanwhile, outraged at not being reinforced by McDowell, McClellan vented his anger in a May 21 letter to his fellow West Pointer and good friend Major General Ambrose Burnside, a prematurely bald but superbly sideburned thirty-eight-year-old from Rhode Island who presently was conducting some successful operations along the coast of the Carolinas: "I expect to fight a desperate battle in front of Richmond, and against superior numbers. . . . The Government have deliberately placed me in this position. If I win, the greater the glory. If I lose, they will be damned forever, both by God and man." By "they" he meant Lincoln and Stanton. The former he deemed a "well meaning baboon," the latter "without exception the vilest man I ever heard of"—or so he wrote Ellen. On the other hand, he believed that he, and he alone, possessed the ability to win the war and save the Union—provided, he always hastened to add in his letter, God so willed it. Which, Burnside also believed, he almost surely did.[3]

The "desperate battle" McClellan predicted to Burnside soon came, but not where or in the way expected. On May 31 Johnston, seeking to exploit the separation of the Army of the Potomac by a rain-swollen Chickahominy, attacked that portion of it south of the river and due east of Richmond. Since he deployed 40,000 troops against 30,000 and had the advantage of surprise and concentration of force, he came close to success; but, as always would be the case with him in the rare instances he took the offensive, in the end he failed. His battle plan proved too complicated for his inexperienced generals, the assailed Federals fought stubbornly, reinforcements (thanks to the initiative of one of McClellan's corps commanders) came to their aid across a rickety bridge spanning the Chickahominy, and Johnston himself fell severely wounded.

Although McClellan had gained a victory—a victory to which he had contributed nothing, not even his presence on the battlefield—Johnston's attack left him more convinced than before that the Confederates greatly outnumbered him. If not, then Johnston, a sensible soldier, would not have attacked! Therefore, McClellan decided to hold where he was until McDowell finally came, all the while constructing more and better bridges across the Chickahominy so that he could rapidly switch units from one side of that stream to the other should the enemy again strike. At the same time, he pelted Washington with pleas for still more reinforcements, among them most of Halleck's army now that it had taken Corinth. Lincoln responded by sending him 20,000 troops, one-half of them from McDowell, which meant that all told 149,000 soldiers had gone to the Peninsula starting in March. Yet on June 20, McClellan reported his "present for duty" strength at 105,000, of which number only 90,000 were "available for combat." Small wonder that Lincoln remarked that sending men to McClellan "is like shoveling fleas across a barnyard—not half of them get there."

Even after all of McDowell's corps joined him, and despite most of Burnside's corps soon becoming available upon its return from North Carolina, McClellan did not intend to storm Richmond, less than five miles distant from the Union front line. Instead, he planned to blast his way into the city with artillery, lots of artillery, including more mammoth siege cannons. This was the method he had prepared to use at Yorktown and before that at Rich Mountain after concluding that Rosecrans's column had been repulsed, perhaps wiped out. It was a slow method, but a sure one and, above all, safe. Probably, too, it would have succeeded against Johnston, who shared McClellan's dislike of pitched battles because of their uncertain outcome and who also persistently badgered his president for more troops. McClellan, though, now faced a different opponent: Robert E. Lee.

Presumably, McClellan welcomed the change. Back in April, having mistakenly concluded that Lee "commanded in our front," he wrote Lincoln so informing him, then stated: "I prefer Lee to Johnston—the former is *too* cautious & weak under grave responsibility—personally brave & energetic to a fault, he yet is wanting in moral firmness when possessed by heavy responsibility & is likely to be timid & irresolute in action."[4]

Rarely, if ever, has a commander been more egregiously wrong about his enemy counterpart, particularly given the fact that McClellan had had ample opportunity to know what Lee did and how he did it while both of them served under Winfield Scott in Mexico. How much so, McClellan soon found out (or should have). First, Lee, thanks to his cavalry under Jeb Stuart, confirmed that the Union right was "in the air"—exposed to an attack in flank and rear. Next, in a bold move, he left 30,000 troops to screen Richmond while leading the rest of his army north of the city and across the Chickahominy, where it was joined by Jackson's corps, brought there from the Shenandoah Valley by rail. On June 26, now 55,000 strong, he advanced against the 35,000-man Federal right wing under Brigadier General Fitz John Porter, McClellan's most-trusted general, his purpose to crush it and cut the Federal supply line by seizing the bridges over the Chickahominy. Porter parried this thrust and then fell back to Beaver Dam Creek, where on the evening of June 26 he repulsed a Confederate onslaught, inflicting heavy losses while suffering comparatively few himself.

Had McClellan promptly delivered an attack with his 70,000 troops south of the Chickahominy, he could have, in the words of one of the Southern generals opposing him, "captured Richmond with very little loss of life," for the 21,000 Rebels actually manning its fortifications were stretched thin.[5] Or, at the very least, he could have reinforced Porter while at the same time faking a full-fledged assault on Richmond—a stratagem that would have compelled Lee to abandon his offensive in order to protect his own supply line and safeguard the Confederate capital.

McClellan considered doing each but ended up attempting neither. Instead, he ordered a "change of base" southward to Harrison's Landing on the James River now that his line of supply to the York River was severed. Convinced more than ever that he was outnumbered two to one—why else would someone so "timid & irresolute" as Lee assail so furiously?—his sole desire became to save his army, his reputation, and his command. Lincoln, he suspected, was seeking an excuse to supplant him with Pope, perhaps even McDowell.

During the next four days the Union forces fought as many battles as they fell back toward the James. In each encounter, except at Gaines' Mill on June 27, they beat off ferocious, albeit poorly co-coordinated Rebel onslaughts, and even there the enemy success was bought at an enormous cost in blood and was barren of strategic significance since the Yankees would have retreated in any event. Then, on July 1 the climax came at Malvern Hill, five miles from Harrison's Landing. Lee, frustrated by his failure to obliterate the Army of the Potomac—a failure in large part caused by a physically and mentally exhausted Jackson not performing with his characteristic energy—hurled forward all the troops he could gather in a desperate effort to overpower the Federals before they could reach the cover of their gunboats on the James. Northern cannons, aligned along the crest of the hill by chief of artillery Henry Hunt, slaughtered them, sometimes ripping holes ten feet wide in their serried ranks with a single projectile. "It was not war—it was murder," later wrote a Confederate division commander.[6]

Several of the Union generals, among them the normally cautious Porter, proposed a counterattack come morning, one supported by their totally dominant artillery. Had it been made, in all likelihood it would have enabled the Federals to obtain the offensive initiative in the same way that Grant seized it on the second day at Shiloh and perhaps with the same outcome. But McClellan, who was absent from the battlefield as he had been during all of the previous encounters, except briefly at Beaver Dam Creek, adhered to his already issued withdrawal order: the next day his soldiers marched in torrential rain to Harrison's Landing, there to fortify and await yet another attack. During what became known as the Seven Days Battles, they had inflicted 20,000 casualties on the enemy while losing 16,000, of which 4,000 were sick or wounded and left behind because of retreating. Not they but their commander had been defeated and so had his three-month campaign to take Richmond—defeated by foes inferior in all respects save leadership at the top and fortitude among the rank and file at the bottom.

McClellan, of course, saw it otherwise. The reason, the only reason, he had not taken Richmond, thereby opening the way to a rapid and victorious end to the war, was that Lincoln and Stanton had deliberately denied him the reinforcements required to overcome Lee's vastly greater numbers. And why had they done this? To McClellan, a conservative Democrat for whom the sole purpose of the war should be the restoration of the Union, the answer to both was obvious and obnoxious: the president and his secretary of war, bowing to the demagogic demands of the abolitionist Radical Republicans, wished to prolong the war so that its objective could become the destruction of slavery and the subjugation of the South. This objective would render restoration impossible by greatly strengthening Southern determination to achieve independence while fatally weakening Northern willingness to continue a conflict that had been perverted into an antislavery crusade. McClellan barely tolerated what he viewed as their military incompetence, but to plunge the nation into a bitter bloodbath over slavery was, to him, unforgivable.

McClellan, moreover, had not hesitated to tell Lincoln and Stanton that they, rather than he, bore the blame for the failure to seize Richmond and for the Army of the Potomac being (so he thought) in dire peril of annihilation. As early as late on the night of June 27, following Gaines' Mill, he telegraphed Stanton an account of the battle wherein he falsely claimed that his soldiers "were overwhelmed by vastly superior numbers even after I brought my last reserve into action" and declared that "you must send me very large reinforcements, & send them at once." He concluded with these words:

> I know that a few thousand men more would have changed this battle from a defeat to a victory—as it is the Govt must not & cannot hold me responsible for the result.
>
> I feel too earnestly tonight—I have seen too many dead & wounded comrades to feel otherwise than that the Govt has not sustained this Army. If you do not do so now the game is lost.
>
> If I save this Army now I tell you plainly that I owe no thanks to you or any other person in Washington—you have done your best to sacrifice this Army.[7]

Shocked by the final paragraph—not only was it grossly insubordinate, but it also in effect accused the secretary of war, the president, and his entire administration of treason—the supervisor of the military telegraph office in Washington deleted it from the deciphered version of the telegram before sending it on to Stanton, who in turn showed it to Lincoln. Had it remained, Lincoln would have had no choice other than to remove McClellan from command and order his court-martial. As it was, upon reading what he received, Lincoln replied, also by wire:

> Save your Army at all events. Will send reinforcements as fast as we can. . . . I feel any misfortune to you and your Army quite as heavily as you feel it yourself. If you have had a drawn battle, or a repulse, it is the price we pay for the enemy not being in Washington. We protected Washington, and the enemy concentrated on you.[8]

This response surprised and puzzled McClellan. Why had not Lincoln relieved him? He could think of only one answer: Lincoln dared not. If he did, then he would have to justify the act, and that in turn would necessitate publishing the telegram, which, as he explained to Ellen when she asked about it, "would have ruined him & Stanton forever," because of the adverse reaction of the Northern public on learning the true reason for the failure of the Peninsula Campaign.[9]

So, believing he now held the upper hand over the president, on July 1 he wired the following to the War Department:

If it is the intention of the Government to reinforce me largely, it should be done promptly, and in mass. I need fifty thousand *50,000* more men, and with them I will retrieve our fortunes. More would be well, but that number sent at once, will, I think enable me to assume the offensive. I cannot too strongly urge the necessity of prompt action in this matter.[10]

This was not a request, it was a demand, and Lincoln responded to it as a father, his patience wearing thin, responds to a child throwing a tantrum:

Allow me to reason with you a moment. When you ask for fifty thousand men to be promptly sent you, you surely labor under some gross mistake of fact. . . . All of Frémont in the valley, all of Banks, all of McDowell, not with you, and all of Washington, taken together do not exceed, if they reach sixty thousand. . . . Thus the idea of sending you fifty thousand, or any other considerable force promptly, is simply absurd. . . . If you think you are not strong enough to take Richmond just now, I do not ask you to try just now. Save the army . . . and I will strengthen it for the offensive again as fast as I can.[11]

On reading this, in particular the phrases "gross mistake" and "simply absurd," McClellan should have realized that far from being intimidated, Lincoln was (to put it mildly) irritated. He thought nothing of the kind. Instead, on July 4 he wired father-in-law and chief of staff Marcy, who had gone to Washington with a letter to Stanton soliciting "rather much over than much less than 100,000 reinforcements," a message stating that he had received "a long telegram from the Presdt which quite discourages me as it shows a fatal want of appreciation of the glorious achievements of this Army, & of the circumstances of the case, as well as of the cause which led to it. I will save this Army & lead it to victory in spite of enemies in all directions."[12]

That same day Marcy met with Lincoln, who had summoned him to the White House on learning that he had told Stanton that the Army of the Potomac might have to "capitulate" given its present situation. That word, said Lincoln sternly, was "not to be used in connection with our army." Taken aback by the president's vehemence, Marcy muttered something to the effect that the term was merely "hypothetical." His answer, he subsequently recorded in a private memorandum, "seemed to afford great relief to the President."[13]

If so, not for long. Later in the day Lincoln received a long telegram from McClellan. In it the general warned that "communications along the James are not secure," that there "are points where the enemy can establish themselves with cannon or musketry and command the river," and that "in case of this or in case our front is broken I will still make every effort to preserve at least the personnel of the Army. . . . Send such reinforcements as you can, I will do what I can."[14]

These words smacked of potential, not just "hypothetical," capitulation. What in fact was the condition of the Army of the Potomac and the intention of its commander? Lincoln decided to go to Harrison's Landing and find out.

He arrived on the morning of July 8, reviewed some of the troops—their morale seemed high—and then conferred with McClellan. Having been notified of the president's coming, McClellan handed him a letter dated July 7 and marked "Confidential." Only the first sentence of the opening paragraph dealt with the military situation: "You have been fully informed that the Rebel army is in our front, with the purpose of overwhelming us by attacking our position or reducing us by blocking our river communications." The rest of this paragraph and most of the ensuing seven paragraphs, some very long, pertained to the political objective of the war. This should be, indeed it must be, solely the restoration of the Union; any "declaration of radical views, especially upon slavery, will disintegrate our present armies."[15]

Lincoln perused the letter, then pocketed it without comment. Already he had decided what to do about slavery: declare all slaves in Rebel-held territory free unless all of the Confederate states resumed their allegiance to the Union by a certain date, which was most unlikely unless they were on the verge of defeat, which certainly was not the case now. He, the president, not McClellan, the failed general, would determine the war aims, and he believed that the majority of Northerners would support adding the abolition of slavery to restoration of the Union as a goal of the war. After all, it was slavery which had brought about the secession and thus the war.

With regard to the Army of the Potomac and its commander, on July 11 Lincoln returned to Washington, having decided to put into effect one of the propositions set forth in McClellan's letter: "In carrying out any system of policy which you may form, you will require a Commander in Chief of the Army; one who possesses your confidence, understands your views and who is competent to execute your orders by directing the military forces of the Nation to the accomplishment of the objects by you proposed." This he did through Stanton, who that same day telegraphed Halleck: "Ordered,

That Major General Henry W. Halleck be assigned to command the whole land forces of the United States, as general-in-chief, and that he repair to this capital as soon as he can with safety to the positions and operations within the department under his charge."[16]

Lincoln's decision to place Halleck at the head of the Union army requires little explanation and less justification. His own attempts at directing military operations in Virginia had proved less than successful, whereas Halleck had achieved enormous success in the West, success that promised still more success. Hence, Lincoln desired a professional to take charge of all Federal forces. Who among all Northern generals possessed such credentials superior to Halleck's? None.

Thus Halleck found himself, so he put it in a letter to his wife, "in General Scott's place"—the place he would have occupied well before had he made it from San Francisco to Washington sooner or Scott remained in that place a little longer. From a personal standpoint, as he also told his wife, it was a "very high compliment," one that placed him on the very top rung of the professional ladder.[17] Yet he probably was sincere, at least up to a point, when he wrote Sherman prior to leaving for Washington that he would have preferred remaining in the West and had accepted his new post because "I must obey orders."[18] Since becoming commander of the Department of the Mississippi he had been free to do what he wished the way he wanted, with little interference from Lincoln and Stanton, and none at all by McClellan, after being reduced to heading just one army, albeit the one deemed most important. Now, in Washington, he would be under the direct supervision of the president and the secretary of war; plus, he would have to deal with McClellan—not a pleasant prospect given their past differences and the present military situation in Virginia.

This prospect soon became actuality. Arriving in Washington on July 23, Halleck met with Lincoln and Stanton, who instructed him to proceed at once to Harrison's Landing and ascertain what should be done with the Army of the Potomac and its commander, whom he was authorized to remove from his post should he judge it necessary. They did not, though, tell him whom they had in mind to replace McClellan. This was Burnside, whose zeal and success while operating along the coast of the Carolinas had gained Lincoln's favorable attention.

The very next day Halleck set out in a steamer for Harrison's Landing accompanied by Burnside, most of whose corps had recently been transferred from the Carolinas to Fort Monroe. On July 25 he met with McClellan, who considered him "my inferior" and his appointment to general in chief "a slap in the face" by Lincoln, whom he viewed (so he wrote Ellen) "with thorough contempt—for his mind, heart & morality."[19] McClellan proposed crossing his army to the south side of the James and then with a quick thrust seizing Petersburg, a town twenty miles south of Richmond wherein all except one of the railroads linking Richmond to the rest of the South terminated, thereby compelling Lee to abandon the Confederate capital in order to supply his army. This scheme Halleck rejected, stating that it could result only in disaster if, as McClellan maintained, Lee possessed 200,000 men, more than enough for him to defend Petersburg while at the same time marching on Washington. McClellan then said that with 30,000 more troops he might have a "chance" of taking Richmond by moving up the north bank of the James and besieging it. No more than 20,000 reinforcements, answered Halleck, were available; would they suffice to take Richmond? He was, replied McClellan, "willing to try it." Halleck thereupon offered him two choices: (1) Attempt to take Richmond after being joined by the 20,000 additional troops, most of whom would come from Burnside's corps; or (2) transfer all of his forces from the Peninsula to Fredericksburg on the Rappahannock, from where they would move on Richmond along with Burnside's corps and Pope's Army of Virginia, both also to be under his command.[20]

Having thus dealt with McClellan, Halleck on July 27 returned, again accompanied by Burnside, to Washington, where he received that same day a letter from McClellan dated July 26 and obviously written after their final meeting. In it McClellan asked for "15,000 or 20,000 men from the West to reinforce me temporarily" and asserted that "the true defence of Washington consists in a rapid & heavy blow given by this Army upon Richmond." Halleck showed the letter to Lincoln, who on reading it decided to abandon the Peninsula Campaign: "If I could send McClellan 100,000 reinforcements, the General would claim that the Confederates had 400,000, and that to advance he would need still more men."[21] Halleck agreed. "General McClellan," he wrote his wife on July 28, "is in many respects a most excellent and remarkable man, but he does not understand strategy and should never plan a campaign."[22]

Unbeknownst to Halleck, on either that same day or the following Lincoln and Stanton met with Burnside in private and offered him command of the Army of the Potomac. Surprised, indeed appalled, Burnside declined the post, declaring that McClellan was a better general than he. Surprised in his turn by Burnside's response—never before had he known a general on active duty to turn down a higher status—Lincoln tried to persuade Burnside to change his mind, but to no avail. Besides being sincere in regarding

McClellan his superior in talent, Burnside felt a strong personal obligation to "Mac" for having in 1858 given him a well-paying job with the Illinois Central Railroad after a business venture of his went bankrupt.[23]

Left with no practical alternative, Lincoln decided to retain McClellan as commander of the Army of the Potomac—for the time being, at any rate— but to go ahead with removing it from the Peninsula to Fredericksburg. To this end, on August 1 he had Halleck direct Burnside, who by then had returned to Fort Monroe, to transport his corps by ship to Aquia Creek, a landing on the Potomac ten miles northeast of Fredericksburg, a movement Burnside promptly executed. Then, on August 3, again per Lincoln's instructions, Halleck ordered McClellan to begin transferring all of his active-duty troops to the same place. For both the president and his general in chief, safeguarding Washington now took precedence over attempting to seize Richmond, and this meant uniting Pope's and McClellan's forces before Lee could exploit their separation.[24]

The order outraged McClellan, who at once protested it, predicting that it "will bring disaster on our cause." But when Halleck replied that the order "will not be rescinded, and you will be expected to execute it with all possible promptness," McClellan proceeded to obey—that is, in his fashion: reluctantly, protestingly, and slowly. "I am," he wrote Ellen on August 10, "satisfied that the dolts in Washington are bent on my destruction." He then asserted that "the result of their machinations will be that Pope will be badly thrashed within two days & that they will be very glad to turn over the redemption of their affairs to me."[25]

McClellan's prediction regarding Pope's fate proved prescient, although not as soon as he anticipated. Lee, on ascertaining that the Army of the Potomac was evacuating the Peninsula, promptly began doing what Lincoln and Halleck feared he would do—take advantage of the division between Pope's and McClellan's forces.[26] First, remaining with Major General James Longstreet's command to cover Richmond, he sent Jackson's corps to strike at Pope's army, which was deployed in the vicinity of Culpeper, only to have the thrust parried at Cedar Mountain on August 9. Jackson's attempt, though, caused Pope to shift eastward and to the south side of the Rappahannock. Next, seeing an opportunity to slice in between Pope and Fredericksburg and thus isolate him from McClellan, whose troops now were arriving in large numbers at Aquia, Lee moved north and again endeavored to turn his left flank, this time with both Jackson's and Longstreet's commands, but again failed when Pope detected this stratagem in time to fall back behind the Rappahannock and then repel Confederate efforts to cross it. Stymied, yet still determined to exploit the separation of the Yankee forces, Lee thereupon resorted to one of the boldest moves of a career of bold moves. While continuing to threaten Pope in front with Longstreet's command, he sent Jackson's "foot cavalry" on a rapid march northward around Pope's right and then eastward deep into his rear, where on August 27 they destroyed an immense Federal supply depot at Manassas Junction, cut Pope's supply line, and placed themselves within striking distance of Washington.

Pope, on learning of Jackson's foray, hastened northward in hope of trapping and crushing him should he head toward the capital. Anticipating such a move, Jackson withdrew to a superb defensive position behind a deep railroad cut northwest of Groveton, a village astride a turnpike leading to Alexandria. At this point, Pope should have gone over to the defensive while waiting to be joined by the Army of the Potomac, which finally had completed evacuating the Peninsula; in fact, some of its units already had joined him or else were on the way to so doing, notably Porter's corps. Had he done this, Lee, who was following in Jackson's wake with Longstreet's command, would have been left with no rational alternative other than to abandon his attempt to smash Pope and take Washington.

Instead, Pope, believing that he had Jackson cornered and that there was no danger of him being joined by Longstreet, followed Jackson and on August 29 delivered a series of uncoordinated assaults on his heavily outnumbered troops, who barely repelled them and perhaps would not have had they not been fronted by the railroad cut. But repel them they did, and by doing so enabled Longstreet's command to come up on Jackson's right during the afternoon, with Lee accompanying it.

At this juncture Pope definitely should have withdrawn toward Washington, especially after belatedly learning of Longstreet's arrival. Why did he not? The surface answer, valid as far as it goes, is that he assumed that Longstreet had come merely to support Jackson and that Lee intended to retreat. Beneath that assumption, though, was an intense desire to defeat Lee. In that way, only in that way, could he put an end to the frustration he had experienced since coming to Virginia at being constantly on the defensive and so achieve with deeds what he had promised in words upon taking command of the newly constituted Army of Virginia: "I have come to you from the West, where we have always seen the backs of our enemies; from an Army whose business it has been to seek the adversary and beat him where he was found; whose policy has been attack and not defense. . . . Success and glory are in the advance; disaster and shame lurk in the rear."[27]

Now, therefore, was the time to attack, to defeat the adversary, and to see the enemies' backs as they fled. Not only would this bring success and glory, it would assure his retaining an independent command—or, quite possibly, supplanting McClellan at the head of all Federal forces in Virginia! Indeed, should he overtake and overcome Lee, that might lead to the North winning the war, in which case . . . well, Pope knew full well the award that awaited victorious American generals in peace.

His mind filled with this glistening vision, throughout the morning of August 30 Pope dismissed as exaggerated all reports and signs that Longstreet was aligned on Jackson's right. He persisted in believing on the basis of the most flimsy evidence that Lee intended to retreat, if not retreating already. Then in the afternoon, having in the meanwhile been joined on his left by Major General Fitz John Porter and expecting the arrival soon of Major General William B. Franklin's corps, also from the Army of the Potomac, he again assailed Jackson.

Jackson's soldiers, protected by the moatlike railroad cut, withstood the Federal onslaught, some of them even throwing rocks after firing their last cartridge. Then Lee unleashed Longstreet's corps. Twenty-five thousand strong, and supported by massed artillery, it slammed into the Union left, crumpled it, and threatened to get between the Federal forces and Washington. To his credit, Pope kept his head, and by shifting units from his right to his left held the Confederates at bay until most of his army escaped across Bull Run via the same stone bridge over which McDowell's routed troops fled back in July 1861.

Thus Pope avoided debacle but not defeat. This, then and afterward, he blamed on others, most of all Porter and McClellan. The former, he charged officially, prevented him from gaining a "decisive and complete victory" on August 29 by disobeying an afternoon order to join him promptly with his 12,000-man corps for an attack on Jackson's right flank and rear. The latter, he informed Lincoln unofficially, had denied him success, or at least a drawn battle, by not sending Franklin's corps to his support on August 30, as repeatedly ordered by Halleck.

There can be no doubt that Porter despised Pope, disliked serving under him, and desired to be back with his good friend "Mac." Yet his personal attitudes did not motivate his performance as a general. The reason he disobeyed Pope's order was that he rightly realized that if he tried to obey it his corps would be exposed to the same near catastrophe it suffered on the afternoon of August 30 when it became the prime victim of Longstreet's assault, an assault he tried in vain to warn Pope against. Finally, his troops played a key role in holding open the Union line of retreat following that assault, and Pope should have credited him with this rather than making him, however sincerely, the scapegoat for his own failure.

McClellan's case is more complex. On the one hand, he too despised Pope. He resented having so much of *his* Army of the Potomac placed under that "fool," and he was delighted by what he deemed to be Pope's "deserved" defeat. On the other hand, he did not intentionally seek to bring about that defeat. The basic cause of his recalcitrance in reinforcing Pope was his reluctance to engage in offensive battle and a consequent desire to concentrate all Federal forces for the defense of Washington, a desire shared by Halleck but not to the extent of denying Pope reinforcements, which, if they did not enable him to gain a victory, would prevent him from suffering a potential disaster.[28]

Once again, too, Lincoln took a different view of the matter. He believed, rightly, that in order to win the war and restore the Union the North needed to fight aggressively and that it, not the South, possessed the stronger armies and should use them accordingly. So believing, on the morning of August 29 he had urged (but not ordered) McClellan to reinforce Pope with "all available forces" while at the same time stating that this was preferable to the alternative proposed by McClellan, which was to "leave Pope to get out of his scrape & at once use all of our means to make the Capital perfectly safe."[29] To Lincoln this language indicated, at the very least, a callous indifference to Pope's fate. Then, during the next three days, he read Halleck's telegrams to McClellan ordering him to hasten Franklin's corps to Pope's assistance and McClellan's evasive, often insubordinate, replies. At the same time, he also saw messages sent by Porter to Burnside, whose troops were guarding the landing at Aquia Creek, wherein the former strongly denounced Pope both as a general and a person. As a result, he concluded, to quote from the diary of his private secretary, John Hay, that "out of envy, jealousy, and spite" McClellan and Porter "wanted Pope defeated" and conspired to have it happen.[30]

So what now to do about the "Young Napoleon"? On the morning of September 2, Lincoln, accompanied by Halleck, went to McClellan's Washington residence and told him that he now was in charge of defending the capital, an assignment that not only left him at the head of the Army of the Potomac but also placed him over all of Pope's troops as they retreated into the District of Columbia, their ranks thinned by 14,000 killed, wounded, captured, and missing.

Later that morning Lincoln met with his cabinet and "in deep distress" informed it of McClellan's new assignment, much to the dismay of most of its members who had signed a petition drafted by Stanton stating that "it is not safe to entrust to Major General McClellan the command of any Army of the United States." Placing him in charge of Washington's defense, protested Secretary of the Treasury Salmon P. Chase of Ohio, formerly a fervent supporter of the general, was tantamount to giving it to the Rebels. McClellan, replied Lincoln, had the "slows" and was "good for nothing" when it came to offensive operations, but no one else could do a better job of reorganizing the army and restoring its morale.[31]

Defending Washington, however, was one thing; defeating Lee or, better still, smashing his army was very much another. To this end, on September 3, Lincoln via Stanton instructed Halleck to organize all available troops not needed for that defense for "active operations" in the field. As always, he was not content merely to hold the enemy at bay; if at all possible, he wished to destroy him.

Halleck received the message that night. At once he rewrote it and sent it to McClellan, whom he directed to "report the approximate force of each corps . . . now in the vicinity of Washington which can be prepared in the next two days to take the field." By doing this he in effect declined to assume command of the Army of the Potomac, from which most of the field force would have to come. His motive for so doing was not what many then thought and most historians since have assumed—namely, fear of the responsibility of commanding the United States' prime army in a campaign that might determine the outcome of the war, as had generals in chief George Washington in the Revolutionary War and Winfield Scott when thrusting from Vera Cruz to Mexico City to win the Mexican War. His reasons were fourfold and, in ascending order of importance, as follows:

First, he was close to physical exhaustion from having gone four successive nights virtually without sleep during the closing days of August and, to make matters worse, he was suffering a severe bout of hemorrhoids.[32]

Second, he realized that in spite of the heavy losses and failure of the Peninsular Campaign, most of the rank and file of the Army of the Potomac still idolized "Little Mac" and so would fight better for him than anyone else.

Third, not only did he expect Lee soon to invade Maryland, but also in Kentucky, a Rebel force headed by Major General Edmund Kirby Smith had routed a 6,500-man Federal contingent headed by "Bull" Nelson and occupied the state capital of Frankfort, from where it menaced Cincinnati. At the same time, another Confederate army under Braxton Bragg was moving on Louisville after sweeping through Middle Tennessee. These incursions, which threatened to undo all that had been accomplished in the West since

February under his direction, had to be dealt with, and only he was in a position to do so, there no longer being a department commander for that region, which he considered to be as strategically and politically important as the East, if not more so.

Fourth and foremost, as general in chief he could not, unlike Washington and Scott, devote himself mainly to commanding the nation's prime army. They, in fact, had no other choice given the means of communication available to them, namely mounted couriers by land and sail-propelled ships by sea. By the time of the Civil War, though, such had ceased to be the case. The telegraph, the locomotive, and the steamship brought into being armies of unprecedented size deployed over a region far surpassing in area all of present-day Western Europe, exclusive of Britain and Italy. They also made it possible and necessary for a general in chief, along with his constitutional superiors, the president and his secretary of war, to oversee the operations of these armies on a scale and to a degree never before equaled, much less exceeded, by the military chieftains of any nation at war.[33]

Hence it was that Halleck became de facto what did not become de jure until the twentieth century when the general in chief of the U.S. army gave way to a chief of staff. This in turn led to his defining his role in terms of two things he would do and two that he refused to do. The first of the former and the problems it entailed he described in a letter written to Sherman shortly before he ceased to be general in chief early in 1864 (but, as shall be seen, in name only):

> The great difficulty of the office of General-in-Chief is that it is not understood by the country. I am simply a military advisor to the Secretary of War and the President, and must obey and carry out what they decide upon, whether I concur in the decision or not. . . . If I disagree with them in opinion I say so, but when they decide it is my duty faithfully to carry out their decision.[34]

The second thing he did was to make every effort to provide the armies in the field with the men and materiel needed to gain the objectives that had been set for them directly by the president or via the secretary of war, to offer their commanders advice and encouragement, and, when he deemed it necessary, to warn them of the personal consequences of being perceived by Lincoln and/or Stanton as lacking in vigor, obedience, or, worst of all, success.

As to the two things he steadfastly refused to do, one was to issue to these commanders *orders* on how to conduct a campaign or wage a battle. Only they, he correctly believed, possessed timely access to accurate information about the enemy's strength, position, and intentions, plus the condition and situation of their own forces. For him in Washington to tell them what to do, when, where, and how would be to transform the ludicrous into the disastrous.

And the other thing he would not do was take command of an army in the field. Even if physically and temperamentally better suited for it than he was, already he had all he could do effectively in supervising, providing for, and advising the heads of all the Union armies, and doing so moreover with a personal staff of only seven officers and sixteen enlisted men, one much smaller than would be assigned to a division in World War II. For him to endeavor to be both general in chief and a field commander almost surely would produce failure in each role. Thus his evasion of Lincoln's attempt to put him in charge of the Army of the Potomac.[35]

Early on the morning of September 5 definite word reached Lincoln that Lee was crossing the Potomac into Maryland. Having suffered 9,000-plus casualties while winning what the Confederates called Second Manassas, and having failed in an attempt to turn the Federal right flank, he decided to invade Maryland, there to obtain badly needed provisions, perhaps spark a prosecessionist uprising, and, by menacing Baltimore and Pennsylvania's capital, Harrisburg, draw the Union army out of its Washington fortifications into the open country, where he hoped to outmaneuver and defeat, even destroy it. And then? Much, indeed all, was possible.[36]

At about 9 A.M. Lincoln and Halleck again visited McClellan's Washington quarters, this time to tell him that he was to pursue, overtake, and crush Lee. Two hours later they departed, whereupon McClellan, confident now that he had prevailed over both of them, ecstatically wrote Ellen: "Again I have been called upon to save the country." He added that "the case is desperate, but with God's help I will try unselfishly to do my best & if he [God] wills it accomplish the redemption of the nation. . . . I still hope for success & will leave nothing undone to gain it."[37]

Possibly even as McClellan penned these lines Lincoln learned that Burnside now was in Washington, having just arrived there with the last of his troops from Aquia Landing. At once he summoned him to the White House and again offered him command of the Army of the Potomac, only to have him again turn it down for the same reason as before: he lacked sufficient ability for too great a responsibility. While disappointed by this answer, it reinforced Lincoln's high regard for Burnside as a person. How nice, because so rare, to find a general not beset by the demon Jealousy! On the other hand, Burnside's rejection of the command either initiated or intensified Lincoln's resentment of Halleck's refusal of that post, for it so happened that when Halleck wrote Sherman that "the office of General-in-Chief . . . is not understood by the country," he had the president in mind more than anyone else, for reasons which will be revealed in due course.[38]

Later, starting at midnight, Burnside had another meeting. It was with McClellan, who told him that he was so angry because Porter and Franklin had been relieved of their corps commands in order to face a court-martial on charges brought by Pope that he intended to demand that Lincoln dismiss Stanton and Halleck, a demand he would support by declaring that unless this were done he would resign from the army.

What McClellan said alarmed Burnside. Aware, as he freshly was, of Lincoln's continued strong desire to relieve McClellan, he realized that any attempt by "Mac" to have Stanton and Halleck removed by threatening to resign if they were not would be sure to result in the president removing McClellan and placing him in command of the Army of the Potomac. This he did not want for reasons other than modesty and friendship. Like Halleck, he believed that most of that army, from generals down to privates, remained loyal to "Little Mac," that they would resent anyone who superseded him, and that consequently it would be difficult, if not impossible, for any successor to succeed as commander. Therefore, he urged, even pleaded with, McClellan not to place any conditions on serving his country in its present crisis. Finally, McClellan agreed to refrain from demanding, at least for the present, the dismissal of Stanton and Halleck. Instead, the following day he wrote to both Lincoln and Halleck requesting that court-martial proceedings against Porter and Franklin be suspended so that they could resume commanding their corps. Instructed by Lincoln to decide the matter, Halleck complied with the request, perhaps figuring that those two generals, if serving under McClellan, would obey orders, something he, like Lincoln, believed they had not done when called on to support Pope.[39]

As for Pope, September 5 also saw him formally relieved of "command" of his now nonexistent Army of Virginia. But what to do with him? The solution came the next day in the form of an urgent request from the governor of Minnesota for Federal military assistance in suppressing a bloody Indian uprising in his state. Lincoln responded by appointing Pope head of a freshly created Department of the Northwest to which he traveled by train on September 9, his Civil War career ended, the consequence of fighting at the wrong time in the wrong place and in the wrong way.[40]

Once it became clear that Washington no longer was in danger, McClellan began moving—slowly—toward Frederick, Maryland, on learning that

Lee had occupied it. He did not find him there, but on September 13 he experienced one of the most extraordinary strokes of luck in all the annals of warfare. Two Indiana soldiers, poking about on the site of a former Rebel camp, found some cigars wrapped in a piece of paper that turned out to be a copy of an order issued by Lee revealing that he had divided his army, with one part under Jackson heading south to take Harpers Ferry, the northern gateway of the Shenandoah Valley, while the rest under Longstreet deployed west of South Mountain toward Pennsylvania.

"Here is a paper," McClellan exclaimed gleefully, "with which if I cannot whip Bobbie Lee I will be willing to go home!" He set his troops in motion, intending to cross South Mountain and get between the Confederate halves and defeat each separately. He moved fast—for him. Alarmed by McClellan's uncharacteristically rapid advance, Lee sent forces to hold the South Mountain passes long enough to regroup his army. On September 14 the Federals fought their way through the passes but took all day to do it. Worse, McClellan relapsed into his customary caution on coming into contact with the enemy, whom he credited with totaling 120,000, maybe more, in number. Not until the evening of September 16 did he post 75,000 of his 95,000 available troops for an attack. By then Lee had all of his army on hand, save a small division left behind by Jackson at Harpers Ferry, where he had captured 12,500 Yankees and garnered immense spoils of war. But even should that division join him in time, Lee would face the Union onslaught with at most 38,000 weary, hungry soldiers, having lost, in addition to the 9,000 casualties at Second Bull Run, at least an equal number to exhaustion and desertion while campaigning in Maryland. Rarely has a commander displayed greater contempt for his opponent than Lee in deciding to offer battle to McClellan.[41]

Rarely, too, has such contempt proved more justified. Instead of attacking simultaneously all along the enemy line, McClellan first struck the Confederate left, then center, and finally right, thereby enabling Lee to shift units from sector to sector, where, just barely and with heavy loss, they managed to repel the Federal assaults, inflicting terrible casualties. Even so, at midafternoon Burnside's IX Corps, which, unlike the other Union formations, had to cross Antietam Creek in order to engage, broke through on Lee's right and swept, virtually unopposed toward the village of Sharpsburg and the sole road by which the Confederates could retreat across the nearby Potomac. But before it reached the road, 3,000 troops from Major General Ambrose Powell Hill's division of the Army of Northern Virginia, the one left behind at Harpers Ferry to dispose of the Yankee prisoners and spoils, arrived on the field, struck the IX Corps's flank, and, aided by surprise and the blue uniforms that many of its men had donned in place of their gray rags, routed it and forced Burnside to fall back to the Antietam.

Yet the capitulation or annihilation of Lee's army remained within McClellan's grasp. Assembled at the center of his line, ready to enter the fray, was the Reserve Corps headed by Porter. Nearby, also available for attack, were at least as many more soldiers who so far had experienced little or no combat. And in front of them stood no more than 29,000 weary, hungry Confederate combatants—less than the number Lee would lead when in April 1865 he evacuated Richmond and Petersburg and set out on the road that led to Appomattox.

All McClellan needed to do was close his hand, turn it into a fist, and then deliver the blow. Standing in his command post atop a hill east of the Antietam and observing the battlefield through a spyglass, he turned toward Porter but said nothing, for the expression on his face clearly asked: "Should we attack?" Slowly Porter shook his head from side to side: "No." It was the answer McClellan desired. Enough, he believed, had been accomplished, and to attempt more would be to play into the hands of Lee, whom he still believed vastly outnumbered him and so quite likely had many thousands of fresh soldiers concealed in the dense woods north of Sharpsburg, ready to pounce.

Acting on these beliefs, and also expecting Lee to attack, McClellan remained on the defensive all through the following day. At night, having sent off his wounded, Lee retreated across the Potomac back into Virginia. McClellan made only a pro forma pursuit. All he ever had hoped to do was to drive Lee out of Maryland and prevent him from invading Pennsylvania. Now this had been done and he was content.[42]

In fact, more than content. "Those in whose judgement I rely," he wrote Ellen on September 18, "tell me that I fought the battle splendidly & that it was a masterpiece of art."[43] Then, the day after Lee withdrew into Virginia, he penned the following to her:

> I feel some little pride in having with a beaten and demoralized army defeated Lee so utterly, & saved the North so completely. Well—one of these days history will I trust do me justice in deciding that it was not my fault that the campaign of the Peninsula was not successful. An opportunity has presented itself through the Governors of some of the states to enable me to take my stand—I have insisted that Stanton shall be removed & that Halleck shall give way to me as Cmdr in Chief. I will *not* serve under him—for he is an incompetent fool. . . . The only

safety for the country & for me is to get rid of both of them—no success is possible with them. . . .

Thank Heaven for one thing—my military reputation is cleared—I have shown that I can fight battles & *win* them! I think my enemies are pretty effectively killed by this time! May they remain so!!⁴⁴

These statements reveal a man divorced from reality by a combination of megalomania and paranoia. If anyone in whose "judgement" he relied told him that his conduct of the battle was "a masterpiece of art," it had to be Porter, Franklin, and others who relied on him to preserve them as generals. The truth is that, in addition to not coordinating his attack and employing his reserves when doing so, which would have given him total triumph, he kept his 4,000 cavalry concentrated behind the center of his battle line, where it was useless, rather than posting it on his flanks, especially the left one, where it could have provided warning of and delayed the advance of Hill's division, thus making it possible for Burnside's corps to block Lee's sole avenue of retreat and forcing him to surrender. As it was, Lee gained a tactical victory in that he held off the Federal onslaught and then did what he would have done even had no battle been fought—return to Virginia now that it had become obvious that he lacked sufficient force to carry out a successful campaign north of the Potomac and that there would be no mass uprising of Marylanders against Northern domination.

Antietam would turn out to be the single bloodiest day of the Civil War, with the Federals suffering 12,400 casualties out of 50,000 men engaged and the Confederates 10,300—one-fourth of the combatants on both sides. Also, in spite of it being for the Union an incomplete victory, it was one of the most, if not *the* most, decisive battles of that war. There are three reasons why this is so, and in order of importance they are as follows:

First, because the North perceived Antietam as a great triumph, it probably prevented the Democrats from gaining control of the House of Representatives in the fall 1862 congressional elections, an outcome that would have made it difficult, perhaps impossible, for the Republicans to achieve their political objectives in waging the war.

Second, Antietam put an end to any serious consideration by the British government of recognizing the Confederacy as a sovereign nation, an action that some of its leaders were pondering, even favoring, prior to the battle, which they viewed as being the reason why Lee abandoned his invasion of the North rather than it being, as it actually was, merely the occasion for his so doing. And unless Britain did it first, the French ruler Napoleon III dared not establish formal diplomatic relations with Richmond even though he desired them; that almost surely would mean war with the United States, a war in which the rapidly growing Yankee fleet would ravage France's merchant marine if it were not sheltered by the Royal Navy.

Third, but most important of all, Antietam enabled Lincoln on September 24 to announce in the glow of victory what he had refrained from publishing while in the gloom of defeat—a "Preliminary Emancipation Proclamation." Dated September 22, its key passage read: "That on the first day of January in the year of our Lord, one thousand eight hundred and sixty-three, all persons held as slaves, within any state, or designated part of a state, the people whereof shall be in rebellion against the United States shall be then, thenceforth, and forever, free."

In other words, Southerners had 100 days wherein to lay down their arms and resume their allegiance to the United States, or else all slaves in those areas of the Confederacy still resisting the authority of the Federal government would cease to be slaves in the eyes of the government. Since this would not happen short of a very unlikely total defeat and surrender of the Rebel armies before January 1, 1863, Lincoln knew full well that with the proclamation he was changing the North's official purpose in waging the war from solely the preservation of the Union to also the destruction of slavery. And he realized, too, that by adding this second purpose not only would he stiffen Southern resistance but also intensify opposition to the war among Northern Democrats, many of whom contended that it was the Republicans, with their antislavery agitation, who had provoked the South into secession. But he had come to believe, as we have seen, that any restoration of the Union without at the same time eliminating the cause of its separation—slavery—would be a farce, a tragic farce.

Among the Democrats who opposed emancipation, at least until after the war ended, was, of course, McClellan, who on reading Lincoln's proclamation in a newspaper dashed off a letter to him asserting that the army would refuse to fight for abolition. But then he showed the letter to one of his division commanders, Brigadier General William F. Smith, who warned him that it would result in his being relieved of command. Not wanting that—a meeting of Northern governors that he hoped would make it possible for him to force Lincoln to dismiss Stanton and Halleck had just convened in Altoona, Pennsylvania—he tore up the letter.[45]

This proved to be a wise act, for the governor's conference, far from calling for the dismissal of Stanton and Halleck, nearly adopted a resolution demanding McClellan's removal.[46] On the other hand, probably it would have made no difference had he sent the letter unless, like the unexpurgated version of McClellan's Gaines' Mill telegram blaming Lincoln and Stanton for his failure to take Richmond, it was so insolent and insubordinate that there would have been no alternative to stripping him of command. First, to relieve him after he had gained what was perceived in the North as a great victory would impair, perhaps fatally, Republican prospects in the forthcoming state and congressional elections. Second, Lincoln already had decided to retain McClellan at the head of the Army of the Potomac in hope that he now would go on the offensive, decisively defeat Lee, take Richmond, and thus put the North well on the way to winning the war.

To this end, on October 1 Lincoln traveled by train to Harpers Ferry, recently reoccupied by Federal troops. During the next several days he frankly told McClellan that he "would be a ruined man if he did not move forward, move rapidly and effectively."[47] McClellan smiled, nodded, and promised to move once his army was ready to move. But when that would be he did not say nor intend to say. "I found the Presdt," he wrote Ellen, "at Harper's Ferry. . . . His ostensible purpose is to see the troops & the battle fields. I incline to think that the real purpose is to push me into a premature advance into Virginia. . . . The real truth is that my army is not fit to advance. . . . These people [Lincoln, Stanton, Halleck] don't know what an army requires and therefore act stupidly."[48]

Lincoln sensed McClellan's recalcitrance and recognized that it stemmed from a belief that he, the president, dared not remove him from command of "my army." Thus on the evening of October 2, while on a hilltop viewing a troop encampment, he suddenly asked a companion what they were looking at. "The Army of the Potomac," came the puzzled answer. "So it is called," said Lincoln, "but that is a mistake. It is only McClellan's body guard."[49]

So what to do about what few anymore called the "Young Napoleon"? Lincoln could think of only one thing, at least for the present. That was to continue prodding him to go after Lee while at the same time providing him, to the extent possible, with all the men and materiel he needed to defeat Lee and take Richmond. Should he accomplish this, not only might it decide the war in the East, it would negate a potential, should it become actual, debacle in the West. There, early in October, Bragg's and Kirby Smith's forces remained deep in Kentucky, and even as Lincoln and McClellan met in Virginia, another Rebel army, headed by Major General Earl Van Dorn, was assailing Corinth in Mississippi, the capture of which would open the way for it to join Bragg and Kirby Smith in Kentucky.

How did it happen that the tide of war in the West, once totally favorable to the North, now flowed so promisingly for the South? The next chapter will seek an answer and also describe how that tide reversed itself.

7

Grant and Rosecrans at Iuka and Corinth

The Birth of a Rivalry

"I AM DOING EVERYTHING IN MY POWER to get new troops into the field and the sky here [in the East] is cleared," wrote Halleck to his wife soon after Pope's forces checked Stonewall Jackson at Cedar Mountain on August 9. "But at the West everything since I left has gone wrong: It is the strangest thing in the world to me that this war has developed so little talent in our generals. There is not a single one in the West fit for a great command."[1]

As witness his unsuccessful attempt to induce Robert Allen, a mere colonel with no combat experience, to replace him as commander of the Department of the Mississippi, obviously Halleck did not deem Grant, the senior major general in the West, qualified for that post. That this was so is understandable. Viewed objectively, Grant's victories owed as much to luck as to skill: flood-level water at Fort Henry, incompetent opponents at Fort Donelson, and at Shiloh a combination of a foe who shot his bolt the first day and the just-in-time arrival of reinforcements that enabled him to go on the offensive the second day, thereby turning what at best would have been a stand-off into the North's greatest battlefield triumph so far of the war. No doubt, Halleck would have agreed with his protégé Sherman's assessment of Grant made in a July 13 letter to his brother-in-law Philemon Ewing: "very brave but not brilliant."[2]

Hence Halleck's decision, prior to going to Washington, to leave the West as he had reorganized it following the occupation of Corinth: Grant again at the head of *his* Army of the Tennessee and commander of the District of West Tennessee; Buell with the Army of the Ohio fully restored to him and the mission of liberating East Tennessee; and Pope's Army of the Mississippi assigned to the District of West Tennessee but now under Rosecrans, whose presence and status shall hereupon, as promised in chapter 5, be explained.

When in March 1862 Lincoln created the Department of the Mississippi, he also made West Virginia part of a new Mountain Department presided over by Frémont. Again reduced to a subordinate, an understandably resentful Rosecrans at once went to Washington in quest of an independent command. Initially, his prospects for receiving one seemed excellent: he and Stanton shared a deep detestation of that "little cuss" McClellan. But then they had a falling out. It began with Stanton wrongly thinking that Rosecrans had dillydallied in guiding a lost division headed by a geographically challenged German immigrant into West Virginia, and it ended when Stonewall Jackson made the Federals pay for Stanton's disregard of Rosecrans's proposal to combine Banks's, McDowell's, and Frémont's armies, instead leaving them dispersed and vulnerable in the Shenandoah Valley. It would be left to Lincoln to act upon Rosecrans's idea when he pulled those commands together and placed them under John Pope. Never one to admit mistakes, Stanton resented being caught in one and so punished Rosecrans by exiling him to the West, where he would be submerged beneath an ever-mounting tide of major generals, hopefully unable to surface.[3]

On May 24 Rosecrans reported for duty to Halleck, who assigned him to Pope's Army of the Mississippi, where, thanks to being its senior brigadier, he took charge of two of its five divisions. In that capacity he participated in the "siege" of Corinth and conducted the "pursuit" of the Confederates after they evacuated the town. Then, as previously noted, on June 15 he replaced Pope as commander of the Army of the Mississippi upon the latter being summoned to Virginia.[4]

Thus he finally headed a large army. This gave him much satisfaction, all the more so because he rightly felt that doing so was long, indeed too long, overdue. Yet there remained two rubs: he still was a brigadier and he continued to lack an independent command, one in which he could decide what to do, when, where, and how, then order it done.

Although there is no evidence that he did, he could have blamed Halleck for his present status without being altogether wrong. It was Halleck who, after failing to persuade Allen to succeed him as commander of the Department of the Mississippi, again divided that portion of the department between the Mississippi River and the Appalachians south of the Ohio River into two independent districts, with one headed by Grant and the other by Buell. And it was Halleck too who assigned Buell's Army of the Ohio the mission of liberating East Tennessee while casting Grant and Rosecrans in a supporting defensive role. Two of his reasons for so doing, apart from appeasing Lincoln's obsession with "liberating" Unionist East Tennessee, have been previously presented: the precarious condition of the rail lines needed to supply a large army advancing farther into Mississippi and concern about the effect of a Deep South summer on the health of troops from the North.

Soon, though, he had two other reasons. One was a hope that should Buell take Chattanooga, this could lead to an invasion of Georgia, which, if successful, would split the Confederacy east of the Mississippi strategically in twain. The second was a belief that there would be no need to attempt to seize Vicksburg, the sole remaining major Rebel fortress on the Mississippi, by an army traversing two-hundred-plus miles of land. It was about to be done and soon in the same way that Columbus, New Madrid, Island No. 10, Port Pillow, and Memphis had been taken—by warships and troopships steaming along on water. Specifically, he expected David Farragut, the captor of New Orleans, to repeat his performance there at Vicksburg, thus severing the Confederacy again, this time between the eastern cis-Mississippi and western trans-Mississippi.

It failed to turn out that way. On July 15, two days before Halleck set out for Washington, Farragut's flotilla of oceangoing wooden warships assailed Vicksburg's fortifications, only to suffer so severe a pounding from their cannons and those of an ironclad named *Arkansas* that it had no choice except to continue back down the river to New Orleans and undergo repairs. Likewise, an attempt by Federal troops to dig a canal across Milliken's Bend to the west of Vicksburg, thereby changing the course of the Mississippi so that ships could steam by the fortress far out of range of its big guns, merely produced a trickle of water too shallow for a rowboat, much less transports and gunboats. If Vicksburg ever was to be taken, it would have to be by an attack on land, not from the river.[5]

Mid-July found Buell closer to Chattanooga than he had been in mid-June but still too far away to have any immediate prospect of reaching it. On a map, he appeared to have with the Memphis & Charleston a splendid supply line of continuous track. On the ground, though, it consisted of a series of segments, the product of Confederate raiders and guerrillas burning bridges, torching trestles, and ripping up rails. Yet, in spite of all, on July 12 he received word that the Nashville & Chattanooga Railroad now was open all the way to Stevenson, Alabama, a mere thirty miles from Chattanooga, thus providing him with an alternate, seemingly more secure logistical conduit.

Not so. The very next day Nathan Bedford Forrest's cavalry struck a large Federal depot on the Nashville & Chattanooga at Murfreesboro, Tennessee, destroyed everything they could not carry away, burned all the nearby railroad bridges, and marched off with 1,100 Yankee prisoners. Buell, who recently had been chastised by Lincoln and Halleck for what they perceived as his all-too-chronic slowness, responded to this raid by sending work crews to repair the damage. This they did, only to have Forrest again break the Nashville & Chattanooga on July 21 near Nashville itself.

Obviously that rail line required protection as well as repair. Hence, Buell placed two divisions along it while the work crews went back to work. On July 29–30 trains packed with rations arrived in Stevenson, which his increasingly hungry and disgruntled soldiers had managed to reach. Finally: On to Chattanooga!

Again, no. July 30 also brought Buell a message from Rosecrans conveying information acquired by Colonel Phil Sheridan's cavalry regiment during a foray into north central Alabama: A large Rebel army headed by Braxton Bragg was on its way to Chattanooga. Buell promptly decided to stay put. It was the best thing to do. Even if he reached Chattanooga before Bragg, which he could not since Bragg's troops, unbeknownst to him, already were entering the town, how long could he stay given the vulnerability of his supply line? And why risk his army when it now was the only large force standing between the Confederates and Nashville? He could think of none and so reacted accordingly.[6]

Bragg's sudden, unexpected-by-the-Federals arrival at Chattanooga would prove to be the most spectacular maneuver by rail of the Civil War. To understand why and how it occurred, it is necessary to go back to Beauregard's stealthy withdrawal from Corinth down the Mobile & Ohio Railroad to Tupelo, Mississippi. There Beauregard, painfully ill from a throat infection, took sick leave without first obtaining Jefferson Davis's permission. Davis, who disliked Beauregard personally, resented his premature claim to total victory at Shiloh, and blamed him for not achieving one, immediately replaced him with Bragg, for whose soldierly qualities he had a high regard dating back to when they had served together during the Mexican War in Zachary Taylor's army and who could be trusted to fight.

This Bragg made ready to do, imposing a regimen of hard drilling and harsh discipline on his troops. Then, after Farragut abandoned his attempt to take Vicksburg, he sent his artillery and wagon trains, along with the soldiers serving them, marching eastward through north Alabama while at the same time loading 30,000 infantry onto trains that carried them via the Mobile & Ohio from Tupelo down to Mobile, from where they traveled by both river and rail to Montgomery, Alabama, then again by trains up through Atlanta to Chattanooga. Behind in Mississippi, he left 18,000 troops under Van Dorn to guard Vicksburg and Sterling Price's Army of the West to confront Grant and Rosecrans in northeastern Mississippi.

On July 31 Bragg conferred in Chattanooga with Major General Edmund Kirby Smith, commander of the Confederate District of East Tennessee, who agreed to cooperate in executing the next stage in Bragg's campaign plan. In essence, this called for Smith to penetrate Kentucky by way of Cumberland Gap and for Bragg to advance from Chattanooga into Middle Tennessee, feint toward Nashville, and then head into Kentucky, where together they would march on Louisville, thereby inspiring a popular uprising against Yankee occupation, drive Federal forces from the state, and establish the political boundary of the Confederacy in the West along the Ohio River. Should they succeed, and they felt confident they would, and if Lee finished off McClellan and then went on to take Washington, then the war would be good as won and Confederate sovereignty recognized by Britain and France, leaving the North no alternative other than to do the same.[7]

Buell's reaction to Bragg's coming to Chattanooga partook more of relief than disappointment. From the outset he had doubted the practicality of seizing that town for reasons both logistical and strategic. Events had demonstrated, indeed continued to demonstrate, the validity of the first concern. Now the presence in Chattanooga of a formidable enemy army brought there by rail all the way from Mississippi proved the same about the second doubt. Even had Buell reached Chattanooga, he could not have remained there. He would have had to evacuate the place in order to avoid being besieged and starved into surrender by Bragg's forces, plus other Confederate contingents sent there in trains from Virginia, where his good friend McClellan obviously had failed to take Richmond and been obliged to retreat.

So Buell abandoned what he now deemed his foredoomed attempt to capture Chattanooga and went on the defensive. To that end, he fell back from Stevenson to Decherd, a village on the Nashville & Chattanooga, and then deployed his army along a line covering the most likely approaches to Nashville, which he expected to be Bragg's target. Hardly, though, had he completed doing this than he received on August 6 a telegram from Halleck warning him that "there is a great dissatisfaction here [in Washington] at the slow movement of your army toward Chattanooga," which was true. Lincoln had declared at an August 3 cabinet meeting that "a McClellan in the army is lamentable, but a combination of McClellan and Buell is abominable."[8]

Faced yet again with a demand that he do what he believed would be disastrous, Buell sought to appease the president by wiring Halleck that "I shall march upon Chattanooga at the earliest possible day."[9] This meaningless promise, of course, merely increased Lincoln's displeasure, and Halleck let Buell know it in an August 9 letter: "I deem it my duty to write you confidentially that the administration is greatly dissatisfied with the slowness of your operations. . . . So strong is this dissatisfaction that I have several times been asked to recommend some officer to take your place."[10]

Perhaps even as Halleck penned these words 600 Confederate cavalry led by Kentucky cavalier John Hunt Morgan descended on Gallatin, Tennessee, a town north of Nashville. There they tore up track and burned bridges of the Louisville & Nashville Railroad, after which they galloped further north. They set fire to a locomotive and ran it into the Big South Tunnel, where it exploded, causing the tunnel to collapse into an immense pile of rock, dirt, and timber. Since a good deal of the supplies Buell received from Nashville came to that city from Louisville, Morgan's foray had the same effect on Buell's logistical situation, albeit not immediately, as had Forrest's raids.

Nor was that all. By the time Halleck's warning reached Buell, Kirby Smith was on the way into Kentucky with 12,000 troops, most of them loaned to him by Bragg. No matter how strongly Lincoln desired it, for the present there could be no liberation of East Tennessee; the need now was to prevent the Rebels from (as they saw it) liberating Kentucky. And because Halleck refused to recommend anyone to replace Buell as commander of the Army of the Ohio, because he knew of no general of sufficient rank who could be relied on to do better, Lincoln decided to refrain from removing Buell for the time being. But why, oh why, did he have so many generals who, rather than go after the enemy, seemed to prefer having the enemy come after them? The war could not be won that way.

On August 28, Bragg with 27,000 infantry advanced northward across the Tennessee, his movement screened by Brigadier General Joseph Wheeler's cavalry. Buell, still assuming that the Confederate objective was Nashville, fell back toward that city and so opened the way for Bragg to enter Kentucky unopposed. Next, on August 30, Kirby Smith's column routed a Union force (if such it deserved to be called) of raw recruits under "Bull" Nelson at Richmond, Kentucky, then occupied Lexington and Frankfort, both within easy striking distance of Louisville and Cincinnati.

News of Nelson's debacle reached Buell on September 1, whereupon he decided to retire into Kentucky with most of his army while leaving three divisions headed by Thomas, who had rejoined the Army of the Ohio, to defend Nashville. Bragg, on the other hand, did not learn of the victory at Richmond until September 5, when he received at Sparta, Tennessee, a dispatch from Kirby Smith accompanied by a plea to join him at Lexington. This message removed any lingering hesitation he had about bypassing Nashville. His goal now definitely became Louisville, to which purpose he wrote Price on September 7 to "march rapidly for Nashville" in the mistaken belief that all five divisions of Rosecrans's Army of the Mississippi were on the way to reinforce Buell.[11]

But before describing what Buell and Bragg did and failed to do on entering Kentucky, we first need to take a look at some simultaneous events in

Mississippi involving four other generals: Grant, Rosecrans, Price, and Van Dorn.

Although glad to have back his Army of the Tennessee, Grant resented being cast in a supporting role to Buell, a role that required him, contrary to his penchant for the offensive, to remain on the defensive. "I have," he wrote Halleck on August 9, "communicated to Gen. Buell several times such information as I had of interest to him, but never received an acknowledgment. I do not know where he is." Even so, he added, "I will try to hold the [railroad] communication with Gen. Buell and be in readiness to reinforce him if it should become necessary."

This, as has been seen, did become necessary and, to put it mildly, the necessity gave Grant another reason to dislike Buell. For in his August 9 letter to Halleck he also stated: "I am anxious to keep the whole of the Army of the Mississippi together, and under the command of Brig. Gen. Rosecrans . . . either to move upon any force that may threaten my front, or to reinforce Gen. Buell. Having so many Maj. Generals to provide commands for, this may be difficult. I regret that Gen. Rosecrans has not got rank equal to his merit to make this easy."[12]

Obviously, Grant had developed a high opinion of Rosecrans. On the other hand, his already low opinion of McClernand had become lower still, made so by what he viewed as exaggerated, even false, claims in his official report about what he did at Shiloh. As a result, by late August his sole desire regarding that ambitious politician-general was to get rid of him, as he already had Lew Wallace, whom he unfairly but understandably blamed for failing to reinforce him during the first day of Shiloh. McClernand, for his part, was equally eager to be free of Grant for reasons also understandable. Early in August he had asked his good friend, Illinois governor Richard Yates, to secure from Stanton permission for him to come to the Prairie State, there to help enlist recruits pursuant to a July 4 call by Lincoln for 300,000 Northern volunteers. This Yates did, and on August 25 Halleck ordered McClernand to "repair to Springfield, Ill., and assist the Governor in organizing soldiers." Two days later, McClernand boarded a northbound train and Grant no longer had to deal with him, at least for the time being, although he hoped it might be forever.[13]

Soon after McClernand's departure orders from Halleck did make it necessary to send to Buell's District of the Ohio three of Rosecrans's divisions, with one of them being a division that Sheridan soon commanded, he having been promoted to brigadier general at the urging of Rosecrans and four of his generals because he was "worth his weight in gold." Grant thereupon asked and received permission from the general in chief to cease trying to guard the Memphis & Charleston east of Corinth and concentrate on protecting the region between that town and Memphis. This he tried to accomplish by posting units of his army along a line running through Tennessee from Memphis to Chewalla and stationing Rosecrans's remaining two divisions, 9,000 strong, at Iuka, Mississippi, a spa astride the Mobile & Ohio only ten miles southwest of Eastport, the most likely place where Price might cross the Tennessee River should he endeavor to reinforce Bragg. He then waited for the Confederates in Mississippi to make their move.[14]

His wait proved brief.[15] Starting early in September he began receiving reports that Price was advancing north along the Mobile & Ohio and that Van Dorn was doing the same via the Mississippi Central Railroad—a name that described its location. Then, on September 16, Rosecrans notified him that Price was at Iuka, from which he had recently withdrawn except for a cavalry detachment. Grant thereupon decided to attack and if possible crush Price before he could continue on to reinforce Bragg, by then in Kentucky, or else join Van Dorn for an attack on Corinth, a possibility he feared even more.

The following day, during which he received a telegram from Halleck urging him to "do everything in your power to prevent Price from crossing the Tennessee River," Grant put into effect a plan that called for Rosecrans to join an 8,000-man force headed by Major General E.O.C. Ord, a newcomer to the Army of the Tennessee, in an attack on Price to be delivered from Burnsville, a village on the Mobile & Ohio seven miles northwest of Iuka. Rosecrans in turn proposed on September 18 that, instead of combining with Ord, he have his column advance on Iuka from the south via the San Jacinto and Fulton roads while Ord moved against Price from Burnsville. Since this stratagem promised to trap Price and so lead either to his capitulation or to his annihilation, Grant promptly agreed to it and instructed Ord to attack Price on the morning of September 19, by which time he expected Rosecrans to be close enough to Iuka to do the same.

Neither Grant or Rosecrans knew, because they could not, that Price no longer intended to reinforce Bragg, at least not with his 14,000-man "Army of the West" alone. On September 14, the day he occupied Iuka, he discovered that two of Rosecrans's divisions still remained near Corinth and also most belatedly received Bragg's September 6 telegram directing him to "move rapidly on Nashville." Unable to decide whether or not to do the latter, he wrote Van Dorn on September 14 and again three days later urging that they unite their forces, crush Rosecrans, and then go into Tennessee.

On September 18 Grant traveled by rail to Burnsville with Ord's troops, and Rosecrans set out eastward for Barnett's Crossing, from which point he intended to swing northward along both the San Jacinto and Fulton roads, thereby blocking Price's sole escape routes from Iuka. But, as so often in war, what appeared easy in the abstract proved otherwise in practice. A civilian guide led one of Rosecrans's divisions (Brigadier General David M. Stanley's) astray, and rain, breaking a long draught, turned dirt roads into mud, producing further delays. As darkness descended, Rosecrans remained twenty miles from Iuka, whereupon he sent Grant by way of a courier line a message that he would not be in position to assail Price's rear come morning but would do so by 1 or 2 P.M. on September 19, and that "when we come in, will endeavor to do it strongly."

Grant received this dispatch at his headquarters in the Burnsville railroad station sometime during the night or early morning of September 19—he subsequently asserted in a report "after midnight"—but not until daylight did he dictate to staff officer Colonel Clark Lagow a note stating that Rosecrans "is behind where we expected him" and directing him "not to be to[o] rapid with your advance [on Iuka] unless it should be found the enemy are evacuating." This note, though, did not reach Ord, who on instructions from Grant was off to the west investigating what turned out to be a false report of a Confederate thrust toward Corinth, until 10 A.M., and he did not return to Burnsville until 4 P.M. He then met Grant, who told him to move his "whole force forward to within 4 miles of Iuka, and there await sounds of an engagement between Rosecrans and the enemy" before attacking Price. But since Grant and he agreed that it would be impossible for Rosecrans to come within striking distance of Iuka until the morning of September 20, most of his force remained near Burnsville. Not only did Grant doubt that Rosecrans could engage Price on the nineteenth, he believed that there might be no need to fight him at all. For around midnight on September 18 he had received a message from the superintendent of the military telegraph office at Cairo stating that "reports from Washington this evening contain intelligence" of a two-day battle "near Sharpsburg" in which the "Entire rebel army of Virginia [had been] destroyed."

Concluding that this surely was true, Grant thereupon arranged, probably via Colonel Lagow, for Ord to send to Price a copy of the message, along with a summons to "avoid useless bloodshed and lay down his arms." As might, indeed should, have been expected, Price took his time before replying, and when he did he declared that he did not "credit the dispatches from Cairo," but even "if the facts were as stated in those dispatches they would only move him and his soldiers to greater exertions in behalf of their country, and that neither he nor they will ever lay down their arms . . . until the independence of the Confederate States shall have been acknowledged by the United States." And thus ended this comedy.

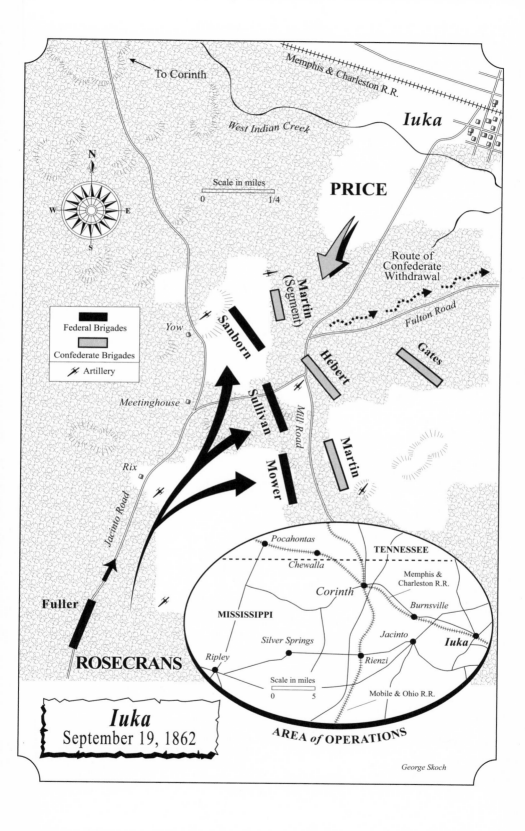

To Corinth

Memphis & Charleston R.R.

West Indian Creek

Iuka

N
W E
S

Scale in miles
0   1/4

PRICE

Route of
Confederate
Withdrawal

Martin
(Segment)

Federal Brigades
Confederate Brigades
Artillery

Sanborn

Yow

Hebert

Fulton Road

Gates

Meetinghouse

Sullivan

Mill Road

Rix

Mower

Martin

Jacinto Road

Fuller

ROSECRANS

Pocahontas

TENNESSEE

Chewalla

Memphis &
Charleston R.R.

Corinth

Burnsville

MISSISSIPPI

Jacinto

Iuka

Silver Springs

Ripley

Rienzi

Scale in miles
0   5

Mobile & Ohio R.R.

AREA of OPERATIONS

Iuka
September 19, 1862

George Skoch

Meanwhile, Rosecrans made good time, the van of his column passing at noon through Barnett's Crossroads only seven and a half miles southwest of Iuka by way of the Jacinto road. There, soon after, Lagow and Colonel T. Lyle Dickey, Grant's inspector general, joined him, having been sent by Grant to inform him that Ord would not attack until he did so first.[16] Both of them urged him to hasten his march—superfluous advice—and also to send Stanley's division headed by Brigadier General Charles S. Hamilton, up the Fulton road, which ran almost due north to Iuka from a hamlet called Cartersville, thereby cutting Price's sole remaining line of retreat southward. This he refused to do for three reasons. First, Stanley would have to march another five miles eastward in order to reach the Fulton road. Second, once on it he would be so widely separated from Hamilton's division that neither could support the other should the Confederates attack either or both. And, third, only one and a half miles south of Iuka, near where the Jacinto and Fulton roads joined, there was a crossroads angling off northeast from the former. Here Hamilton could rapidly reach the latter and thus block Price's line of retreat while being in close supporting distance of Stanley. Rosecrans also took it for granted that as soon as Ord heard the sound of his guns he would join in the fray, thereby removing Price from the chessboard of the war in the West—not as great a victory, to be sure, as that just rumored to have been won in the East over Lee, news of which had also been conveyed to him and his troops, yet one that should help Buell to at least parry Bragg and also reduce, if not eliminate, any threat to Corinth.

After conferring with Lagow and Dickey, Rosecrans sent by his courier line a dispatch marked "12:40 P.M.," wherein he notified Grant that he had reached Barnett's Crossroads and was pressing on to Iuka. This he continued to do, but more slowly than he had anticipated, his march being harassed by Confederate cavalry. Even so, by about 3:30 P.M. the van of the lead brigade of Hamilton's division, which like Stanley's consisted of only two small brigades, arrived within two miles of Iuka and were almost at the crossroads leading to the Fulton road.

Then one of Price's two infantry divisions suddenly struck it, driving it back and capturing nine cannons before it could be reinforced, whereupon it rallied and beat back the enemy onslaught. Fierce fighting then ensued, with both sides losing heavily in proportion to the number of troops engaged, until darkness descended. Rosecrans, after withdrawing Hamilton's division and replacing it with Stanley's, sent by courier a dispatch to Grant: "We met the enemy in force. . . . The engagement lasted several hours. . . . You must attack in the morning and in force."

Late that night Price retreated from Iuka by way of the Fulton road. Ironically, had the Federals not menaced him he would have done this in any event come the morning of September 20, the reason being that late on the night of September 18 he had received an order from Van Dorn, who now commanded all Confederate forces in Mississippi, to link up with him for an attack on Corinth. He had remained in Iuka on the nineteenth solely to load his wagons with Yankee military stores left behind there, owing to the failure of one of Rosecrans's cavalry officers to set fire to them before fleeing the place on discovering the approach of Price's army.

At 8 A.M. Rosecrans, upon being told by some of its residents that Price had evacuated Iuka, occupied the village, skedaddling some lingering Confederates with cannon fire. Grant had received Rosecrans's 12:40 dispatch from Barnett's Crossroads during the night and had directed Ord to move closer to Iuka and attack as soon as Rosecrans did. When Ord arrived at 10 A.M., Rosecrans asked him, "Why did you leave me in the lurch?" Ord answered by handing Rosecrans a crumpled sheet of paper. It bore Grant's dispatch, scribbled by Lagow, instructing Ord not to be too rapid when advancing toward Iuka because Rosecrans "is behind where we expect him." Neither Grant nor he, Ord added, heard any sound of battle coming from the south yesterday afternoon and evening, the consequence of a strong wind blowing from the northwest.

There can be no reasonable doubt that Ord spoke the truth. What motive could Grant and he have had for deliberately exposing Rosecrans to defeat and his troops to a debacle? None. Furthermore, even had Grant and Ord heard the din of combat south of Iuka, as did members of an advance detachment two miles from the place, in all likelihood it would have made no difference. Price's other infantry division was quite capable of fending off Ord's force, which owing to detachments had been reduced to no more than 5,000, and it could not have engaged the Confederates before it became too dark to have done so. Likewise, had either Hamilton's or Stanley's divisions gone up the Fulton road, neither was strong enough to have blocked for long Price's 14,000 troops, who could have easily overpowered or surrounded it or both. The blunt truth of the matter is that the only way the plan that Grant adopted at Rosecrans's suggestion for eliminating Price's army, and not merely obliging it to retreat, could have succeeded was for there to have been no Rebel cavalry patrolling the southern approaches to Iuka. But there was. As a result, the plan, which depended on surprise for success, turned into the military equivalent of shooting an arrow into the air, only to have it fall somewhere in Berkley Square.

At noon Grant rode into Iuka, where, in response to a 9:45 message from Rosecrans asking, "Why did you not attack this morning?" he too told Rosecrans that the sound of the previous day's fighting south of Iuka did not reach him. He then toured the battlefield with Rosecrans, agreed that it had been best to keep Hamilton's and Stanley's divisions together, and then telegraphed Halleck a brief account of what had happened at Iuka, one that stated, "I cannot speak too highly of the energy and skill displayed by General Rosecrans."[17] As far as Grant was concerned, Iuka was simply a case of a good plan going bad because of chance and circumstance, and he attached no blame for this to Rosecrans.

Rosecrans took a different view of the matter. He believed that Iuka was a repeat of Rich Mountain, that once again a commanding general had denied him the success he had earned and the credit he deserved. "The failure of proper cooperation," he wrote his wife, Anna, on September 22, "unfortunately lost us the capture of Price and his entire army, which would have been inevitable had the attack from the west side been duly made." Not even his promotion to major general, notification of which he received on September 20, provided much compensation. "I shall accept it," he informed Anna, "as an act of tardy justice."[18]

In sum, Rosecrans felt that once more he had been deprived, this time by Grant, of the opportunity to perform the leading role in securing a victory that surely would have led to his obtaining what he so desperately desired and had so long rightly deserved—independent command of a major army. Deprived, moreover, because Grant, he had learned from Ord, had spent all of October 19 in Burnsville, where instead of aggressively pressing Price he had passed most of the day vainly endeavoring to induce that "old woodpecker" to surrender on the basis of what since then had proved to be a very exaggerated report of Lee's defeat, if such it was, in Maryland. No doubt, Grant was a hard fighter on the battlefield, but off of it he was careless, as witness his being surprised by enemy attacks while away from his troops at Donelson, Shiloh, and now for a third time in a row at Iuka, where he did not even know that an attack had taken place until he became a near victim of it. Not, Rosecrans decided, an impressive record. Rather, it was evidence that Grant, like McClellan, was a lucky dog.

Throughout the Iuka operation, Grant was perhaps concerned more about safeguarding Corinth than he was about Halleck's behests to prevent Price from reinforcing Bragg. With Price's escape from the trap set for him at Iuka, the likelihood, which soon became a certainty, that he would now join Van Dorn for an incursion into West Tennessee increased the danger to Corinth. Therefore, Grant assigned Rosecrans the mission of defending that town and reinforced him with two small divisions from Ord's command. Also, he transferred his headquarters from Corinth to Jackson, Tennessee, to be in a better position to direct the movements of all of his army. Once Van Dorn and Price were repelled or, better still, eliminated, he would no longer have to play strategic second fiddle to Buell. He hoped to strike at Vicksburg via the Mississippi—a strike to be spearheaded by gunboats.[19]

Meanwhile, at Corinth, Rosecrans prepared to resist Van Dorn should he attack there.[20] This Van Dorn did on the morning of October 3, after first feinting a thrust into Tennessee, then swinging back into Mississippi to approach Corinth from the northwest with his 22,000-man Army of West Tennessee, which consisted of Price's two infantry divisions, another infantry division headed by Major General Mansfield Lovell, and Brigadier General Frank C. Armstrong's cavalry, the ones who had alerted Price to Rosecrans's advance on Iuka. Van Dorn expected to surprise Rosecrans and, in the belief that only 15,000 Federals held Corinth, overpower him, after which he would sweep through West Tennessee into Kentucky, there to join Bragg in "liberating" that state.

He was mistaken on both counts. Not only did Rosecrans know he was coming and from where, he also had increased his strength to 22,000 by calling in various detachments and had bolstered Corinth's defenses with a line of breastworks anchored by cannon-mounting redoubts called "batteries" fronted by ditches. In addition, he made use of fortifications built by Beauregard north of Corinth by placing two of his four divisions behind them with instructions to offer sufficient resistance to cause Van Dorn to deploy his forces and thus reveal where he intended to deliver his main assault.

By midafternoon that became clear, whereupon Rosecrans sent his chief of staff, Lieutenant Colonel Arthur Ducat, to Hamilton, who had borne the brunt of Price's surprise attack at Iuka, with a verbal order to swing his division, which was on the extreme Union right and not facing any Confederates, to turn about and strike Van Dorn's left flank and rear—a move suggested by Ducat. Hamilton, though, refused; he wanted a written order, probably because should the battle turn into a Union disaster, which he believed it would, he could not be blamed. Ducat informed Rosecrans of Hamilton's demand, Rosecrans dictated and signed the order, and Ducat returned with it to Hamilton, who read it and then said he did not understand it. In fact, it contained the word "left" where "right" should have been used. Ducat explained this to Hamilton, but to no avail: he wanted clear, precise instructions.

So again Ducat rode back to Rosecrans, then again back to Hamilton, this time with a sketch map illustrating the flank attack. Hamilton looked at it, said he now understood what was wanted, and even moved one of his two brigades into position for the flank attack, only to have to recall it when it verged off in the wrong direction to counter what in actuality was a nonexistent enemy threat. At this point, Hamilton declared that it soon would be too dark to fight. He was right, as Rosecrans himself admitted when Ducat informed him of Hamilton's new reason for doing what he manifestly wanted to do: nothing. All that could be done now was to withdraw to the new line of fortifications and hope to repel the Confederates when they attacked in the morning.

Repelled they were, but not easily. First one, then the other of Price's divisions stormed forward. A portion of the second even managed to break through a Union weak point and swarm into the streets of Corinth until a counterattack drove it out. Had both divisions attacked simultaneously and Lovell's division joined in the assault, Van Dorn might have taken Corinth. As it was, he gained nothing save the loss of one-fourth of his army killed, wounded, captured, and missing.

In the afternoon the Confederates began retreating. Rosecrans sent out cavalry to track them and detachments to collect their wounded and large numbers of willing prisoners, but did not pursue. His troops, who had suffered 2,500 casualties, were physically and psychologically exhausted. So was Rosecrans, having slept no more than two or three hours during the past seventy-two. At daylight the next day his army set out after Van Dorn, having been reinforced the previous evening by five regiments headed by Brigadier General McPherson, who had been dispatched from Jackson, Tennessee, via (most of the way) the Mobile & Ohio by Grant, who also had sent 5,000 men under Hurlbut to aid in smashing the already half-wrecked enemy.

Wishing to maintain telegraphic contact with Grant, and having issued detailed instructions to his generals on how to conduct the pursuit, Rosecrans remained throughout the morning in Corinth. It proved to be a mistake. Hamilton took the wrong road, another division commander ignored orders to keep wagons at the rear of his column, and the other two halted on discovering they were alone. Not until Rosecrans arrived on the scene did the pursuit truly get under way.

Even so, the Federals came close to bagging Van Dorn, who, on approaching the Hatchie River at Davis Bridge late in the afternoon, found the west bank occupied by Hurlbut's division, now under the command of Ord, to whom Grant had assigned the mission of directing all the Federal forces, Rosecrans's included, seeking to finish him off. Fortunately for his rapidly dwindling army—hundreds of its soldiers were surrendering or deserting— five miles to the south lay a dam that could be, and soon was, converted into a makeshift bridge. To this he fled after posting a rearguard to keep the Yankees on the west bank of the Hatchie as long as prudently possible, then crossed it during the evening and night, with the rear guard being the last to do so. Hurlbut, who had resumed command of his division on Ord being wounded, pursued not. "I am," he notified Grant, "out of rations," and have "too much in crippled wounded men and dead artillery horses to follow." In truth, owing to Ord's overaggressive attack across Davis Bridge, Hurlbut had suffered heavy losses. But the true reason he abandoned the chase was that he was too drunk to go on, despite what should have been a sobering-up punch from a teamster whom he tried to stop from beating a horse.[21] That much, at least, was to his credit.

Rosecrans, once more his vigorous (some would say too vigorous) self, continued to pursue. At noon on October 6, he telegraphed Grant: "The enemy are totally routed, throwing everything away. We are following sharply." And in the evening he informed Grant that the Confederates were heading toward Holly Springs and that "we shall follow them." Did Grant, he asked, have orders for him? "You will," Grant replied, "avail yourself of any advantage and capture and destroy the Rebel army to the utmost of your power."[22]

Encouraged by these words, Rosecrans the following day pushed on across the Hatchie after the fleeing Rebels, even though his own troops, like them, suffered from a shortage of food and water, the latter as a consequence of a long summer drought that had dried up springs and streams. Many soldiers on both sides forced civilians to provide them with provender and sometimes plundered or smashed things that were not edible or drinkable. Such went against the orders of the generals, but it is captains, lieutenants, and sergeants who enforce such orders, and fewer and fewer of them bothered to do so.[23]

In the afternoon, Rosecrans telegraphed another, longer, more portentous message to Grant. Basically, it asked him to have Hurlbut and Sherman join his pursuit; for supplies, rolling stock, and reinforcements to be sent from the North; and declared that "it is of the utmost importance to give the enemy no rest day or night but push him to Mobile and Jackson [Mississippi]." In sum, Rosecrans proposed transforming Van Dorn's repulse and rout into a campaign designed to take Vicksburg, which would cease to have any direct rail connection with the rest of the Confederacy once Federal forces reached the Southern Mississippi Railroad at or near Jackson, less than forty miles east of the fortress.[24]

Grant became angry when he read Rosecrans's proposal. As during the Iuka fiasco, Rosecrans in effect was telling him what to do and how to do it. He tolerated it then but not this time. Besides, he had his own ideas about

Vicksburg. "We can do nothing with our weak forces," he wired Rosecrans, "but fall back to our old places. Order the pursuit to cease."[25]

This reply reached Rosecrans at midnight, October 7, by which time his advance, headed by McPherson's contingent, was within thirty-five miles of Holly Springs, a town on the Mississippi Central Railroad and the main Confederate supply base in northern Mississippi.

Dismayed, Rosecrans promptly dictated to Ducat a long telegraphic response, the essence of which stated: "We have defeated, routed, and demoralized the army which holds the lower Mississippi Valley. . . . The effect of our return to old position will be to permit them [the Confederates] to recruit their forces, advance and occupy their old ground, reducing us to the occupation of a defensive position, barren and worthless." However, "If, after considering the matter, you still consider the order of my return to Corinth expedient, I will obey it and abandon the chief fruits of victory."[26]

Grant's initial impulse on perusing these words was to tell Rosecrans to turn back to Corinth at once, and that orders were to be obeyed, not debated. Instead, on the morning of October 8 he notified him that he would submit to Halleck the matter of continuing the pursuit, presumably confident that in view of the general-in-chief's ponderous advance on Corinth and failure to conduct a vigorous pursuit of Beauregard following its fall he would uphold him, not Rosecrans.[27]

Then, later in the day, he received a message from Hurlbut: "I have just heard from Holly Springs [*probably from a spy*]. There are no [Confederate] forces there. All left on Sunday [October 5]. . . . I am of opinion that the route of Van Dorns army is complete."[28] This report should have caused Grant at least to wait until he heard from Halleck before deciding definitely what to do with Rosecrans. It did not. Instead, he again ordered him to return to Corinth. Rosecrans, hoping that Halleck would endorse continued pursuit, ignored the order. This Halleck did. "Why order," he wired Grant, "a return of your forces? Why not reinforce Rosecrans & pursue the enemy into Mississippi, supplying yourself on the country?"

Halleck's answer probably surprised Grant but did not change his mind. After nearly three months of experience, he knew that while Halleck as general in chief might make suggestions, he never issued orders to field commanders regarding the conduct of ongoing military operations. Because of that knowledge, he had felt confident that Halleck would not override his decision to suspend the pursuit of Van Dorn. That confidence now having been confirmed, he once more ordered Rosecrans to return to Corinth. At the same time, he informed Halleck, "On reflection I deem it idle to pursue farther without more preparation and have for a third time ordered his [Rosecrans] return."[29]

Realizing that he had been left without any alternative, Rosecrans obeyed the order. Then and afterward, though, he passionately believed that had he been permitted to continue advancing and been reinforced, as he had urged Grant to do, by Hurlbut's division, Sherman's two divisions, and six regiments stationed at Jackson, Tennessee, not only could he have completed the destruction of Van Dorn's army but gone on to take Vicksburg. This would open up the entire Mississippi to the North and set the stage for Union victory in the war as a whole, as only Bragg's and Kirby Smith's small armies would have remained to challenge Federal power west of the Appalachians, Confederate forces in the trans-Mississippi being too small and dispersed to constitute a serious menace. "We were," he wrote following the war, "about six days march from Vicksburg and the country along the Mississippi Central . . . was a corn country—a rich farming country—and the corn was ripe."[30]

Which general, Grant or Rosecrans, was right about attempting to go on to Vicksburg? A definite answer, of course, cannot be made, the attempt never having been made. And the only certain thing about war, being as Clausewitz observed, is uncertainty. Yet, as shall be seen in due course, probably the prospect of taking Vicksburg was superior in October 1862 to what it proved to be two months later.

Two things, however, are certain when it comes to the performances of Grant and Rosecrans during the last half of September and the first week of October. One is that both of them sometimes acted as much, if not more, out of personal considerations as they did strategic. Rosecrans sought to conceive, then play the starring role in conducting operations that would produce great victories and lead to his heading a major, independent army. Grant, on the other hand, had his own aspirations, with the prime one being to capture Vicksburg in a campaign designed and directed by himself. Also, he found Rosecrans's penchant for proposing plans centered about himself increasingly annoying, indeed presumptuous. What he wanted were subordinates who, while capable, were subordinate and therefore would execute his orders without quibbling or endeavoring to replace his plans with their own. To this end, he resolved, after stopping Rosecrans's pursuit of Van Dorn, to put that overambitious and under-obedient general in his place—or, should that fail, dispose of him.

The other aspect of Grant's and Rosecrans's performances as summer gave way to autumn in 1862 was their effect on the course of the war in the

West. First, the shattering of Van Dorn's army at Corinth permanently put the Confederates on the defensive in Mississippi, and the Federals on the offensive, with Vicksburg being the focus for both sides. Second, this in turn had a profound impact on Bragg's and Buell's fortunes in Kentucky and led to Rosecrans achieving the command status so long deserved but denied. It also led to Phillip Sheridan taking his initial stride toward becoming one of our "victors in blue." These, along with more specimens of the ironies of war and quirks of those who wage it, shall provide the topics of the next chapter.

Lincoln and His Generals. A fanciful and refashioned picture of harmony among the victors, masking their rocky relationship, with Meade, as at Appomattox, nowhere to be found. Courtesy of the Library of Congress.

Ulysses S. Grant, mounted. Triumphing over adversity, this man won in the end.
Robert U. Johnson and Clarence C. Buel, eds., *Battles and Leaders of the Civil War*
(New York: Century Co., 1884–1887), 4:178.

Grant. Warts and all, he was a man who made the most of his luck and his breaks, which, added to his skill, determination, and political savvy, put him on the path to the presidency. John Fiske, *How the United States Became a Nation* (Boston: Ginn and Co., 1904), 205.

William T. Sherman. Successful at war, shaky in combat, and a tremendous writer of fiction offered as fact, Sherman's memory still burns in the hearts of many a Southerner, as well as some critics. John Fiske, *How the United States Became a Nation* (Boston: Ginn and Co., 1904), 235.

Philip H. Sheridan. This fiery little Irishman proved a driven fighter with a sense of the dramatic, earning him the status of Grant's favorite general, which served him well always. Robert U. Johnson and Clarence C. Buel, eds., *Battles and Leaders of the Civil War* (New York: Century Co., 1884–1887), 4:503.

George H. Thomas. Far better on the battlefield than in his relationships with Grant and Sherman, this steady sledgehammer's pride masked a prickly ego easily slighted. Robert U. Johnson and Clarence C. Buel, eds., *Battles and Leaders of the Civil War* (New York: Century Co., 1884–1887), 4:442.

George G. Meade. The gruff grumbler enjoyed true greatness at Gettysburg, never to ascend those heights again, leaving him to grouse and snap at those around him. Robert U. Johnson and Clarence C. Buel, eds., *Battles and Leaders of the Civil War* (New York: Century Co., 1884–1887), 3:242.

Henry W. Halleck. Well suited for desk duty but a failure in the field, this intellectual pioneered the role of chief of staff, yet failed to command and was reduced to meddling in Grant's business. Robert U. Johnson and Clarence C. Buel, eds., *Battles and Leaders of the Civil War* (New York: Century Co., 1884–1887), 1:276.

John M. Schofield. A late bloomer in command, he found battlefield success just in time to jump upon the victors' bandwagon, driven by Grant and Sherman, ensuring postwar rewards. Robert U. Johnson and Clarence C. Buel, eds., *Battles and Leaders of the Civil War* (New York: Century Co., 1884–1887), 1:293.

William S. Rosecrans. A skilled commander, beloved by his men, he wielded a sharp sarcastic pen and possessed a talent to offend, marking him for obscurity in the wake of battlefield setbacks. Robert U. Johnson and Clarence C. Buel, eds., *Battles and Leaders of the Civil War* (New York: Century Co., 1884–1887), 1:136.

8

Rosecrans at Stones River

How a Near Disaster Became a Much-Needed Union Victory

HAD BUELL WON A BATTLE AT PERRYVILLE? Or had he not? He was unsure. In fact, the battle nearly ended before he discovered it was taking place. To make matters more curious, his Confederate counterpart, Bragg, did not realize until the fighting drew to a close that he faced a Federal army so far superior in numbers to his own available force that unless he retreated he would be destroyed despite having been victorious.

But before relating how this remarkable situation came about, we need first to examine what preceded it. To begin with, on deciding that Louisville and not Nashville was Bragg's target, Buell marched rapidly to Bowling Green, Kentucky, where his army could be supplied via the Louisville & Nashville Railroad and also be in position to intercept Bragg. At the same time, Bragg set out for Kentucky after ordering Price to cross the Tennessee and attack Nashville. He planned, indeed expected, Kirby Smith's forces, still in the Lexington-Frankfort area, to join him in an assault on Louisville, the capture of which would place the Stars and Bars on the Ohio River and open the way (or so he thought) for the Bluegrass State to join the Confederacy in body as well as spirit and impel hordes of eager Kentuckians to swell his ranks, to which end he had brought along numerous wagons packed with rifles.

It did not turn out that way. Short of supplies, without hoped-for reinforcements from Mississippi, and with more Yankees now inside Louisville than he had troops outside of it, on September 23 Bragg abandoned the offensive and went over to the defensive. It was a wise decision. By then Buell's veterans had begun entering the city, with the final units arriving on the twenty-ninth, there joining 36,000 freshly raised Federals manning burgeoning fortifications.[1]

On the morning of the same day, two events occurred in Louisville pertaining to generals of the Army of the Ohio. Each took place at the Galt House, the city's premier hotel and source of Sherman's favorite whisky. First, in the morning, Brigadier General Jefferson Columbus Davis, a prewar regular army officer who had risen from the ranks rather than been anointed by West Point, entered the lobby. Accompanied by Republican Governor Oliver P. Morton of Indiana and another Hoosier named Thomas Gibson, he accosted Major General "Bull" Nelson and demanded that he be returned to the post he had held in Louisville before being deprived of it by Nelson for insubordination. Nelson refused. Davis thereupon flipped a crumpled hotel calling card into Nelson's face, and Nelson responded by slapping Davis across the face with the back of his hand—not a light blow, given that Nelson owed his sobriquet of "Bull" to standing six feet four and weighing well over 300 pounds. Nelson then headed toward the stairs leading to his room while Davis procured a pistol from Gibson, then followed Nelson and shot him in the chest, killing him. Although arrested for murder, Davis not only escaped punishment but also was never tried and soon returned to duty, thanks to the potent political clout of Morton. It helped, too, that Nelson had many enemies, even among his fellow Kentuckians. While vigorous and enterprising, he tended to be overbearing and arrogant, causing some to dub him "Bully" in lieu of "Bull."[2]

The other event was less dramatic but much more significant. Shortly after Nelson's slaying, a messenger from Washington delivered to Buell, who also was staying at the Galt House, an order from Lincoln. Sent via Halleck, it removed Buell from command of the Army of the Ohio and replaced him with Thomas. Buell promptly summoned Thomas to his room and showed him the order. To his surprise, Thomas declared that he would not accept the command. Doing so, he explained, would be unfair both to Buell and to himself, what with the army about to fight a battle. Then a new order arrived from Lincoln canceling the one just received and which probably had been brought about by Halleck. Buell thereupon displayed his gratitude for Thomas's forbearance by appointing him second in command of the Army of the Ohio, the same meaningless post that had nearly driven Grant to despair and the end of his military career.[3]

On October 1 Buell set forth from Louisville with 55,000 troops divided into three corps marching southward along as many roads, while another Union column of 22,000 headed by Brigadier General Joshua Sill advanced east on Frankfort in a diversionary move designed to pin down Kirby Smith's forces. Chance and circumstance, though, not generalship, determined what ensued, with the main factor being a shortage of drinking water caused by a prolonged drought. Thus, early on the morning of October 8, having been informed that potable pools of water existed on the bed of Doctor's Creek near the hamlet of Perryville, Major General (well, a captain acting under the impression he was a major general) Charles Gilbert ordered Sheridan to secure control of the creek, which he did. This in turn triggered a battle, during which the Confederates outflanked and drove back Major General Alexander McCook's corps, inflicting heavy casualties on it.

Throughout most of the day Buell remained unaware of this fighting, which lasted until nightfall. The reason lay in his obsession with discipline. While advancing toward Perryville on October 7 he came upon some blue-clad soldiers foraging in a farmhouse garden, whereupon he ordered them to rejoin their regiment. All obeyed save one. Angered, Buell rode over to him and shouted at him to stop. Startled, the soldier tried to grab the bridle of Buell's horse, causing it to rear up and fall on its back, Buell still astride. He could have been killed; instead, he suffered crippling injuries that necessitated his taking to an ambulance and led to his headquarters being in a tent far to the rear of the embattled Union. To make matters worse, the tent happened to be in an "acoustic shadow" zone similar to the one that prevented Ord from hearing the sound of Rosecrans's engagement south of Iuka.[4]

As a result, not until 4 P.M. did Buell discover that his left wing was waging a fierce battle and order the rest of his army to attack. But Crittenden's corps on the right allowed itself to be bluffed into halting, then falling back, by 1,500 Rebel cavalry. The sole aid provided McCook by Gilbert's corps came from Sheridan's division, which helped beat back a final enemy assault. Then, with the coming of night, Bragg retreated, having decided to join forces with Kirby Smith in an attempt to counter the now nonexistent threat of Sill's column, which after occupying Frankfort had swerved southwestward to bolster Buell.

Thus ended the Battle of Perryville, as it became known. In it 15,000 Confederates facing—potentially—at least 50,000 Federals came close to crushing one-third of the latter. Yet while a tactical victory, strategically it was a defeat for Bragg and he knew it. Not only had he suffered 4,000 casualties, Kirby Smith and he, with a combined strength of little more than 40,000, now faced what he estimated, accurately enough, as twice that number of Federals. And, worse, Buell was in position, if he moved fast enough, to block a retreat out of Kentucky by way of Cumberland Gap.

For these reasons, and also because a mere 2,500 Kentuckians had enlisted in his and Kirby Smith's armies, Bragg on October 12 decided to return to Tennessee via the Cumberland Gap and began doing so the next day, Kirby Smith following. Buell pursued, but so slowly and cautiously that twice he passed up excellent opportunities to smash or at least inflict serious damage on the Confederates, whom he thought totaled more than twice their actual number. As a consequence, on October 28 Bragg rode to the crest of Cumberland Gap, looked back, and saw Polk's corps ascending, followed by Hardee's, Kirby Smith's army, and Wheeler's cavalry. He had escaped.

But that was not all. Fifty-five days previously, Bragg had set out from Chattanooga hoping, indeed expecting, to restore the Stars and Bars above Nashville. Instead, his tattered, battered army—Kirby Smith at once headed for Knoxville—now became the sole barrier between the Federals and Chattanooga, the gateway to northern Georgia and Alabama. In sum, after going on the offensive in the autumn of 1862 to regain what had been lost during the winter and early spring, Confederate forces in Tennessee, along with those in Mississippi, again found themselves on the defensive and destined to remain so for nearly another year.

Buell, on learning that Bragg had reached Cumberland Gap, ceased his "pursuit," during which he had taken two weeks to traverse sixty-five miles. Continuing, he notified Halleck, would be to enter "almost a desert" where the "limited supply of forage is consumed by the enemy as he passes." Therefore, he added, his army would return by way of Louisville to Nashville, which he considered to be not merely the best base for a move into East Tennessee but also the only one from where this could be done with sufficient strength and supplies to remain there against an inevitable Confederate counterthrust.

In taking this stance, Buell realized the obvious—that he was going counter to Lincoln's obsession with liberating East Tennessee. More than that, he expected to be relieved, perhaps even desired it. If so, he was not disappointed. On October 30 he received an order from Halleck, acting on instructions from the president, removing him from command.[5]

Thus ended Buell's military career. Although he may have been, as Sherman described him in the same letter wherein he wrote that Grant was "very brave but not brilliant," the "best soldier" among the top West Point–trained generals serving in the West, he fell far short of being a good army commander.[6] Like his friend and patron McClellan, he feared failure too much to be successful and unlike him possessed no talent for securing the affection of his troops, most of whom had come to hate him because of his rigid discipline and aloof manner. Finally and fatally, he lacked what Napoleon rightly deemed to be the sine qua non for a successful general: *bonne chance* (good luck). Having his horse fall on him and being unaware as he was at Perryville because of an acoustic freak that a third of his army was engaged in a ferocious encounter stand as prime candidates for bad luck in the endless annals of warfare—and both occurred within a span of twenty-four hours.

As October drew to a close, Lincoln pondered whether also to relieve Mc-Clellan. For a month now he had been urging him to advance into Virginia overland toward Richmond while having Halleck and Quartermaster General Montgomery Meigs do all that could be done to provide the Army of the Potomac with the means to defeat Lee and/or take the Rebel capital. All of this, though, had been to no avail. McClellan had no desire to take on Lee again, whom as always he credited with double his actual strength, until spring. At that time he would return to the Peninsula with his army bolstered by reinforcements from the West. However, these were military operations that he looked upon as a distraction from winning the war in the East and by himself.

Two considerations prevented Lincoln from doing what he would have preferred to do—sack the so-called Young Napoleon. One was that he knew of no general in the East of sufficient rank qualified and willing to take his place, given Burnside's and Halleck's refusals. The other was political. Come November 4 the Northern states would complete their gubernatorial, legislative, and congressional elections. Should McClellan be removed before then, it would make worse the already bleak Republican prospects in these elections, for he was highly popular among the Democrats, many of whom saw him as their 1864 presidential candidate. Hence, Lincoln decided to give him one final chance. Should he by November 4 gain a victory over Lee or be in position to achieve it, then he would retain command of the Army of the Potomac. But if not, he would be dismissed.

Meanwhile, McClellan, having become aware of Lincoln's growing impatience, began crossing the Potomac into Virginia on October 26, his target Culpeper Court House, on what would become his supply line, the Orange & Alexandria Railroad. "If," he wrote Ellen while the crossing took place, "you could know the mean and dirty character of the dispatches I receive [from Lincoln, Stanton, and Halleck], you would boil over with anger. . . . But the good of the country requires me to submit to all this from men whom I know to be greatly my inferiors socially, intellectually & morally! There never was a truer epithet applied to a certain individual than that of the 'Gorilla.'"[7]

Unlike with McClellan, replacing Buell posed no problem, given his unpopularity among the rank and file of the Army of the Ohio and his total lack of political potency; indeed, Governor Morton of Indiana warned Lincoln that unless he were removed it would be disastrous for the Republicans in his state. The sole question was who should be his replacement—Thomas or Rosecrans? Since the former had refused to supersede Buell, Lincoln decided to "let the Virginian wait" and assign the post to the latter, whose aggressiveness in pursuing Van Dorn's shattered forces into Mississippi, with Vicksburg his target, favorably impressed him. Thus on October 23 the telegraph brought Rosecrans at Corinth an order from Halleck: "You will immediately repair to Cincinnati where you will receive orders. . . . Go with the least possible delay."[8]

The implication of this somewhat cryptic message was clear to Rosecrans; he was to replace Buell. This prospect, of course, delighted him. It meant that he would become what he should have been long before—head of a major army. Also, it meant escape from an increasingly intolerable relationship with Grant, one made more so by Grant's response to a recent request by him for more cavalry arms. This he found so insulting that on October 21 he wired Grant the following:

> I am amazed by the tenor of your dispatch—You have no truer friend no more loyal subordinate . . . than myself—Your dispatch does me the gravest injustice. I now say to you if you have any suspicions at varience with this declaration . . . either from the influences—the suspicions or jealousies of mischief makers[,] winesellers & mouse catching politicians or from any other cause I ask you to tell me so frankly & at once as a favor to myself & the service.[9]

Rosecrans's forthcoming assignment also pleased Grant, who likewise learned of it on October 23 via a message wired to him by Halleck. Now he would be rid of that insufficiently subordinate general without having to relieve him of command of what little remained of the Army of the Mississippi, something he had decided to do that very day, a decision triggered by Rosecrans's October 21 telegram, to which he had immediately replied in kind:

> My dispatch was but a proper reply to yours of this date and others from you equally objectionable. The leaky lecture of some in your staff or in confidential relation to you as evidenced by newspaper correspondents and their attempt to keep up an invideous distinction between the armies of Miss and the Tenn. are detrimental to the good feeling that should exist between officers & men as well as improper and should not be allowed.[10]

To what extent Rosecrans's and Grant's charges against each other were valid is unknowable but at the same time irrelevant. The essential fact is that they made them and thus widened further the gap between them—a gap that continued to grow until it turned into an unbridgeable chasm.

On October 26 Rosecrans took leave of the Army of the Mississippi, command of which passed on to Hamilton, and set out for Cincinnati, where he arrived two days later. Waiting for him were Halleck's orders, or to be more exact Lincoln's orders as conveyed by Halleck. They placed him in charge of a newly designated Department of the Cumberland, consisting of all of Kentucky and Tennessee east of the Tennessee River and as much of northern Georgia and Alabama as he might be able to occupy; gave the Army of the Ohio the absurd designation "XIV Corps"; directed him to proceed "immediately" to Buell's headquarters in Louisville and relieve him; and set two "great objects" for his operations in the field: "First, to drive the enemy from Kentucky and Middle Tennessee; second, to take and hold East Tennessee." Halleck closed by declaring that "I need not urge upon you the necessity of giving active employment to your forces. Neither the country nor the Government will much longer put up with the inactivity of some of our armies and generals."[11]

From Cincinnati Rosecrans went to Louisville, where he conferred with Buell at the Galt House. On November 1 he traveled by train to Bowling Green and formally assumed command of the XIV Corps. His first task was to placate Thomas, who on learning that Buell was being replaced by him, his junior as a major general, had protested to Halleck and asked to be assigned to a different military theater, preferably Texas. This he accomplished by telling Thomas, as he had Halleck, that his commission had been backdated from September 17, 1862, to March 21, 1862, thereby making him the senior major general, and then by offering Thomas the choice of being either second in command or else head of the "Center" of the XIV Corps, which had been divided into three groups, with the other two being a "Left Wing" and a "Right Wing," led respectively (if not effectively) by McCook and Crittenden thanks solely to seniority. Thomas, having already experienced under Buell the meaninglessness of being second in command, chose the latter alternative and thus began a relationship that would be of great significance for both Rosecrans and himself.[12]

Rosecrans's next step was to reinforce the garrison at Nashville. By so doing he countered a threat to that city by Bragg, who reportedly was at Murfreesboro with 25,000 troops. At the same time, he began preparing for an offensive aimed at taking Chattanooga. Not only did he, like Buell, consider liberating East Tennessee a logistical impossibility, he believed it to be a strategic one as well, given the ability of the Confederates to rush reinforcements to Kirby Smith at Knoxville by way of the East Tennessee &

Virginia Railroad. On the other hand, should he seize Chattanooga, Richmond would have to focus on defending Georgia and Alabama, a region far more important to its war effort than East Tennessee.[13]

November 4 also saw the final election returns come in from the Northern states. Although the Democrats gained the governorship of New York and control of the Indiana and Illinois legislatures, the Republicans retained a majority in Congress. Such being the case, Lincoln felt free to do what he had resolved to do should McClellan by then have failed to defeat Lee or at least bring him to bay. Since this was the case—he had spent eleven days crossing the Potomac and creeping into Virginia, making it easy for Lee to confront him with Longstreet's corps far short of his initial objective of Culpeper Court House while retaining Jackson's corps in the Shenandoah, where it was in position to repeat the same flanking maneuver that had been used against Pope—on November 5 Lincoln instructed Halleck to issue an order replacing McClellan with Burnside.

Two days later Brigadier General Catherinus Buckingham, a member of Stanton's staff, delivered the order to Burnside, who after first protesting accepted it since it was an order from the president and not a behest, as in the past. Then he and Buckingham went to McClellan's tent, which they reached at 11 P.M., and the latter handed the order to McClellan, who read it, then said to Burnside, "Well, Burnside, I turn the command over to you."[14]

After his visitors left, McClellan reported what had just happened in his nightly letter to Ellen, adding that "Poor Burnside feels dreadfully, almost crazy—I am sorry for him, & he never showed himself a better man or truer friend than now."[15] Evidently, as McClellan penned these words it did not occur to him that they contradicted what he had written Ellen on September 29 while preparing his report on Antietam: "I *ought* to rap Burnside *very* severely & probably will—yet I hate to do it. He is very slow & is not fit to command more than a regiment."[16]

In that report, though, he did not "rap" Burnside. This he saved for a later account of all of his military operations, designed to promote his presidential aspirations. In it he blamed Burnside for the failure to destroy Lee's army at Antietam. Such was McClellan's friendship.

Rosecrans was not the only Union general assigned a departmental command in the West during the autumn of 1862. The others were Major General Samuel Curtis, who was rewarded for his victory at Pea Ridge and subsequent seizure of Helena, Arkansas, on the Mississippi by being placed in command of the Department of the Missouri consisting of Missouri, Kansas, and as much of Arkansas as he could occupy; Major General Nathaniel Banks, who headed the Department of the Gulf embracing New Orleans and Baton Rouge and potentially the coastal portions of Alabama and Texas; and Grant, who on October 25 assumed command of the Department of the Tennessee, the new name that had been given to the District of West Tennessee.

Behind this new arrangement lay two intertwined factors. First, although he pretended otherwise, Lincoln continued to exercise a high degree of control over the Army of the Potomac with regard to what it did, where, when, and under whom, as witness his replacement of McClellan by Burnside. Second, as noted in the previous chapter, Lincoln's focus on operations in the East left Halleck free to set objectives and supervise operations in the West, with the principal limitations on him being Lincoln's obsession with liberating East Tennessee and a desire to establish a Union government in Louisiana—a desire that explains why political general Banks, despite his miserable military record, replaced another politician-turned-general, Ben Butler.

We know what Halleck directed Rosecrans to do in his department. What, though, did he want Grant to do in his? On October 26 Grant wrote him to find out. After pointing out that Halleck had "never mentioned to me any plan of operations in this Department," and that he was ignorant of the missions assigned to Rosecrans and Curtis, he stated that by withdrawing the troops stationed at Corinth, and with the assistance of a "small reinforcement at Memphis," he would "be able to move down the Mississippi Central" and "cause the evacuation of Vicksburg and . . . to capture or destroy all the boats in the Yazoo river."[17]

Not until October 30 did Grant receive a response from Halleck, and then it took the form of a reply to an October 29 telegram from him, which, instead of speaking of an offensive directed against Vicksburg, declared that the "Rebels [in Mississippi] have been largely reinforced & are moving precisely as they did before the last attack [on Corinth]." It concluded with "Reinforcement not arrived—." Moreover, Halleck's response consisted merely of this: "Reinforcements for your army are moving from Wisconsin, Minnesota, & Illinois."[18] Then, on November 2, Grant wired Halleck a message wherein he made no mention of an impending enemy attack but again spoke of invading Mississippi: "If found practicable I will go on to Holly Springs and may be Grenada completing Railroad & Telegraph as I go."[19]

In turn Halleck, upon receiving this message, signaled his approval of Grant's "plan of advancing upon the enemy as soon as you are strong enough for that purpose." He then added: "The Minn.-Wisconsin regts.

Should join you very soon & the Governor of Ill. has promised ten regts. this week. I have directed Genl Curtis to reinforce Helena [Arkansas] & if their [Federal forces in Arkansas] cannot operate on Little Rock they can cross the [Mississippi] river and threaten Grenada. I hope for an active campaign on the Miss. this fall."[20]

How to explain this enigmatic exchange of telegrams between Grant and Halleck—enigmatic because Grant assumes he has Halleck's permission to attempt to take Vicksburg before Halleck actually gave it in a subsequent telegram. The probable answer consists of a single word, or, to be precise, one name: McClernand. Upon obtaining leave late in August to raise troops in Illinois, McClernand spent three weeks there. He then went with Governor Yates to Washington, where, apart from accompanying Lincoln on his visit to the Army of the Potomac early in October, he remained for a month. During this period he sought, both personally and through influential friends, command of an expedition to be composed of newly recruited soldiers from Illinois and other midwestern states that would have as its goal the capture of Vicksburg.[21] In this he seemed to succeed, for on October 21 he received the following from Stanton:

> Ordered, That Major-General McClernand be, and he is, directed to proceed to the States of Indiana, Illinois, and Iowa, to organize the troops remaining in those States and to be raised . . . and forward them . . . to Memphis, Cairo, or such other points as may hereafter be designated by the general-in-chief, to the end that, when a sufficient force not required by the operations of General Grant's command shall be raised, an expedition may be organized under General McClernand's command against Vicksburg.
>
> The forces so organized will remain subject to the designation of the general-in-chief, and be employed according to such exigencies as the service in his judgement may require.[22]

Appended to the order was a note written by Lincoln authorizing McClernand to show it, "though marked confidential," to governors and even others whenever "he believes so doing to be indispensable to the progress of the expedition, in the success of which I feel a deep interest."[23]

The key aspect of the order is that while it ostensibly placed McClernand in command of an expedition to take Vicksburg, it actually left the choice of that commander to Halleck by recognizing, to the point of redundancy, his authority as commander in chief to do this. Nor did Lincoln's postscript in any way counter this, for obviously neither Halleck nor, for that matter,

Grant were "governors" or "others" to whom McClernand "in his discretion" could show the order.

So why did Lincoln via Stanton seemingly assign McClernand to head a Vicksburg expedition while at the same time making it very easy for Halleck and Grant to prevent him from performing that role, something he surely realized they would do given their obvious dislike of that particular political general? The probable answer is that although he correctly believed that McClernand would do a good job of providing troops for a Vicksburg expedition, he also rightly realized that should Halleck and Grant be denied the power inherent in their rank and status to forestall Mc-Clernand taking charge of such an expedition they both would tender their resignations in protest, leaving him with no practicable alternative other than to revoke the "confidential" order so that they would withdraw them. In sum, the order was a ploy by Lincoln to obtain soldiers needed to capture Vicksburg—a ploy that cast McClernand in the role of dupe. Lincoln may have been saintly in ways, but he did not lack at least a soupçon of Machiavellianism.[24]

Halleck knew of the "confidential" order, having been directed by Stanton to meet with McClernand prior to its issuance, presumably for the purpose of telling him about it.[25] And Grant soon learned of it, as witness a letter sent to Sherman on October 29 by Colonel William S. Hillyer, one of Grant's top aides, stating that "from newspaper and other reports it is probable that McClernand will go to Helena and lead whatever expedition may move from there, and report to Curtis." Since Grant instructed Hillyer to write this letter, obviously he was aware from the sources it indicated that McClernand had been authorized to head some sort of expedition to begin in Curtis's Department of the Missouri but was uncertain as to its objective, although he must have suspected that it was Vicksburg.[26]

Early in the second week of November, Grant finally learned definitely what McClernand's target and base of operations would be. The source of this information was First Lieutenant James H. Wilson, a twenty-five-year-old West Point graduate who joined his staff on November 8 as chief topographical engineer. While in Washington awaiting an assignment, Wilson had met with McClernand, who, in trying to recruit him for his staff, told him of the Lincoln-Stanton order. Wilson told this to Grant, who on November 10 telegraphed Halleck, who had refrained from telling him of the order because he believed he should not do so until McClernand actually began to act on it: "Am I to understand that I lay here [in Tennessee] while an Expedition is fitted out from Memphis or do you want me to push as far South as possible?"[27]

Halleck's answer, which came the following day, could not have been more pleasing to Grant yet at the same time not at all surprising: "You have command of all troops sent to your Department, and permission to fight the enemy where you please."[28] Two days later, Union cavalry occupied Holly Springs, a town on the Mississippi Central Railroad about twenty-three miles deep into Mississippi via that line.[29] Thus began what proved to be Grant's first campaign to take Vicksburg.

While Grant in Tennessee made ready for a foray into Mississippi aimed at Vicksburg, in Virginia Burnside developed a plan designed to take Richmond.[30] On November 10 he completed it and sent it by courier to Halleck, who in turn passed it on to Lincoln—further evidence that he deemed the Army of the Potomac to be the president's personal purview—and then on November 12 and 13 visited Burnside at Warrenton, Virginia, in company with Quartermaster General Montgomery Meigs and Chief of Military Railroads Herman Haupt. Not until November 14 did Burnside receive Lincoln's decision in the form of a telegram from Halleck: "The President had just assented to your plan. He thinks it will succeed, if you move very rapidly; otherwise not."

Burnside's plan called for abandoning the attempt to move against Lee by way of a railroad that the Confederates again could cut in the Union rear. Instead, he would advance on Richmond by crossing the Rappahannock at Fredericksburg, thereby gaining access to a rail supply line linked to Aquia Landing on the Potomac while obtaining access to a railroad leading to Richmond. To this end, Halleck, anticipating Lincoln's approval of Burnside's plan, already had ordered the commander of the Engineer Brigade in Washington to have all of the pontoon bridges there transported on barges down the Potomac to Aquia Landing.

What ensued and why is so complex and controversial that any attempt to describe it fully would require an excessive amount of space. Suffice it to state, though, that, through no fault of his, it was not until December 8 that Burnside had enough pontoons available to order his engineer troops to lay five bridges across the Rappahannock at Fredericksburg come the morrow. By then, Lee, who initially had been puzzled by Burnside's swerve southeastward from the Orange & Alexandria Railroad to the upper bank of the Rappahannock opposite Fredericksburg, had ordered both Longstreet's and Jackson's corps to resist the Federals.

At this point, an obvious question arises: Should Burnside, no later than late November, have scrapped his plan to cross the Rappahannock at Fredericksburg, since the essential condition for its success as set forth by

Lincoln—swift execution—had manifestly not been achieved? The answer also is obvious: Yes. But it is an answer based on a knowledge that Burnside did not possess because he could not possess it—the consequence of his crossing, although it has been contended that he should have foreseen it. As it was, on November 26 at Aquia Landing and again two days later in Washington, he discussed with Lincoln the prospects at Fredericksburg. The sole outcome was a memorandum wherein Lincoln suggested to Halleck that 25,000 troops be stationed on the Rappahannock across from Port Royal, seventeen miles below Fredericksburg, so as to threaten Lee's railroad supply line to Richmond. In all likelihood, Lincoln thought that a crossing at Fredericksburg might succeed—the Army of the Potomac outnumbered the Army of Northern Virginia two to one—but even should it fail, this would be better than making no attempt at all, since that would be akin to McClellan marching up the hill only to turn around and march down it without firing a shot.

Many, perhaps too many, books have been written about the Battle of Fredericksburg—or, to be more accurate, the one-sided slaughter at Fredericksburg. For the purpose of this account, all that needs to be reported is that owing to the fierce resistance of a Mississippi brigade posted in Fredericksburg it took the Federals two days (December 11–12) to lay their pontoon bridges, cross to the other side of the Rappahannock, and deploy for an attack; that on the afternoon of December 13 they assaulted the Confederate defense line only to be repelled everywhere save for a brief, shallow penetration by Major General George Meade's division; that Lee dared not counterattack because Union cannons would have pulverized his troops; and that two days afterward Burnside returned to the other side of the Rappahannock, his 113,000-man army having suffered 12,653 killed, wounded, and missing while inflicting 5,377 casualties on approximately 58,000 Rebels, only 20,000 of whom were fully engaged.[31] In sum, measured in blood, Fredericksburg was for the Federals the most one-sided major encounter of the Civil War.

Lincoln could have, and many then and since have declared he should have, removed Burnside from command. But this he did not. After all, he shared the responsibility for the slaughter; besides, with whom could he replace Burnside? Hence he instructed Burnside to try again, employing a different strategy. The main thing was to keep on fighting. Only by fighting could the war be won, the Union be restored, and slavery be abolished.

Mid-December found Grant at Oxford, Mississippi, a village on the Mississippi Central south of the Tallahatchie River and thirty miles from Holly

Springs to the north. He had halted the advance of his 30,000-man army in order to stockpile more supplies at Holly Springs. Meanwhile, Sherman organized at Memphis 21,000 troops, two-thirds of them sent there by McClernand, prior to loading them aboard steamboats and heading down the Mississippi in an attempt to take Vicksburg from the river while Grant moved on it by land, thereby defeating or at least tying down the 16,000 Confederates opposing him under the command of Lieutenant General John C. Pemberton, who had superseded Van Dorn.[32]

This plan, however, almost immediately threatened to go awry. On December 18 Grant received a telegram from Halleck instructing him to divide his forces, which henceforth would be known as the Army of the Tennessee, into four corps and stating, "It is the wish of the President that General McClernand's corps shall constitute a part of a river expedition and that he shall have the immediate command under your direction."[33] Obviously, this meant that unless Sherman set out for Vicksburg soon—very soon— McClernand might arrive in Memphis and, owing to his seniority in rank, take over the Mississippi expedition from Sherman. How, then, to prevent such a calamity? His solution, promptly put into effect, was to write a letter to McClernand, who still was in Illinois, informing him of Halleck's instructions and implying, but not explicitly indicating, that McClernand on reaching Memphis would head the Mississippi expedition. This done, he then sent a telegram to Sherman wherein he again urged him to head for Vicksburg before McClernand showed up in Memphis.[34]

Neither message, though, reached their destinations in time to make any difference—but this made no difference either. The reasons are three. First, starting on December 18 and continuing until December 26, Nathan Bedford Forrest's raiders struck the Mississippi Central at and about Jackson, Tennessee, ripping up track and tearing down telegraph wire, with the result that Grant's letter to McClernand and his telegram to Sherman took weeks to reach them.

Second, Sherman needed no prompting from Grant to hasten his sortie down the Mississippi. He knew full well that if the despised McClernand showed up in Memphis before he left for Vicksburg he would become subordinate to him. Therefore, on December 20 he began steaming southward in transports crammed with infantry, artillery, and the requisite supplies for both.

And third, not until December 27 did McClernand show up in Memphis, for not until December 23 did he finally obtain, after several requests and complaints, Stanton's permission to cease organizing troops and go forth to lead them. Also, he seems to have continued assuming that Lincoln's postscript to the "confidential" order placing him in command of a Vicksburg expedition assured him of such a command since he delayed his departure from Illinois to do what he presumably could have done earlier—marry the sister of his deceased first wife. Only on reaching Memphis did he realize the need for haste and so steamed out of there on December 30 in hope of overtaking Sherman in time to supersede him before he attacked Vicksburg and perhaps captured it—and even then he brought along his bride.[35]

He was too late. So, for that matter, was Sherman, but for a different reason and with a different outcome. On nearing Vicksburg, his troop strength increased to 32,000 by the addition of two divisions headed by Brigadier General Frederick Steele, who had joined him at Helena, he dutifully decided to execute an order from Grant to wreck what appeared on a map to be the last remaining rail link between the eastern and western portions of the Confederacy (respectively called cis-Mississippi and trans-Mississippi), a sixty-mile-long railroad that ran from Monroe, Louisiana, to the Mississippi across from Vicksburg. To this end, therefore, instead of joining Porter's gunboats in the Yazoo, on Christmas Day he halted his transports near the mouth of that bayou-lined river while one of his brigades tore up track along that line. This achieved, the following day his ships steamed into and up the Yazoo, accompanied by Porter's flotilla, in quest of a place to land and attack. On December 27, thinking he had found it and perhaps further motivated by a premature report that McClernand was on the way from Memphis, he disembarked his four divisions at Chickasaw Bluffs and two days later delivered a two-brigade assault on an entrenched enemy line in an attempt to break through to Vicksburg three miles to the south.

The outcome was a small-scale repetition of Fredericksburg. Only nine Union regiments managed to engage the enemy, and they suffered 154 killed, 757 wounded, and 528 missing (mostly prisoners) while inflicting on the Confederates a mere 207 casualties. According to one of his division commanders prior to the attack, Sherman told one of his aides "that we will lose 5,000 men before we take Vicksburg, and may as well lose them here as anywhere else." If this be true, then Sherman indeed was a "fighting prophet," albeit in this instance his prediction erred on the low side.

After spending two more days vainly seeking a better place to attack, Sherman abandoned his attempt to take Vicksburg—an attempt that lost any chance it may have had of success when he chose to spend Christmas Day with most of his army afloat in its transports while a brigade wrecked the railroad from Monroe, Louisiana, that terminated on the west bank of the Mississippi. Had he gone straight at Vicksburg on December 25, he would have stood an excellent chance of capturing it, for not until the afternoon and night of the twenty-sixth did the Confederate troops who repelled him on the twenty-ninth reach the town.[36]

Where did they come from? From Pemberton's army opposing Grant in northern Mississippi. But why did not Grant, by resuming his advance, prevent Pemberton from sending reinforcements by rail to Vicksburg? Because on December 20 Van Dorn, now commanding a cavalry division, swooped down on Holly Springs, took prisoner its garrison, and then torched its enormous stockpiles of food, forage, and ammunition, causing Grant to abandon his overland campaign in Mississippi. Also, owing to Forrest's simultaneous raid around Jackson, Tennessee, Grant had no way of promptly notifying Halleck, much less Sherman, of his situation.

Soon, though, he made a discovery, one that eventually proved of great value to him and eventually Sherman too. This was that an army, so long as it operated in a region not too thinly populated, could live off of the land or, to be more precise, supplement and even go without its regular rations by taking food from the farms, barns, and cellars of civilians. In fact, many of his soldiers already were doing this contrary to stern but rarely enforced orders issued by him at the outset of the campaign. Now, acting on his very different orders, foragers spread out across a fifteen-mile-wide area in the vicinity of Holly Springs and began collecting enough edibles that, so Grant wrote in this *Memoirs,* his army could have "subsisted off the country for two months." This, he added, "taught me a lesson."[37]

Here let us examine the assertion put forth toward the end of the preceding chapter, to wit that "probably the prospect of taking Vicksburg was superior in October 1862 than it proved to be two months later," and, as shall be seen in chapter 10, it turned out to be during the winter and spring of 1863. Or, to state it another way, were Rosecrans and Halleck justified in urging Grant to continue the pursuit of Van Dorn's army deep into Mississippi all the way to Vicksburg, so that the Union troops could be "subsisted off the country"? The answer is yes. In October the farmers and planters of Mississippi either had brought in their harvests or were so doing and thus provender would have been quite abundant for invaders, perhaps more so than it was in December.

Likewise, the prospect of the Federals being able to overcome Confederate resistance while on the way to Vicksburg, and then to take it once they got there, was far superior in October to what it proved to be in December. Not only was Van Dorn's army demoralized and increasingly depleted by desertion as a consequence of its bloody defeat at Corinth, it would also have to defend against a Union army invigorated by victory. Assuming that Grant had acted on Rosecrans's proposals, he would be reinforced by

Sherman's two divisions, Hurlbut's division, and six recently arrived new regiments, which would give him a more than two-to-one advantage over Van Dorn. Also, the troops would be united instead of split into two widely separated forces, which was the case in December, when Forrest's foray into Tennessee prevented communication by telegraph. As a result, they had to depend on dispatches sent by boats and trains, with both tending to be slow and unreliable.

Last but not least, assuming that Grant took personal command of his army, as he surely would have since Rosecrans was junior in rank to Sherman, who never before had headed more than a division in combat (Shiloh), he would not have encountered the virtually impregnable fortifications that existed on Vicksburg's landward side in May 1863 that led to a forty-seven-day siege that ended only when the Confederates had no alternative to surrender save starvation. Not until after Sherman's failed attempt at Chickasaw Bluffs did the commandant of Vicksburg, Major General Martin L. Smith, begin erecting full-fledged fortifications against attack by land as well as by water. Furthermore, apart from the troops manning the river batteries, its garrison consisted of only 1,800 infantry, 200 cavalry, and the cannoneers of six artillery batteries. So vulnerable did Smith consider Vicksburg to be if attacked by land that on September 30, 1862, he wrote Van Dorn that it was "at the mercy" of Steele's 12,000-man force at Helena—so much so that he wondered why Steele did not swoop down and take the place.[38]

In war, to paraphrase Clausewitz, the sole certainty is uncertainty. Yet had Grant acted on Rosecrans's proposal to pursue Van Dorn's remnants with all available Union troops, a proposal supported by Halleck—who never has been accused of rashness—it is quite possible that he could have captured Vicksburg in October 1862, an outcome that would have made the subsequent history of the Civil War fundamentally different from what it is.

Of course, this is speculation, yet it is legitimate speculation. History cannot be confined and therefore is not confined to endeavoring to relate accurately what happened; it must and hence often does deal with what might have happened if certain things had occurred or not occurred. Besides, doing this is enjoyable for the writer of history and, evidently, for the reader of it also.

On December 29, the day that Sherman's assault at Chickasaw Bluffs might have succeeded had not troops from Pemberton's army arrived at Vicksburg just in time to repel it, Rosecrans's army, 44,000 strong, began advancing on Murfreesboro. Not until Christmas Day did he decide that he could do this with a reasonable prospect of success. At Murfreesboro, he believed, Bragg's army came close to equaling, if not surpassing, his own field force.[39] But the main reason he had waited until now to move against Bragg is that it would have been foolish to have done so until he had the means in rations and munitions either to wage a great battle or else continue advancing should Bragg fall back. And this in turn required repairing the Louisville & Nashville Railroad so that it could provide an adequately reliable supply line again and then safeguarding it against the sort of Rebel cavalry raids that had rendered it incapable of performing this vital function. To these ends he stationed infantry detachments at various points along the Louisville & Nashville, employed engineer troops to reopen the tunnel destroyed by Morgan's cavaliers, organized his own cavalry into two divisions commanded by Brigadier General David Stanley, and armed most of his troopers with breech-loading carbines in hope this would make them a better match for the Confederate horsemen.

Meanwhile, like Buell before him, he came under mounting pressure from Lincoln, through Halleck, to engage Bragg—pressure that increased as November gave way to December. "The President," Halleck wrote him on December 4, "is very impatient at your long stay in Nashville. . . . Twice I have been asked to designate some one else to command your army. If you remain one more week in Nashville, I cannot prevent your removal." To this, Rosecrans replied: "If my superiors have lost confidence in me, they had better at once put some one in my place and let the future judge the propriety of the change. . . . To threats of removal or the like I must be permitted to say that I am insensible."

Finally, on December 25 Rosecrans decided to set out from Nashville. He had only twenty days' rations available, the consequence of continued Confederate cavalry raids on the Louisville & Nashville, but they would suffice, and the weather promised to be good. Better still, by then he knew that Forrest had gone into West Tennessee and that Morgan was heading into Kentucky, leaving only Wheeler's cavalry to deal with. In a night meeting with Thomas, Crittenden, McCook, and his division commanders, Rosecrans outlined his plan. Rather than head directly toward Murfreesboro, only thirty miles to the southeast, most of the army would swing southwest, then pivot southeastward, forcing the Confederates either to give battle or else retreat in order to preserve their rail connection to Chattanooga. He expected them to do the former, in which case, he declared, "Press them hard! Drive them out of their nests! Make them fight or run! *Fight them! Fight them!* Fight, I say!"

Bragg did give battle, but not where nor how Rosecrans anticipated. Instead of facing the Federals north of Murfreesboro behind Stewart's Creek, an excellent defensive position twelve miles northwest of Murfreesboro, on December 30 he deployed all of his 38,000 men, save Wheeler's cavalry, about a mile west of the town along the east bank of Stones River. Somewhat surprised, yet pleased that Bragg had not retreated, Rosecrans formed his army facing the enemy, with McCook's wing on the right, Thomas in the center, and Crittenden on the left. He then instructed Crittenden and Thomas, come dawn December 31, to assail Bragg's right, outflank and overpower it, then in conjunction with McCook drive whatever remained of the Rebel forces from the field.

In concept it was an excellent plan, especially since the Confederates, like the Federals, had not entrenched or constructed other defensive works, such yet not being standard practice in the Civil War except when protecting some strategically vital place such as Nashville, Louisville, Corinth, or Vicksburg. Even so, Rosecrans never executed it. The reason: Bragg put its mirror image into effect first by striking McCook's wing in the darkness of early morning, surprising and routing some Union units, then turning the Federal right flank. One of McCook's generals, though, prevented total disaster—Sheridan. Informed by Brigadier General Joshua Sill, who had carried out the successful fake attack on Frankfort while Buell experienced frustration at Perryville, that large numbers of Rebels were present only a few hundred feet from his brigade, Sheridan took a look himself. He then went to warn McCook of the peril, only to be told by that incompetent that there was no danger. Knowing otherwise, Sheridan thereupon returned to his division and readied it for the impending onslaught.

It soon came and with terrific impact. Still, Sheridan's troops inflicted heavy casualties on their assailants while suffering the same themselves. Among them was Sill, who was shot through the heart. But the Confederates, thanks to overlapping the Federal right flank, steadily pushed back McCook's wing until by late morning it faced southwest along a line paralleling the Nashville & Chattanooga Railroad, thereby turning Rosecrans's battle line into a "V," with its sides meeting in what became known as the Round Forest. And, to make matters worse, Wheeler's cavalry, circling clear around the Federal army, destroyed two of its wagon trains carrying ammunition. In sum, Bragg seemed to be on the verge of victory, Rosecrans on the brink of disaster.

Astride a magnificent steed, Rosecrans responded by galloping up and down the right wing's battle line, rallying troops, summoning reinforcements, and redeploying units. Beside him rode his new chief of staff, Colonel Julius Garesché—rode, that is, until a cannon projectile decapitated him, splattering Rosecrans with blood and brains. Whether Rosecrans's heroics helped or hindered is debatable, but in either case the Federal right held while the Confederate left shot its bolt. Perceiving this, Bragg thereupon ordered Polk to have Breckinridge's division attack the apex of the Federal front in the Round Forest; if it could be cracked open, then both Yankee wings could be struck in the rear. But Polk, as was his wont, sent in Breckinridge's troops piecemeal, with the result that they were repulsed, one attack after the other, by the defenders of the forest, a brigade headed by Colonel William Hazen, a thirty-two-year-old West Pointer destined to become one of the top Northern combat commanders.

Night, which descended early on this final day of 1862, brought cessation to the carnage. Meeting with his generals in a log cabin, Rosecrans asked whether the army should stand or retreat. Some favored the first, others the second, most voiced no opinion. Rosecrans thereupon conducted a personal reconnaissance, then returned and declared: "Gentlemen, we have come to fight and win this battle, and we shall do it."[40]

As it turned out, no serious fighting took place on New Year's Day. Bragg, notified by Wheeler that Yankee wagon trains were heading toward Nashville, concluded that Rosecrans intended to do the same; after all, it was standard practice for an army about to retreat to send its wagons rearward first. Such, though, was not the case in this instance. The Federals merely were foraging for food, many of them having been reduced to a handful of parched corn or in some cases cooking slices of flesh cut from dead horses. Otherwise, they prepared for battle by fortifying their lines. To the same end, Rosecrans also sent Colonel Sam Beatty's division to occupy the high ground above McFadden's Ford on the east bank of Stones River so as to forestall the Confederates from doing this. Neither he nor anyone else foresaw that he thus set the stage for the decisive event of the battle.

Clouds concealed the sun on January 2 but did not hide from Bragg the continued presence of Rosecrans's army. Hence, following a reconnaissance, he ordered Breckinridge to seize with his division the hill held by Beatty; it then would be used to enfilade the Union left with artillery fire. Breckinridge protested. He too had surveyed this hill and discovered that not only was it strongly defended, but that even if taken it would be exposed to enemy cannons atop a higher elevation on the other side of the river.

Bragg ignored him. The attack, he added, must be made at 4 P.M., less than an hour before it became dark, thereby preventing an enemy counterattack. Reluctantly, indeed resentfully, Breckinridge assembled his division.

Then, at the designated time, a signal cannon boomed and its four brigades, formed into two lines of battle, each four ranks deep, moved forward. Beatty's troops greeted them with rifle and artillery fire, inflicting heavy losses, but by sheer determination abetted by chance and circumstance they swarmed up the hill, driving its defenders across the river. It seemed that Bragg had been right.

Not so. Observing the flight of Beatty's men, Crittenden ordered his chief of artillery, Captain John Mendenhall, to cover them with his cannons. This Mendenhall more than did. Assembling fifty-seven big guns of various poundage and caliber, he struck the oncoming Confederates with perhaps the most devastating barrage of the Civil War, killing and wounding hundreds of them and causing those who could to flee. It had been Breckinridge who had been right—no consolation to him. "My poor Orphans! My poor Orphans!" he cried, referring to his Kentucky brigade, one-third of whose men failed to return from the charge, among them their commander.

On January 3 Bragg, having been informed by Wheeler that Rosecrans was receiving reinforcements, began a retreat that did not end until he reached the Elk River, nearly fifty miles south. Rosecrans made no attempt to pursue and waited until the following day to occupy Murfreesboro. Sleet, which turned the roads into quagmires, made it impossible to overtake Bragg. More to the point, of the 43,400 troops of all arms he had as of December 31, 13,249 had been killed, wounded, captured, or simply gone no one knew where while inflicting a total loss of 10,266 on Bragg's 37,712 soldiers.[41] Thus Stones River, or Murfreesboro, as the Confederates called it, equaled Shiloh in numerical casualties and surpassed it in proportional casualties for both sides. On the other hand, it was not nearly as decisive militarily as Shiloh, which led to the Federals securing control of all of western Tennessee, driving the Confederates into Mississippi, and opening up the way at least potentially to Chattanooga and Vicksburg. Stones River, in contrast, merely resulted in Bragg withdrawing to a much stronger position and in Rosecrans, for logistical reasons, not again advancing against him until six months later.

Yet, while not decisive in a strategic sense, Stones River had some very important political and personal consequences. First, coming after Burnside's bloody fiasco at Fredericksburg, Sherman's abysmal failure at Chickasaw Bluffs, and the sudden collapse of Grant's campaign in Mississippi, it came as a bright ray of sunshine through dark clouds for the Republicans, especially those in the Midwest, where the Democratic-controlled legislature of Indiana threatened, according to Governor Morton, to adopt a resolution recognizing the Confederacy, and where Yates of Illinois feared an antiwar insurrection in the southern part of the state. Second, it forestalled renewed proposals in Britain by prominent politicians to acknowledge Southern independence, proposals they never again made. Third, and most of all, it enabled the Emancipation Proclamation to go into effect in the wake of a Union victory instead of still another defeat, this one a debacle.[42]

As for the personal consequences, let us begin by fulfilling a long-postponed promise to relate the pre–May 1862 career of Philip Sheridan, a career that on the surface makes it seem even more unlikely than Grant's pre–April 1861 career that he would become one of the victors in blue, with a fame and status exceeded only by those of Grant and Sherman. Born in March 1831 in (perhaps) Ireland or (maybe) a ship to the United States or (conceivably) in New York, he grew up, all five feet five inches of him, in Ohio, got into West Point in 1848 thanks to the original appointee failing the entrance exam, and graduated near the bottom of the class of 1853 because of being suspended a year for "a quarrel of a belligerent character" with a cadet officer (he tried to stab him with a bayonet). He then spent eight years in an infantry regiment as a second lieutenant before the advent of war in 1861 resulted in his being promoted to captain, at which rank he served as quartermaster for Curtis's army in the Pea Ridge Campaign. He then became a major in the same capacity for Halleck during the siege-march on Corinth until he was appointed colonel of a cavalry regiment and then commander of a division with the rank of brigadier general. Ever active, he opened the battle of Perryville and helped prevent the Union left from suffering worse than it did, but it was his wariness and skillful defensive fighting that saved Rosecrans from disaster at Stones River on December 31, 1862, an outcome that Rosecrans rewarded by recommending him for promotion to major general, a rank he thereupon attained on March 16, 1863, ten days after his thirty-second birthday.[43] There were other young major generals in the Union army, a few even younger, but none of them possessed a more potent nonpolitical patron than Rosecrans now had become.

His prestige, already high owing to Iuka and Corinth, soared far higher with Stones River. Thus the *Chicago Tribune* in a headline hailed his "Complete Victory" there, the *Cincinnati Gazette*'s account of the battle praised his "splendid generalship," and the reporter of the *Louisville Journal* accompanying his army wrote, "Of all our commanding generals, he is the only one that knows how to fight a battle." Better yet, from a practical standpoint, Halleck telegraphed him that his "victory was well earned and one of the most brilliant of the war." Even Stanton informed him that "there is nothing you can ask within my power to grant to yourself or your heroic command that will not be cheerfully given." Best of all, Lincoln wrote him: "God bless you, and all with you. Please tender to all, and accept for yourself, the nation's gratitude for your and their skill, endurance, and dauntless courage."[44]

In sum, Rosecrans, who in September had found himself reduced to commanding two understrength divisions and in October barely escaped losing even them in spite of, or perhaps because of, his victory at Corinth, now found himself in January 1863 higher on the ladder of military prestige than any other Northern general, including Grant, whose status had slipped with his near debacle at Shiloh and then sunk lower still with the collapse of his attempt to take Vicksburg.

Would he rise higher, even to the very top? The answer to this question will come in chapters 10 and 11, for the chronology of events requires that we return to the East and then to the West.

9

Meade at Gettysburg
How to Win by Staying Put

UNDERSTANDABLY, INDEED INEVITABLY, the Fredericksburg fiasco caused many of the Army of the Potomac's generals to conclude that Burnside should be removed from command.[1] Soon after the battle two of them journeyed to Washington, where they so told Lincoln, who in turn summoned Burnside to the White House, where, on December 31, he informed him of what the generals had said. Outraged, Burnside asked for their names, but Lincoln refused to provide them. Burnside thereupon described a new plan he had conceived for taking Richmond, one that called for crossing the Rappahannock downriver from Fredericksburg, and requested the president's approval of it. This, too, he did not receive, Lincoln stating that he wished to discuss the matter with Stanton and Halleck.

On New Year's Day morning Burnside went to the White House, where he found the president accompanied by Stanton and Halleck. He handed a letter to Lincoln, who read it and then returned it to him without comment. For in it Burnside declared that since he had lost the confidence of his generals "I ought to return to private life"—an indirect way of saying that he wished to be relieved of command of the Army of the Potomac and be allowed to resign his commission. Instead of responding to this request, Lincoln asked Halleck to express his opinion of Burnside's new plan for taking Richmond. This, though, Halleck refused to do, stating that only a commander in the field possessed the knowledge needed to judge whether or not a military operation involving combat stood a reasonable chance of success.

With this the meeting ended, but not Lincoln's desire to obtain Halleck's views on Burnside's plan. To this end he penned a note to Halleck, the key passage of which read: "You know what General Burnside's plan is, and it is my wish that you go with him to the ground, examine it as far as practicable, confer with the officers . . . [and] in a word, gather all the elements for forming a judgment of your own, and then tell General Burnside that you do approve or that you do not approve his plan. Your military skill is useless to me if you will not do this."[2]

At the White House New Year's Day reception, Lincoln gave this letter to Stanton, who at a reception held at his residence passed it on to Halleck. Returning to his office, Halleck addressed to Stanton his reply to Lincoln, a reply wherein after repeating his reason for not expressing his views on the validity of Burnside's plan, he concluded with these words: "I therefore respectfully request that I may be relieved from further duties as General-in-Chief."

Following the White House reception and after signing the Emancipation Proclamation, Lincoln received from Stanton Halleck's resignation. After reading it, he wrote on his copy of his request for Halleck's advice on what Burnside should do: "Withdrawn, because considered too harsh by General Halleck." Stanton then notified Halleck of the president's response, whereupon Halleck withdrew his request to be relieved, after which he resumed attending to such matters as Grant's seemingly precarious situation in Mississippi, Sherman's expedition to Vicksburg, and McClernand's pursuit of that expedition, all the while hoping for reliable word about Rosecrans's advance on Murfreesboro. He had more than enough to deal with in the West without becoming the de facto commander of the Army of the Potomac in the East, which is what he would become if he did what Lincoln had asked him to do.

Burnside, back with his army, decided to proceed with making another effort to defeat Lee or at least drive him back to Richmond. But rather than cross the Rappahannock downriver from Fredericksburg, he chose to take advantage of some fords upstream, thereby lessening his dependence on pontoons. To this end, on January 20 he set forth with his army in hope of turning Lee's left flank. Almost at once it began raining, a persistent, torrential rain that turned the roads into muddy streams, wherein wagons, cannons, and pontoons became haplessly bogged and mules drowned. After two days Burnside had no choice other than to call off what became known as the "Mud March."

Finding himself unable to wage war against the enemy in front, in bitter frustration he turned against the foes in the rear—the Army of Potomac generals who sought to have him dismissed from command. After drawing up a general order that expelled Hooker and three other generals from the United States army and relieved five more, among them Franklin, on January 23 he telegraphed Lincoln that he was coming to Washington. This he did, not once but twice, with the second visit taking place on January 29.

There and then Lincoln told him that he had been replaced as head of the Army of the Potomac by Hooker. The president's decision, while unpleasant for Burnside—with cause, he detested Hooker—was not unexpected;

indeed, it came as a relief, for the responsibility of commanding the North's main army and his humiliating failures had devastated him both physically and emotionally. Hence, assuming that his January 1 offer to resign his commission now had been accepted, he reacted to Lincoln's statement by asking if he was free to return at once to his Rhode Island home. No, came the answer; he remained in the army and would see further service.

Which he did and, as shall be seen, with mostly unfortunate results. In twice declining command of the Army of the Potomac on the grounds that he was unqualified for the post, he spoke the truth, as was demonstrated on the battleground, or, to be more exact, the killing fields at Fredericksburg. On the other hand, Lincoln displayed poor judgment by in effect forcing him to assume command of the Army of the Potomac. A commander who lacks self-confidence will not inspire confidence in his generals or achieve success, but instead will almost guarantee failure.

Lincoln put Hooker in charge of the Army of the Potomac with misgivings.[3] He knew that Hooker had been the leader of the generals who sought to depose Burnside, and he knew too that Hooker had declared that the nation needed a dictatorship, presumably with himself as dictator. Yet his appointment of Hooker to supersede Burnside is understandable, indeed perhaps was inevitable. No other general in the Army of the Potomac matched Hooker's combat performance, a performance that had caused him to be dubbed (thanks to a newspaper flub) "Fighting Joe." His professional pedigree was also impressive: West Point, class of 1837; promoted to brevet lieutenant colonel during the Mexican War for gallantry; commissioned a captain in the regular army in 1848; and appointed the following year as assistant adjutant general of the Pacific Division, with headquarters at San Francisco.

In 1853, not having obtained further promotion, although now nearly forty, because Winfield Scott disliked him—while in Mexico he had sided with Gideon Pillow in a quarrel with Scott—he left the army to take up farming in Sonoma County, California, at which he failed. At the same time, he succeeded in gaining what evidently was a well-deserved reputation for persistent drinking and frequent womanizing that resulted in two other ex-army officers also residing in California to form a low opinion of him. Their names were Henry W. Halleck and William T. Sherman.

With the advent of war in 1861, he made his way to Washington in quest of a generalship, only at first to fail: General in Chief Scott saw to that. Then came First Bull Run. McClellan replaced Scott and soon came a brigadier generalship for Hooker, who proceeded to distinguish himself with hard, aggressive fighting in the Peninsular Campaign, at Second Bull Run, and above all at Antietam, where his corps—by then he was a major general—came close to crushing the Confederate left wing. Next, at Fredericksburg, where he headed one of Burnside's three "Grand Divisions," he again distinguished himself, this time not for fighting but rather for refusing to fight when it became all too obvious that to do so was to engage in mass suicide.

Thus, as January 1863 drew to a close, Hooker, who less than two years before had sunk to a social status lower even than Grant's at that time, found himself at the head of the North's premier army with the assignment of overcoming Lee and taking Richmond—outcomes that most Northerners and Southerners believed would result in the termination of the war, the restoration of the Union, and the abolition of slavery. Should he achieve this, he would not only ascend to the highest peak of military prestige but also become a prospective presidential candidate.

Well aware of what he stood to win by winning against Lee, Hooker devoted the remainder of winter and the beginning of spring to rebuilding the Army of the Potomac in numbers, efficiency, and morale. By April it totaled 134,000 well-drilled and well-equipped troops backed by 404 cannons; possessed eight corps (the "Grand Divisions" had been abolished), one of which consisted of 11,000 cavalry, giving it for the first time a mounted force capable of combating Stuart's cavaliers on equal terms; and its officers and men felt confident of victory under Hooker's leadership. Unlike Burnside, who became haggard under the (for him) crushing weight of top command, the tall and stalwart "Fighting Joe" radiated confidence both in himself and in success.

On April 27 Hooker initiated what would become known as the Battle of Chancellorsville. His plan was excellent. Taking advantage of Lee's army having been reduced to 60,000 by Longstreet being in southeastern Virginia, where with two of his divisions he was engaged in a futile attempt to retake Suffolk from the Federals, it called for threatening Lee in front at Fredericksburg with two corps and a division while sending the cavalry corps under Major General George Stoneman and the rest of the infantry, 81,000 strong, sweeping around his left flank and into his rear. If all went well, Lee either would be forced to beat a hasty retreat to Richmond or else be trapped, in which case his army would have to surrender to avoid obliteration, Richmond would be taken, and the war would be as good as won.

At first all did go well, albeit Stoneman's troopers did no serious damage to Lee's rail supply line, their primary mission. On the afternoon of April 30, Major General Henry Slocum's XII Corps, followed by Major General

Oliver Otis Howard's XI Corps, reached Chancellorsville, basically just a brick manor house located at a crossroads amidst a dense forest appropriately called the Wilderness. So far, scant resistance had been encountered, Meade's V Corps was within supporting distance, and Brigadier General Daniel Sickles's III Corps soon would be. All that Hooker, who now arrived at Chancellorsville, needed to do was to continue advancing eastward toward Fredericksburg, a mere eleven miles distant, and Lee would have to fall back toward Richmond in order to escape being assailed on front, flanks, and rear by twice his strength, plus being cut off from Richmond, his supply base.

Instead, Hooker halted at Chancellorsville, and when he resumed advancing come morning, May 1, an attack by two Confederate divisions caused him to fall back to Chancellorsville, where he ordered his troops to fortify. That night, Lee and Jackson conferred. They decided to have Jackson, with 24,000 troops, swing around to the Union rear west of Chancellorsville and strike it—strike it hard—while Lee, with two divisions, menaced the enemy from the east and another division continued to hold off the Yankees at Fredericksburg.

In the early morning Jackson began marching. Several times the Federals noticed his column, and twice Hooker directed Howard, whose XI Corps guarded the rear, to take due precautions against an attack from the west. However, Howard, a thirty-two-year-old West Pointer who had lost his right arm during the Peninsular Campaign, thinking that the Confederates were retreating, paid little heed to these warnings, with the result that when Jackson struck at 6 P.M. he routed the XI Corps. Then, seeking as always to inflict maximum damage, Jackson conducted a mounted reconnaissance with members of his staff. Some of his own soldiers, in the near-dark twilight mistaking his party for Yankee cavalry, fired on it. Three bullets hit Jackson, who survived but lost his left arm, and eight days later his life.

Jeb Stuart, the senior available major general, took command of the flanking force and at daylight resumed its onslaught. The Federals, fighting behind log barricades and backed by artillery stationed atop Fairview, site of Chancellorsville manor, initially withstood the Rebel assaults. But then they had to fall back, the consequence of running out of cartridges because Hooker, in quest of greater mobility, had replaced ammunition wagons with pack mules who balked at coming under fire.[4]

Next, Stuart assembled thirty-one cannons on a hill to the southwest of Fairview, a hill Hooker had ordered to be evacuated early that morning and from which the Confederates now bombarded Fairview. Before long, one of their projectiles, a solid shot, struck a wood pillar on the front porch of Chancellorsville manor against which Hooker was leaning, knocking him unconscious. He soon revived but remained incapable of exercising competent command. Even so, the chief surgeon refused to declare him unfit, and the army's senior major general and head of the II Corps, Darius Couch, refrained from taking command because Hooker, upon regaining consciousness, had told him to withdraw the whole army back across the Rappahannock—and this in spite of it having two corps totaling 35,000 troops ready, eager, and in position to strike Stuart's force and the two divisions being directed by Lee in their exposed flanks. Such Hooker did during the next three days, as also did the troops that had crossed the river at Fredericksburg. In round numbers, Federal losses came to almost 16,500, of which 6,000 were listed as captured or missing, but of which a very high percentage were deserters. The Confederates, for their part, suffered 12,500 casualties, nearly 11,000 of them killed or wounded, twice the Union percentage and the price of fighting mostly on the offensive. Their main loss, of course, was Jackson; he was irreplaceable.[5]

Thus ended the Battle of Chancellorsville. For the Federals it was a classic case of defeat being snatched from the jaws of victory, with Hooker doing the snatching by halting when he should have continued advancing and by failing to employ one-fourth of his available troops. Officially and publicly he blamed the defeat on certain of his generals, in particular and with some truth Howard and Stoneman. But after he directed Couch to retreat back across the Rappahannock, he told Meade that he wished he had never been born and said that he was tempted to turn over command of the army to him![6] And when, several weeks after the battle, Major General Abner Doubleday asked him why he lost the battle, he answered: "For once I lost confidence in Hooker, and that is all there is to it."[7] In sum, "Fighting Joe" ceased to be a fighter when as head of the Union's main army the fighting did not go the way he had planned.

By losing at Chancellorsville when he should have won, Hooker also lost the confidence of Lincoln, who following the battle offered command of the Army of the Potomac in succession to four of its major generals: Couch, John Reynolds, Sedgwick, and Winfield Scott Hancock.[8] All of them, though, declined the post, leaving Lincoln no practical alternative (or so he thought) other than to retain Hooker—at least for the time being.

Meanwhile, Lee prepared to invade again the North. To this end he reorganized the Army of Northern Virginia into three infantry corps of three divisions each: Longstreet's, Lieutenant General Richard S. Ewell's, and Lieutenant General Ambrose Powell Hill's. These, along with Stuart's cavalry, provided him with close to 80,000 troops, most of them veterans. Such a force, he believed, would enable him to gain a victory on Northern soil that would cause the British and French to recognize Southern independence and bolster the antiwar movement in the North. Also, he hoped to nullify by a great triumph in the East the impending fall of besieged Vicksburg in the West.

Early in June, Ewell's corps began marching toward the Potomac by way of the Shenandoah Valley, with Longstreet's corps following by the same route east of the Blue Ridge that Jackson took when flanking Pope in August 1862.[9] This left only Hill's corps confronting the Army of the Potomac at Fredericksburg. Hooker thereupon proposed to Lincoln—on replacing Burnside, he had asked and obtained Lincoln's permission to deal directly with him, bypassing Halleck, whom he knew to be a personal enemy—that he "pitch into" it, only to have the president react negatively. So, too, did Halleck, which should have alerted Hooker to the fact that he no longer enjoyed a special relationship with Lincoln. Both the president and his general in chief cautioned him to keep between Lee and Washington, and this meant heading north, staying parallel to Longstreet.

Prevented from attacking Hill, Hooker went ahead with another operation he had conceived. This was to have his cavalry, now headed by Major General Alfred Pleasonton, "disperse and destroy" Stuart's cavaliers assembled near Culpeper Court House. On June 9, Pleasonton, with 7,500 troopers supported by 3,000 infantry, crossed the Rappahannock and fell upon Stuart at Brandy Station. There ensued the biggest cavalry battle of the Civil War, one that ended with Pleasonton retreating back across the Rappahannock. Physically, the Confederates could and did claim a victory. Psychologically, however, the Federals won. Not only had they held their own in the fighting and sometimes more, but they had taken Stuart by surprise, something for which Southern newspapers criticized him, much to his vexation.

The following day Hooker, perhaps buoyed by Pleasonton's near success, telegraphed another proposal to Lincoln. It called for the Army of the Potomac to move on and take Richmond, thus "giving the rebellion a mortal blow." Shocked, Lincoln promptly wired back: "I think *Lee's* army and not *Richmond,* is your true objective point." Now left with no alternative, Hooker instructed his corps commanders to prepare to march northward, keeping the army between the Confederates and the capital.

During the next twenty days Lee's legions crossed the Potomac into Maryland. On the way, Ewell's corps killed, wounded, or captured nearly 5,000 Yankees whose commander, contrary to Halleck's instructions, tried to make a stand at Winchester in the Shenandoah Valley. Also, Longstreet switched over to the west side of the Blue Ridge and followed Ewell and Hill into Pennsylvania, where the former threatened the state capital of Harrisburg and briefly occupied Carlisle and York before turning back to link up with the rest of Lee's army. Only Stuart's cavalry remained east of the mountains, so hard pressed by Pleasonton that it could not perform its prime mission of informing Lee of the location and strength of the Federal forces. Realizing this, and maybe seeking to redeem Brandy Station, Stuart thereupon obtained from Lee a somewhat vague authorization to ride yet again around the Army of the Potomac, then join him in Pennsylvania, where he would seek out the Federals for a decisive battle on enemy soil.

All the while, Hooker moved steadily north through north-central Virginia and then into Maryland, performing his assignment of covering Washington. His main concern, though, was his troop strength, or rather lack thereof. In addition to Chancellorsville's huge casualties, the Army of the Potomac had been badly depleted by the discharge of two-year and nine-month units, with the result that its number of present-for-duty soldiers had declined to 90,000. Hoping to in part remedy this, on June 26 he telegraphed Halleck soliciting the services of the 10,000-man garrison at Harpers Ferry, a place that, on the basis of what happened there during the Antietam Campaign, he deemed indefensible and hence a strategic liability instead of an asset. Halleck refused the request. Hooker, declaring that a garrison "is of no earthly account there," then asked that the matter be referred to Stanton and Lincoln. But before he received a response, he learned that the commander at Harpers Ferry had been directed by Halleck to "pay no attention to General Hooker's orders."

This confirmed what he already had suspected: Lincoln, Stanton, and most of all Halleck wished to replace him. Hence, he made it easy for them to do so. "I earnestly request," he wired Halleck, "that I at once be relieved from the position I occupy." Halleck promptly relayed this "request"—it actually was a resignation—to Lincoln, who just as promptly issued an order relieving Hooker and replacing him with Meade. Early on the morning of June 28, a messenger from the War Department delivered the order to Meade at Frederick, Maryland. Meade in turn showed it to Hooker, who not only expected it but, in all likelihood, welcomed it. The task of defeating Lee and preventing him from quite possibly winning the war for the Confederacy now belonged to Meade.

Prior to Fredericksburg no one would have predicted, much less expected, Meade to become the commander of the Army of the Potomac.[10] There was no reason why anyone should. Born in 1815 in Spain of well-to-do American parents, he entered West Point at the age of sixteen, graduated from there an undistinguished nineteenth in the class of 1835, and then resigned his commission one year later to become a civil engineer, only to prosper so little that he rejoined the army in 1842 as again a second lieutenant in the Corps of Topographical Engineers. His service in the Mexican War also was undistinguished, and following it his career remained routine. But, as with so many other West Point–trained regular army officers, both active and former, the advent of war in 1861 opened doors of opportunity for him through which he passed successfully, one after another, until at Fredericksburg his division was the sole one *almost* to break through the Confederate line, albeit at great cost and with two bullet holes through his hat. Promoted to major general and put in command of a corps, he had no chance to take part in the fighting at Chancellorsville, yet this did not prevent Reynolds, Couch, and Slocum from urging Lincoln to replace Hooker with him—an urging that led Lincoln to do exactly that.

In sum, despite a lack of McClellan-like personal magnetism—his soldiers called him "Old Four-Eyes" because he wore spectacles except when posing for photos—he was a hard, determined fighter who was unlikely to lose a battle out of a Hooker-like loss of self-confidence and smart enough not to persist in a Burnside-like attempt to do the impossible even after it became clear that it was not possible. As to whether he possessed Napoleon's essential attribute of luck, the answer to this question will come in due course. Suffice for the present to state that he already had been lucky when it came to Lee—luckier than he knew, luckier than he ever could have hoped for.

This luck consisted of two occurrences, both taking place on June 28, the day he assumed command of the Army of the Potomac. One was a report from that army's Bureau of Military Information, an organization established by Hooker and probably his most valuable contribution to the Union war effort in the East. According to data supplied to it by a citizen of Hagerstown, Maryland, through which the Army of Northern Virginia recently had passed, Lee had at most 80,000 troops backed by 275 cannons. Since both figures came close to absolute accuracy, Meade knew what he faced with his 90,000 men, who soon would be bolstered by Halleck with units from Washington's garrison and Harpers Ferry, something he had refused to do for Hooker. The second stroke of luck took the form of Stuart capturing 150 Union wagons and their teams near Rockville, Maryland, and deciding to bring them along with him as he circled around the Army of the Potomac—a decision in accordance with his orders from Lee, but which resulted in greatly slowing his march and causing Lee, who was at Chambersburg,

Pennsylvania, with Hill's and Longstreet's corps, to remain ignorant of the whereabouts of the Army of the Potomac. All he knew, thanks to a spy employed by Longstreet, was that it had a new commander—Meade—and that five of its corps had crossed the Potomac into Maryland. Probably he regretted that "Mr. F. J. Hooker," as he contemptuously referred to his opponent at Chancellorsville, had been replaced, but that the Federals were advancing faster toward Pennsylvania than he hitherto thought startled him. At once he sent an order to Ewell to rejoin the rest of the army, and on June 29 he began marching with Hill's corps, followed by two divisions of Longstreet's corps, southeastward from Chambersburg along a road leading to a town named Gettysburg.

June 30 found Meade fourteen miles southeast of Gettysburg, in Taneytown, Maryland, a small town where he experienced another stroke of luck. It again came from the Bureau of Military Information and again consisted of an estimate of Lee's strength, a more recent one based on what pro-Union inhabitants of Hanover, Maryland, saw when the Rebel horde marched through their village. According to them, Lee's army numbered at least 100,000 rather than at most 80,000. Since this gave Lee nearly as many soldiers as his own 104,000—reinforcements from Washington had arrived and more were on the way—Meade decided to withdraw to a defensive position along a ridge behind Pipe Creek a short distance to the south of Taneytown. He therefore instructed his chief of staff, Major General Daniel Butterfield, whom he had inherited from Hooker, to draw up an order to that effect, with copies to be delivered to the corps commanders. However, Butterfield, perhaps because of insufficient copyists, failed to complete the order, which consisted of twenty-one paragraphs, before darkness descended.

This proved to be a fortunate event. On the morning of June 30 at Cashtown, Pennsylvania, eight miles east of Gettysburg, Major General Henry Heth, head of the lead division in Hill's corps, ordered Brigadier General Johnston Pettigrew to go on to Gettysburg and gather all the men's shoes in the town's stores, as many of his soldiers were barefoot or close to it. This task Pettigrew, with three regiments and a gaggle of wagons, set forth to do. But as he neared Gettysburg the same spy who had informed Lee by way of Longstreet that the Federals had crossed the Potomac into Maryland warned him that Yankee cavalry were approaching the place. Pettigrew thereupon halted and sent word of the spy's sighting to Heth. Continue on, came Heth's response—only some easily routed militia could be in Gettysburg. Pettigrew resumed his march only again to halt when his advance pickets reported that the bluecoats in Gettysburg were regular

Yankee cavalry. This time Pettigrew, aware of an order by Lee not to bring
on a battle until the whole army had been united, returned with his troops
and wagons to Cashtown.

Heth, though, refused to believe that Federal cavalry could be as far
north as Gettysburg, a view supported by Hill, who declared that Lee had
told him that Meade's army was at least twenty miles southeast of the town.
Hence, soon after dawn on July 1 Heth's division set forth for Gettysburg,
encountered Brigadier General John Buford's division of Army of the Potomac cavalry, and the biggest, bloodiest, and most momentous battle of the
Civil War got under way.

More has been written about this battle, at any rate in English, than any
other battle in all of history, and the flow of books and articles concerning
it shows no sign of abating. To describe it here in a manner even remotely
complete would require more space than can be afforded in a book dealing
not with losers in gray, but with victors in blue. Therefore, what follows is
a compact account of the Battle of Gettysburg designed to demonstrate how
and why Meade won it and so became one of those victors in blue.

During the early morning of July 1, Buford's cavalry division held Heth's
division at bay thanks to their carbines and to being posted on high ground
nearly a mile northwest of Gettysburg astride the Chambersburg Pike.[11]
Shortly before 10 A.M., two brigades from Reynolds's I Corps arrived on
the scene. Reynolds, who already was present, thereupon ordered them to
deliver a counterattack. Although a bullet struck Reynolds dead, this attack
repelled Heth and brought a lull in the fighting. During it, all of the I Corps,
now headed by Major General Abner Doubleday, deployed to the east of
Gettysburg, in the process relieving Buford's troopers. At the same time, the
XI Corps, which Reynolds had summoned to Gettysburg along with the XII
Corps, took position on the I Corps right and north of the town. Howard,
being the senior major general present, assumed command of both corps,
the XII Corps not yet having come up.

Late in the morning Heth again attacked, only again to be repulsed. Soon,
however, two of Ewell's divisions, Major General Robert Rodes's and Major
General Jubal Early's, approached Gettysburg, the first from the north, the
second from the northeast. After forming battle lines, they advanced to the
attack, as did Heth's battered but still belligerent troops, who were backed
by another of Hill's divisions. Although two of Rodes's brigades floundered
owing to the ineptitude of their commanders, Early's assault routed most of
the XI Corps, which in turn caused the I Corps, its right flank now exposed,
to fall back.[12] As this took place, Major General Winfield Scott Hancock,

now head of the II Corps in place of Couch, who had taken command of the Pennsylvania Militia, arrived with an order from Meade to take charge of all Union forces presently at Gettysburg. Upon surveying Cemetery Hill due south of Gettysburg, which the remnants of the XI Corps now occupied, and Cemetery Ridge, an elevation extending southward from Cemetery Hill, the upper part to which the badly battered I Corps had retreated, Hancock declared them the "strongest point to fight a battle," then sent a dispatch to Meade stating that "we can fight here."

So it was that Meade and Lee became engaged in what promised to be a decisive battle, perhaps *the* decisive battle, at a place and in a manner that neither of them expected nor desired.

Such is war.

Toward dawn on July 2 Meade joined his army, having spent the previous day at Taneytown overseeing its transfer to Gettysburg and arranging for it to be supplied there. On learning via dispatches from Buford and Reynolds that the Confederates were endeavoring to seize Gettysburg, he had declared that they must not be allowed to do so, for if they did they then would be able to strike in almost any direction owing to the numerous roads radiating from it. Hence his primary concern after arriving on the battlefield was to ascertain whether his forces occupied a naturally strong defensive position and, if so, were properly deployed to hold it. He quickly approved the first, albeit because there was no practicable alternative to it; as to the second, he conducted a personal inspection. This proved fortunate because when he toured the Cemetery Hill sector he discovered that a short distance to the southeast of it there was a higher eminence called Culp's Hill, whence enemy artillery could rake Cemetery Ridge with enfilade fire, rendering it untenable. To forestall this he had Henry W. Slocum's XII Corps and elements of the battered I Corps occupy the hill while linking up with the XI Corps on its left, causing the Union battle line to resemble, as anyone writing about the Battle of Gettysburg must by long tradition point out, a fishhook—an inverted one (this author's attempt at originality).

The morning and much of the afternoon passed with little or no aggressive action by the Confederates, a lull that provided Meade with ample time to bring up and position all of his army, save John Sedgwick's VI Corps, which, having the longest distance to march from Maryland, remained on the way. Then, a bit before 4 P.M., two of Longstreet's divisions, 14,500 strong, attacked the Union left. Had Sickles's III Corps been in the position assigned to it by Meade at the south end of Cemetery Ridge, the attack probably would have stood little chance of success, Lee having ordered it in the erroneous belief, based on an ill-conducted reconnaissance by one of his staff officers, that the Union left flank was open. But Sickles, a political general whose military incompetence matched his colossal conceit, had in defiance of Meade's repeated directions advanced his corps westward from Cemetery Ridge to a peach orchard near the Emmitsburg Road, thereby exposing both of his flanks, creating two gaps in the Federal defense line, and uncovering Little Round Top, a hill at the south end of the ridge, which if seized by the enemy would make all of Cemetery Ridge untenable and produce the defeat, perhaps the destruction, of the Army of the Potomac. Fortunately for the Federals, Brigadier General Gouverneur Warren, the army's chief engineer, perceived the undefended condition of Little Round Top and hastened two brigades to it just in time—barely—to beat back— also barely—a Rebel attempt to take it. Likewise, units under the command of Hancock rushed to the support of Sickles's isolated corps and drove back the Confederates surging around it, but not before they wrecked the III Corps and Sickles lost his right leg to a cannon ball—a loss that was a gain for the Army of the Potomac and the Union cause since it took him out of the war for good.

Indeed, the closest the Confederates came to a battle-winning success on July 2 came on the Union right flank. There, in the evening, Major General Edward Johnson's division of Ewell's corps took all of Culp's Hill, save the crest, the consequence of all of the XII Corps, except one brigade, having gone to reinforce the left. The remaining brigade, fighting behind log breast-works, checked Johnson's advance and contained the damage. In sum, Lee, while inflicting heavy losses on the Federals thanks to Sickles's ineptitude, also suffered severe casualties and failed to achieve the decisive victory he desired and for a while thought he was attaining.

Late that night Meade met with his top generals in his headquarters, a small farmhouse located a short distance behind the center of the Union battle line. Whether, come tomorrow, to go on the offensive or remain on the defensive was the question. All favored the latter—which is what Meade already had decided to do. He also believed that Lee would try to break through the middle of this front, having been repulsed at both ends.

Such proved to be the case, but not immediately. On the morning of July 3, Ewell intended to renew his effort to seize the crest of Culp's Hill, to which end he had reinforced Johnson's division with troops from Early's division. This time, though, the Confederates encountered most of the XII Corps, which, under the acting command of Alpheus Williams, had returned to the hill during the night and not only repulsed all attacks but reoccupied most of it.

Next, toward noon, 163 Confederate cannons aligned along Seminary Ridge opened up on the II Corps, which was under the acting command of Brigadier General John Gibbon, Hancock being in overall command of the Federal center. Many of the Rebel shells either failed to explode or else overshot the ridge. At first, none of the Union gunners responded, having been instructed by Brigadier General Henry Hunt, the Army of the Potomac's Chief of Artillery, to remain silent so as to preserve their shells and solid shot for use against the enemy infantry once it emerged from the woods along Seminary Ridge. However, Hancock, fearing that his troops might become demoralized if the Rebel cannonade was not answered, ordered the II Corps chief of artillery, Captain John Hazard, to fire back, which he did. Hunt, realizing that Hazard felt that he had to obey his immediate superior, made no attempt to stop him, and all of the rest of the Federal artillery—far greater in number and power than Lee's—continued to comply with his instructions.

After several hours of firing, and with their supply of long-range projectiles nearly exhausted, the Confederate guns became silent, and close to 15,000 Southern infantry emerged from the woods atop Seminary Ridge in two large, multiranked formations. The northern one consisted of six brigades headed by Pettigrew, who had taken over from a wounded Heth and was followed by two brigades under Major General Isaac Trimble. To the south, separated from Pettigrew's and Trimble's troops by a wide gap, came Major General George Pickett's division of Longstreet's corps, three large brigades composed entirely of Virginians and supported on its right rear by two brigades from Hill's corps. All of the Union cannons thereupon opened fire, shredding the oncoming Rebels with shells and solid shot, the latter sometimes mangling whole rows as they bounded along after striking the ground. Still they kept coming, closing up the holes in their lines as they did so. Next, as they drew near enough, Hunt's gunners switched to canister, the equivalent of giant shotgun blasts. This, along with enfilade fire from an Ohio regiment, sent Pettigrew's troops reeling backward and caused Trimble's to halt and then also fall back.

Pickett's division, despite increasingly heavy losses, continued onward. Then it came under a devastating rifle fusillade both in front and flank as it swerved leftward to strike Hancock's corps. Soon it ceased to exist as an organized force. Only a few hundred survivors of Armistead's brigade kept going, their target a salient in the Union line marked by a little clump of trees. Led by Armistead, his hat atop an upraised sword to guide them, they reached it and pierced it, only to be shot, bayoneted, and clubbed until just a mere remnant remained, whereupon those still on their feet dropped their rifles and raised their hands. So too did hundreds of others who never reached the clump of trees and realized that to try to return to Seminary Ridge would be suicidal. Among the dying lay Armistead, West Point class-mate and close friend of Hancock, who also had been wounded, painfully but not fatally.

Thus ended what became known in history and legend as Pickett's Charge—a somewhat unfair appellation given that most of the soldiers who made it came from Hill's corps and were not under Pickett's command. At about the same time it took place, another young general, a Northern one, began a career that would lead to him also passing into history and legend. He was George Armstrong Custer, West Point class of 1861, where he finished last, and who only five days before had been jumped from first lieutenant to brigadier general and placed in command of a cavalry brigade. In that capacity he figured prominently in a clash that took place three miles east of Gettysburg when Jeb Stuart, who finally had rejoined the Army of Northern Virginia on July 2, to a cool reception from Lee, tried to cut off a hoped-for Union retreat but was forced to retreat himself by the once-despised Yankee cavalry. Like Pickett, with whom he shared many traits, Custer was destined to give his name to a military disaster, a disaster that is second only to Gettysburg in the ever-increasing number of books written about it. Defeat, if the right kind, can make a general, if he is the right kind, immortal. Witness Cambronne at Waterloo.

Thus ended too the Battle of Gettysburg, the biggest and bloodiest of the Civil War. In it the Federals suffered slightly over 23,000 killed, wounded, and missing—more than one-fourth of the troops they had on the field—and the Confederates lost at least 23,000, nearly one-third of their total fighting strength. This was more than they could afford to lose and not win the battle, a battle that if they had won would have at the very least com-pensated for the debacle at Vicksburg and at most led to victory in the war.

So why did they lose? Beginning then with Southern participants and continuing to this day in the writings of many historians, the answer often sought and found lies in what the Army of Northern Virginia's general did, did not do, or should have done, starting with Lee and including Longstreet, Ewell, Hill, and Stuart. And some of them, among them Douglas Southall Freeman, generally deemed the greatest of all Civil War historians, found the basic cause of Confederate defeat in the death of Stonewall Jackson: "If I had had Stonewall Jackson with me," Freeman quotes Lee as saying to a cousin shortly before his own demise in 1870, "I should have won the battle of Gettysburg." He then asserts: "That statement must stand. The darkest scene in the great drama of Gettysburg was enacted at Chancellorsville when Jackson fell."[13]

Possibly this is true. Certainly Jackson was superior in military talent to Longstreet, Ewell, and Hill. Yet to attribute Lee's defeat at Gettysburg to Jackson not being there is to continue to focus on what the Confederates did or did not do while ignoring what the Federals did and did not do—in particular, a Federal named George Meade. It was Meade who, on learning from Buford and Reynolds that a strong Rebel force was approaching Gettysburg, at once began hastening his whole army there. Likewise, he made the definite decision to make a stand on Cemetery Hill and Cemetery Ridge. But most of all, unlike McClellan during the Seven Days, he did not retreat from victories gained by repelling enemy attacks. Instead, he stayed put, thereby taking advantage of the fundamental fact of the Civil War battlefield, to wit that the advent of the rifled musket and rifled cannon rendered the defense tactically superior to the offense, with the result that throughout that war the attacking army rarely prevailed, and when it did it was because of overwhelming numbers, an enemy blunder, or sheer good luck. At Gettysburg, Meade, although he did not know it, outnumbered Lee; he made no serious mistakes, or at least none that were not remedied in time; and, on the whole, Dame Fortune smiled on him. On the other hand, Lee, having failed on July 1 and 2 to turn the Union flanks, attempted to penetrate his opponent's center with a frontal assault and paid the price—a price, to repeat, the Confederacy could ill afford. Or, as one of Lee's generals put it when after the war he was asked why Lee lost at Gettysburg, "I think the Yankees had something to do with it."

That general was in a position to know. His name was George Pickett.[14]

Meade spent the morning of July 4 preparing to renew the battle should Lee resume his attacks. He need not have. Lee's sole desire now was to return to Virginia. To that end, during the afternoon and night the Army of Northern Virginia began retreating toward Williamsport, Maryland, a small town on the upper bank of the Potomac, where it had crossed that river when advancing northward.

Not until early the next day did Meade discover that Lee was gone, this time heading southward. Yet he did not begin a pursuit until July 6. His reasons were organizational, logistical, and prudential, with the last being the product of a belief on his part that despite its heavy losses Lee's army might still outnumber him, a belief based on the Bureau of Military Information's report that it entered Pennsylvania with 100,000 men and his corps commanders stating that altogether they had only 56,000 infantry available for combat, the consequence not only of casualties but also of large-scale straggling and what in a later war would be called "bugging out."

Meade's delay in pursuing Lee intensified Lincoln's already existing irritation with him, an irritation aroused by a general order that Meade had issued to his army on July 4, which declared that "the commanding general looks to the army for greater efforts to drive from our soil every vestige of the presence of the invaders." To Lincoln, this seemed like the "old idea of driving the rebels out of Pennsylvania and Maryland, instead of capturing them."

Lincoln's desire to trap Lee increased on July 7 with the receipt of definite word that Grant had taken Vicksburg and with it 29,000 Confederate prisoners. At once he sent a note to Halleck telling him of the "certain information" about Vicksburg and stating, "Now, if General Meade can complete this work so gloriously prosecuted so far, by the literal or substantial destruction of Lee's army, the rebellion will be over." Halleck in turn telegraphed the contents of the note to Meade, who promptly replied, "I most earnestly desire to try the fortunes of war with the enemy this side of the [Potomac] river . . . but I should be wrong not to frankly tell you of difficulties encountered." These difficulties included constant rain, consequent muddy roads, weary and often barefooted soldiers, a vigilant enemy rearguard, and the absence of some of his best generals, among them Reynolds, Hancock, and Gibbon, who also was wounded on July 3.

Then the incessant rain became, in effect, pro-Union. It caused the Potomac at Williamsport to rise to a depth of thirteen feet, making it unfordable, and since Lee's pontoon train, which he had left at Falling Waters on the Virginia side after entering Maryland, had been almost totally destroyed by Federal cavalry operating out of Harpers Ferry, his sole way of crossing was a small cable ferry capable of carrying only a few men or a couple of wagons at a time. Thus he had no choice when his army reached Williamsport other than to halt there until a makeshift pontoon bridge could be built. This he did while his troops constructed a line of fortifications.

On July 12 Meade deployed his army opposite Lee's. The question then became whether or not to try to storm the enemy's fortifications. After taking a look at them, and being under ever-stronger pressure from Lincoln to prevent Lee from escaping into Virginia, he decided to make the attempt. But, as was his practice, that evening he consulted his seven corps commanders plus Pleasonton, Chief of Engineers Warren, and his new chief of staff, Brigadier General Andrew Humphreys. Five of the corps commanders adamantly opposed it, and since their votes carried more weight than those in favor, Meade stated that he would conduct a thorough personal reconnaissance of the Confederate lines before making a final decision. He did so and then ordered four of his corps to probe, not attack, the enemy defenses come tomorrow, and if they found them vulnerable endeavor to breach them.

Early on the morning of July 14 Yankee skirmishers moved cautiously toward the Rebel works only to discover that they were empty. Starting at twilight on the thirteenth and continuing throughout the night, almost all of Lee's army had crossed the Potomac on the new pontoon bridge or else waded its now subsided water. Only the remnants of two Confederate divisions remained on the Maryland side across from Falling Waters. Two Union cavalry divisions, Buford's and Brigadier General Judson Kilpatrick's, attacked them, mortally wounded Pettigrew, and took about 1,000 prisoners, but the rest under Heth escaped across the pontoon bridge, which they then cut loose. In sum, the Army of Northern Virginia escaped to fight many another day.

Lincoln, on learning of this via a telegram from Meade, exclaimed to his secretary John Hay: "We had only to stretch forth our hand and they were ours." He also expressed the same sentiments to Halleck, who in turn wired Meade: "I need hardly say to you that the escape of Lee's army without another battle had created great dissatisfaction in the mind of the President."

On reading these words, Meade telegraphed Halleck that "the censure of the President conveyed in your dispatch of 1 P.M. this day is, in my judgment, so undeserved that I feel compelled most respectfully to ask to be immediately relieved from command of this army." Halleck's reply, made at Lincoln's behest, was both terse and negative: "My telegram, stating the disappointment of the President at the escape of Lee's army, was not intended as a censure, but as a stimulus to an active pursuit. It is not deemed a sufficient cause for your application to be relieved."

Lincoln continued to believe, as have many historians since, that on July 12–13 Meade threw away a golden opportunity to crush the Army of Northern Virginia and thus achieve a victory that, coming on the heels of Vicksburg and removing the South's main army from the military chessboard, would have soon ended the war with the Union restored and slavery on the way to total extinction. Meade, for his part, concluded upon touring the Confederate fortifications on July 14, that an attack on them would have resulted in a bloody repulse, a judgment also supported by many historians.

Which view is correct? Almost surely the second.[15] Although Meade then had, by rounding up skulkers and receiving reinforcements, 80,000 troops, Lee still possessed around 50,000, quite enough when fighting behind earthen ramparts six feet wide at the top and containing embrasure for artillery arranged in a fashion to sweep assailants in murderous cross fire. Even a probe would have remained such, and a very brief one at that. Neither the Northern officers nor their men had any desire to emulate Pickett's charge.

At Gettysburg, Meade, by remaining on the defensive and on the whole leading skillfully, won a battle that, to repeat, had he lost might have offset for the Confederacy the debacle at Vicksburg—or perhaps, indeed, accomplished more than that. Now he faced the challenge of waging offensive war against Lee in Virginia. How he met it and with what results shall be addressed in due course, but not until after we first discover how Grant captured Vicksburg, Rosecrans seized Chattanooga, Thomas prevented the destruction of Rosecrans's army at Chickamauga, and Grant secured Chattanooga once and for all, thereby opening the way, so it would turn out, to Northern victory in the war as a whole.

10

Grant Victorious at Vicksburg

How to Win by Causing Your Enemies to Defeat Themselves

HAD SHERMAN TAKEN VICKSBURG? Or had he failed? So Grant wondered as 1862 gave way to 1863, with his army still in northern Mississippi and still living, quite well thank you, off the country. According to the *Grenada (Mississippi) Appeal*, it had fallen to the Federals. But on January 7, telegraphic communications having been restored between Washington and Holly Springs, Halleck wired him that "Richmond papers of the 5th and 6th say that Sherman has been defeated and repelled from Vicksburg. Every possible effort must be made to reenforce him."[1] Which, wondered Grant, was correct?

The answer came on January 9 in a dispatch Sherman had sent from Napoleon, Arkansas, to Memphis; it had then been telegraphed from there to Grant. In essence, it stated that he had been repulsed.[2] So that was that. But why was Sherman at Napoleon, 145 water miles up the Mississippi from Vicksburg instead of still near that fortress? Grant decided to go at once to Memphis and find out, and unless there was good reason for not doing so, send him back to the Vicksburg area, where he would be in position to assist Banks's forces as they came up to the river from Louisiana.

The next day Grant traveled by train to Memphis, where on January 11 he received a message from McClernand that gave the reason why Sherman was at Napoleon. Now in command of the Vicksburg expedition, owing to his seniority in rank as a major general, the former congressman intended to attack Arkansas Post, a Confederate fort located near the mouth of the Arkansas River. This information infuriated Grant. "Genl. McClernand has fallen back to the White river," he wired Halleck, "and gone on a wild goose chase to the [Post] of Arkansas." Next he penned a letter to McClernand declaring, "I do not approve of your move on the Post of Arkansas whilst the other [on Vicksburg] is in abeyance. . . . Major General Banks has orders from Washington to cooperate in the reduction of Vicksburg, and if not already off that place may be daily expected. You will therefore keep your forces well in hand at some point on the Mississippi River where you can communicate with Gen. Banks on his arrival."[3]

Halleck, upon reading Grant's telegram calling McClernand's sortie up the Arkansas River a "wild goose chase," transmitted the following to him on January 12: "You are hereby authorized to relieve Gen. McClernand from command of the expedition against Vicksburg, giving it to the next in rank [Sherman], or taking it yourself." Grant, who received this message the same day it was sent, at once directed Chief of Staff Rawlins to notify McClernand that Sherman, not he, now headed the Vicksburg expedition. This Rawlins did in a letter that no doubt he wrote with as much pleasure as Grant felt in having him write it.[4]

But before it or Grant's letter to McClernand could be dispatched, another telegram from Halleck arrived, one which quoted a telegram sent by McClernand to Halleck on January 11 from "Post of Arkansas." In essence, it reported that on the afternoon of January 11 his "Army of the Mississippi," supported by Porter's gunboats, "stormed the enemy's works, took a large number of prisoners, variously estimated at from 7,000 to 10,000, together with all of his stores, animals, and munitions of war."[5]

On reading this it is quite possible Grant gritted his false teeth. Obviously, even if not strategically justified, McClernand had gained a significant victory, one made all the more so by Burnside's debacle at Fredericksburg and Sherman's repulse at Vicksburg. To remove him from command and replace him with Sherman now had become a political impossibility no matter how justified militarily. Hence, Grant decided to send neither his letter nor his order to McClernand. Instead, he wrote another letter to him wherein he expressed disapproval of his Arkansas Post foray and directed him to return to the vicinity of Vicksburg so as to be in position to "cooperate with Banks should he come up the river."[6]

This letter reached McClernand on January 16. "I take," he at once wrote in angry response, "the responsibility of the expedition against Post Arkansas, and had anticipated your approval of the complete and signal success which crowned it, rather than your condemnation. . . . Having successfully accomplished the object of this expedition, I will return to Milliken's Bend, according to my intention, communicated to you in a previous dispatch, unless otherwise ordered by you."[7]

It was not, to put it mildly, a tactful letter. McClernand did not intend it to be. With good cause he considered Grant, along with Halleck and Sherman, to be a personal enemy. Therefore, as soon as he completed the foregoing letter he penned one to a person he deemed a friend—Lincoln: "I believe my success here is gall and wormwood to the clique of West Pointers who have been persecuting me for months. . . . Do not let me be destroyed, or what is worse, dishonored, without a hearing. [H]ow can General Grant at a distance of 400 miles intelligently command the army with me? He cannot do it. It should be made an independent command, as both you and the Secretary of War, as I believe, originally intended."[8]

Quite likely the steamboat carrying McClernand's letters passed the one transporting Grant downriver, he having decided to deal directly with the presumptuous politician. On January 18 he landed at Napoleon, where most of the "Army of the Mississippi" had gone after destroying the Confederate fortifications at Arkansas Post. He met first with Sherman, who revealed why the expedition to Arkansas Post took place: he himself proposed it to McClernand! Grant thereupon changed his opinion of the "wild goose chase"; after all, it did produce a victory, one that more than compensated for the losses at Chickasaw Bluffs in that it put out of action nearly 5,000 Rebel soldiers, the great majority of them prisoners. Then, in company with Sherman and Porter, he conferred with McClernand, whom he ordered to return to Milliken's Bend to prepare to change the course of the Mississippi, by digging a canal across it, so that it would no longer flow by Vicksburg. He did not, however, notify McClernand that he intended to assume personal command of operations around Vicksburg, an intent strengthened, supposing it could become any stronger, by Sherman and Porter telling him, prior to his heading back to Memphis, that neither the army nor the navy possessed confidence in McClernand's military ability.[9]

Arriving back in Memphis on the night of January 20, the ensuing day Grant wired Halleck a short telegram informing him of his visit to Napoleon, of his sending McClernand back to Milliken's Bend, and of his plan to "cut" a new canal through it, adding: "The work of reducing Vicksburg will take time but it can be accomplished."[10]

This message he followed with a lengthy letter of the same date to Halleck that went into more detail about digging the new canal and the difficulties involved before turning to two other subjects. The first pertained to what he believed was necessary to success in taking Vicksburg: placing both banks of the Mississippi under one commander in so far as operating against Vicksburg was concerned—himself. The second had to do with McClernand:

> I regard it as my duty to state, that I found there was not sufficient confidance felt in Gen. McClernand as a commander, either by the Army or the Navy, to insure him success. Of course all would cooperate to the best of their ability but still with a distrust.

This is a matter I made no enquiries about but it was forced upon me. As it is my intention to command in person, unless otherwise directed, there is no special necessity of mentioning this matter, but I want you to know that others besides myself agree in the necessity of the course I had already determined upon pursuing.[11]

Grant expected these assertions and proposals to meet with Halleck's approval. They did. In contrast, the letter McClernand sent to Lincoln complaining that the "clique of West Pointers" had deprived him of his independent command received this response in a January 22 letter from the White House: "I have too many *family* controversies (so to speak) already on my hands, to voluntarily, or so long as I can avoid it, take up another. You are now doing well—well for the country, and well for yourself—much better than could possibly be, if engaged in open war with Gen. Halleck. Allow me to beg, that for your sake, for my sake, & the country's sake, you give your whole attention to the better work."[12] It was good advice. Would McClernand act on it?

During the evening of January 29, Grant and his staff came ashore at Young's Point on Milliken's Bend. In the morning, he proclaimed via Rawlins that he was assuming "immediate command of the expedition against Vicksburg," and that henceforth all of his orders would be issued directly to the corps of the Army of the Tennessee—McClernand's XIII, Sherman's XV, and McPherson's XVII (the XVI Corps, headed by Hurlbut, remained in Tennessee). In sum, McClernand's "Army of the Mississippi" ceased to exist.[13]

McClernand at once protested to Grant, citing the Lincoln-Stanton order giving him permission to conduct the Vicksburg expedition. In turn, Grant replied, "I have seen no order to prevent me from taking immediate command in the field . . . and I have received another from the Gen.-in-Chief of the Army authorizing me directly to take command of this Army." McClernand thereupon asked Grant to forward his protest to Halleck, Stanton, and Lincoln. This Grant did, along with a letter containing this passage: "if Gen. Sherman had been left in command here such is my confidance in him that I would not have thought my presence necessary. But, whether I do Gen. McClernand injustice or not, I have not confidance in his ability as a soldier to command an expedition of the magnitude of this one successfully."[14]

Neither Lincoln nor Stanton nor Halleck responded to McClernand's protest.[15] At this point he should have finally realized what a careful reading of the Lincoln-Stanton order authorizing him to conduct an independent expedition against Vicksburg would have made clear to him upon receiving it—that his doing so depended on Halleck allowing it and that there was no chance of this happening. "Whom the gods would destroy," declares an ancient Greek axiom, "they first make mad." In McClernand's case, they made him so mad with ambition that they blinded him to reality.

Having so far in this chapter focused on the war between Grant and McClernand, it now becomes necessary to deal with the Vicksburg Campaign in the same fashion as the Battle of Gettysburg has been described—succinctly—and for the same basic reason: to wit, because of the huge amount that has been written and continues to be written about it, probably more than any other military operation to occur in the West, with much if not most of it being mere rehashes of previous writings. Furthermore, the primary purpose of this book is not narration but interpretation designed to demonstrate why certain battles or campaigns were decisive in determining the outcome of the Civil War and thus the status, then and afterward, of the Northern generals who won them or in some cases lost them. So now, seeking a brevity compatible with clarity, what follows is an account of how and why Grant took Vicksburg, followed by a short and somewhat unorthodox exploration of what his victory achieved for the North and for him.

Throughout February and well into March, Grant tried four ways to get his army close enough to Vicksburg by water so that he could attack it by land.[16] None succeeded. An ever-rising level of the Mississippi, caused by almost constant rain, obliterated the new canal across Milliken's Bend without changing the course of the river. Likewise, three different attempts by Porter's gunboats endeavoring to find a way for troop transports to reach by rivers, lakes, and bayous the rear of the Walnut Hills north of Vicksburg, where Sherman had suffered his bloody December 29 repulse, also failed, the final one barely escaping entrapment and destruction.

Late March found Grant no closer to taking Vicksburg than he had been in late December. It seemed, therefore, that he had only two options left: return to Memphis and again advance overland through Mississippi, or else repeat Sherman's attempt to break through the Confederate Walnut Hills defenses by an all-out assault with his entire army by way of Chickasaw Bayou. Although Sherman advocated the first alternative, Grant rejected it out of fear that a pull back to Memphis would adversely affect the morale of his troops and the Northern people. As for the other option, he correctly concluded that it would probably produce a bigger fiasco than Sherman's attack.

So Grant again pondered the problem of taking Vicksburg. As he did so, a new, daring, yet simple solution took form in his mind, one that he proceeded to implement. First, late in March, McClernand's corps, soon followed by McPherson's, began marching southward along the Louisiana bank of the Mississippi while Sherman's remained northeast of Vicksburg at Milliken's Bend in order to keep the Confederates uncertain of Union intentions. Because his route was as much swamp as it was land—rain had virtually washed away the dirt roads—McClernand made slow progress, yet by the second week of April he reached New Carthage, well below Vicksburg. Next, on the night of April 16, seven of Porter's gunboats, a ram, and three transports protected by stacks of cotton bales on their decks—their crews dubbed them "cottonclads"—ran by Vicksburg's water batteries with the loss of only one transport. Six nights later, six transports made the run, again with only one loss. Now Grant had the means to put his army across the Mississippi and on land south of Vicksburg.

To that end, he ordered McClernand and McPherson to resume their southward march while having Sherman fake an assault on the Walnut Hills and sending Benjamin Grierson's cavalry brigade on a raid through central Mississippi, all the way to Baton Rouge, Louisiana. Then on March 29, after McClernand and McPherson reached Hard Times, Porter's gunboats attacked Grand Gulf, Mississippi, in hopes of securing a landing place on the east bank of the river. They silenced the Confederate batteries but failed to destroy them, whereupon Grant, who now personally directed the XIII and XVII Corps, sent both downriver to Deshroon's Landing, on the west bank from where the transports ferried them over to the undefended village of Bruinsburg. Grant wrote in his *Memoirs:*

> I felt a degree of relief scarcely equaled since. . . . I was now in the enemy's country, with a vast river and the stronghold of Vicksburg between me and my base of supplies. But I was on dry ground on the same side of the river with the enemy. All the campaigns, labors, hardships, and exposures from the month of December previous this time that had been made and endured were for the accomplishment of this one object.[17]

Wasting no time, Grant set out at once for Grand Gulf, his purpose to secure a better base of operations than tiny Bruinsburg. This he achieved on May 3, in the process driving off a Confederate division that Pemberton had sent to prevent him from so doing. Next, upon learning that it would be weeks before Banks attacked, much less took, Port Hudson, he decided to strike northeast from Grand Gulf toward the railroad between Vicksburg and Jackson, thereby forcing Pemberton's army to sally forth from Vicksburg to defend its sole supply link to the rest of the Confederacy, whereupon he would defeat and, if possible, destroy it, after which he could turn west to storm or else besiege Vicksburg, supposing it remained garrisoned. As to how his own army would feed itself so far from its base at Grand Gulf, that was simple: live off the land.

During the next nine days, Grant's soldiers scoured the countryside, collecting wagons, buggies, carriages, and the animals to pull them. Into these vehicles they piled the basic necessities—ammunition, hardtack, salt, and coffee—and formed them into a peculiar but highly mobile supply train. This done, on May 12 Grant, his strength up to 40,000 with the arrival of most of Sherman's XV Corps, set out for Edward's Station on the railroad between Vicksburg and Jackson.

Pemberton had close to 40,000 troops, quite enough to block or even defeat Grant. His problem was that he could not concentrate them into one fighting force. At least 8,000 had to be kept at Vicksburg to man its land and water batteries, and another 4,000 were stationed at Jackson to guard the two rail lines intersecting it and the facilities that went with them. Consequently, and because of other detachments deemed necessary, he managed to muster a field force of no more than 19,000 troops.

Help, though, was on the way—or so he thought. Determined to hold both Vicksburg and Port Hudson in order to preserve the sole remaining link, such as it was, between the eastern Confederacy (cis-Mississippi) and the western Confederacy (trans-Mississippi), Jefferson Davis had begun transferring troops from the Atlantic coast and other less-threatened areas to Mississippi and directed Joseph Johnston, whom in December he had placed in overall command between the Appalachians and the Mississippi, to take personal charge of these troops for the purpose of aiding Pemberton to hold Vicksburg.

Pemberton, who credited Johnston with far greater strength than he actually possessed, assumed that Grant of necessity was heading for the Yazoo River so as to establish a logistical link with the North and thus would expose his rear to a devastating attack by Johnston and himself. He assumed wrong. On May 12, while still on the way to Edward's Depot, Grant received word that McPherson had encountered a strong Rebel contingent at Raymond, a village to the southeast of that town. At once he decided to eliminate any threat from there and prevent reinforcements from reaching Pemberton. To this end, on May 13 he moved on Jackson with McPherson's and Sherman's corps while dispatching McClernand's corps to Bolton Depot to block any attempt by Pemberton to attack him in the rear.

On the evening of May 13, Johnston arrived by train in Jackson with only a couple thousand troops and was greeted with the not-so-cheerful news

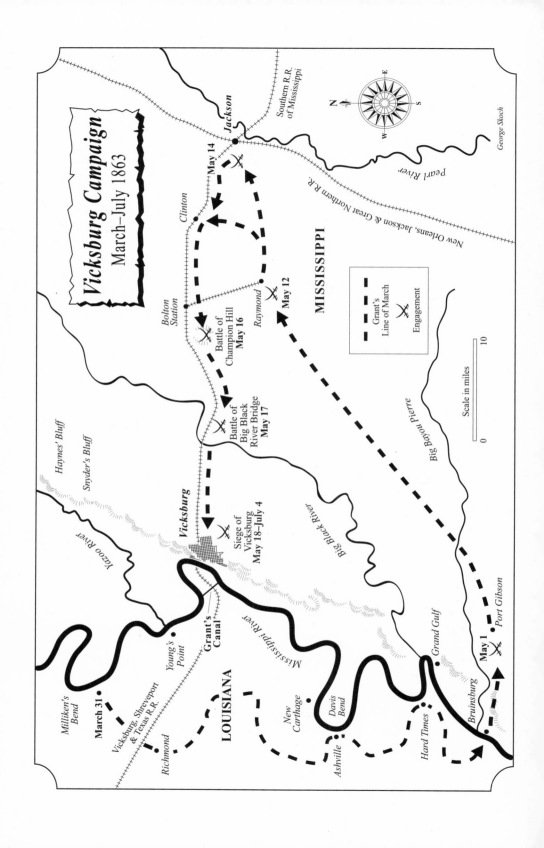

Vicksburg Campaign
March–July 1863

Grant's Line of March
Engagement

Scale in miles
0   10

MISSISSIPPI

Jackson
Southern R.R. of Mississippi
May 14
Clinton
Bolton Station
Battle of Champion Hill May 16
Raymond
May 12
New Orleans, Jackson & Great Northern R.R.
Pearl River
George Skoch

Battle of Big Black River Bridge May 17
Vicksburg
Siege of Vicksburg May 18–July 4
Haynes' Bluff
Snyder's Bluff
Yazoo River
Big Black River
Big Bayou Pierre

Grant's Canal
Young's Point
Vicksburg, Shreveport & Texas R.R.
Mississippi River
Milliken's Bend
March 31
Richmond
LOUISIANA
New Carthage
Ashville
Davis Bend
Hard Times
Grand Gulf
May 1
Port Gibson
Bruinsburg

that a large Federal force was at Clinton. He thereupon sent by courier an order to Pemberton, who was with his field army, to attack the enemy at Clinton. Grant, however, did not give Pemberton time to do this. Late on the morning of May 14, he had Sherman and McPherson assail Jackson. Johnston, hopelessly outnumbered, retreated after a short delaying action, seven miles north to Tugaloo. Grant refrained from pursuit. Having accomplished his purpose of keeping Pemberton and Johnston apart, his target now became Vicksburg. The next day he turned west with McPherson's corps while Sherman's men happily executed Grant's instructions to destroy Jackson "as a railroad center and manufacturing city of military supplies."

Meanwhile, Pemberton, responding to Johnston's order to attack the Federals at Clinton, marched toward that village with 17,500 troops (he left behind a brigade to guard the railroad bridge over the Big Black River). But before he got there he learned that an estimated five Federal divisions were at Raymond in position to do three things, none pleasing to contemplate: hit his little army on the right flank, cut it off from Vicksburg, or dash there and overwhelm the garrison. Hence, he conferred with his division commanders. They advised turning south to slice Grant's supply line, thereby forcing him to retreat back to Grand Gulf. He adopted this plan, which was theoretically sound. The flaw in it, of course, was that Grant had no supply line to cut.

This Pemberton had no opportunity to discover. During the night he received another message from Johnston, whom he had notified of his intention to sever Grant's communications. Johnston disapproved of this move and still wanted Pemberton to go to Clinton, where they would join forces, the Federals having gone from there. Pemberton therefore set out for that village, but before he went far his cavalry scouts reported that heavy enemy columns were approaching from the east and southeast. Quickly he began deploying his troops, which with the addition of a division from the Walnut Hills totaled about 23,000, along the crest of Champion Hill, a naturally strong position astride the road to Vicksburg, and waited for the Federals to attack.

They did so with a total strength of 29,000, consisting of McClernand's and McPherson's corps, both still under Grant's personal direction. Initially, the fighting favored the Federals, with Logan's division of the XVII Corps and Brigadier General Alvin Hovey's division of the XIII Corps overpowering the Confederate left and threatening to turn it. But then a counterattack by Major General John Bowen's Missouri-Arkansas division smashed one of Hovey's brigades and threatened to break through. Enfilade fire from sixteen of McClernand's cannons, however, halted Bowen, then a charge by a fresh XVII Corps division drove him back. Without reserves, Pemberton had no choice other than retreat.

In the battle, one of the truly decisive engagements of the Civil War, Grant's army suffered 2,500 casualties and Pemberton's nearly 4,000, plus the loss of Major General William Loring's division, which being unable to cross a creek in its rear, made its way to Johnston's force. More important, Grant now was firmly established between Pemberton and Johnston. As one of his soldiers wrote home that night, "Vicksburg must fall."

Pemberton continued retreating until he reached the Big Black River. Here, on its east bank and within a horseshoe bend of the river, he had previously prepared a strong, semicircular line of fortifications that covered a railroad bridge. He hoped to hold this line long enough for Loring, whom he did not know was on the way to join Johnston, to rejoin his army. For this purpose, he posted Bowen's division in the fortifications along with Brigadier General John C. Vaughn's brigade from Vicksburg's garrison. His only other division, which had been badly cut up at Champion Hill, took position on the west bank of the river.

Grant started in pursuit of Pemberton at dawn on May 17. A few hours later he came in sight of the Confederate works and found them so formidable that he decided to outflank them instead of attacking frontally. Hence, he instructed McClernand and McPherson to feint an assault and sent Sherman's corps, which had just come up, to cross the Big Black upriver at Bridgeport and move against the enemy's rear. However, before this maneuver could be executed, Brigadier General Michael Lawler's brigade of the XIII Corps surged forward on its own initiative in a real attack against the Confederate left. Vaughn's troops, evidently surprised by such aggressiveness, panicked and fled, creating a gap in Pemberton's defense line and causing Bowen's men to do the same. Most managed to escape across the river on the planked-over railroad bridge before Pemberton had it set afire, but they left behind 551 dead and wounded, along with 1,200 prisoners. Union casualties came to only 279, and the last obstacle between Grant and Vicksburg had been eliminated.

Pemberton retreated to Vicksburg's landward fortifications, in the process abandoning the now-useless works on Walnut Hills. Contrary to some critics, he did so not solely because President Davis had ordered him to hold the town until Johnston broke any siege, but also because he believed that it was too late to follow the course urged by Johnston in a message received on May 17: evacuate the place and march northeast to join him. An attempt to do this now, he correctly realized, almost surely would result in the destruction of his army and the loss of Vicksburg. On the other hand, if he defended Vicksburg long enough, Johnston would have time to gather sufficient strength to defeat or drive away Grant. Such, he felt confident, could be done. By withdrawing the forces stationed on Walnut Hills, he had almost 29,000 combat troops to put into the fourteen-mile-long semicircular chain of forts, bastions, and trenches that ringed Vicksburg's landside, and a stockpile of food to keep them fighting for at least a month and probably longer if sparingly rationed. His prime worry, following the disgraceful rout at the Big Black River bridge, was whether they would fight the way Southern soldiers normally fought.

He soon found out. Grant crossed the Big Black on the night of May 17 by means of an improvised bridge, invested Vicksburg the next day, and on the nineteenth attempted to storm it in the belief that the Confederates indeed were demoralized by their recent defeats. He was wrong, and Pemberton found that he had no cause to worry. Behind their log and dirt bulwarks and supported by 102 well-sited cannons, his troops stopped the Union assault cold, and with it 941 Yankees. Their own loss came to less than 200.

Two days later Grant tried again. His soldiers, he reasoned, would be unwilling to settle down to the long drudgery of a siege unless convinced that there was no quick way to take Vicksburg. What happened convinced them. With one exception, none of the attacking units so much as reached the Rebel earthworks, much less penetrated them, and casualties totaled 3,199, whereas Pemberton lost less than one-sixth that number.

Five of McClernand's regiments, all from Lawler's brigade, the one that broke through the Confederate line at Big Black River, provided the exception. They planted their flags on the parapet of the Rebel Railroad redoubt; some of them even entered it. McClernand thereupon notified Grant: "We have part possession of the Forts, and the stars and stripes are floating over them. A vigorous push ought to be made all along the line." Grant ignored the message. Not until receiving more pleas from McClernand, another of whose brigades had reached an enemy fort, did Grant order Sherman and McPherson to renew their attacks. They did so, but to no avail. Likewise, one of McPherson's divisions that Grant personally sent to bolster McClernand failed to accomplish anything, it being belatedly and poorly employed. Soon Confederate counterattacks repelled all of McClernand's storming parties, save those killed or captured. Total Federal losses came to 3,189; Confederate, to about 500.

Possibly the Union assaults would have succeeded, as McClernand then and afterward contended, had they been focused on a few objectives selected for their potential vulnerability and supported by strong reserve forces, which would have quickly followed up the initial foray with another. But, given the Civil War dominance of the defense over the offense, this is certainly uncertain. In any case, as has been noted, Grant conceived of the second attempt to storm Vicksburg as a prelude to a siege. (It will be recalled that he planned to take Fort Donelson by siege until a totally unexpected Confederate breakout attempt made it possible to capture it without one.)[18]

Besieging Vicksburg also gave Grant an opportunity to do what he long had desired to do once circumstances became propitious: get rid of McClernand and replace him with a professional soldier who could be counted on to be a subordinate, not a rival. To this end, on May 24 he telegraphed Halleck the following about the assault and the heavy losses incurred: "Gen. McClernand's dispatches misled me as to the real state of facts and caused much of the loss. He is entirely unfit for the position of Corps commander both on the march and on the battle field. Looking after his Corps gives me more labor, and infinitely more uneasiness, than all the remainder of my Dept."[19]

Grant already possessed the authority to relieve McClernand from his command thanks to a telegram sent to Stanton by Charles A. Dana, a New York newspaper editor whom Stanton had made his personal agent (a nice term for spy) when it came to providing him with confidential information about the conduct and character of army commanders in the West. Yet Grant decided, after considering the matter further, to postpone the removal of McClernand until Vicksburg fell, whereupon he would ask him to take a leave of absence. After all, McClernand had powerful political connections, including, for all Grant knew, the president, and while the siege was in progress it made little difference who headed the XIII Corps.[20]

Then, on the evening of June 16, Sherman read in a Memphis newspaper an order issued by McClernand to his troops in which he praised their performance during the second assault on Vicksburg and declared the reason it failed was because there had not been a "simultaneous and persistent attack all along our lines."[21] In the morning, Sherman sent the newspaper to Grant, along with a letter stating that the publication of such an order without first submitting it to Grant violated a War Department regulation. Grant, realizing that he now had a legal and not just a personal reason for relieving McClernand, immediately dispatched him a letter asking if the newspaper copy of his order was authentic. Aware that he faced dismissal, McClernand replied that it was, then added: "I regret that my adj. [adjutant] did not send you a copy [of the order] as he ought & I thought he had."

Grant, of course, did not accept this obviously dubious excuse. Upon reading it, he had Rawlins write an order relieving McClernand and replacing him with General E.O.C. Ord, who, having recovered from the wound he suffered back in October, had rejoined the Army of the Tennessee. Rawlins then gave the order to James H. Wilson, now a lieutenant colonel, to deliver to McClernand. Attired in his dress uniform and accompanied by an armed escort, Wilson went to McClernand's headquarters, where he arrived at 2 A.M. Informed of Wilson's presence, the significance of which he realized, McClernand donned his full uniform and then sat down at his desk, whereon he placed his sword. Wilson handed him Grant's order, at the same time saying that he had been instructed to see to it that it was read and understood. McClernand put on his spectacles, scanned the document, and then declared: "Well sir! I am relieved! By God sir, we are both relieved!"

The following day, McClernand headed back to Illinois. From there he wrote Lincoln, again protesting Grant's treatment of him, again to no avail. Lincoln was not going to take any action adverse to Grant, a commander standing on the verge of a great victory in the West, a victory badly needed by the North after suffering in the East two humiliating defeats and presently facing another Confederate invasion headed by the seemingly invincible Lee.

McClernand had some legitimate grievances. Contrary to Grant's claims, his XIII Corps performed well during the campaign that led to the siege of Vicksburg, especially in the decisive engagements at Champion Hill and Big Black River. Had he remained silent, content to be what he was, a corps commander, perhaps he could have remained so. Unfortunately for him, unrealistic ambition and the ways he sought to realize it made an enemy out of a man who too had ambition, an ambition that was becoming not at all unrealistic.

On July 4—a date perfect in its historic serendipity!—Pemberton surrendered Vicksburg and his army. He did so with ill-grace but had no other rational choice. His half-starved soldiers hovered on the brink of full-fledged starvation, the Federals had burrowed to within yards of his fortifications and even beneath them to stack explosives, and there could be no hope of rescue by Johnston, who had been able to muster only 25,000 troops, whereas reinforcements had increased Grant's strength to 75,000. This time, though, Grant made no demand for unconditional surrender. Instead, he paroled his 30,000-some prisoners, which meant that they were not to perform any military service until exchanged for a like number of Federals in Southern prisons, as provided for by an agreement between Washington and Richmond covering such matters. This, Grant telegraphed Halleck, "leaves troops and transports ready for immediate service."[22]

Obviously, Grant did not intend to rest on his laurels. He deserved those laurels. His Vicksburg Campaign is one of the most brilliant to be conducted by any commander, Northern or Southern, during the Civil War—indeed, perhaps *the* most brilliant, given the obstacles he overcame, his rapid marches, bold maneuvers, and the swift succession of victories he gained to cut Vicksburg off from the rest of the Confederacy and so doom it and its defenders to surrender, a surrender soon followed by the capitulation of Port Hudson's 5,000-man garrison as it realized that continued resistance against Banks's besieging force no longer served any purpose.

But if brilliant in its execution, how decisive was the Vicksburg Campaign in its results?[23] Less, far less, than customarily claimed by historians past, present, and probably future. Thus, although Lincoln famously said after Vicksburg's fall that "the father of waters now flows unvexed to the sea," not until after the war did commercial shipping on the Mississippi return to its prewar norm, it being too risky and unprofitable prior to then. Likewise, the Confederate loss of Vicksburg did not deprive the cis-Mississippi of troops, arms, and beef from the trans-Mississippi for the very good reason that virtually none of these things were coming from there before the loss. Also, while the taking of Vicksburg, coming as it did simultaneously with Meade's victory at Gettysburg, gave a great boost to Northern morale, little more than a year later (as shall be described) antiwar and propeace sentiment in the North became so strong that Lincoln feared McClellan might win the presidency on a Democratic platform, declaring the war unwinnable and calling for a suspension of hostilities as a means of inducing the South to return to the Union, with the matter of slavery to be settled afterward. And, last but not least, as shall be seen too, following the fall of Vicksburg, Grant soon found himself unable to undertake a new campaign, one aimed at the very strategic and economic heartland of the Confederacy, which, if successful, as it almost surely would have been, probably would have brought the war to a victorious conclusion for the North in 1863 or at the latest early 1864, barring an extremely unlikely epic victory by Lee leading to his seizing and holding Washington.

What truly proved most decisive about the Vicksburg Campaign was that it made the general who conceived and conducted it, Grant, manifestly the most successful Union commander. None other could come close to matching his record of victories either in number or importance. And since Meade had disappointed Lincoln by failing to destroy Lee's army, his sole potential rival in reaching the top rung of the military ladder was Rosecrans, to whom we shall return in the next chapter.

11

Rosecrans Takes Chattanooga
and Grant Takes a Fall

As January 1863 gave way to February, Rosecrans, whose forces now possessed an official name—The Army of the Cumberland—faced in Tennessee the same problem Grant confronted in Mississippi: how to get at the enemy.[1] Grant's eventual solution, we know, was to transport his troops by water to a place where they could move against Vicksburg on land while living off that land. In contrast, Rosecrans, to reach his prime target of Chattanooga, had to advance seventy-some miles through a region of hills, ridges, and mountains, most of it so barren that it barely supported its own sparse population, while overcoming a formidable foe whose strong fortifications could be approached only through long and narrow passes, and with his sole railroad supply line exposed to Confederate cavalry superior to his own both in quantity and quality.

So how to do it? His solution, when it came to preparation, was fourfold: (1) transforming Murfreesboro into an advance supply base, one fortified by a fortress bristling with cannons; (2) increasing his field army by reinforcements and the return to duty of wounded or sick soldiers until it substantially outnumbered Bragg's forces, although he did not realize this; (3) accumulating enough wagons and mules to haul them so as to provide two weeks of rations for his troops and sufficient ammunition to fight two major battles; and (4) developing a mounted arm capable of preventing the Confederate cavalry from destroying his wagon trains.

When winter gave way to spring, Rosecrans had achieved the first two objectives but not the third and fourth, despite an incessant flow of telegrams to the War Department pleading for more wagons, mules, horses, and cavalry, plus "revolving rifles"—a shoulder-arm version of the Colt revolver—with which to equip his troopers. Worse, from the standpoint of personal consequences, his persistence succeeded only in adversely affecting his relations with Stanton and Halleck. Thus a message to the former, wherein he made the mistake of referring to a year-old grievance, caused the secretary of war to renege on a promise to furnish him with the North's entire output of "revolving rifles." His repeated requests for better weapons for his cavalry eventually provoked Halleck into telling him that his "cavalry is as well armed as that of Grant and Curtis"—an assertion no doubt true but also irrelevant, in that Curtis in Missouri had to deal mainly with guerrillas armed with pistols and that Grant in Mississippi had almost no tactical need for cavalry, whereas Rosecrans faced 12,000 Confederate horsemen led by the likes of Forrest, Morgan, Wheeler, and—until he was killed by a woman's irate husband on May 7—Van Dorn.[2]

Disgusted but not discouraged by Stanton's and Halleck's rejection of his requests for better weapons for his cavalry, Rosecrans soon discovered a way to obtain them thanks to the enterprise of Colonel John T. Wilder, a well-to-do Indiana businessman turned soldier. Having with his 4,000-man infantry brigade easily repulsed a Rebel cavalry attack on Munfordsville, Kentucky, during Bragg's invasion of the Bluegrass State back in the summer of 1862, only to have to surrender on discovering that he was surrounded by Bragg's entire army, he had decided upon returning from a two-month captivity to transform his brigade into a mounted one. This he did, and while doing it he witnessed a demonstration of a new repeating rifle. Bearing the name of its inventor, Christopher Spencer, it fired seven .52 caliber bullets in rapid succession, then could be quickly reloaded by inserting a tube containing another seven cartridges through a slot in its stock. He immediately asked Rosecrans's permission to equip his brigade with it and immediately obtained it, whereupon he used his credit with a Hoosier bank to raise the money needed to purchase the requisite number. Few realized it at the time, but the battlefield dominance of the single-shot, muzzle-loading musket, even a rifled one, was in the process of becoming doomed.[3]

Halleck, on learning of the conversion of Wilder's brigade into mounted infantry, notified Rosecrans that it would make "neither good infantry nor good cavalry." Rosecrans ignored this platitude, it being obvious that Halleck did not realize that the rank and file of Forrest's and Morgan's divisions fought on foot, it being virtually impossible to reload and accurately aim the long-barreled rifles with which they were equipped while mounted on a frightened, rearing horse. But he reacted differently to a March 1 message from the general in chief. Prompted by Lincoln and Stanton, both desiring an offensive victory that would offset the depressing effect of the repulses at Fredericksburg and Vicksburg on Northern morale—Stones River, after all, was basically a defensive victory—Halleck sent identical letters on that date to Grant, Hooker, Rosecrans, and Major General Horatio Wright, commander of the Department of the Ohio, embracing Kentucky and the Midwest. They read: "There is a vacant major generalship in the Regular

Army and I am authorized to say that it will be given to the general in the field who first wins an important and decisive victory."[4]

Since Grant, Hooker, and Wright were unlikely to gain such a victory in the foreseeable future, the letter in fact was directed solely at Rosecrans. He realized this and resented it: "As an officer and a citizen," he answered Halleck on March 5, "I feel degraded to see such auctioneering of honor. Have we a general who would fight for his own personal benefit, when he would not for honor and the country? He would come by his commission basely in that case and deserve to be despised."[5]

Rosecrans should have refrained from replying so bluntly to Halleck and through him to Stanton and Lincoln. All it did was strengthen their perception of him as unwilling to engage Bragg in spite of three months having passed since Stones River. But he was temperamentally incapable of not responding to what he deemed to be false or insulting allegations. Ultimately, as shall be seen, this would prove unfortunate for him.

March and April passed with the Army of the Cumberland still at Murfreesboro. By April it fielded 68,000 combat and combat-support troops organized into Thomas's XIV Corps, McCook's XX Corps, Crittenden's XXI Corps, a Reserve Corps headed by Major General Gordon Granger, two cavalry divisions under Stanley, and a Pioneer Brigade and an army regiment, neither of which existed in any other Union army.[6] Halleck, aware of Rosecrans's strength, which was exceeded among Federal forces only by the Army of the Potomac, thereupon began demanding, not merely urging, Rosecrans to move against Bragg. In so doing he again spoke for Lincoln, who on May 28 telegraphed Rosecrans the following: "I would not press you to any rashness, but I am very anxious that you do your most, short of rashness to keep Bragg from getting off to help Johnston against Grant."[7] With Hooker's recent fiasco at Chancellorsville, Lincoln believed a defeat of Grant in Mississippi would be a calamity, not only militarily but also politically, in that it would bolster the antiwar Democrats, now known as Copperheads, but also prevent the liberation of East Tennessee from Rebel domination.

"Dispatch received," replied Rosecrans. "I shall attend to it."[8] But his army remained motionless. The best way, in his opinion, to forestall Bragg from reinforcing Johnston was to threaten him with an attack while not making one, for if he did attack him and was repulsed, then Bragg would be free to join Johnston. Furthermore, he still thought, mistakenly, that Bragg outnumbered him, whereas in actuality the Army of the Tennessee totaled only 42,000, with Morgan having gone off on what turned out to be a disastrous raid into Indiana and Ohio and most of Van Dorn's erstwhile division sent from Middle Tennessee to bolster Johnston.[9]

Five days passed, whereupon Halleck, again on Lincoln's instruction, wired Rosecrans: "Accounts received here indicate that Johnston is very heavily reinforced by Bragg's army. If you cannot hurt the enemy now, he will hurt you soon."[10] Then, without waiting for Rosecrans to respond to this rather cryptic warning, Halleck ordered the sending of tens of thousands of troops to Vicksburg from Missouri, West Tennessee, and the Department of the Ohio, now headed by Burnside. As a result, by mid-June Grant had at his disposal 75,000 men, more than enough to keep Pemberton inside Vicksburg and to fend off any attempt by Johnston to rescue him from the outside.

It was a rescue attempt that Johnston did not intend to make in any case. His forces numbered only 24,000, including 5,200 from Bragg, and since most of them had come to Mississippi by rail, they lacked sufficient transport, provisions, and ammunition to traverse the thirty miles of devastated land separating them from the Big Black River, where on its west bank Sherman with 25,000 men had been posted to prevent them from crossing. All that Johnston could do, so it turned out, was send Pemberton a message on July 3 informing him that "I hope to attack the enemy in your front about the 7th" by way of a "diversion," and calling on him to "cut your way out, if the time has come for you to do this." The message reached Pemberton after he surrendered.[11]

Rosecrans, for his part, realized that unless he took action soon against Bragg, he too might be stripped of troops to provide still more for Grant, a possibility that turned into a probability on the receipt of a June 2 telegram from Halleck stating, "If you can do nothing yourself, a portion of your troops must be sent to Grant." Hence, after fending off Halleck by wiring him that "the time appears now nearly ripe" to begin "a movement, which, with God's blessing, will give us some good results."[12] Then, on the night of June 8, he met with his seventeen corps and division commanders and handed to each a document containing five questions, with the key one being the fourth: "Do you think an immediate advance advisable?" All of them answered no. This, they in essence declared, would produce a defeat which would lead to Bragg joining Johnston to attack Grant. "General," counseled Crittenden, "you should not move with less than 100,000 infantry and at least 6,000 to 10,000 cavalry. Mr. Stanton is either crazy or bent upon the destruction of this army." McCook concurred with regard to the number of soldiers required, as did Thomas, but differed as to Stanton: "He is a natural born fool." Rosecrans, despite his deep dislike of the secretary of war, rejected Crittenden's and McCook's opinions of Stanton. "He is neither a knave nor a fool, but he fears that the [Lincoln] administration will go to pieces without victories, and he is so impatient for them that he doesn't stop to consider how they are won."[13]

Having obtained from his generals what he wanted and, no doubt, expected, on June 11 Rosecrans telegraphed Halleck a tally of their answers to his questions, then he added: "No one thinks an advance advisable until Vicksburg's fate is determined. . . . I therefore counsel caution and patience at headquarters [in Washington]. Better wait a little to get all we can ready to insure the best results, if by doing so we . . . observe a great military maxim, not to risk two great and decisive battles at the same time."[14]

Halleck answered the following day: "I do not understand your application of the military maxim 'not to fight two great battles at the same time': it will apply to a single army, but not to armies acting independently of each other." Moreover, he continued, "there is another military maxim, that 'councils of war never fight.'" He concluded, though, by stating that if Rosecrans was "not prepared to fight Bragg, I shall not order you to do so, for the responsibility of fighting or refusing to fight must rest upon the general in immediate command." Halleck also warned Rosecrans that the "prolonged inactivity" of his army "is causing much complaint and dissatisfaction, not only in Washington, but throughout the country."[15]

Thus, Halleck adhered to his policy of allowing field commanders to decide when, where, and how to engage the enemy, and he was quite correct in warning Rosecrans of the mounting pressure from Washington (i.e., Lincoln and Stanton) and from "throughout the country" (i.e., the Republicans) for him to give battle to Bragg. What is puzzling, given his great knowledge of military lore, is his assertion that the maxim not to fight two battles at the same time has to do with one army doing so, whereas it is obvious that Rosecrans was referring to his and Grant's armies. Perhaps it was a consequence of his being preoccupied with Lee's impending northward thrust and getting rid of Hooker before it occurred, or possibly he had ingested a little too much opium to treat his hemorrhoids. In any case, it also puzzled Rosecrans, which may explain why he waited until June 21, an unusually long time for him, before sending a reply to Halleck. In it, after dryly commenting that for a single army to "fight two great battles simultaneously would be, by the way, a very awkward thing to do," he promised to attack Bragg "if we have a strong prospect of winning a decisive battle . . . and upon the ground I shall select."[16] In other words, he remained determined to fight Bragg at a time and place of his own choosing, no matter how much pressure Washington put on him.

Lincoln and Halleck were not the only ones pressing Rosecrans to engage Bragg and soon. Another was Brigadier General James Garfield, who in January had replaced Garesché as Rosecrans's chief of staff. Only thirty-one, tall, and impressively handsome, Garfield, thanks to a sharp mind fueled by keen ambition, had risen from the depths of poverty to secure a college degree, become headmaster of a private school (today's Hiram College), gain a seat in the Ohio senate, take the lead in recruiting a regiment after the outbreak of war, become its colonel, command a brigade that defeated a Confederate force in eastern Kentucky, and then secure promotion to brigadier general and assignment to the Army of the Cumberland, where Rosecrans, finding him personally and intellectually congenial, soon named him his chief of staff.[17]

But now he wanted political power and stood on the verge of achieving it, having been elected as a Republican in the fall of 1862 to the U.S. House of Representatives. Should the Army of the Cumberland with him as its chief of staff prevail over Bragg and capture Chattanooga, thus securing Union control of Tennessee, his prestige would be enhanced in the House once he took his seat there, which would be in December 1863.

This concern possibly explains, at least in part, why Garfield asked Rosecrans's permission to respond to the five-question circular and also why he alone among all of the Army of the Cumberland's generals urged an immediate move against Bragg. In a memorandum dated June 12, 1863, and occupying nearly four pages of the *Official Records,* he first presented strictly military reasons for so doing, with the main one in essence being that whether or not Grant took Vicksburg, "Johnston will send back to Bragg a force sufficient to insure the safety of Tennessee [Chattanooga]" for the Confederates. Next he contended that "a sudden and rapid movement would compel a general engagement, and the defeat of Bragg would be in the highest degree disastrous to the rebellion" while delivering, given the "turbulent aspect of politics in the loyal states," a "decisive blow against the enemy at this time of the highest importance in the success of the Government [Republicans] at the polls." And last, but not necessarily least, he in effect warned Rosecrans that unless he took advantage now of Bragg's present reduced strength brought on by reinforcing Johnston, he would soon be relieved of command because the "Government and the War Department believe that this army ought to move against the enemy; the army desires it; and the country is anxiously looking for it."[18]

Garfield's ponderous memorandum angered Rosecrans, who considered it to be a breach of friendship. It also offended him professionally, and with good reason. The duty of a chief of staff was not to propose operational plans to his commander; rather, it was to assist him in implementing those plans, plans conceived by him. As for being relieved from command, Rosecrans, of course, knew full well that he stood in danger of this happening—but he remained resolved to do what he regarded to be the right thing militarily, regardless of the potential personal cost.[19] Besides, who could replace him? Buell? Burnside? McClellan? Grant? In the case of the last, not now, certainly!

Just two days after receiving Garfield's unwelcome advice there came to Rosecrans yet another telegram from Halleck. It read: "Is it your intention to make an immediate movement forward? A definite answer, yes or no, is required."[20] This time, Rosecrans realized, he truly was on the brink of being relieved. But he also was almost ready to advance on Bragg, something he already had decided to do once it became evident that Grant would take Vicksburg in at most three weeks, which surely Johnston could not prevent given Grant's strong reinforcements. Hence he wired Halleck: "If immediate means tonight or tomorrow, no. If it means as soon as all things are ready, say five days, yes."[21]

Twice five days passed before Rosecrans ordered an advance. Then, over the ensuing dozen days, he conducted a superb campaign of maneuver based on cunning, deception, and daring. First he forced Bragg's army to fall back to its advance base at Tullahoma by faking an attack on its left wing at Shelbyville while delivering its main thrust against its right wing at Wartrace by way of Hoover Gap, where Wilder's brigade penetrated the long, narrow gap and then repulsed a Confederate counterattack owing to its Spencer firepower, a feat that gained it the name of the Lightning Brigade. Only constant rain, which turned the dirt roads into mud, then slime, and finally into a close cousin to quicksand, prevented him from gaining Bragg's rear. As it was, Bragg barely escaped across the Elk River to Chattanooga, in the process burning the bridge that spanned it and so escaping further pursuit. Union causalities came to a mere 570, while the Confederates lost nearly 2,000, the majority of them prisoners, many of whom, being East Tennessee Unionists, surrendered voluntarily.[22]

Did Lincoln or Stanton or Halleck congratulate Rosecrans on his near-bloodless success, one that drove Bragg's army from Middle Tennessee and opened the way for Burnside to invade East Tennessee? No. Grant's capture of Vicksburg, along with Meade's victory at Gettysburg, eclipsed in Washington the flight of Bragg's still intact army back to Chattanooga. With "Lee's army overthrown" and "Grant victorious," Stanton telegraphed Rosecrans on July 7, "you and your noble army now have the chance to give the finishing blow to the rebellion. Will you neglect the chance?"[23]

Stung by Stanton's hectoring tone, Rosecrans answered sarcastically: "Just received your cheering dispatch announcing the fall of Vicksburg and confirming the defeat of Lee. You do not appear to observe the fact that this noble army has driven the rebels from Middle Tennessee. . . . I beg in behalf of this army that the War Department may not overlook so great an event because it is not written in letters of blood."[24]

Rosecrans's reply is understandable. Yet it would have been better for him and his army had he made none at all. He should have realized that deeds speak more persuasively than words. Not until he occupied Chattanooga and decisively defeated Bragg would he have gained a victory that, while it would not equal Vicksburg and Gettysburg in its political impact on the North, could surpass them in its potential strategic effect.

Throughout the reminder of July and on into August, Rosecrans labored to ready the Army of the Cumberland for another and longer bound southward, one that would take it to Chattanooga and beyond. All the while, Halleck, expressing the desires of Lincoln as conveyed to him either directly or through Stanton, continued to urge Rosecrans to advance immediately while warning him that unless he did so Johnston would join Bragg to crush him. Actually, though, there was no danger of this occurring. The day before Pemberton's surrender, Grant ordered Sherman to reoccupy and complete the destruction of Jackson. This he soon did, in the process driving Johnston further eastward into Mississippi. There Johnston was perfectly content to stay, being totally without desire to join forces with Bragg, for if he did so, then he also would become field commander of the Army of the Tennessee, a responsibility he preferred to avoid. Of course, Lincoln did not know this; but also, of course, the real reason why Rosecrans again was being badgered to move at once against Bragg lay in Lincoln's obsession with liberating East Tennessee and then bringing all of the Volunteer State back into the Union.[25]

Matters came to a head, or seemed to, when at noon on August 4 Halleck telegraphed Rosecrans: "Your forces must move forward without further delay. You will daily report the movement of each corps till you cross the Tennessee River."[26] Five hours later Rosecrans replied that he had been "making all preparations, and getting such information as may enable me to do so without being driven back, like Hooker" at Chancellorsville, then added, "I wish to know if your order is intended to take away my discretion as to the time and manner of moving my troops."[27]

The following day Halleck answered: "The order for the advance of your army, and that its movements be reported daily, is preemptory."[28] Rosecrans thereupon played what he, no doubt, already had conceived to be his

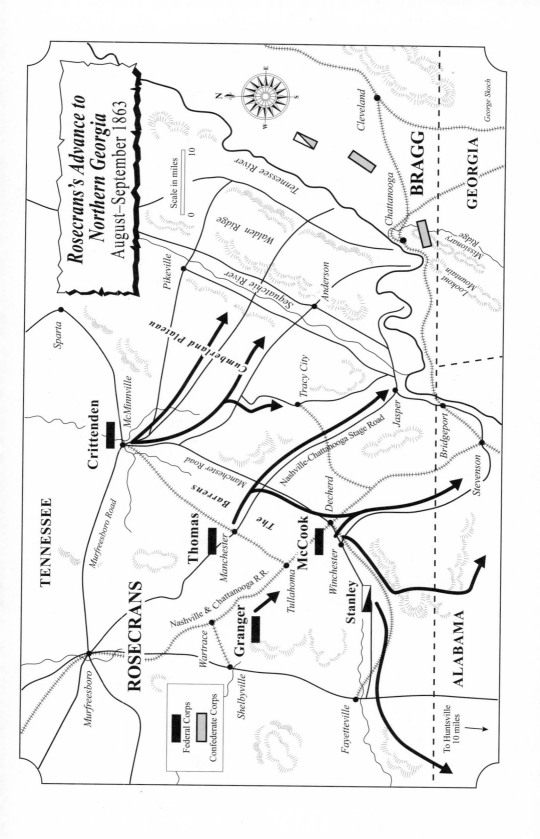

Rosecrans's Advance to
Northern Georgia
August–September 1863

Scale in miles

Federal Corps
Confederate Corps

TENNESSEE

GEORGIA

ALABAMA

ROSECRANS

BRAGG

Murfreesboro

Sparta

McMinnville

Crittenden

Thomas

Granger

McCook

Stanley

Nashville & Chattanooga R.R.

Wartrace

Shelbyville

Manchester

Tullahoma

Winchester

Fayetteville

Decherd

Pikeville

Tracy City

Anderson

Jasper

Bridgeport

Stevenson

Chattanooga

Cleveland

Cumberland Plateau

Walden Ridge

Sequatchie River

Tennessee River

Lookout Mountain

Missionary Ridge

Murfreesboro Road

Manchester Road

The Barrens

Nashville-Chattanooga Stage Road

To Huntsville
10 miles

George Skoch

ace in the hole. Summoning Thomas, Crittenden, McCook, and Stanley to his headquarters, he read to them Halleck's order, adding that it originated with Stanton. Then he read his reply to the order. In it he stated that "arrangements for beginning a continuous movement" on Chattanooga "will be completed and execution begun by Monday next [August 10]." But, he concluded, "to obey your order literally would be to push our troops at once into the mountains on narrow and difficult roads, destitute of pasture and forage, and short of water, where they would not be able to maneuver as exigencies may demand, and would certainly cause ultimate delay and probably disaster. If, therefore, the movement which I propose cannot be regarded as obedience to your order, I respectfully request a modification of it, or to be relieved from the command."[29]

Rosecrans's ploy succeeded. Faced with a choice between relieving him or allowing him to conduct a campaign which could lead to the capture of Chattanooga, the restoration of Tennessee to the Union, and possibly the destruction of Bragg's army and the opening of Georgia and Alabama to Federal invasion, what else could Lincoln do other than retain him in command? Besides, the only other general of sufficient rank, experience, and ability readily available to replace him was Thomas, who had turned down command of the same army when offered it before and who was known to be on friendly terms with Rosecrans. Indeed, had Thomas been offered the command, he would have rejected it, for along with Crittenden, McCook, and Stanley he supported Rosecrans's response to Halleck's declaration that the War Department's orders were "preemptory." "That's right!" he exclaimed after Rosecrans read it. "Stick by that and we will stand by you to the last!"[30]

Another general who listened to Rosecrans read his reply to Halleck reacted quite differently. He, of course, was Garfield, who as before was present and as before disagreed with the commander he served. This time, however, he did not make his disagreement known to Rosecrans. Instead, on July 27 he penned a letter to Secretary of the Treasury Salmon P. Chase, the top Ohio Republican and one of the most influential members of Lincoln's cabinet:

> I cannot conceal from you the fact that I have been greatly tried and dissatisfied with the slow progress we have made in the department [of the Cumberland] since the battle of Stones River. . . . The army has grown anxious with the exception of its leading generals, who seem blind to the advantages of the hour. . . . I was the only one who urged upon the general [Rosecrans] the imperative necessity of striking a blow at once.

. . . My personal relations with General Rosecrans are all I could desire
. . . but I beg you to know that this delay is against my judgment and
every wish. . . . If this inaction continues long I shall ask to be relieved
and sent somewhere where I can be part of a working army.[31]

A chief of staff, to put it mildly, should not write such a letter to anyone,
much less to an influential member of the president's cabinet. By doing it,
Garfield betrayed the commander he was duty-bound to serve. As a professional politician, he in effect claimed to possess a strategic wisdom superior
to such professional soldiers as Thomas and Rosecrans. He did not. And his
assertion that if the Army of the Cumberland continued to be inactive then
he would ask to be relieved so that he could be with a "working army" was
nonsensical given that in a few more months he would have to resign from
the army in order to take his seat in the House of Representatives.

Early on the morning of August 16, Rosecrans launched his new offensive. This time he had Crittenden's corps fake a turning movement around
Bragg's right while using Thomas's and McCook's corps to turn the left
by crossing the Tennessee River to the southwest of Chattanooga, in the
process entering Georgia and Alabama. Realizing that he again had been
outmaneuvered and fearful of having his rail connection to Atlanta severed, Bragg then attempted to cut Rosecrans's supply line only to fail for
the very good reason that Rosecrans had none. Meanwhile, Crittenden,
with Wilder's Lightning Brigade again providing the spearhead, occupied
Chattanooga on September 9, Bragg having evacuated it and retreated into
Georgia in order to avoid being trapped there the same way Pemberton was
trapped in Vicksburg.

Thus, in little more than three weeks, with little fighting and few casualties, Rosecrans conducted one of the most brilliant military operations of
the Civil War both in conception and execution, an operation that, unlike
Grant's Vicksburg campaign, took place in a region where for the most part
it was impossible for a large army to live off the land. All he now needed
to do, he believed, was what he already had determined to do: continue his
offensive with a view to smashing Bragg's army and going on to Atlanta, the
seizure of which would open the way for a strike toward the Atlantic. Should
that succeed, the Confederacy would be reduced in economic and strategic
essence to Virginia and the Carolinas. And he, Rosecrans, would become
the North's premier general. Or so he desired, perhaps even expected.

On September 9, the day Rosecrans's troops began marching into Chattanooga, Grant lay flat on his back in a New Orleans hotel room.[32]

To explain how he became thus recumbent, it is necessary to go back to July 3. On that day he instructed Sherman, who was guarding against the nonexistent threat of an attack by Johnston, to "drive Johnston from the Mississippi Rail Road . . . and do the enemy all the harm possible."[33] This, as noted earlier, Sherman did, employing for the purpose of his XV Corps, Ord's XIII Corps, and two divisions from Burnside's IX Corps, the last being the reinforcement ordered by Halleck in May from Burnside's Department of the Ohio. Outnumbering Johnston more than two to one, he forced him to evacuate Jackson on July 16, then on July 17 he began destroying most of the town along with the railroads bisecting it.[34]

The very next day Grant received the appointment to major general in the regular army Halleck had offered back in March to the department commander in the West who first gained a decisive victory. This meant that he now possessed the highest permanent rank of any active field commander in the Union army. And soon after he also received, for the first time ever, a personal letter from Lincoln. Dated July 13, it read:

My Dear General

    I do not remember that you and I ever met personally. I write this now as a grateful acknowledgement for the almost inestimable service you have done the country. I wish to say a word further. When you first reached the vicinity of Vicksburg, I thought you should do what you finally did—march the troops across the neck, run the batteries with the transports, and thus go below; and I never had any faith except a general hope that you knew better than I, that the Yazoo Pass expedition and the like could succeed. When you got below and took Port Gibson, Grand Gulf, and vicinity, I thought you should go down the river and join General Banks; and when you turned northward east of the Big Black, I feared it was a mistake. I now wish to make the personal acknowledgment that you were right and I was wrong.[35]

This oft-quoted letter usually, if not always, is presented as if it contained nothing but unstinted praise of Grant's conduct of the Vicksburg Campaign. It did not. After expressing his "grateful acknowledgment" for Grant's capture of Vicksburg, most of it is devoted to pointing out things that Grant did that Lincoln thought, correctly, he should not have done because they would not succeed. Only in the last two sentences does Lincoln state that in not joining Banks and by moving northward when east of the Big Black was Grant "right" and he, the president, "wrong."

Perhaps this explains why Grant did not thank Lincoln for his letter. In any case, he had other matters on his mind. Following the fall of Vicksburg and subsequent surrender of Port Hudson, he assumed that his troops needed a long period of rest and recuperation, all the more so when Sherman's contingent returned with many of its rank and file suffering from exhaustion and/or sunstroke. But soon most of them recovered, even became reinvigorated. Realizing this, he conceived a new campaign, one in which most of his army would be transported by boats to New Orleans, from where it would move by way of Pascagoula on the Gulf Coast to Mobile, capture it, and then proceed along the Alabama River to Selma, next over to Montgomery, and finally to Atlanta, the taking of which, with its factories and rail connections, would reduce the Confederacy from a strategic and economic standpoint to Virginia and the Carolinas.

Unfortunately, launching such a strike from New Orleans posed a jurisdictional problem: Louisiana lay in Banks's Department of the Gulf. But a July 18 message from Banks seemed to dispose of it: "It is my belief that Johnston, when defeated by you, as I am confident he will be, will fall back upon Mobile. . . . The capture of Mobile is of importance second only in the history of the war to the opening of the Mississippi. I hope you will be able to follow him. I can aid you somewhat by land and sea, if that shall be your destination."[36]

All that Grant now needed to launch an expedition to Mobile and beyond was Lincoln's approval by way of Halleck. He did not obtain it. Responding to a message from him to go after Mobile, transmitted the same day Banks sent his positive message, Halleck on July 22 wired Grant: "Before attempting Mobile I think it will be best to clean-up a little. Johnston should be disposed of; also Price [now operating in Arkansas]. . . . This will enable us to withdraw troops from Missouri, Vicksburg, and Port Hudson . . . [and] also assist General Banks in cleaning out Western Louisiana. When these things are accomplished there will be a large available force to operate either on Mobile or Texas."[37]

Halleck concluded this de facto rejection of Grant's proposed Mobile operation by stating that the "navy is not ready for co-operation" in conducting it, and that it would not be until Fort Sumter, which had been under Federal siege since spring, fell, whereupon "iron-clads can be sent to assist at Mobile."

Upon receiving this five days later—still no direct telegraphic connection existed between Washington and Vicksburg—Grant felt disappointed but did not despair; this he never did. Then, on August 1, Banks paid him a hasty visit, immediately following which he wrote another dispatch to be wired from Memphis to Halleck: "Mobile can be taken from the Gulf Department, with only one or two gunboats to protect the debarkation [of troops]. I can send the necessary force. With your leave, I would like to visit New Orleans, particularly if the movement against Mobile is authorized."[38] Some days later came Halleck's response, transmitted on August 6, to Grant's proposal: "There is no objection to you visiting New Orleans. The orders through you to General Banks will indicate what operation next is to be undertaken."[39] The order, dated August 8, sent via Grant to Banks and signed by Halleck, read: "There are important reasons why our flag should be restored in some part of Texas with the least possible delay."[40]

Why this was so Grant probably did not learn until at least a week later in a letter from Lincoln dated August 9: "I see by a dispatch of yours that you incline quite strongly toward an expedition against Mobile. This would appear tempting to me also, were it not that, in view of recent events in Mexico, I am greatly impressed with the importance of re-establishing the national authority in Western Texas as soon as possible. I am not making an order, however; that I leave, for the present at least, to the General-in-Chief."[41]

The final sentence of this letter is, of course, absurd, being merely another example of Lincoln's pretense that Halleck, not he, set the objectives for Union armies. Otherwise, though, the letter explains why Lincoln wanted to raise the Stars and Stripes in Texas. Taking advantage of the American Civil War, Napoleon III of France had transported an army to Mexico with the object of establishing there a puppet government, and Lincoln sought to counter this violation of the Monroe Doctrine by placing U.S. forces in Texas, a move designed to send a warning to "Napoleon Le Petit" while avoiding an armed clash with France—avoid it, that is, until the Union had been restored and America would be free to employ its now formidable military might, both on sea and land, against France.

Restoring the Union, of course, was Lincoln's fundamental objective in waging the Civil War. This explains, as has been noted, his taking advantage of McClellan's ostensible victory in western Virginia to convert that region into the state of West Virginia. It motivated his obsession with liberating Unionist East Tennessee. It was the reason why he endeavored to have his top political generals, Benjamin Butler and Banks, establish a state government in Louisiana in spite of the vast majority of its inhabitants being strongly pro-Confederate. It also led to General Frederick Steele occupying Little Rock on September 10, 1863, as a first but necessary step toward bringing Arkansas back into the Union. And, along with sending a warning message to Napoleon III, he believed that landing Federal troops in Texas would cause that state to return voluntarily to its pre-1861 allegiance.

Grant, after reading Lincoln's letter, abandoned all notion, for the foreseeable future, of advancing by way of Mobile, Selma, and Montgomery to take Atlanta and instead set out to board a steamer for New Orleans, where he arrived on September 2, to confer with Banks. Two days later, after a luncheon banquet at a plantation near the city and accompanied by Banks and a number of other officers, he rode back to his hotel astride a large, temperamental horse, one that only a superb horseman such as he could manage, which so far he had done masterfully. But as he approached a railroad, far ahead of the other members of his party, a locomotive came steaming around a bend, sounding its whistle. The horse reared up then toppled over on its left side, Grant still in the saddle, and crashed onto the cobblestoned street, knocking Grant unconscious.[42]

At first everyone thought he was dead. However, when the horse was pulled off him, he regained consciousness, whereupon he was taken to his room at the St. Charles Hotel. There he lay flat on his back, his left side and leg badly swollen, suffering pain, he wrote in his *Memoirs,* "almost beyond endurance."[43] After a day or two, though, the pain disappeared, and while he remained bedfast he could chat with his many visitors.

He continued to lie in bed for nearly two weeks before traveling by steamboat back to Vicksburg, where, along with wife Julia and his youngest son, he stayed in a mansion but still could not stand, much less walk, unaided. No doubt, he kept track of Rosecrans's operations by way of newspapers. As he perused them did he wonder if it would be this once highly regarded, now loathed, general who, after taking Chattanooga, would go on to Atlanta, thus doing what he had hoped to do—penetrate the Southern heartland? In any case, this is certain: On September 22 he received via Hurlbut in Memphis a telegraphed order, dated September 15, from Halleck stating that "all the troops that can possibly be spared in west Tennessee and on the Mississippi river should be sent without delay to assist Gen. Rosecrans on the Tennessee River."[44] Why this order came to Grant when it did and with what consequences will be described in the next chapter.

12

Rosecrans and Thomas at Chickamauga

The Fortunes and Misfortunes of War

FOLLOWING BRAGG'S EVACUATION OF CHATTANOOGA and its occupation on September 9 first by Wilder's Lightning Brigade and then by one of Crittenden's divisions, Rosecrans had two options.[1] One was to regroup his army there, rest and resupply it, and then resume advancing, presumably in conjunction with Burnside, a portion of whose forces entered Knoxville on September 2. The other was to continue his southward thrust with the twin goals of smashing Bragg's army and taking Atlanta.

He chose the second. Why? Perhaps he wished to avoid being yet again badgered from Washington to pursue Bragg regardless of logistical factors. Or maybe he thought that Bragg's troops, in particular the Tennesseans, were so demoralized by their repeated retreats and now by the virtual evacuation of the entire Volunteer State that they would be easy prey. In any case, having received what he deemed to be reliable reports that Bragg was withdrawing by way of Resaca and Dalton, both on the Atlantic & Western Railroad, with the intention of concentrating at Rome in northwest Georgia, where he would be in position to strike him in the rear should he advance on Atlanta, he decided to do to Bragg what Bragg evidently intended to do to him.

Hence, at 10 A.M. on September 9, he had Garfield pen this order to Thomas, whose four-division XIV Corps constituted the Union center: "The general commanding directs you to move your command as rapidly as possible to LaFayette and make every exertion to strike the enemy in flank, and, if possible, cut off his line of escape."[2]

Thomas, although he favored a halt at Chattanooga, promptly endeavored to conduct this operation, employing for the purpose his lead division, commanded by Major General James Negley. Almost as promptly, Negley found himself, as he marched along the road leading to LaFayette, confronted by Dug Gap, a long, narrow gorge through Pigeon Mountain, five miles northwest of the town. Not only was the gap blocked by all sorts of obstructions, but also, according to a captured Confederate officer and local civilians, a strong Rebel force, perhaps three infantry divisions, defended it and other passages through the mountain. At once, Thomas, who accompanied Negley, instructed him to assume a defensive posture; then he sent a dispatch to Rosecrans informing him of the situation, stating: "I hope to drive the enemy beyond Pigeon Ridge [Mountain] by tomorrow night."[3]

Since in the meantime Rosecrans had established his headquarters in Chattanooga, the courier carrying this message did not deliver it to him until after midnight. Still confident that Bragg was on the run, he refused to credit Thomas's report. "Your advance," he had an aide-de-camp write Thomas, "ought to have threatened LaFayette yesterday evening"—an indirect, yet curt, way of telling the big Virginian that he was being spooked by a nonexistent enemy threat.[4]

Even as this complaint made its way to Thomas, the Confederates provided more-than-ample proof that it was unjustified. First, Cleburne's division, which defended Dug Gap, cleared away the obstructions. Then it attacked so fiercely that Thomas reinforced Negley with some of Major General Absalom Baird's division and at 4 A.M. on September 12 wrote Rosecrans that, in spite of this, Negley was obliged to fall back, adding: "All information goes to confirm that a large part of Bragg's army is opposed to Negley."[5]

This report, plus other indications, convinced Rosecrans that the Confederate Army of Tennessee, far from being weak, demoralized, and on the run, was strong, aggressive, and on the attack. And this, in fact, was the case. By the second week of September, Bragg had been reinforced by 8,000 men withdrawn from Knoxville, 9,000 more sent from Mississippi by Johnston, and unknown but probably large numbers of paroled prisoners from Vicksburg. Furthermore, on the way from Virginia by rail through the Carolinas into Georgia were two divisions of the Army of Northern Virginia, led by John Bell Hood and LaFayette McLaws, headed by Longstreet and totaling close to 12,000. Once they arrived, Bragg would have 71,000 troops with which to engage Rosecrans's 58,000, who were presently spread out across thirty-some miles of mostly mountainous terrain with few roads, none of them good.

In sum, instead of the hunter, Rosecrans had now become the hunted, with his army exposed to being cut off from its base, which basically remained in Nashville, and destroyed piecemeal. Indeed, had one of Bragg's division commanders, Major General Thomas Hindman, obeyed his orders, Thomas's corps already would have been assailed by superior Confederate forces front, flanks, and rear, thus almost surely destroyed.

Rosecrans, who knew that Bragg had been reinforced by Simon B. Buckner and had received "intimations" that troops from Johnston and Lee were on the way to Georgia, finally realized his danger on September 13, and so began concentrating his army while calling on Halleck for reinforcements, in particular from Burnside. Halleck at once responded by telegraphing both Burnside and Grant to go to Rosecrans's assistance. But it availed naught. Burnside, who, of course, was much nearer, lacked both the will and the means to go to Rosecrans's assistance.[6] On the other hand, the message to Grant, which called on him to send all of his available forces to "cooperate with Rosecrans and Burnside," did not reach him at Vicksburg until nearly two weeks after it was transmitted, in spite of it having been placed in a package labeled "Important dispatches, to be delivered immediately," because the steamer that picked it up at Cairo did not deliver it to Vicksburg until September 25.[7] Yet even had it reached Grant on September 16, the earliest date possible, this would have made no practical difference.

The reason is that Rosecrans, having succeeded in uniting his three corps, stood ready on September 18 to give battle to Bragg along the west bank of the west branch of Chickamauga Creek, which supposedly derived its name from an Indian word meaning "River of Death," a sobriquet it earned on September 19, when at dawn Confederate attackers splashed across its various fords, determined to crush their blue-uniformed foes. The fight soon became ferocious, with each side gaining and losing, suffering and inflicting heavy casualties. On the whole the Army of the Cumberland held its position, but after nightfall it adjusted its line, one screened by a dense forest wherein the Federals cut down hundreds of trees and converted them into log breastworks, now standard practice for blue and gray infantry when on the defensive.

Like he had at the end of the first day at Stones River, Rosecrans held a council of war in his headquarters, a small log cabin known as the Widow Glenn House. During it Thomas dozed most of the time in his chair, having gone without sleep during the past forty-eight hours. Whenever asked for his advice by Rosecrans, he answered, "I would strengthen the left," where he held the line, before returning to the arms of Morpheus. Should the Confederates turn or penetrate the Union left, they then would cut the whole army off from Chattanooga. To prevent this, Rosecrans instructed Garfield to draw up orders that placed Thomas in command of what in effect became the Federal left wing while he himself took charge of the right, consisting of Crittenden's and McCook's corps. Thomas had control of six of the ten divisions on the field.

While Rosecrans conferred with his generals, Bragg met with some of his, among them Polk and Longstreet. Also, he formally organized his army into a "Right Wing" and a "Left Wing." The first, composed of five divisions, he put under the command of Polk, with orders to pounce on the Yankee left come daylight in an attempt to do to it what Thomas obviously expected the Rebels would try to do. The other wing, Hood's and McLaws's divisions from the Army of Northern Virginia, plus three divisions of the Army of Tennessee, Bragg assigned to Longstreet. In essence, its role, as conceived by Bragg, was to pin down the Federal right. Longstreet, though, had more than that in mind. Much more.

Daylight came on September 19. Yet not until nearly 10 A.M. did units of Polk's Right Wing attack, the consequence of orders going astray, not understood, or undelivered. Meanwhile, almost equal confusion reigned on the Federal right, in large part because Rosecrans, who had obtained little if any sleep during the night, was as he looked—a very weary man. Then came a request from Thomas to be reinforced by Negley's division, battered but still battle-worthy following its encounter at Dug Gap. Rosecrans promptly obliged by instructing Crittenden to have Brigadier General Thomas Wood's division, which was in reserve, replace Negley's. Wood, a West Pointer with a long but at best mediocre battle record, moved forward only to halt on a ridge behind Negley's position. Seeing this, and knowing that Thomas needed him, Negley had a staff officer inform Wood that he was supposed to relieve him. This the officer did, only to have Wood declare, "I am ordered to post my troops on this ridge." The officer thereon headed back to Negley but on the way met Rosecrans and told him of his meeting with Wood. Infuriated, Rosecrans immediately rode to the ridge, where he denounced Wood for his disobedience, a denunciation laced with profanity and delivered in the presence of Wood's staff. Although seething with resentment, Wood remained silent, and when Negley's troops moved out, his moved in behind their breastworks.

What ensued next would have been comic had its outcome not been tragic for both Rosecrans and the Army of the Cumberland. First, toward 10:45 A.M., Captain Sanford Kellogg, aide-de-camp and nephew of Thomas, acting on his own initiative, personally notified Rosecrans that Major General Joseph Reynolds's division of the XIV Corps was unsupported on its right, thus leaving a gap on the Union left. This was false. Brigadier General John Brannan's division of the same corps, although in echelon to Reynolds's right rear, nevertheless covered that flank. But Kellogg, who had made a hasty reconnaissance, believed this was correct, and Rosecrans understandably

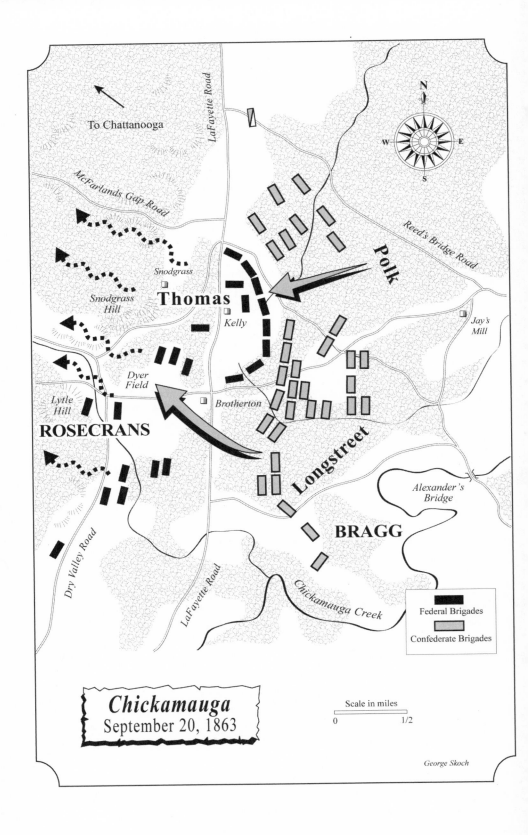

To Chattanooga

McFarlands Gap Road

LaFayette Road

Reed's Bridge Road

Snodgrass

Polk

Snodgrass Hill

Thomas

Kelly

Jay's Mill

Dyer Field

Brotherton

Lytle Hill

ROSECRANS

Longstreet

Alexander's Bridge

BRAGG

Dry Valley Road

LaFayette Road

Chickamauga Creek

Federal Brigades

Confederate Brigades

Chickamauga
September 20, 1863

Scale in miles
0   1/2

George Skoch

assumed the same. Hence, he told one of his aides, Major Frank Bond, to write an order directing Wood to "close to the left of Reynolds and support him." Bond thereupon inscribed the following:

Brigadier-General Wood, Commanding Division,
    The general commanding directs that you close up on Reynolds as fast as possible, and support him.

Rosecrans, preoccupied with redeploying Crittenden's and McCook's troops so that they would fill the gap that would be created by Wood shifting leftward to link up with Reynolds, did not read the order but instead passed it on to one of Crittenden's staff officers, Lieutenant Colonel Lyne Starling, who was on horseback, and asked him to deliver it to Wood, remarking as he did so that Wood was to "close to the left on Reynolds and support him."

A few minutes later, Starling galloped up to Wood and handed him the order. Wood read it, then said that there was no vacancy between his and Reynolds's divisions. "Then," declared Starling, "there is no order," meaning that Wood need not attempt to do what was impossible and implying that he should ask Rosecrans for a clarification of the order, which could be quickly done since Rosecrans's command post was only six hundred yards away.

Wood, though, was in no mood, to put it mildly, to ask anything of Rosecrans. Or, to put it strongly, he resented the tongue-lashing he had received from Rosecrans and desired revenge. Disregarding protests from some of his own brigade and regimental commanders, and ignoring the fact that a "considerable enemy force" faced him in the dense forest along his front, he pulled his division from the battle line and marched it northward around to the rear of Brannan's division. Behind he left a half-mile-wide hole in the Union right.[8]

Even as Wood did this, Longstreet's Confederates advanced into the hole, swept aside a brigade still present, overpowered the hopelessly outnumbered Federals who tried to stop them, and then routed the Union right wing, despite desperate efforts by Rosecrans, Crittenden, McCook, and Garfield to rally it and make a stand. Realizing that he and the others were engaging in the futile, Rosecrans told Crittenden and McCook to follow their fleeing soldiers until they passed through McFarland's Gap a few miles southwest of Chattanooga, whereupon they could rally and reorganize them. Next he instructed Garfield as what to do on reaching Chattanooga while he himself went to join Thomas. Garfield replied that it would be better for Rosecrans to go to Chattanooga while he checked on Thomas—as only the army's commander could issue the orders needed in this time of crisis. Rosecrans agreed and headed for Chattanooga.

Meanwhile, Longstreet turned north to join Polk in attacking the Federal left, his object to achieve total Confederate victory, after which not only Chattanooga but also Knoxville and Nashville might have the Stars and Bars waving over them again. By deploying units from Brannan's, Negley's, and Wood's divisions eastward along the south slope of Horseshoe Ridge, so-called because of its shape, Thomas held him at bay until early afternoon. Then Longstreet, having brought up most of his full force, threatened to turn again the Union right flank. Should he succeed, he would cut off Thomas from Chattanooga, leaving him with no rational choice other than to surrender so as to prevent his troops from being slaughtered.

At this critical juncture, Dame Fortune, who all day so far had frowned on the Army of the Cumberland, smiled. Acting entirely on his own initiative, Granger personally led a division of the Reserve Corps to the imperiled flank and repelled the surprised Confederates with a counterattack, driving them back. Longstreet, as did Polk, continued to throw in fresh brigades and divisions, but the Federals continued to hold.

Toward midafternoon Garfield arrived at Thomas's command post, having traveled there by way of a road that passed through Rossville, a village located some four miles southeast of Chattanooga on a road that passed through a gap in Missionary Ridge. After conversing with Thomas, he sent, to be telegraphed from Rossville, a dispatch to Rosecrans. In it he reported, accurately enough, that "Thomas holds nearly his old ground of the morning." He added: "I think we may in the main retrieve our morning disaster. I never saw better fighting than our men are now doing. The rebel ammunition must be nearly exhausted. Ours is fast failing. If we can hold out an hour more it will be all right . . . . I think you had better come to Rossville tonight and bring ammunition."[9]

But before Rosecrans, now in Chattanooga, received this message, at 4:15 P.M., he wired an order to Thomas directing him to assume command of all Union field forces, and with Crittenden and McCook "take a strong position" at Rossville. "I will," he added, "examine the ground here and make such dispositions for defense as the case may require and join you. Have sent ammunition and rations."[10]

This order reached Thomas fifteen minutes later. His initial reaction was to disregard it. "It will ruin the army," he told Garfield, "to withdraw now. This position must be held until night." Soon, however, he changed his mind, a change prompted by a rapidly dwindling ammunition supply and a potential Confederate breakthrough on his extreme right, which, should it occur, would cut off his forces from Chattanooga and leave him with only two choices: capitulation or extermination. So, starting at 5 P.M. and continuing on into the night, division after division pulled away and headed for Rossvillle via the LaFayette road.

The Confederates made no attempt to prevent or block Thomas's withdrawal. The reason is simple: Bragg, Polk, and Longstreet all assumed that the Federals would remain where they were. Not until well after sunup did they discover that their Yankee antagonists had gone, leaving behind only their dead and those too badly wounded to move, plus thousands of rifles and three dozen cannons, most of them presumably spiked or otherwise rendered unusable.

So ended the Battle of Chickamauga. In it the Army of the Cumberland suffered. Out of 58,000 soldiers involved, a total of 16,170 were casualties, of which nearly 5,000 were missing and probably prisoners. Precise figures for the Confederate loss do not exist, but the best estimate puts it at close to 18,500 of the 66,000 troops available to Bragg, with only 1,500 placed in the missing category.[11] Among Civil War battles, only the three-day slaughter at Gettysburg produced a bigger butcher bill.

What, though, did the Confederates achieve strategically with their tactical triumph? The answer is, surprising as it may seem, merely another chance to gain what they failed to gain on September 20, 1863—a truly decisive victory over the Army of the Cumberland. But an explanation of why this was so will be postponed, because it must be. After all, this is a book about the victors in blue, not the losers in gray. And one of the victors, Rosecrans, most unexpectedly on his part, had become a loser. How, then, did he react to this reversal?

He came close to breaking down both physically and emotionally. The first was inevitable. For at least three days and nights he had gone with little, if any, sleep. As to the second, it is understandable. Having finally consolidated his widely separated corps and deployed them along a topographically strong line rendered stronger still by log breastworks, he had good cause for being confident that his army would again repel the Rebel onslaught, after which he either could go over to the offensive or remain on the defensive until Burnside did what he knew Halleck had repeatedly ordered him to do—come to his assistance.

Instead, somehow the enemy in great force had broken through the center of his battle line and routed most of Crittenden's and McCook's corps, driving all of their troops save the thousands shot or captured in headlong, panic-stricken rout back toward Chattanooga. Why did this happen? What went wrong? Would Thomas experience the same fate as befell Crittenden and McCook?

Yet, despite all, he kept going and on the whole functioned well. Thus, on reaching Chattanooga, and in spite of having to be helped from his horse, he quickly issued the orders he had asked Garfield to deliver, took measures leading to the rallying of Crittenden's and McCook's troops, and, as has been seen, instructed Thomas to fall back to Rossville, thereby ending the battle with his army still intact and capable of tenacious resistance.

These things accomplished, at 5 P.M. he wired Halleck:

> We have met with a serious disaster, extent not yet ascertained. Enemy overwhelmed us, drove our right, pierced our center, and scattered troops there. Thomas, who had seven divisions, remained intact at last news . . . . Every available reserve was used when the men stampeded. Burnside will be notified of the state of things at once, and you will be informed.[12]

Rosecrans's message of defeat was not the first to reach Washington. An hour before he sent it Charles A. Dana, who recently had shown up at Rosecrans's headquarters to perform the same sort of mission he had while with Grant, and who had been caught up in the rout of Crittenden's and McCook's corps, transmitted to Stanton the following telegram:

> My report today is of deplorable importance. Chickamauga is as fatal a name in our history as Bull Run . . . . Our soldiers turned and fled. It was wholesale panic. Vain were all attempts to rally them. Our wounded all left behind . . . . Enemy not yet arrived before Chattanooga.[13]

Stanton, of course, showed this report to Lincoln after it was decoded. No doubt, it alarmed the president, yet he decided to wait until he received word from Rosecrans before acting. Although what it stated was alarming, at least it indicated that the Chickamauga defeat was not total, that Rosecrans might be able to hold on at Chattanooga until reinforced, whereupon the defeat could be transformed into a victory that would assure Union control of Tennessee and open the way into Georgia.

After telegraphing the president, Rosecrans continued to issue orders, dictate dispatches, and receive reports. The most important of the last came at 9 P.M. from Garfield and was delivered by Granger:

General Thomas has fought a most terrific battle and has damaged the enemy badly. . . . The disaster to the right . . . must be considerable in men and material. . . . The rebels have, however, done their best today, and I believe we can whip them tomorrow. . . . The troops are now moving back, and will be here [Rossville] in good shape and strong position before morning.[14]

Upon reading this, Rosecrans instructed Crittenden and McCook, who by now had rallied in both body and spirit their corps, to join Thomas at Rossville, which they proceeded to do. Then came a telegram from Lincoln, sent at 12:35 A.M., September 21, in response to Rosecrans's "serious disaster" message:

Be of good cheer. We have unabated confidence in you and in your soldiers and officers. In the main you must be the judge as to what is to be done. If I was to suggest, I would say save your army by taking strong positions until Burnside joins you, when I hope you can turn the tide. . . . We suppose some force is going to you from Corinth, but for want of communications we do not know how they are getting along. We shall do our utmost to assist you.[15]

Presumably, Lincoln's expression of "unabated confidence" pleased Rosecrans. On the other hand, he could only have felt skepticism about Burnside joining him and must have been puzzled by his statement, "We suppose some force is going to you from Corinth." What force? And when would it arrive?

As related at the close of the previous chapter, on September 22 Grant received at Vicksburg a September 15 telegram from Halleck ordering him to send without delay "all the troops that possibly can be spared in west Tennessee and on the Mississippi River to assist Gen. Rosecrans on the Tennessee River." On reading it, Grant, of course, realized that Washington wanted him to reinforce Rosecrans quickly and strongly. The problem was that he could do neither. More than half of his army had been loaned to Banks and Steele for purposes more political than strategic in Texas and Arkansas. Furthermore, a summer drought had rendered long stretches of the Tennessee and Cumberland rivers unnavigable, limiting the route by which reinforcements could be sent from Vicksburg to Chattanooga. First, four divisions under Sherman traveled aboard steamboats to Memphis. Then, from there they traveled by rail to Corinth, from where they began marching eastward along roads paralleling the Memphis & Charleston, laying track as they went in order to be supplied.[16]

Obviously, Sherman would not make it to Chattanooga, supposing he made it at all, in time to be of any help to Rosecrans. Likewise, efforts by Lincoln and Halleck to have Burnside go to Rosecrans's aid had failed and were sure to continue failing because, to repeat, Burnside had neither the means nor the desire to do this.

Realizing these realities, Stanton decided to deal with them in a realistic fashion. On the night of September 23, he met with Lincoln, Halleck, and several fellow cabinet members to whom he proposed transporting 30,000 troops from the Army of the Potomac by rail to Tennessee, where they would reinforce the Army of the Cumberland after first restoring its railroad supply line from Murfreesboro. Both the president and the general in chief doubted this could be done, with the latter declaring that it would require forty days to move that many soldiers from Virginia to Tennessee. Stanton thereupon summoned Colonel Daniel C. McCallum, superintendent of military railroads. After making some rapid calculations, McCallum, who prior to the war had been superintendent of the New York & Erie Railroad, announced that such a troop movement could be executed in seven days. Lincoln thereupon gave his approval, and on September 25 Howard's XI Corps and Slocum's XII Corps, 15,000 troops in all, began boarding trains. Accompanying them in a private car was Hooker, who had been placed in command of both corps by Stanton. Although he despised "Fighting Joe" personally, Stanton recognized that he had been a capable corps commander.

Thus, thanks to Stanton and Lincoln, as September drew to a close a strong reinforcement was on its way, potentially at least, to Rosecrans. But when it came to leading both, it and the Army of the Cumberland, in battle, Stanton had in mind another general from Ohio who also headed an army in the West. His name was Grant.

Slocum's and Howard's corps did not begin arriving in Tennessee until eight days after they set out, thus only taking a day longer than McCallum had calculated. Yet their rapid trip would have been an exercise in futility had Bragg during those days smashed the Army of the Cumberland or drove it from Chattanooga.

Why did he not? The answer is that he made no attempt to do so. His reasons were three: (1) Two days of slaughter along the Chickamauga had reduced his effective infantry strength to a bare 36,000, less than he credited Rosecrans with having, which was a bad guess, as the Army of the Cumberland now numbered a mere 32,000 battle-worthy soldiers; (2) he believed he could starve Rosecrans, who on September 22 withdrew all of his army close to Chattanooga at the urging of Thomas, who contended that the Rossville position was flankable, into either evacuation or capitulation; and (3) he therefore decided to devote himself for the present to getting rid of generals in his own army whom he considered incompetent and/or personal enemies, starting with Polk and soon including Lieutenant General Daniel Harvey Hill, who after the Tullahoma campaign had replaced Hardee as the Army of Tennessee's other corps commander.[17]

In sum, throughout the remainder of September and well into October, Bragg was more interested in waging war against certain of his own generals than in engaging Rosecrans in what he deemed to be not only an unnecessary but also an uncertain battle in its outcome given what rapidly became the formidable nature of the Federal fortifications.

On October 10 Grant, now able to move about on crutches, received at Vicksburg a message from Halleck: "It is the wish of the Secretary of War that as soon as General Grant is able to take the field he will come to Cairo and report to [the War Department] by telegraph."[18] At once he set forth on a steamboat, accompanied by Rawlins and the rest of his staff, for Cairo, where on October 16 he notified Halleck of his arrival and in turn was ordered to proceed to the Galt House in Louisville. This he did by train, stopping in Indianapolis for the night on October 11. In the morning, as his train pulled out of that city, it suddenly stopped and returned to the station. A short, bespectacled, white-bearded man entered his car. It was Stanton, who informed him that he now headed the newly established Military Division of the Mississippi, consisting of the Departments of the Ohio, the Tennessee, and the Cumberland, plus Arkansas.[19]

Behind this new organization, which gave Grant a command of a region far surpassing in size that of any other Union general, were a number of conditions, situations, and motivations. Chief among the first was a pressing need to place that area under the overall supervision of one chieftain, something it had lacked since Halleck's call to Washington. To be sure, Halleck had continued to function de facto in that capacity, but he also had to deal with operations in the East and the trans-Mississippi West, whereas someone now was needed who could give full attention to the needs of the armies stationed between the Appalachians and the Mississippi. Grant, manifestly, was the one most suited by experience and success to do this.

Second, the situation at Chattanooga, owing to the near disaster of the Army of the Cumberland at Chickamauga, would become a horrific calamity for the entire Union cause should that army be forced to surrender in order to escape starvation. Who better to prevent this than Grant, who had turned apparent defeat at Donelson and Shiloh into great victories? Furthermore, among all Northern generals he was the only one to have won at Fort Donelson and, above all, at Vicksburg, offensive campaigns of major strategic significance. (At Antietam, it will be recalled, McClellan allowed himself to turn what could have been a war-winning victory into a war-prolonging tactical defeat.)

Last, but not least, indeed most of all, Rosecrans's attitude and conduct following Chickamauga caused Lincoln to lose confidence in him. As to why, much has been written, with most of it emphasizing negative allegations regarding Rosecrans in reports by Dana to Stanton and a letter of the same type by Garfield to Chase, who as a consequence joined the secretary of war, Secretary of State William H. Seward, and Secretary of the Navy Gideon Welles in urging the president to relieve Rosecrans.[20] No doubt, these cabinet members did influence Lincoln, but in all likelihood the prime reason Lincoln came to distrust Rosecrans were messages from that general himself.

These alternated between outbursts of extreme pessimism—"We are about 30,000 brave and determined men; but our fate is in the hands of God; in whom I hope"—and expressions of equally extreme optimism: "We hold this point, and I cannot be dislodged except by very superior numbers and after a great battle." But most disturbing of all from Lincoln's standpoint was an October 3 proposal by Rosecrans to "offer a general amnesty to all officers and soldiers in the rebellion," if Chattanooga was held "in such strength that the enemy are obliged to abandon their position, and the elections in the great [Northern] States go favorably" for the Republicans.[21]

Not only was this putting the cart before a nonexistent horse in the form of large reinforcements actually reaching Chattanooga, it also dealt with political matters, something Lincoln resented generals doing as a consequence of his experience with McClellan. Then came on October 6 a telegram from Dana to Stanton, which, of course, Lincoln read. "I judge," it stated, "from intimations that have reached me that in writing his own report [on Chickamauga] General Rosecrans will elaborately show that the failure in this great battle rests on the Administration; that is, on the Secretary of War and General-in-Chief, who did not foresee Bragg would be re-enforced, and who compelled him to move forward without cavalry enough, and very inadequately prepared in many other respects."[22]

The only "intimations" by which Dana deduced the nature of Rosecrans's report came from Dana himself. Rosecrans was not so foolish as to accuse or even imply that the administration was responsible for his defeat. What he did was to give the real reason for the defeat by stating that, owing to the "unfortunate mistake" of Wood, "a gap was opened in the line of battle, of which the enemy took instant advantage."[23] As has been demonstrated, what Wood did and why was worse, far worse, than a "mistake." He should have been court-martialed and at the very least stripped of his rank and dismissed from the army.

Lincoln, of course, did not, because he could not realize this, for not until January 1864 did Rosecrans himself discover the full truth of what Wood did and did not do on the morning of September 20, 1863, at Chickamauga.[24] What Lincoln did know, or rather felt, was that he lacked confidence in Rosecrans's self-confidence. Rosecrans, he told his private secretary, John Hay, had since Chickamauga acted "confused and stunned like a duck hit on the head."[25] Hence he decided to replace him with a general in whom he did have confidence. To this end, on October 16, following the Ohio state election, in which the Republican candidate for governor defeated the Copperhead Democrat aspirant Clement L. Vallandigham by a large margin, he informed his cabinet that he intended to establish a Military Division of the Mississippi with Grant as its commander. The cabinet approved, but when Stanton proposed putting Thomas at the head of the Army of the Cumberland, Lincoln refused, asserting that he preferred not to do this himself. The cabinet thereupon agreed to have Stanton draw up two sets of orders, with one leaving Rosecrans in command and the other assigning Thomas to that post.

It was these two orders that Stanton next handed Grant. Grant chose the second, as, no doubt, Stanton expected, for he knew full well Grant's strong dislike of Rosecrans. On the other hand, the orders surprised Grant, who had assumed that Sherman would supersede Rosecrans on reaching Chattanooga. But now Sherman would head the Army of the Tennessee, a post Grant believed his friend long had deserved and which would be more appropriate than commanding the ill-starred Army of the Cumberland.[26]

The next day, having arrived in Louisville and taken a room at the Galt House, Grant in the afternoon, for the first time since his New Orleans mishap, went horseback riding. Although he had to be helped onto the saddle, once in it he rode well and proved to himself and others that he no longer needed to travel in a carriage when not hobbling about on crutches. But on returning to the Galt House, he met a very agitated Stanton, who had just received a telegram from Dana asserting that Rosecrans was about to evacuate Chattanooga. Like many of Dana's reports concerning Rosecrans, this was false—or, to be more accurate, a deliberate lie. Stanton, however, believed it, as he believed anything derogatory about Rosecrans, and therefore urged Grant to inform Thomas immediately that the Department of the Cumberland was now part of the new Military Division of the Mississippi headed by himself and that he, Thomas, commanded the Army of the Cumberland. This Grant did via the telegraph, then added: "Hold Chattanooga at all hazards. I will be there as soon as possible. Please inform me how long your present supplies will last, and the prospect of keeping them up."[27] Soon came Thomas's reply. After enumerating the rations on hand at Chattanooga, it concluded with these words: "I will hold the town till we starve."[28]

On reading this, Grant realized that he must go to Chattanooga as quickly as possible. Hence, the following day he and his staff boarded a private train, their destination Stevenson, Alabama, where the Nashville & Chattanooga linked up with the Memphis & Charleston.[29] Again, as at Donelson, Shiloh, and Vicksburg, he found himself in a situation where the sole alternative to victory was disaster—a disaster that would enable the Confederates to regain most of what they had lost thanks to those victories.

13

Grant at Chattanooga
How to Win a Battle Contrary to Plan

AT DUSK ON OCTOBER 19, ROSECRANS, having spent most of the day visiting hospitalized soldiers and surveying his lines, returned to his headquarters.[1] On the desk, he found Grant's order replacing him with Thomas. He immediately sent for the Virginian and when he arrived handed him the order. As he read it, Thomas turned pale and began breathing hard. Then, upon finishing it, he started to declare that he would not obey it, only to have Rosecrans stop him. "George . . . we are in the face of the enemy. No one else can safely take my place now; and for our country's sake you *must* do it." Heaving a deep sigh, Thomas said he would do it—but solely out of a sense of duty. Rosecrans then spent the rest of the evening conferring with Thomas and also with Major General Joseph Reynolds, the Army of the Cumberland's new chief of staff, Garfield having left the army to take his seat in the House of Representatives—a seat that provided the springboard for his becoming, briefly, president of the United States. (A disgruntled office-seeker shot and mortally wounded him in a Washington railroad station.)

Early in the morning, Rosecrans, accompanied by two personal aides and the Catholic priest who served as his personal chaplain, set out on horseback for Stevenson, Alabama, the closest place where he could board a train to begin a journey to Cincinnati, where he had been ordered to report. His route was the same by which the besieged Army of the Cumberland was receiving its supplies—a fifty-five-mile dirt trail northward of Chattanooga that meandered through a wilderness of wooded hills, climaxed by a high, steep elevation called Walden Ridge. Until early October it had sufficed, but a devastating raid on it by Wheeler's cavalry, wherein hundreds of mules were slaughtered and the wagons they pulled burned, reduced the flow of food and fodder to Chattanooga to an erratic trickle, with the result that soldiers became perpetually hungry and horses began to resemble equine skeletons. It was this situation that Thomas referred to when he answered Grant's query about holding Chattanooga, declaring, "I shall hold the town till we starve."

Rosecrans arrived in Stevenson toward evening on October 21. Soon afterward he learned that Grant also was there, in a private railroad car. At once he paid him a brief visit. During it, according to Grant's *Memoirs,* he "made some excellent suggestions as to what should be done" to enable reinforcements, rations, ammunition, and forage to reach Chattanooga by a more rapid and reliable route. "My only surprise," Grant commented sarcastically, "was that he had not carried them out."[2]

Why had Rosecrans "not carried them out"? The answer, like Edgar Allan Poe's "Purloined Letter," should be obvious, but for that very reason has never been discovered, at least to the knowledge of this historian.

Here is the answer.

On the morning of October 19, Rosecrans set forth with a couple of his aides and his new chief of engineers, Brigadier General William "Baldy" Smith, to search for a crossing over the Tennessee River by which an adequate quantity of supplies and reinforcements could be delivered reliably to his army. Smith was anxious to resuscitate a once-promising military career that had been derailed early in 1863 by too-active politicking while with the Army of the Potomac; playing a minor role in the Gettysburg campaign, he now hoped for a chance to redeem himself as a staff officer. As Rosecrans and his aides stopped off to visit, as he daily did, hospitalized soldiers, Smith went on to take a look at one of the possible crossing points, only to find it hopelessly inadequate. He continued on to Brown's Ferry, a no-longer-used crossing on the east bank of the Tennessee where it loped northward. After examining it for an hour, he concluded that it would be an excellent place to lay a pontoon bridge. On the other side of the river there was a road that passed through Lookout Valley to Kelley's Ferry, only seven miles distant, where steamboats coming from Bridgeport could land troops and supplies, which could be transported in wagons to Chattanooga by way of a pontoon bridge across Brown's Ferry. Also, a mere two dozen Confederates guarded the Brown's Ferry crossing, and the enemy snipers stationed on the opposite shore were few in number and widely spread, and therefore quite vulnerable to a nocturnal surprise attack by a superior force.

Shortly after Smith's discovery, Rosecrans joined him. After being told of it, he—who also, let it be remembered, was a West Point–trained engineer—examined Brown's Ferry and agreed it was the solution. He then headed back to his headquarters in Chattanooga. There he found, as has been related, Grant's order replacing him with Thomas as commander of the Army of the Cumberland, whereupon he summoned the "Rock of Chickamauga" and informed him, much to his distress and then anger, that he now headed the Army of the Cumberland.

Why is it—or, at least, why should it be—obvious that Rosecrans told Grant of Brown's Ferry? What other plan could Rosecrans have told Grant about during their short visit in Stevenson? The only plan for making it possible to deliver adequate rations for soldiers and sufficient provender for horses in Chattanooga called for doing so by way of Brown's Ferry. When relating in his *Memoirs* how Rosecrans told him of his plan for supplying the Army of the Cumberland at Chattanooga, Grant wrote, "My only surprise was that he had not carried them out"—thereby unknowingly and very unintentionally demonstrating that the plans Rosecrans described involved Brown's Ferry, plus the many preparations Rosecrans long had under way to execute such plans.[3]

Grant's education about the situation he now faced continued on October 22 and 23 as he and his entourage, which now included Dana, made their way via the Walden Ridge "road" to Chattanooga. Not only did he behold the hundreds of wrecked wagons and thousands of dead mules that cluttered it, during the second day, his horse slipped and fell on its left side, but owing to the mud he was not further injured. Obviously, should the Walden Ridge route remain the sole supply line to Chattanooga, the Army of the Cumberland soon would be faced with a choice between capitulation or starvation.

On the evening of October 23, Grant entered Thomas's headquarters, where he was expected, but not so soon. He hobbled to a chair next to the fireplace and sat down, rainwater dripping from his cape and forming puddles on the floor. Neither he nor Thomas, nor anyone else, spoke; it was as if they all were strangers who by sheer chance had met and knew not what to say. Finally, James Harrison Wilson broke the silence. "General Thomas, General Grant is wet and tired, and ought to have some dry clothes. . . . He is hungry besides, and needs something to eat. Can't your officers attend to these matters for him?"

Thomas, coming out of his reverie, if such it was, offered Grant dry clothes and ordered food to be brought to him.[4] Grant declined the first, ate the second, and then asked Thomas to describe the military situation and the prospects of his army. Thomas spoke briefly—reticence, along with great physical endurance, steady nerves, and enormous determination were traits he shared with Grant. He then called upon Smith to explain how supplies and reinforcements could be brought to Chattanooga by way of Brown's Ferry.

This Smith happily and ably did. When he finished, some of the other generals present expressed skepticism. Not so Grant. After asking Smith a series of to-the-point questions, he closed the conference by stating that come morning he would ride out to Brown's Ferry with Thomas and Smith. If he found the latter's plan feasible, it would be carried out as soon as possible. He then went to an adjoining bedroom, where, in all probability, he quickly fell asleep. The ability to do this and remain asleep was one of his assets, an asset not shared by McClellan, Rosecrans, and Sherman, all of whom had hyperactive intellects.

Come morning, Grant, Thomas, and Smith rode to Brown's Ferry. There Grant soon decided that the Rosecrans-Smith plan was sound and authorized Smith to execute it. Such he did on the night of October 26–27 with less difficulty and greater success than even he had anticipated. As a result, on the twenty-seventh a steamboat was able to transport supplies from Bridgeport to Kelley's Ferry, where they were loaded on wagons that carried them across the newly laid pontoon bridge at Brown's Ferry to Chattanooga. At the same time, Hooker, with Howard's XI Corps and Brigadier General John Geary's division of Slocum's XII Corps (Slocum refused to serve under Hooker and so was placed in charge of guarding the Nashville & Chattanooga with Alpheus Williams's division), moved into Lookout Valley, where Geary fended off a feeble attempt by the Confederates to restore their blockade. In sum, the Army of the Cumberland, although it continued to be on short rations and lacked sufficient horses to move its artillery, now had ample ammunition and no longer was in danger of starving.

Yet it still lacked enough troops to drive Bragg's army from the heights of Lookout Mountain and Missionary Ridge. Having realized that such would be the case, on October 25 Grant sent by courier an offer to Sherman to stop repairing the Memphis & Charleston Railroad as he marched—Rebel cavalry and guerrillas made this as much an exercise in futility as when Buell endeavored to do the same—and hasten with his command to Stevenson. From there, he would make his way via Bridgeport to Chattanooga. Once he arrived, Grant felt confident, Bragg could be defeated and Union control of Tennessee assured. Indeed, it might be possible to go over to the offensive in Georgia or Alabama.

Unknown to Grant, because unknowable, Bragg's prime priority was, and continued to be, waging war against most of his own top generals rather than the Federal generals opposing him. Starting on September 22, with Horseshoe Ridge still carpeted with corpses, and continuing well into October, he relieved Polk, D. H. Hill, and Hindman of their commands, deprived Buckner of the Department of East Tennessee by abolishing it, and caused Forrest to tender his resignation from the Confederate army by assigning his troopers, most of whom he had recruited, to Wheeler, whom he despised as incompetent, an attitude strengthened by Wheeler being badly routed by Yankee horsemen soon after his Walden Ridge raid. Concerned about losing the services of Forrest and having received complaints from his long-time friend Polk, Jefferson Davis first sent an aide-de-camp to report on the situation in the Army of the Tennessee and then visited it himself.

After talking with Bragg and his insubordinate subordinates, he held a meeting at which Longstreet, Hill, Buckner, and nearly a dozen other high-ranking generals voiced their opinion of Bragg, who also was present. Without exception, they declared that he no longer possessed their confidence and should be relieved. Yet, in spite of this, Davis retained Bragg in command, with his main reason being that the sole full generals in the Confederacy available to replace him were Johnston and Beauregard, both of whom he strongly disliked for personal reasons. Evidently, he did not so much as consider giving the post to Longstreet, who very much desired it and resented having to serve under Bragg, whom he viewed with contempt as both a man and a commander.

In the end, Hardee, who had left the Army of Tennessee to serve in Alabama and Mississippi, returned to take over Polk's former corps while Polk replaced Hardee; Breckinridge, who had refrained from denouncing Bragg at the meeting with Davis, although he probably had more cause to do so than anyone else, became commander of a corps consisting of troops that hitherto had served under Hill and Buckner; and Longstreet remained at the head of the two divisions he had brought from Virginia, plus a third assigned to him by Bragg. As for Hill, his military career virtually came to an end because he had lost the confidence not only of Bragg but also of Lee; and while Cheatham, whom Bragg blamed for the failure to defeat Rosecrans on the first day at Stones River, retained his division, most of his Tennessee troops, who adored him, were shunted off to other divisions.

The net result of these changes was an army wherein the majority of its corps, division, brigade, and regiment commanders disliked and distrusted their commander, an attitude that trickled down to the lower ranks. And to make the bad worse, owing to the rickety railroad supply line that stretched for more than a hundred miles from Atlanta, the ordinary soldiers suffered nearly as much from hunger and the increasingly inclement weather as did those of the Army of the Cumberland—so much so that ever larger numbers of them began deserting to the Federals.

Not until November 3, though, did Bragg commit his climactic act of military folly. On that day, he ordered Longstreet to march his Virginia divisions to Knoxville, there to capture it and in the process either do the same to Burnside's army or else cause it to flee back into Kentucky, thus regaining

East Tennessee for the Confederacy and opening the way for the redemption of the Volunteer State from Yankee thralldom. To be sure, Bragg acted on instructions from President Davis, but he did so gladly, even though it meant depriving his army of 12,000 first-class soldiers, so eager was he to be rid of Longstreet.[5]

Unlike Bragg, Grant did not wage war against his generals and refrained from making more changes than already had taken place in the Army of the Cumberland prior to his arrival in Chattanooga. The main one, apart from Thomas replacing Rosecrans, occurred soon after Chickamauga when the War Department (Stanton) removed Crittenden and McCook, then consolidated their corps into a IV Corps headed by Granger. Also, John M. Palmer, being its sole major general, succeeded Thomas as commander of the XIV Corps, and Stanley ceased to hold any command at all, having been put on sick leave, something that should have been done prior to the Chattanooga Campaign, wherein the contribution of his cavalry was negative. As for Hooker, Grant disliked having him in charge of the XI and XII Corps because he believed he had been insufficiently aggressive in supporting the Brown's Ferry operation, but since Lincoln had given him the command, he realized it would be best to allow him to keep it.

Above all, though, Grant wanted Sherman to come, the sooner the better. This desire intensified when he learned that Longstreet was moving against Knoxville, and Washington (Lincoln, Stanton, Halleck) began bombarding him with telegrams urging him to do something to help Burnside. Finally, misconstruing a proposal from Smith for a demonstration against the northern end of Missionary Ridge into attacking it, on November 7 he ordered Thomas to assault it not "one moment later than tomorrow morning."

The order horrified Thomas. The few horses he still had were too weak to haul artillery, and his troops remained on half rations when they got any at all, for although the "Cracker Line" between Bridgeport and Chattanooga now was open, the actual arrival of food and fodder was erratic owing to the incompetence of the chief commissary officer of the Department of the Cumberland. Smith, on being shown the order by Thomas, reacted to it the same way, and both agreed to find a good reason not to obey it. To that end, they reconnoitered the Confederate line along Missionary Ridge and discovered what they hoped to discover: that it extended too far north to be outflanked with the available force, and a frontal attack unsupported by artillery would be suicidal. They then went to Grant and told him this, adding that turning Bragg's right flank could best be done by Sherman's force when it came. Grant thereupon revoked the order, an order which is the second worst one he ever issued. (We shall in due course learn of the worst one.)

Sherman was coming, but slowly, very slowly. The reason was that to reach Stevenson he had to traverse a hundred miles of some of the most rugged and barren terrain in northern Alabama, all the way encumbered by hundreds of wagons carrying rations for 30,000 troops and fodder for thousands of horses and mules. There could be no living off this country, only starving in it.

Not until November 17 did Sherman, traveling ahead of his army, reach Bridgeport, where he received a telegram from Grant to come at once to Chattanooga. Such he did, first by steamboat, then on horseback, arriving at Grant's headquarters shortly after dark on the eighteenth. After exchanging some jovial banter with him, Grant stated that Chief Engineer Smith had discovered a way by which Bragg's right flank could be turned with results potentially disastrous for the Confederates, and that come morning he, Thomas, Rawlins, and Smith would show him how it could be done.

At dawn the five generals rode eastward along the north bank of the Tennessee to where South Chickamauga Creek emptied into it. Along the way, Smith commented that the hills they were passing would shield Sherman's forces from enemy observation once they crossed Brown's Ferry onto Moccasin Point. Then, on reaching a hill overlooking the mouth of South Chickamauga Creek, Sherman and Smith dismounted and crept down to the bank of the Tennessee, where Smith pointed at the northern end of Missionary Ridge. Supposing his troops crossed the river before dawn, he asked Sherman when they would be able to attack it. Sherman surveyed the ridge through his field glass and replied that he would take it by 9 A.M.

The generals thereupon rode back to headquarters, where Grant canceled, as no longer necessary, a plan by Thomas to have Hooker seize Lookout Mountain. He ordered Howard, whose corps constituted two-thirds of Hooker's force, to come by way of Brown's Ferry to Moccasin Point, where he would be in position to reinforce either Thomas or Sherman. Thomas, however, was to remain on the defensive while Sherman delivered the victory strike.

With the Army of the Tennessee now in the Stevenson-Bridgeport area, Grant assumed that within a few more days it would reach Moccasin Point. His assumption turned out to be mistaken. Sherman had his army march to Brown's Ferry the same way it had trekked across Mississippi and Alabama, the wagon train of each division lumbering along behind it, thus setting the pace, a very slow one, for his whole army. As a result, by the time his fourth division reached Brown's Ferry, the pontoon bridge had been so badly damaged by log rafts floated down the Tennessee by the Confederates that it could not cross, which in turn led to Jefferson C. Davis's division of the Army of the Cumberland being assigned to Sherman.

Bragg, of course, knew that Sherman had reinforced Grant. But displaying his abundant talent for jumping to the wrong conclusion, he decided that Grant intended to send Sherman to rescue Burnside at Knoxville. Thus, he ordered Major General Patrick Cleburne to bolster Longstreet with his and Buckner's divisions. Also, acting on the assumption that the Federals in Lookout Valley posed no serious threat to Lookout Mountain, he instructed Major General Carter Stevenson, whose division now occupied that impregnable-looking height, to deploy his four brigades along what would be a twenty-mile picket line. Stevenson, with Hardee's consent, ignored this absurdity.

On the morning of November 23, Grant, having been informed that Confederate deserters stated that Bragg intended to withdraw from Missionary Ridge and Lookout Mountain, presumably for the purpose of crushing Burnside and then blocking the Nashville & Chattanooga Railroad, instructed Thomas to have Granger conduct a reconnaissance-in-force against Orchard Knob, a Confederate-occupied hill about one-half mile from the base of the ridge. Thomas did as directed, whereupon Granger ordered Wood and Sheridan to move against Orchard Knob, which they soon did, with Howard's corps supporting them on the left and Brigadier General Absalom Baird's division of the XIV Corps doing likewise on their right. Altogether, 25,000 Federal troops marched forward as if on parade. Surprised by this display, and assuming that it was indeed just a parade, the two Alabama regiments posted on the knob as pickets at first did not fire. When they did, it was too late, with those who did not flee either raising their hands in surrender or being shot down if they attempted to fight.

Bragg, as astonished by what had happened as his unfortunate pickets, made no counterattack. Instead, he ordered approximately one-half of the troops stationed behind log and dirt breastworks at the base of Missionary Ridge to withdraw to its crest, there to entrench. He brought up dozens of cannon to support this new line and summoned reinforcements for Breckinridge, whose corps defended the south half of the ridge. Last, but far from least, he dispatched a message to Cleburne, whose division was at Chickamauga Station awaiting a train to join Longstreet at Knoxville, instructing him not to go there, as all except one of Buckner's brigades already had done, but instead to report to him at his headquarters. Although he believed that Grant would not be so rash as to attack the center of his line, he had a hunch that Grant wished to distract his attention from his right flank, which in fact was weakly held and to which he already had sent Walker's Division of Hardee's Corps.

As November 23 gave way to the twenty-fourth, Sherman's soldiers began crossing to the south bank of the Tennessee in pontoon boats paddled

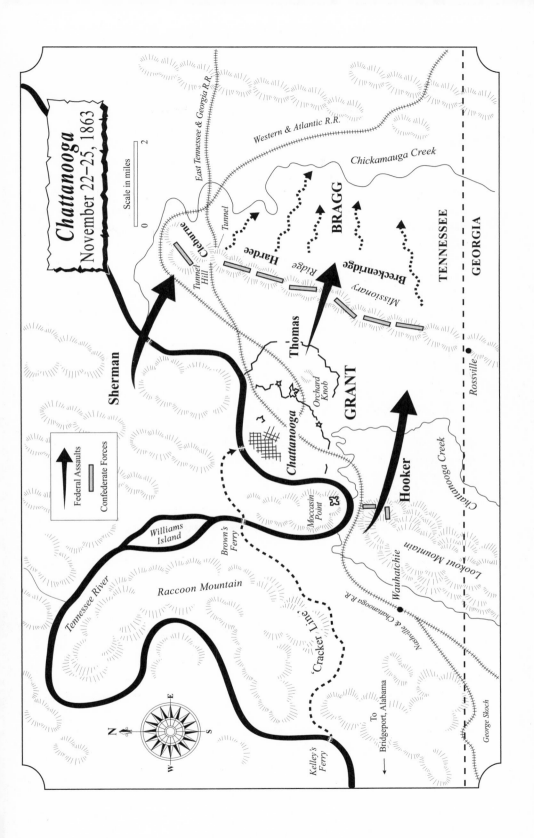

Chattanooga
November 22–25, 1863

Scale in miles

Western & Atlantic R.R.

East Tennessee & Georgia R.R.

Chickamauga Creek

Tunnel

BRAGG

Cleburne

Tunnel Hill

Hardee

Missionary Ridge

Breckenridge

TENNESSEE

GEORGIA

Sherman

Rossville

Thomas

Orchard Knob

GRANT

Chattanooga

Federal Assaults

Confederate Forces

Moccasin Point

Hooker

Williams Island

Brown's Ferry

Raccoon Mountain

Tennessee River

'Cracker' Line

Wauhatchie

Lookout Mountain

Nashville & Chattanooga R.R.

Chattanooga Creek

To Bridgeport, Alabama

Kelley's Ferry

N E S W

George Skoch

by Smith's engineer troops, who also began laying a pontoon bridge across
the river. By dawn most of them were on that side and one of his units had
captured a small Confederate picket force, gaining thus the advantage of
surprise. But, instead of advancing to seize the north end of Missionary
Ridge at 9 A.M., as he had told Smith he would, he entrenched. Not until
early afternoon did he order his three Army of the Tennessee divisions to
advance on what he perceived to be the north end of Missionary Ridge
about one and a half miles distant and occupy it. This they did, but not until
after sunset. By means of a signal lamp, Sherman notified Grant that come
morning he would sweep down the ridge, rolling up Bragg's right wing.
Grant in turn telegraphed Halleck word of Sherman's success.

This was not the only good news that Grant soon would report to Washington. To his astonishment, Hooker, whom he had authorized after all to
attack Lookout Mountain, managed to reach and hold its crest in what
became known as the "Battle Above the Clouds," but which actually was
a large-scale skirmish among the clouds. Thus, November 24 ended with
the Federals seemingly in position to crush both of Bragg's flanks unless
he retreated during the night, something Grant believed he almost surely
would do. Hence, when daylight came he was surprised, yet pleased, to find
Bragg's troops still in their fortifications along the south half of Missionary
Ridge. This meant that he now had an excellent opportunity not merely to
cause Bragg to retreat but also to trap his whole army, leaving him with just
two alternatives: capitulation or extermination. To this end, he instructed
Hooker to cross to the east side of Chattanooga Creek, which flowed between the ridge and Lookout, and then "operate against Bragg's left and
rear." He let stand the order he had sent to Sherman at midnight, which was
to "attack the enemy at the point most advantageous from your position at
early dawn."

Unlike Grant, Sherman felt pessimistic as the sun ascended. For he saw
what he had not seen before—to wit, that far from being on the north tip of
Missionary Ridge, he held a height dubbed Billy Goat Hill, separated from
the true beginning of the ridge, Tunnel Hill, by a deep, steep ravine. This
portion of the ridge was not continuous, as he had assumed, but consisted
of a series of separate hills. In sum, he was in the wrong place, a situation
he blamed on bad maps, but which were actually a product of his failure to
conduct a reconnaissance prior to his belated advance the previous day.

So he did the only thing he could do other than nothing, which was to
try to take Tunnel Hill, only to fail for two reasons. One was that it was defended by Cleburne's division, probably the best fighting outfit in the Army
of Tennessee, Bragg having sent it there during the night. The other was that

Sherman contented himself with sporadic, ill-coordinated attacks, each at most with a single brigade. Not until 3:30 P.M., and then more by accident than design, did parts of several Union brigades manage to launch an assault up a hill so steep that Cleburne's artillerymen could not depress their cannon sufficiently to blast the oncoming Yankees, and his infantry had nearly run out of cartridges. So how to stop them? The answer was a spontaneous charge down the hill, which so surprised the Federals that most of them fled. Those who did not were shot down, bayoneted, or became one of 500 prisoners.

At this point, Sherman ceased his assaults, despite having 23,000 men on hand who had not been engaged at all, among them Jefferson C. Davis's division and most of Howard's corps, which Grant had sent to bolster him on seeing large Confederate reinforcements heading north along Missionary Ridge. Perhaps Sherman feared a repeat of the bloody fiasco at Chickasaw Bayou. In any case, only twice again during the rest of the war did he attempt large-scale frontal assaults, and both turned into dismal fiascoes.

Meanwhile, Grant became increasingly frustrated and impatient. Along with Sherman's failure to achieve the expected at the north end of Missionary Ridge, early afternoon found Hooker unable to move against the south end because he had to halt to construct a new bridge across Chattanooga Creek, the Confederates having burned the old one. Finally, at 3 P.M. Grant directed Thomas to order Granger's corps to seize the Rebel rifle pits at the base of the ridge. In spite of suspecting that Grant's purpose was to assist Sherman even if it meant heavy casualties for his own troops, Thomas nonetheless obeyed.

At 3:40 P.M., Wood's and Sheridan's divisions surged forward, supported on their flanks by two divisions from Palmer's XIV Corps. To the surprise and then the delight of the advancing Federals, the Confederates manning the rifle pits offered only token resistance before fleeing up the ridge. With shouts of triumph Wood's and Sheridan's soldiers poured into the abandoned trenches. Quickly, though, they discovered that they occupied a deathtrap, the rear of these trenches being exposed to the fire of the enemy artillery atop the ridge. The best way, indeed the only practical way, to escape being slaughtered was to continue onward and upward.

Such they did, at first only a few scattered regiments, next whole brigades, and finally all of them. Beholding their surge, Grant reacted to it with fear and anger—fear that it would end in a deadly debacle, anger that it was taking place. "Who," he asked Thomas, "ordered those men up that ridge?" "I don't know," answered Thomas. "I did not," he added. Grant next questioned Granger: "Did you order them up?" "No," replied Granger. "They started without orders. When those fellows get started all hell can't stop them." "Well," muttered Grant, "somebody will suffer if they don't stay there."

To stay there at the top of Missionary Ridge, they first had to get there. Such they did. By chasing the fleeing Confederates up the ridge, they made it difficult, often impossible, for those atop it to fire at them without hitting their own men. Many if not most of the fugitives collapsed out of sheer physical and emotional exhaustion on reaching the crest, thereby weakening rather than strengthening the defense. Once the attackers came close, Rebel cannoneers found it impossible to lower the barrels of their big guns sufficiently to fire into instead of over the oncoming Yankees. Last but not least, because the engineer officer whom Bragg had placed in charge of laying out a defense line atop Missionary Ridge had constructed it along the topographical crest instead of the tactical one below it, the soldiers manning it were silhouetted against the sky, making them easy targets for the rifles of the attackers once they came within range and had clear fields of fire.

Consequently, what should have been improbable became close to inevitable—the near total rout of Bragg's center, which in turn led to the flight of his whole army first to Ringgold, then to Dalton in Georgia. Behind it were a mere 2,000 or so killed and wounded, but more than 6,000 prisoners, 7,000 castaway rifles, and 39 cannons. In contrast, the Federal forces, in spite of being the attacker, suffered only 684 killed, 4,329 wounded, and a mere 329 captured or missing, of which total almost one-fourth (1,346) occurred in Sheridan's division. On the other hand, Sherman's entire Army of the Tennessee had suffered only 1,695 casualties.[6]

Furthermore, at Missionary Ridge the Army of the Cumberland, against all odds and contrary to Grant's plans, expectations, and even desire, achieved on its own initiative the most complete battlefield victory so far of the Civil War, and it did it by making a frontal assault, something that, as we have seen and will continue to see, rarely succeeded during what euphemistically is sometimes called the "War Between the States." This was its revenge for its undeserved defeat at Chickamauga, and, ironically, the general responsible for that defeat, Wood, performed a major role in gaining the victory, although Sheridan and his troops took the leading part in bringing it about.

Grant, of course, received credit for the victory, which surpassed Vicksburg in its actual and potential impact on the subsequent course and outcome of the war because it assured Union domination of Tennessee and opened the way to Atlanta, outcomes far more important strategically and politically than establishing, either in whole or part, Northern control over Arkansas, western Louisiana, and Texas, goals destined never to be achieved until after Lee's surrender at Appomattox Court House on April 9, 1865. And, of course, the routing of Bragg's army at Missionary Ridge also enhanced Grant's already existing status as the North's best because most successful commander. It also made inevitable what soon he would become—the North's top general in rank and assignment, with the mission of winning the war by doing what so far no Union general had done: wage a campaign against Lee in Virginia that would result in the capture of Richmond, along with the surrender and/or destruction of the Army of Northern Virginia.

14

While Grant Fails to Defeat Lee, Sherman Invades Georgia

Circling around to Move Forward

IN ALL LIKELIHOOD GRANT WOULD HAVE PURSUED Bragg's now badly demoralized and heavily outnumbered army after Chattanooga had it not been for two occurrences. First, a staunch stand at Ringgold by Cleburne's stalwarts against Hooker's contingent enabled Bragg's wagon train to reach Dalton, Georgia, a strong defensive position located at the junction of the Western & Atlantic and the East Tennessee & Georgia railroads. Second, and more important, on November 25 Grant received Lincoln's response to a telegram from him describing the progress made as of the evening of November 24 at Chattanooga: "Well done. Many thanks to all. Remember Burnside."[1]

Obviously, Lincoln felt more concerned about Burnside and Knoxville than about allowing the Confederates in Georgia to escape and regroup. Moreover, upon pondering the matter, Grant concluded that while he possessed enough troops to finish off Bragg, he lacked sufficient supplies and transport to chase him all the way to Atlanta, as he almost surely would have to do. Therefore, he ordered Granger to hasten with his corps to the relief of Burnside. Then, when Granger tarried to give his troops time to recuperate from their spontaneous attack on Missionary Ridge, Grant placed Sherman in command of the expedition, to which were added the XV Corps plus Howard's and Jefferson C. Davis's divisions. He wanted subordinates who could be counted on to be subordinate.

If down on Granger, whom he found to be, putting it mildly, eccentric in his behavior, Grant was highly impressed by "Baldy" Smith's conception (as he erroneously thought it to be) and execution of the Brown's Ferry operation and his reconnaissance that made possible the attack on Bragg's right flank. Therefore, he urged Lincoln, with eventual success, to promote Smith to major general: "Recent events have entirely satisfied me of his great capabilities."[2] What Grant did not realize was that Smith had hopes that went beyond what he soon became, a corps commander serving in Virginia.

On December 6 Sherman and Granger, riding ahead of their troops, reached Knoxville. There they discovered that Longstreet had attempted to storm the town on November 27, only to be repulsed with heavy loss by its formidable fortifications, fortifications designed by Burnside's chief of engineers, Captain Orlando M. Poe.[3] Also, they saw pens filled with cattle and were entertained at a sumptuous banquet where the main course was turkey. Disgusted—obviously Burnside's army had not been in any imminent danger of starvation—Sherman the following day headed back to Chattanooga with his troops, leaving behind Granger so that his contingent would be available to help counter another attempt by Longstreet, reinforced by Lee, to take Knoxville, something Lincoln needlessly feared.[4]

Meanwhile, Grant revived his plan to invade the Deep South. After pointing out to Halleck in a December 7 letter that winter weather and logistical factors made it impossible to advance on Atlanta from Chattanooga until spring, he proposed to employ troops that otherwise would remain idle to seize Mobile by way of New Orleans, then "make a campaign into the interior of Alabama, and, possibly, Georgia." Such a move, he added, "would secure the entire states of Alabama & Mississippi, and a part of Georgia or force Lee to abandon Virginia & North Carolina. Without his force the enemy have not got Army enough [in the West] to resist the army I can take."[5]

Ten days later Halleck received and replied to Grant's letter. He approved of Grant's proposal—but with two provisos that made it impossible to implement. First and foremost, sufficient forces must remain available to prevent Longstreet, if reinforced by Lee, from taking Knoxville and/or Cumberland Gap. (Rumor had it that Ewell's corps was on the way to East Tennessee.) That Halleck could actually raise such a possibility suggests the degree to which Lincoln, Stanton, and Halleck had lost faith in Meade's ability to conduct offensive operations to keep Lee pinned in Virginia. Second, Banks needed to be provided with sufficient strength to ensure that he would be able to advance up the east bank of the Red River supported by Porter's gunboats and supplied by a fleet of cargo ships to Shreveport, thereby obtaining Union domination of western Louisiana and opening the way into Texas, where Lincoln expected (unrealistically) the Unionists there to gain control. In sum, Grant could go after Mobile and the rest, but not until other objectives, more political than strategic in nature, had been achieved.[6]

Grant realized this and so again shelved his plan to penetrate Alabama and Georgia by way of Mobile and settled for doing three things he believed could be done as well as should be done. First, he continued to maintain a force in East Tennessee capable of preventing Longstreet, if he was reinforced by Lee, from taking Knoxville and/or Cumberland Gap. To this end, he placed Brigadier General John Foster in command of the Army of the Ohio, Burnside having been relieved from that post in order to recruit his IX Corps, which had dwindled to less than 4,000, to full combat strength. When Foster suffered a severe injury, Grant replaced him with Major General John M. Schofield, whose promptness in sending troops from his Department of Missouri to Mississippi during the siege of Vicksburg had favorably impressed him. On the other hand, Granger's erratic and sometimes alcohol-influenced behavior so displeased Grant that he replaced him with Howard as head of the IV Corps, having developed a far more favorable opinion of that one-armed general than he had among peers in the Army of the Potomac, owing to his poor performances at Chancellorsville and Gettysburg.[7]

Second, Grant sent Sherman back to Vicksburg with instructions to conduct a raid on Meridian, Mississippi, a small town 150 miles to the east bisected by two railroads, one connecting it southward to Mobile, the other eastward to Selma, Alabama, which along with Atlanta was the main source of Confederate military supplies in the West. Sherman's prime mission was to destroy enough of both lines so that the Confederates could not use them to reinforce Mobile or to place a force on the east bank of the Mississippi once the Army of the Tennessee returned to Chattanooga to participate in the campaign to take Atlanta. Upon reaching Meridian, their trail marked by plundered and burned houses and villages, Sherman's troops proceeded to rip up miles of track, then bend the rails double over bonfires. They then returned to Vicksburg with Sherman, boasting that both rail lines were permanently destroyed. The Confederates, however, possessed devices to straighten the rails and then re-lay them. By April both lines were functioning again, and the workshops in Meridian, which had been burned along with almost all of the other buildings, once more were producing.[8]

Third, Grant did what Lincoln, via Halleck, directed him to do: order Sherman to supply 10,000 troops from the Army of the Tennessee for Banks's Red River expedition. As has been noted, Grant opposed this foray and so did Banks, but the president was commander in chief, and even the North's most victorious general knew he must obey him. War, after all, is "politics by other means" (Clausewitz), and Lincoln wished not only to bring all of Louisiana and Texas under Union control but also to put U.S. troops in position to enforce the Monroe Doctrine after the Confederacy had been subdued.[9]

On March 3 Grant received what he had expected for more than a month: an order to come to Washington to be commissioned a lieutenant general.[10] This would make him the top general of the U.S. army with a rank held before only by George Washington (Winfield Scott's lieutenant generalship was brevet, hence honorary). This meant that he would be at the head of all Federal forces, a position rendered formal on March 9, when Lincoln handed him his new commission in a ceremony held at the White House. Henceforth, he would be subordinate solely to Lincoln or else to Stanton when conveying orders from the president.

The appointment was no accident. In August 1863 Grant expressed relief when a plan to transfer him east to replace Meade fizzled. "Here I know the officers and men and what each Gen. is capable of as a separate commander. There I would have all to learn. . . . Besides," he added, mindful perhaps of the reception accorded John Pope in 1862, "more or less dissatisfaction would necessarily be produced by importing a General to command an Army already well supplied with those who have grown up with, and been promoted, with it." Moreover, having just secured a major generalship in the regular army, Grant was in no hurry to risk his newly won laurels in the political morass that was Virginia. It would be left to his Galena congressman, Elihu B. Washburne, to outline the terms for putting Grant in charge of affairs in the East—by promoting him to lieutenant general and placing him in overall command of all the armies of the United States. It was with that in mind that Washburne had introduced the bill reestablishing the rank. Other Republicans, worried that Lincoln might reward the do-nothing Halleck with a third star, wanted to specify Grant as the recipient of the new rank, in the process disregarding constitutional niceties.

At first, Lincoln did not rush to support Washburne's bill. Initially, he thought it best to keep Grant in the West. On the eve of an election year, he had no interest in elevating a potential rival for the presidency to top rank, especially now as George B. McClellan's name was being broadcast about as a possible presidential candidate. It was a sign of Grant's political intelligence that he hurried to reassure people that he had no interest in running for political office, and he made sure that Lincoln would get that message through back channels. Once Lincoln knew about Grant's intentions, he signaled his approval of the bill, Republicans dropped the notion of specifying Grant in the legislation, and the bill became law on February 29, 1864.

Grant no sooner received his commission than he headed to Brandy Station, Virginia, to visit George G. Meade at his headquarters. Meade assumed he had come to replace him as head of the Army of the Potomac with

Sherman or perhaps Baldy Smith (who accompanied Grant on his visit). He had good reason to do so. Throughout the remainder of the summer of 1863, and on into autumn and winter, he had failed to carry out a single major successful offensive operation against Lee, and he had even been maneuvered by the "Gray Fox" all the way back to the vicinity of Washington. Small wonder that Lee, albeit reluctantly, agreed to send Longstreet with two of his divisions to bolster Bragg, or that even after Bragg's debacle at Missionary Ridge and Longstreet's repulse at Knoxville, the Federals, among them Lincoln, Stanton, and Halleck, feared and for a while actually believed that Ewell's corps was about to reinforce Longstreet, which would have left Lee with only Hill's corps and Pickett's still badly depleted division and Stuart's cavalry to oppose the entire Army of the Potomac.

Therefore, Meade told Grant that he need not hesitate to name a new commander for the Army of the Potomac, thinking that it would be someone who had served under him in the West, most likely Sherman. As for himself, he "would serve to the best of my ability wherever placed," adding that "the work before us was of sufficient importance to the whole nation that the feelings or wishes of no one person should stand in the way of selecting the right men for all positions." Meade's offer to step aside favorably impressed Grant, who promptly assured him that he had not thought of replacing him, especially with Sherman, who "could not be spared from the West."[11] Within days, however, events and experiences caused Grant to tinker with this arrangement in a different way, one designed to deal at least as much with the political enemy in the rear as with the gray-clad one in front. Prior to receiving his new commission, he had intended to return to the West, where he would direct operations against Atlanta. But after arriving in Washington, he quickly realized that as general in chief he needed to be in quick and constant contact with Lincoln, Stanton, and Halleck, whose exact role had become ambiguous. He also saw how politicians were prone to meddle with military affairs firsthand: after meeting Meade at the headquarters of the Army of the Potomac in Virginia, he returned to Washington with Meade, who was on his way to testify before the Joint Committee on the Conduct of the War, which wanted him to admit that he had nothing to do with the victory at Gettysburg. By now, the stories of politicians interfering with military affairs and generals taking their grievances to Washington were common knowledge. Someone had to bring an end to that meddling. Yet at the same time Grant did not want to be in the capital, a place he perceived quite correctly as a nest of political intrigue. So what to do?

Grant's answer was to stay in the East and establish his headquarters in the field alongside Meade. This would become an awkward arrangement, but it might soften resentment in the Army of the Potomac to being taken over by an outsider from the West whose victories had come against, to put it mildly, opponents inferior to Bobby Lee's Army of Northern Virginia. Halleck would remain in Washington as a glorified chief of staff, a communications link between Grant, his civil superiors, and his military subordinates. Removed from real responsibility, Halleck lost no time in offering advice, interfering with orders, and second-guessing plans, which made his presence in Washington problematic, as soon became evident. To make his new job easier, in fact possible, Grant placed Sherman in charge of the Military Division of the Mississippi while at the same time assigning McPherson command of the Army of the Tennessee. By doing this he essentially reduced to just one the general (Sherman) with whom Halleck would have to deal in the West (Banks, of course, remained truly answerable only to Lincoln). Sherman would face Johnston, while Grant would confront Lee, and each general would make sure that the Confederates would find it impossible to shift reinforcements between Georgia and Virginia without fatally compromising their efforts to fend off the chief Union offensives. As for Missouri, Arkansas, and Kansas, they were of small consequence unless ineptitude on the part of the commanders posted in those states threatened to cause failure east of the Mississippi, particularly in Virginia and Georgia, where Grant not only hoped but also expected to win the war no later than late summer. For the moment, generals such as Rosecrans would suffice to keep the Rebels in check.[12]

Grant and Sherman devoted the rest of March and all of April to preparing for their campaigns. Grant faced the task of revising a plan he had once proposed to comport with political realities. Back in January, Halleck, then still general in chief, had queried Grant about his ideas on how to approach the war in Virginia. Grant responded by advising that the Union armies set aside their obsession with striking directly at Richmond and fighting in Virginia. Better, he argued, to strike at North Carolina directly, taking Raleigh and Wilmington, and severing Virginia's connection to the Confederate heartland. Lee would have to leave Virginia to counter this threat. While Grant would leave a force adequate to shield Washington, his main field armies would live off the North Carolina land, encourage alienated North Carolina whites to abandon the Confederacy altogether, and liberate thousands of black slaves.

Halleck had rejected that plan; although, with the force available to Grant in March 1864, it was indeed doable. The Lincoln administration and its foremost military adviser remained wedded to an overland approach in Virginia designed to defeat Lee's army in battle and threaten Richmond in that order. Any water-borne approach smacked of McClellan, and Lincoln refused to consider such a move. So Grant devised another plan within the constraints imposed by the authorities in Washington. He devised a four-pronged offensive against Lee. One Union column, under Franz Sigel, would make its way south through the Shenandoah Valley, taking it out of the war as a source of Confederate supplies and denying the Confederates a route to use to invade the North. A second column would operate in southwest Virginia, wrecking railroads and securing other resources, including salt, which was essential to preserving food. A third force, the newly formed Army of the James, under the command of Benjamin F. Butler, would make its way up the James River to threaten Richmond and sever the Confederate capital's rail connections southward, a goal that could be achieved in large part by capturing Petersburg. Finally, the Army of the Potomac would move south against Lee, drawing its supplies from the various rivers and inlets that flowed into Chesapeake Bay, seeking to pin Lee in place or turn his right flank in order to threaten Richmond. Faced with the loss of the Confederate capital, Lee would either have to withdraw from central Virginia to repel Butler or come out and fight Meade: he would be caught between converging columns, and, if each Union force fulfilled its assignment, the war in Virginia might end by the summer. That last condition proved more challenging than expected, because in two cases Grant had to rest content with trusting generals who owed their commands to their perceived political importance and not to their military skill: Butler and Sigel. If they failed to do their part, Grant's task would become more difficult.[13]

During this period, Grant's misgivings about Banks's Red River foray were realized. On April 8 at Sabine Crossroads, less than forty miles from Shreveport, a Confederate force led by Major General Richard Taylor, son of General and President Zachary Taylor, attacked and drove back Major General A. J. Smith's division, the contingent supplied to Banks by the Army of the Tennessee. Although a counterattack by Smith the next day came close to routing Taylor, Banks ordered a retreat by his 30,000-man army. He had no other choice. David D. Porter, whose gunboats and transports accompanied Banks along the Red River, had to fall back owing to a rapid decline in the depth of that river, thereby making it impossible for Banks to supply his troops. Not until May did Banks make it back to New Orleans. By that time his forces were too demoralized to attempt a strike at Mobile, and Smith's troops were needed in West Tennessee, where Forrest posed potentially a serious threat to the sole rail supply line of Sherman, by then deep into Georgia.[14]

The only other obstacle Grant had to face was the Army of the Potomac. Although Grant had known several of its leading generals in the peacetime army (Hancock and he had been together at West Point), he did not en-counter many friendly faces at various headquarters. Many officers were skeptical about Grant. They claimed that he had won in the West against second-rate Confederate generals: how would he do against Bobby Lee? For his part, Grant sensed that so long as generals in the Army of the Poto-mac nursed a fear of Lee, they were already half beaten. Someone needed to take this army in hand and make it fight to the utmost on the offensive, something it had never done (Gettysburg was a defensive victory). Generals inveighed and intrigued against each other, and if many officers and men welcomed the departure of the XI and XII Corps the previous September, they were unhappy when Meade chose to consolidate the remaining five infantry corps into three, eradicating the I and III Corps as independent or-ganizations. The spring campaign would also mark the return of Ambrose Burnside and his IX Corps to Virginia, just over a year after that general had left the army in humiliation after the twin disasters of Fredericksburg and the Mud March. Meade cared little for Burnside; Hancock was still try-ing to recover from his Gettysburg wounds; John Sedgwick was still smart-ing from his association with McClellan; and Gouverneur Warren found that it was harder to command a corps than he had anticipated. Only when it came to the cavalry did Grant bring along his own field commanders, in-cluding feisty Phil Sheridan and James H. Wilson, who was new to combat command.

There was also one final consideration to contemplate as one looked southward across the Rapidan and Rappahannock that spring. Even as Grant prepared for an advance that would take the army through the very terrain used by Stonewall Jackson to outflank them the previous May—a scrubby undergrowth of forest named the Wilderness, where unburied bod-ies, skeletons, and skulls served as haunting reminders of what lay ahead—he knew that just over half of the men who had signed up for three years of service in 1861 were looking forward to their last months in uniform. There were replacements to be had, including volunteers enticed to join to cash in on the bounties offered for enlistment (and reenlistment), and conscripts who were not the most enthusiastic or committed of soldiers, but the fact remained that over half of the army's most skilled veterans were counting the weeks, days, and hours before they would head home. It remained to be seen how they would fight as the time grew near for their discharge.

On May 4 the Army of the Potomac began crossing the Rapidan to engage yet again the Army of Northern Virginia. Grant's force numbered 118,000, of which 12,000 consisted of cavalry headed by Sheridan and 20,000 in Burnside's newly recruited IX Corps, which consisted of four divisions, one of them black troops, the first to serve in any Federal army as a consequence of large numbers of white veterans not reenlisting. When added to the presence of conscripts and new recruits, the result was a qualitative decline in the Army of the Potomac notwithstanding its quantitative resurgence. In contrast, the Army of Northern Virginia remained formidable, if not more so. Having no term limits on their service, Lee's regiments consisted of war-hardened, battle-wise veterans supplemented by a thin but steady trickle of replacements who, if they lived long enough, also became skilled at killing and surviving.

Starting on May 5, Grant, after abandoning any notion of marching through the Wilderness to flank Lee out of his Mine Run position, decided to stand and fight in the thickly wooded area, hoping to turn Lee's right flank. Instead, Lee blocked this thrust. The next day, in a counterattack led by Longstreet, he began rolling up the Federal left. But like Jackson at Chancellorsville in the same Wilderness, for which the battle became named, some Southern soldiers fired on Longstreet's retinue, thinking it Yankee cavalry. A bullet struck "Old Pete's" right arm, for all intents and purposes terminating his combat career. That evening another Confederate attack crashed into the Union right at dusk, causing a momentary panic. Generals scattered about headquarters in panic, while Grant, smoking a cigar, watched. Finally, an officer approached him and excitedly exclaimed that Lee was once more up to his old tricks, just as he had been the year before, and disaster was just moments away. After all, the officer continued, he knew what Lee would do. Everyone did. It always seemed that in Virginia the Confederate commander waited for just the right moment to seize victory from the jaws of defeat. Why would it be any different now?[15]

Grant had spent the last several days watching the Army of the Potomac move and fight. He did not know what to expect from these generals, but he was at last beginning to learn. He had arrived at the Wilderness wearing white kid gloves, a sword and scabbard clanging at his side, the very picture of a commanding general. Now the sword was among headquarters baggage, a ceremonial nuisance. The kid gloves had been shredded into tatters, a casualty of Grant's whittling away at twigs and sticks with a penknife as he awaited news from the front. It was a way for him to settle his nerves as he wondered about the Army of the Potomac's ability to fight. His stock of cigars had also suffered: he had gone through nearly two dozen that day alone, a sign of how he had puffed away in an effort to relieve his anxiety.

Now, as he heard out the panicky officer, something finally snapped deep within. Taking the cigar from his lips, he let loose. "Oh, I am heartily tired of hearing about what Lee is going to do," he barked. "Some of you always seem to think he is suddenly going to turn a double somersault, and land in our rear and on both our flanks at the same time. Go back to your command, and try to think what we are going to do ourselves, instead of what Lee is going to do." The officer shrank away, and Grant resumed smoking his cigar.[16]

Even so it seemed the Army of the Potomac again had been defeated, and its soldiers assumed that Grant, like his forerunners, would retreat northward. The men were used to the old pattern. They assumed wrong. On May 7 Grant ordered an advance again by way of Lee's right flank to Spotsylvania Court House, which, if reached before the Confederates, would cut them off from Richmond. As the men pulled out of line and prepared to march, they did not know their destination. As they reached the crossroads, they knew that if they turned left, it was yet another retreat. But they turned right, moving southward, advancing. The men cheered Grant, and Grant told them to hush, lest they alert the Confederates as to what was going on. He planned to be first to Spotsylvania.

Only good luck and happenstance prevented this from occurring. First Major General Richard Anderson, who by seniority of rank had taken command of the wounded Longstreet's corps, decided to continue on to Spotsylvania Court House instead of halting north of it as instructed by Lee. At the same time, Sheridan's cavalry encountered Gouverneur Warren's V Corps trudging along the same road, with the result each became entangled with the other. Consequently, the Confederates reached Spotsylvania before the Federals. Nearly two weeks of bloody combat followed, highlighted by an assault on May 12 against a salient in Lee's line where the contending armies clashed in literal hand-to-hand combat. Grant reminded Washington that he was determined to "fight it out on this line if it takes all summer."[17]

Before long he had reason to change his mind. While at Spotsylvania, news came to him that Sigel had been defeated in the Shenandoah Valley, with the victorious Confederates now reinforcing Lee's army. The advance in southwestern Virginia had faltered and come to naught. Nor was there any good news from the James River, for Butler, after a promising beginning, had shown that field command was beyond his capabilities, and his corps commanders, Baldy Smith and Quincy Gillmore, were no better (although the three excelled at squabbling with each other). The promise of a threat against Richmond dissolved. If Grant wanted to pin Lee against Richmond or bring him out in the open, he would have to do it himself, and that meant moving again, not fighting it out at Spotsylvania.[18]

Even that would not be easy. During the first two weeks of fighting, Grant learned more about his own subordinates than he learned about Lee. To be sure, his Confederate counterpart had proven a worthy adversary, one far better than Grant's previous opponents, but if Grant had been unable to defeat him, he had failed to defeat Grant or even stop him in place, and in a few instances he had been lucky that it had not been worse. However, Meade seemed to feud with everyone, earning his reputation as an old snapping turtle. Warren proved better at complaining than fighting, and Burnside simply struggled to keep up. A sharpshooter's bullet felled Sedgwick at Spotsylvania, and it would take some time for his replacement, Horatio Wright, to get up to speed, while Hancock, whose II Corps often bore the brunt of the fighting, was clearly not the commander he once was, and was simply the best of a mixed lot. When Meade and Sheridan had clashed over who was responsible for the traffic jam that had allowed Lee to win the race to Spotsylvania, Grant chose to resolve it by allowing Sheridan to make good on his promise to whip Jeb Stuart, a pledge that deprived Grant of cavalry to reconnoiter the enemy's position.

Struggling with these command problems, and frustrated by the failure of the other component parts of his overall plan of campaign, Grant decided to leave Spotsylvania and move around Lee's right once more, hoping to draw the Confederate out into the open. Lee did not take the bait: indeed, at the North Anna River, he nearly trapped Grant's army astride the river in two places, but illness prevented him from taking advantage of the opportunity. Little did Lee know that events at Union headquarters would play to his advantage. Meade erupted upon hearing that Sherman, reporting on his progress in Georgia, hoped that the Army of the Potomac would do its part. For weeks Grant had found himself taking a more direct role in managing the Army of the Potomac as well as Burnside's IX Corps, a separate command. Now, in the wake of Meade's outburst, Grant decided to place Burnside directly under Meade's command and let Meade direct his army once more, with reinforcements to come from Baldy Smith's XVIII Corps, which would do more good under Meade than under the stalemated Butler.[19]

In trying to resolve one dysfunctional command situation, Grant merely succeeded in creating another, for, as the Army of the Potomac approached the area where Robert E. Lee had first attacked it in June 1862, another disaster loomed. The two armies clashed near a small crossroads called Cold Harbor on June 1. Grant, believing that the fight had gone out of the Confederates, attempted to launch a major assault the next day, but poor staff work meant that Smith's men did not reach the jump-off position in nearly enough time. Thus, Grant left it to Meade and his generals to prepare for a massive assault, three infantry corps strong, in the early hours of June 3. Realizing this, many Federals pinned to their uniforms strips of paper inscribed with their names (dog tags remained to be invented), as they had in other cases when they were preparing to launch an assault.

The result was a horrific disaster, although not quite as bad as legend would have it. Meade and his subordinates failed to make adequate preparations for a successful assault. There was no reconnaissance of the Confederate position, and each corps was left on its own, resulting in an uncoordinated assault. Meanwhile, the Confederates used the delay to their advantage, and by the time the waves of Union troops moved forward before dawn on June 3, they found themselves marching straight into the teeth of a skillfully fortified position. After mere hours those soldiers who could and desired to scrambled back to whence they came. The rest carpeted the terrain between the rival lines, a carpet far thicker near the Federal positions than the Confederate. Most of them were dead or wounded. Many of them, though, lay there by choice until night so that they could creep back to their trenches. All in all, Grant lost some 7,000 in killed, wounded, and prisoners during the entire day of combat, of which half (3,500) came during the morning assaults. Over time, confusion would warp these estimates until it was not uncommon to read of 7,000 men falling in an hour or even thirty minutes. Some commentators even confused Union losses for all twelve days, some 12,000 men, with the fighting on June 3. Yet so sensitive was Meade to the need to command his own army that on the day after the charge he bragged to his wife that he had been in charge all day. Regardless of who was to blame, and despite the wildly exaggerated reports of losses that have been inserted into narratives as gospel truth, Cold Harbor remained a ghastly mistake that came to characterize how the campaign as a whole would be viewed by many people, then and later. Writing to his father in London, Charles Francis Adams, who had denounced Hooker for consorting with whores, wrote that Grant "has literally marched in blood and agony from the Rapidan to the James."[20]

Grant's next move, although another flanking one, targeted neither Lee nor Richmond but Petersburg, where all of the railroads supplying the Army of Northern Virginia and the Confederate capital from the deeper South converged. Should he seize and hold it, Lee's sole rational choice would be an attempt to escape into North Carolina. From the campaign's beginning, Grant had anticipated that he might have to cross the James, and he had made preparations for such an eventuality, perhaps mindful of how the failure to ensure the arrival of bridging equipment had doomed Burnside's fall 1862 offensive. Slowly, Grant pulled away from Cold Harbor, broke contact with Lee, and headed south to cross the James, leaving Lee puzzled as to what his foe intended to do.

This time Grant's stratagem came close to success but yet again failed. Why? Because of the Wilderness, Spotsylvania, and, above all, Cold Harbor. Faced again with the prospect of assailing Rebel fortifications covered by abatis and lined with cannon, the Federals advanced, when they advanced at all, with a caution that often resembled timidity. This gave Lee, who for once had been outgeneraled, time to rush strong reinforcements to Beauregard, who had done a superb job of making his weak contingent seem far stronger. Hence, another Union defeat; hence, another deadlock.

In sum, Grant had come up against an opponent who, for the first time, equaled if not surpassed him in audacity and determination, whose troops worshiped him, and who realized that if they were defeated then so was the Confederacy. For these reasons, and owing to flaws he inherited in the Army of the Potomac on taking de facto command of it, Grant failed to attain the decisive victory he sought and even expected. Instead, he found himself engaged in a siege that, should it persist long enough, might cause the North to lose the will to win the war. He had pledged "to fight it out on this line if it takes all summer." Now he would find it necessary to fight it out on a much longer line, not only all summer but also throughout the fall, the winter, and on into spring. Again, defense had prevailed over offense.[21]

As Grant commenced operations against Lee, Sherman prepared to move. On May 7 he ordered an advance on Dalton, Georgia, against the Army of Tennessee, now headed by Joseph Johnston, Bragg having resigned his command soon after the Missionary Ridge fiasco, which, with his customary probity, he attributed to Breckinridge being drunk.[22] Grant's instructions to Sherman called for him to crush Johnston's forces, after which he was to occupy Atlanta, then take Montgomery, Selma, and ultimately Mobile. Sherman, though, saw his mission as basically to prevent Johnston from reinforcing Lee by forcing him to defend Atlanta, thereby assisting Grant to dispose of Lee and thus win the war. Since Grant felt confident that he indeed would finish off Lee and thereby reduce the rest of the war to little more than a mopping-up operation, he tacitly permitted Sherman to do as he wished. Possibly, too, he realized that this was as much as could be expected of Sherman, given what he did, or rather failed to do, while on, or trying to get on, Missionary Ridge.

Johnston, for his part, intended to do against Sherman what he had done while opposing McClellan on the Peninsula and again when endeavoring to prevent Pemberton from being trapped in Vicksburg—trade territory for time in which to obtain both the strength and the opportunity to strike the enemy a winning blow. Furthermore, he now had available a general whom he thought capable of delivering such a blow: John Bell Hood. It was he who led the assault that broke through Rosecrans's right wing at Chickamauga. But, while doing this, a .58 caliber minié ball shattered his right thigh bone, necessitating an amputation that reduced his leg to a four-and-a-half-inch stump. Even so, he was able to walk with the aid of crutches and an artificial leg. He could also ride a horse, after being hoisted into the saddle, his wooden foot placed into a stirrup, and his person and his crutches strapped to the steed. Moreover, in spite of his terrible wound, he retained the aggressiveness that he had displayed at Gaines Mill, Second Manassas, Antietam, and, above all, Chickamauga, where his contribution to Southern victory gained him promotion to lieutenant general, making him, at thirty-two, the youngest Confederate general of that rank. As soon as Johnston learned of the promotion, he telegraphed the War Department in Richmond: "Lieutenant General Hood is much wanted here."[23] Now he had him, commanding one of the two corps into which he had reorganized the Army of Tennessee, the other being Hardee's, and he was greatly pleased.

Sherman, well aware that a combination of nature and Rebel fortifications rendered Dalton impregnable to frontal assault, adopted a plan proposed by Thomas that called for outflanking Johnston by way of Snake Creek Gap, a narrow passage through a mountain ridge to the south and west of Dalton, and then cutting the Western & Atlantic Railroad, Johnston's sole supply line from Atlanta, by ripping up track above Resaca, a village on the north bank of the Oostanaula River about thirteen miles due south of Dalton. But instead of having the Army of the Cumberland, which with its 77,000 men comprised more than two-thirds of Sherman's combat strength, conduct this operation with one or two of its three corps, he assigned it to McPherson's Army of the Tennessee, which had present only two of its corps, both badly understrength.

On May 9 McPherson passed through Snake Creek Gap and headed for Resaca. The nearer he approached it, though, the slower he went. Owing to detachments to protect his wagon train, which he had left in Snake Creek Gap, his striking force had been reduced to little more than 10,000. Worse, the roads were more numerous and went in different directions than the ones on his map. Increasingly, he feared being attacked by a superior Confederate force coming from the north and so left detachments to guard against this. By the time he came within sight of Resaca he had only one brigade available to strike the railroad. Then an enemy battery, or so he thought, opened up on its flank, whereupon he ordered a retreat back to Snake Creek Gap. A small detachment of cavalry accompanying him tore down some telegraph wires connecting Resaca with Dalton, but lacking the tools for it did not dislodge so little as a single rail.

On learning of McPherson's failure the following day, Sherman instructed all of his army except Howard's IV Corps to march on Resaca by way of Snake Creek Gap. This, of course, proved too late. Johnston, realizing that he was in danger of being cut off from Atlanta, fell back to Resaca. There Polk, who now headed the Army of the Mississippi, reinforced him with three infantry divisions and one of cavalry, bringing his strength up to at least 70,000.

May 14 and 15 witnessed fierce fighting as both armies sought to turn the other's right flank. However, one of Sherman's divisions managed to cross the Oostanaula by way of a pontoon bridge, thereby threatening to gain the Confederate rear and causing Johnston to retreat from Resaca during the night.

Thus ended the first phase of the Atlanta Campaign, which set the pattern for the next two months. Again and again Johnston would take up a strong defensive position, and again and again Sherman would find a way to outflank him, obliging him to retreat yet again. Not until May 19, with his army approaching the Etowah River, did Johnston attempt a large-scale attack. Seeking to take advantage of the Federals pursuing him in three widely separated columns, he deployed Hood's and Polk's Corps near Cassville, his intent to smash Hooker's column as it marched along a single road. Fortunately for Hooker's troops, a large force of Federal cavalry suddenly appeared on a road leading to Hood's and Polk's rear. Although in fact they were merely on a raid, Johnston, on being notified of their presence, could only assume that they might be the vanguard of a strong enemy infantry force and so did what he did—cancel the attack and withdraw across the Etowah River, his army now only fifty miles from Atlanta.

Sherman did not pursue. Instead, he halted north of the Etowah to rest and reinforce his army, which in addition to casualties had found it necessary to detach a large number of troops to guard his increasingly long and hence vulnerable supply line. Not until May 23 did he resume advancing. His target was Marietta, by way of Dallas (Georgia, of course), thereby avoiding the mountainous terrain to the northwest of Marietta and putting his army in position to move against that town, which was situated on the Western & Atlantic and only a short distance from the Chattahoochee, the last major river between him and Atlanta. He wrote to his wife, Ellen: "No doubt we must have a terrible battle at some point near the Chattahoochee," but "I think I have the best army in the country, and if I can't take Atlanta and stir up Georgia considerably I am mistaken."[24]

In theory, it was an excellent plan. In practice, it suffered from two flaws. One, it took Sherman's army away from the Western & Atlantic and thus made it dependent for supplies on its wagon trains. Two, the Confederate cavalry quickly discovered the move, with the result that Johnston posted his army east of Dallas in a region offering numerous excellent defensive positions. In sum, for Sherman to reach Marietta, he now had to either break through or swing around a strongly fortified Army of Tennessee.

He failed to do either. He blamed the failure on Hooker, whom he accused of displaying insufficient aggressiveness against what he alleged to be a small Confederate defensive force at New Hope Church. This was false. That force consisted of Hood's corps plus Hardee's nearby. Hooker assaulted as soon as he possibly could, Alpheus Williams's veterans in the lead, but gained only meager results. The truth was that Sherman refused to believe that Johnston faced him with full strength. And he disliked and distrusted Hooker for personal reasons from their time together in California before the war, just as Halleck's distaste for Hooker dated from their time on the West Coast.

On into early June both armies attacked and counterattacked, all to no avail. For the Confederates it meant strategic success; for the Federals it threatened disaster as they began to run dangerously low on food and fodder. Finally, Sherman, despite stubborn enemy resistance, was able to withdraw his army to Acworth on the Western & Atlantic, where it was bolstered by Major General Frank Blair's two-division XVII Corps, which had been on furlough, and by another division of the XV Corps, more than making good its losses.

What, pondered Sherman, should be done next? The answer, he decided, was to move directly on Marietta. Starting June 14 he did this by instructing Thomas, whose three corps continued to constitute the Union center, to push his way between Pine and Kennesaw Mountains, a thrust he believed would cause Johnston to retreat and hence open the way to Marietta. It did cause Johnston to fall back, but to a much stronger line anchored on his right by Kennesaw Mountain. On the other hand, it led to Bishop General Polk's quick and gory demise, with Sherman unintentionally responsible. Observing some Rebel officers standing atop Pine Mountain obviously surveying his operations, he ordered Howard to have a battery fire at the "saucy" Confederates.[25] Shortly thereafter, three projectiles ripped toward the crest of Pine Mountain in rapid succession. The second eviscerated Polk. Loring, whom we last saw escaping from Pemberton's fiasco at Champion Hill, assumed command as senior major general of what still was titled pro forma the Army of Mississippi but which de facto had become the third corps of the Army of the Tennessee.

Throughout the ensuing two weeks, Sherman vainly endeavored to dislodge the Confederates from their Kennesaw Mountain stronghold by his now standard tactic of outflanking them. Johnston countered by extending his defense line until it stretched eight miles southward from the mountain.

Frustrated by his inability to advance, on June 24 Sherman sought to take advantage of Johnston's increasingly thin line with a three-pronged frontal attack by one division of the Army of the Tennessee and two divisions of the Army of the Cumberland. As might have been expected, the Confederates easily repelled the assault, inflicting approximately 3,000 casualties while suffering a mere 300 themselves.

Sherman blamed the failure on the Army of the Cumberland, concerning which he had written to Grant a week previously: "My chief source of trouble is with the Army of the Cumberland, which is awful slow. A fresh furrow in a ploughed field will stop the whole column, and all begin to intrench." However, in his official report on the Atlanta Campaign composed three months later, he took "full responsibility" for the failure. On the other hand, in a letter to Halleck dated July 9 he asserted that had "the assault been made with one-fourth more vigor, mathematically, I would have put the head of George Thomas's whole army right through Johnston's deployed lines." All of these statements are false.[26]

Proof of this comes from a message Sherman sent Thomas late in the evening. Having received a report from Schofield that one of his division commanders, Brigadier General Jacob D. Cox, who had served under Rosecrans in West Virginia, had found a way to turn the Rebel left flank, which did not extend as far south as hitherto thought, Sherman proposed moving on Fulton, a stop on the Western & Atlantic about seven miles south of Marietta. "How far," responded Thomas, "is Fulton from Olley's Creek? Will we have to cross any other streams of much size? When do you wish to start?" "Nickjack," replied Sherman, "the only stream to cross. Time for starting day after tomorrow." Thomas then queried, "What force do you think moving with? If with greater part of the army, I think it decidedly better than butting against breastworks twelve feet thick and strongly abatised."[27]

Sherman, of course, chose the Army of the Tennessee to make the flanking move. By nightfall of June 30, wagons loaded with ten days' rations, it was ready to set forth come tomorrow. Then, during the night, Sherman received a fortuitous telegram from Halleck: "Lieutenant General Grant directs me to say that the movements of your army may be made entirely independent of any desire to retain Johnston's forces where they are. He does not think that Lee will bring any additional forces to Richmond, on account of the difficulty feeding them."

Thus Sherman suddenly found himself on the eve of potentially the decisive phase of his campaign relieved of what hitherto he had considered his most essential task—namely, keeping such strong and constant pressure on

Johnston that the Confederates would be unable to transfer troops from Georgia to Virginia. Henceforth, he could conduct operations solely on the basis of his own situation and not worry about how they might affect Grant. Moreover, and even of greater importance, by directing Sherman to act independently in Georgia, Grant in essence admitted that he had no expectation of overcoming Lee in the foreseeable future. This meant that Sherman's campaign, which both he and Grant had deemed subsidiary to the one in Virginia, now possessed equal status.

Indeed, should the stalemate at Richmond and Petersburg persist long enough, conceivably Sherman's campaign might attain primary status. For if Union victory could not be gained in the East, it would have to be achieved in the West, or else not at all. Grant's failure to defeat Lee and/or take Richmond, and the huge losses suffered in his effort to do so, were causing growing numbers of Northerners, especially Democrats, to join with Copperhead leader Clement Vallandigham in declaring the attempt to restore the Union by force a failure, and that the sole way to do this was to offer the South peace, with slavery still legally intact—an offer which shall be dealt with in a later, more appropriate context.

15

Grant Remains Stymied, Sherman Takes Atlanta

Decision in the West

(June–September 1864)

GRANT BLAMED "BALDY" SMITH for the initial failure to take Petersburg and with it Richmond. He was right: a more determined attack by Smith on Petersburg's strong but weakly manned fortifications on June 18 almost surely would have succeeded. But he was wrong to think that Smith and his troops, following their bloody repulse at Cold Harbor, had the will, or the heart, to repeat it. (Hancock's corps performed no better when it tried to break through to Petersburg.) The harsh truth of the matter is that Grant, unlike any of his predecessors as the commander (de facto) of the Army of the Potomac, had maintained the offensive in spite of defeats and penetrated deep into Virginia, but in so doing he suffered such hideous losses that most of his troops, from generals down to privates, no longer possessed the will to make frontal assaults against a fortified foe—especially in cases where Union enlistments were about to expire, giving men yet another reason to save their own skin. The odds for success were too low, the chance of death, wounds, or capture too high.[1]

What, though, to do with Smith, who had been unable to overcome his fear and that of his troops of another bloody hecatomb to smash through to Petersburg and thus to a victory that would have led to the defeat of Lee and with it ultimate Union victory? Grant's answer was to appoint him commander of the Army of the James, a two-corps force so titled because of it being posted east of Richmond on the south bank of that river only a short distance from Richmond but facing Rebel fortifications so formidable that Grant likened its situation to "being corked in a bottle." By doing this, he would be rid of its present head, Major General Benjamin F. Butler, known in the South as "Beast Butler" owing to his having, while in charge of New Orleans in the spring of 1862, issued an order stating that any female insulting Union soldiers "shall be treated as a woman of the town plying her avocation," and whose military exploits consisted of employing troops to put down civilian mobs. Grant planned to leave Butler as titular head of a department while removing him from field command of troops. Butler may not have been a skilled field commander, but he was a wily politician who was highly popular among Radical Republicans and War Democrats. Hence, when he learned what Grant had intended him not to learn—that he was about to be displaced—he queried Grant in a fashion that made it clear that he would not go easily. Grant, not wanting another battle in his rear—Lee in front was enough—promptly denied that he had any such intent, despite having obtained, albeit reluctantly, consent from Stanton and Lincoln for his scheme. Indeed, Butler knew that Lincoln was unpopular with many Radical Republicans at the moment, for the president had just decided to set aside a Radical proposal for Reconstruction, the Wade-Davis bill, and had just accepted the resignation of Radical favorite Salmon P. Chase as secretary of the Treasury. To offend Butler at this critical juncture invited even more trouble. Smith, on discovering that he was to remain a corps commander, protested vehemently and persistently to Grant, whereupon Grant told him, "You talk too much." Indeed he did. During the past month Smith had freely criticized Meade's handling of the Army of the Potomac, especially at Cold Harbor, building upon his previous reputation as a troublemaker. At a time when Grant had his hands full with squabbling among his generals, Smith's ranting proved too much to take, and Grant decided to relieve him of command.

Smith retreated to the sidelines in Vermont, where he criticized Grant freely, spread stories about his drinking, and wrestled with health problems. His war was over. Years later, Smith characterized Grant in rather unflattering terms: "Ability ordinary; sense of responsibility, utterly wanting, except so far as his personal interests were concerned; professional acquirements absolutely wanting, so far as related to the direction of movements, and conduct of battles. He was malignant in his hatred, but would forgive for a consideration. Utter disregard of truth where his own interests were concerned; the moral qualities drowned in rot-gut whiskey." It would seem that Smith developed a dislike for Grant.[2]

At least Grant had rid himself of Smith. He remained stuck with Butler, whose seniority meant that should Grant have cause to leave the Richmond-Petersburg front, Butler as ranking officer would be in overall command. He also had to react to a Confederate thrust against Washington, a story better left for the next chapter, but which caused Grant some concern as he dealt with a fretting president and the always second-guessing Halleck. Although

Early failed to take Washington, it looked bad for Union fortunes to have a Confederate force north of the Potomac, and Grant had to dispatch the VI Corps as well as another corps earmarked for Petersburg to bolster the Washington defenses. It would be some time until Grant could straighten out that mess, as we will see. He had his hands full as it was with Meade and his corps commanders. Hancock, whose II Corps had shouldered an increasing amount of the burden of offensive operations, was ailing, and he would never again be superb. Gouverneur Warren continued to be a source of trouble and discord as commander of the V Corps, although matters had settled down a bit between Warren and Meade. Nor could Grant find a way to resolve the friction between Meade and Ambrose Burnside, who simply seemed overmatched by the task before him.[3]

Never was this problem more evident than at the end of July, when Burnside looked to implement what at first seemed to be a promising plan to break the stalemate of the Petersburg siege. Colonel Henry Pleasants of the Forty-eighth Pennsylvania Volunteer Infantry and his men, many of whom had been miners, proposed to dig a shaft under the Confederate lines, fill it with explosives, and literally blow a hole in the Rebel entrenchments. Union soldiers would then exploit the opening, coming through on the edges of the resulting crater, and then outflank Confederate defenders right and left, rolling up the Rebel line and opening the way to Petersburg and ultimate victory. The war might well end that summer after all.[4]

This approach was not a new one: Grant had approved such operations during the siege of Vicksburg. But it was perhaps the most ambitious one, and it promised to provide decisive results. Moreover, Burnside offered a novel twist: he would employ Edward Ferrero's division of African American soldiers to spearhead the assault. After all, they had not seen much combat action. They were fresh, enthusiastic, and not jaded by weeks of making pounding frontal attacks. Burnside and Ferrero had the men rehearse the assault plan, although the division's other duties limited the effectiveness of the training. Divisions of white soldiers would follow in the wake of the assault and complete the work of the miners and Ferrero's men.

It all sounded like a good idea until George G. Meade got involved. He thought the plan stood little chance of success, an opinion accentuated by his ill-concealed reservations about the fighting ability of black soldiers. Sensitive to newspaper criticism in the aftermath of the setbacks during the Overland Campaign, he argued that if the assault failed, the army and its commanders would come under criticism for sacrificing black soldiers as cannon fodder. In truth, Meade thought that black soldiers would come up short, and that the assault would fail if they were used at all. Given the condition and morale of the available white soldiers, this was simply unfair: surely the experiences of the last several months suggested that it was time to give Ferrero's men a chance and Burnside his full support. Otherwise, it was better not to attack at all.

Aware of the brittle political environment, Grant agreed with Meade's reasoning. That was a mistake (Grant had at other times expressed faith in the fighting abilities of black soldiers), and it was not the only one he would make. He failed to supervise Meade's dealings with Burnside, with the result that Burnside did not get all he had asked for to make the operation a success. He also failed to intervene when a frustrated Burnside, deprived of the opportunity to use Ferrero's men in the vanguard of the assault, resorted to the bizarre expedient of having his remaining division commanders draw straws, which left the incompetent James H. Ledlie in charge of the first wave. It was as if Burnside simply lost interest in the operation. Grant knew of Ledlie's shortcomings, which included a tendency to imbibe on the battlefield, but did nothing. He did, however, try to thin out the Confederate defenders in front of Petersburg by having Hancock cross the James and threaten Richmond in order to draw Confederates to its defense.

The story of the digging of the mine and the challenges encountered by the diggers makes for an engrossing but oft-told story. By the night of July 29, all was in place. Grant came down to witness the explosion firsthand, and after a tense delay, the mine exploded in the early morning of July 30, casting Confederates skyward. Opportunity beckoned, but Burnside stumbled. The men in the first wave lacked proper equipment and failed to clear the obstacles before them in timely fashion; Ledlie believed his job was to provide himself with a flask, which he used to the utmost. Meanwhile, his men poured into the crater itself and found it impossible to get out of it. Stunned at first, the Confederates rallied, counterattacked, and soon found themselves shooting fish in a barrel. Ferrero's division was thrown into the fray, and instead of opening the way to Petersburg, the black soldiers found themselves mowed down in cold blood, sometimes the victims of the panic of their own white comrades who were making their escape. The Confederates did not hesitate to shoot down black soldiers as well, even those trying to surrender, evidence that such behavior was not limited to Nathan Bedford Forrest's men at Fort Pillow, Tennessee, the previous April.

The entire operation was part atrocity, part fiasco, and a total disaster. It did not take long for Union commanders to point fingers at each other. Burnside had fumbled an opportunity, in part because Meade meddled with it, failing to give him the requested supplies and revising the role assigned to Ferrero's men. Yet Meade avoided censure, while Burnside paid for the defeat with his command: he spent the rest of the war, like Smith, watching from the sidelines. Grant somehow also escaped criticism, then or since, although he made his share of mistakes. He knew that Meade and Burnside could not work together, and he had good reason to believe that Burnside's planning was not what it should have been, if for no other reason than the evidence provided by his past performance. Two days after the assault, Grant wired Halleck that it was "the saddest affair I have witnessed in this war. Such opportunity for carrying fortifications I have never seen and do not expect again to have." He added that "had instructions been promptly obeyed . . . Petersburg would have been carried."[5] If a chance had been frittered away, it was in part because Grant had allowed incompetence to fester and failed to adopt a hands-on attitude featuring direct supervision. It was not the first time Union soldiers had paid the price for the squabbling of their superiors, but it was among the most tragic and costly. No wonder Grant fell ill soon afterward, especially as he met Lincoln the day after the disaster to discuss other command problems.

Thus the last best chance to break the stalemate at Petersburg and Richmond had passed. For months to come, Grant would extend his lines and launch offensive thrusts in an effort to wear Lee down, but without decisive result. If he had achieved the goal of pinning Lee in place, depriving the Confederate Colossus of his ability to disrupt the progress of Union arms through daring counterattacks, he had failed to do more than neutralize his counterpart. That would not be enough in an election year. Yet, even as Grant regretted what had happened at the Crater, he was learning of progress elsewhere, outside Atlanta, where Sherman had at last reached the outskirts of the city. It would be left to Sherman to do what Grant had failed to do, strike the blow that would sway the sentiments of Northern voters and pave the way to victory.

For even as Grant pondered his options in front of Petersburg that July, Sherman was on the move again in Georgia. His flanking movement to the east of Kennesaw Mountain succeeded, causing Johnston to retreat toward, then to, and ultimately across the Chattahoochee River, a scant seven miles north of Atlanta with its factories, warehouses, rail yards, and an iron mill that made it to the western Confederacy what Richmond was to the eastern—a prime source of the means to wage war. Thus, for Jefferson Davis this new withdrawal by Johnston without so much—or so little— as attempting to attack Sherman was too much to take. Davis wanted in Georgia a commander who would attack—and attack hard. So on July 18 he replaced Johnston with Hood, who throughout the campaign had been sending him letters deploring Johnston's lack of aggressiveness. Whatever else he might lack, aggressiveness was a trait Hood possessed in abundance, as he had displayed during the Seven Days, at Antietam, on Gettysburg's second day, and, above all, at Chickamauga, where he lost a leg while winning a battle.

Two days later, Hood struck Hooker's XX Corps and a small portion of Palmer's XIV Corps at Peachtree Creek, a tributary of the Chattahoochee due north of Atlanta, in hope of forcing them to surrender in order to escape being driven into that river. At first, he seemed on the verge of victory. Then, Federal artillery, summoned by Thomas, repelled the assault with severe loss (about 2,500) and no gain. Meanwhile, Sherman, having ordered troops of the Army of the Tennessee to rip up miles of track of the Georgia Railroad northeast of Atlanta, advanced on that city with his right flank guarded by Schofield's "army" and two divisions of Howard's IV Corps (the other division was with Thomas). Opposing McPherson were only about 5,000 of Wheeler's cavalry fighting dismounted (most of them had long since discarded their sabers) and a few thousand Georgia militiamen, most of them either teenagers or men too old or decrepit for regular service. However, McPherson, equaling if not excelling the caution he had displayed in moving out from Snake Creek Gap, advanced so slowly that Hood had time to cancel an attack by Cleburne's division, which had been held in reserve at Peachtree Creek, and hasten it to hold McPherson at bay on the outskirts of Atlanta until darkness descended.

Not until midnight did Sherman receive word from Thomas of the encounter at Peachtree Creek. Nor, for that matter, did he visit the XX Corps until the morning of July 21. On being told that it had lost upward of 1,200 men, most of them in Alpheus Williams's division, he commented, "Oh, most of 'em will be back in a day or two." So offended was one of Thomas's staff officers by this remark that he felt "a strong urge to shoot Sherman."[6]

Having received reports of Confederate forces marching southward, Sherman on the morning of July 22 assumed that Hood was vacating Atlanta. He instructed McPherson to occupy the town and send Dodge's XVI Corps to tear up more track of the Georgia Railroad. McPherson, still cautious, asked and received Sherman's permission to postpone doing the first but did do the second. That proved fortunate. Shortly after 12 P.M., two divisions of Hardee's corps, their march having been delayed by mud and swamps, struck what otherwise would have been the totally open Union rear, only to encounter the XVI Corps, whose scouts had alerted it to the enemy approach. It beat back the Rebel thrust, inflicting heavy losses, particularly with the fire of one of its regiments equipped with Henry repeating rifles, ancestor of the famed Winchester. At the same time, the Army of the Tennessee's wagon train eluded Wheeler's cavalry.

Meanwhile, though, the rest of Hardee's corps, spearheaded by Cleburne's stalwarts, entered the gap between the XVI and XVII Corps and assaulted the latter both in flank and rear. The attackers came upon McPherson in the open, accompanied by only two aides: he tried to escape by galloping away, only to be shot dead from his saddle. Even so, Blair's veterans held on grimly to a commanding height known as Bald Hill, sometimes facing northeast, other times southwest, and piling up Rebel corpses in heaps while suffering heavy losses themselves.

Last, but far from least, two divisions of Cheatham's division struck Brigadier General Morgan L. Smith's division astride the Georgia Railroad due east of Atlanta, taking the poorly deployed Yankees by surprise, capturing a battery of rifled artillery, and threatening to break through. Schofield and Howard, whose troops still adjoined the Army of the Tennessee's right, offered to go to Smith's aid. Sherman refused, subsequently explaining that this would have been resented by his beloved Army of the Tennessee. Instead, he assembled all of Schofield's artillery and personally directed a devastating bombardment on the attackers. At the same time, Logan, now acting commander of the Army of the Tennessee, personally led a fierce counterattack that transformed the Confederate success into another dismal failure, a failure that cost Hood at least 5,000 casualties—casualties that could not be replaced either in quantity or quality. Federal losses came to about 3,500, with most of them suffered by Blair's XVII Corps, with Sherman weeping over the death of McPherson.

Following what became known as the Battle of Atlanta, Sherman placed Howard in command of the Army of the Tennessee. Later he would claim that Thomas advised passing over Logan in favor of Howard, but Sherman also questioned whether the politician Logan could do as well as the professional Howard. This, of course, angered Logan, who with good cause believed that he had earned that post on the field of battle, but, since he also felt confident that he would gain in peace as a politician what had been denied him in war because he was not a West Pointer, he made no protest. Not so Joe Hooker. Outraged at being passed over in favor of a general not only junior to him in age and seniority of rank, but also whom he held, not without cause, responsible for his defeat at Chancellorsville, he promptly tendered his resignation as commander of the XX Corps. Sherman, relieved that Hooker wanted to be relieved, promptly replaced him as head of the XX Corps with its senior brigadier, Alpheus Williams, pending the arrival of Henry W. Slocum from Vicksburg.

Having failed to capture Atlanta by striking from the northwest, Sherman next sought to take it by switching the Army of the Tennessee, as always his favored offensive instrument, to the northeast of that city, with its target being the Atlanta & Macon Railroad, a line running due south from the city and now Hood's main and almost sole line of supply. Thanks to his cavalry, Hood quickly perceived Sherman's intent and so instructed Lieutenant General Stephen D. Lee, who now headed Hood's former corps, to parry this impending thrust.

Lee, who at age thirty now was a lieutenant general, struck the Yankees on July 28 at what became known as the Battle of Ezra Church, mainly because there was nothing else to name it after except a road with the unusable name of Lickskillet. An alternate name that never took with historians was the Battle of the Poor House. Lee would have reason to forget the battle's name, in any case, because the Yankees turned back his attack with relative ease. Confederate casualties came to 4,000–5,000; Federal, to one-fifth of that. Lee blamed the repulse on his troops being insufficiently aggressive and subsequently resolved to remedy this fault, with results that will be seen. Howard pondered following up his defensive victory with an offensive thrust but—probably very fortunately—quickly abandoned the notion. Sherman, who prior to Lee's assault had smiled at Howard for taking precautions against an enemy attack, sought to have Jefferson C. Davis's division of the nearby XIV Corps strike the rear of Lee's corps, only to find Davis sick in bed. Learning of Sherman's desire, Davis rose from his bed, dressed, mounted his horse, and then immediately fainted and fell off it. Another XIV Corps general set out with a division to strike Lee in the flank but got lost in the woods and so went in the wrong direction. Given the never-ending flood of books on Civil War battles, it sparks curiosity to note that, as far as this author knows, there is no published book devoted to relating the story of the Battle of Ezra Church. There should be; told the right way, it would make an interesting, perhaps even amusing story.

But this did not end the comedy, or, to be more precise, the military farce, being performed east of Atlanta. After pondering the matter, Sherman decided to cut the Macon Railroad farther south at Utoy Creek by way of the Sandtown Road. To this end, he ordered Schofield with his XXIII Corps to swing around to that point and instructed Palmer with his XIV Corps to reinforce Schofield. From a strictly military standpoint, this was an excellent move. But from a practical one, it could not have been worse. An indignant Palmer, like McClernand a political general, believed (not without cause) that he was senior in his major general's rank to Schofield, and promptly tendered his resignation. Sherman endeavored to persuade Palmer to obey, and Palmer said he would, but then he did so in such a way that Sherman had no choice other than to accept Palmer's resignation and to direct Jefferson C. Davis to take command of the XIV Corps. Meanwhile, Schofield, with his tiny corps, tried to reach the Macon Railroad, only to be stymied on August 4 at Utoy Creek by an abatis of fallen trees so deep and thick that his troops were unable to penetrate it, much less break through to the railroad.

For most of the rest of August, Sherman endeavored with artillery bombardment and cavalry raids to force Hood out of Atlanta. Neither succeeded, and it seemed more and more that he, like Grant at Richmond and Petersburg, was stalemated. Certainly that is how it appeared to Lincoln. Hence, on August 23 he summoned his cabinet members to the White House and had them sign, unread, the following statement: "This morning, as for some days past it seems exceedingly probable that this Administration will not be re-elected. Then it will be my duty to co-operate with the President-elect so as to save the Union between the election and the inauguration, as he will have secured his election on such ground that he cannot possibly save it afterwards."[7] These were the words of a skilled politician who had assessed the situation and found it depressing.

That same day, Sherman held what for him was a rare, perhaps unprecedented thing—a council of war of his top generals. To them he presented a plan based on an outline prepared by Thomas. In essence, it called for leaving the XX Corps, now headed by Slocum, entrenched along the south bank of the Chattahoochee, while the rest of his army swung farther southward with a view to reaching and ripping up the Macon Railroad, thereby forcing Hood either to evacuate Atlanta or else again sally forth to attack the Union spearhead, which, of course, would be the Army of the Tennessee. Should he do neither of these things, then Sherman intended to circle clear around Atlanta, in the process again wrecking the oft-wrecked Georgia Railroad.

On August 28 the Army of the Tennessee, having swung far to the southwest, reached the Montgomery–West Point Railroad near the hamlet of Fairburn, Georgia. Although the Confederates now rarely, if ever, used this line to supply Atlanta, the next day Sherman put one-third of the Army of the Tennessee to work tearing up twelve miles of track and then, after heating the rails over bonfires, twisting them around tree trunks and telegraph poles, thereby making sure that they never could be re-laid. Since it was, to put it mildly, unlikely that the Confederates would endeavor to rebuild a rail line that was in enemy-held territory, Sherman evidently wished to make the improbable impossible.

The following day, August 30, the Army of the Tennessee headed south-westward with orders to halt at Fairburn Place, only four miles from Jones-boro, a straggling village astride the Macon Railroad. At midafternoon it reached this destination only to discover that it provided insufficient drink-ing water. Hence, Howard had it march on until it crossed the Flint River about a mile from Jonesboro. Putting caution foremost—a lesson he had learned, and learned well, at Chancellorsville—he deployed his troops along the crests of a series of ridges overlooking the village. He also sent Sherman a dispatch informing him of his location, adding that his artillery could strike trains attempting to chug their way to Atlanta.

From this point onward any attempt to describe in general terms what oc-curred and why with regard to military operations pertaining to Jonesboro on August 31 and September 1 would be in vain. The tale would soon be-come so tediously complicated that most readers soon would either become confused or else cease to be readers. Besides, the author has performed that task elsewhere, and has no stomach to repeat it.[8] Thus, what follows will generally be general and confine detailed description to where it is neces-sary, even obligatory.

First, let us return to August 28–29 with a brief but necessary word per-taining to Hood. On learning that all of the Federal forces, save those en-trenched north of Atlanta, had abandoned their fortifications, he leaped to the jolly conclusion that Wheeler's raid had left them so short of rations that they were retreating northward so as to stave off starvation. But when his troops explored the Yankee trenches, they found more left-behind food in them than their own normal rations. Also, he soon ascertained that except for the XX Corps all of the Union army was to the southeast of Atlanta, and that its objective probably was the Macon Railroad. But just where on that line would Sherman strike? Until Hood knew that—and could also be sure that Sherman was not feinting toward the railroad and not again seeking to seize Atlanta, this time by striking it on its weakly fortified south side—all Hood could do was wait for reliable intelligence as to Sherman's movements and intentions.

That came on the evening of August 30 in the form of a report from the Confederate cavalry informing Hood that Howard's Army of the Tennes-see was on the west side of the Flint River near Jonesboro. Immediately, Hood directed Hardee to march his and Lee's corps to that town and in the morning drive Howard's forces into that river, following which Lee would return to Atlanta and join Stewart's corps in attacking the rest of Sherman's army from the north, thereby striking its rear, while Hardee assailed it from the south. As on July 20, 22, and 28, Hood sought to smash Sherman, not merely repel him.

Again he failed. Although Hardee's corps reached Jonesboro on the morning of August 31, Lee's corps, which had a longer march to make, did not arrive there until early afternoon, having left hundreds of stragglers behind. By then, Howard, whose 20,000 troops at least equaled Hardee's effective force, had ample time to construct more-than-ample fortifications. Only by a military miracle could the Confederates have breached the Federal line. No such miracle occurred. Instead, Howard's veterans, with Logan's XV Corps doing most of the fighting—or, to be more accurate, killing—easily repulsed the ill-coordinated Rebel assaults, inflicting approximately 2,300 casualties while suffering a mere 172 themselves. It was by far a more one-sided slaughter than even Ezra Church. The only thing that prevented it from being worse was the refusal of many Confederate units, including elite ones, to press forward when they came under fire.

Shortly after midnight a courier arrived at Hood's Atlanta headquarters, bringing word of Hardee's repulse. It had to come by courier because, even as Hardee vainly endeavored to drive Howard's forces away from the Macon Railroad, portions of the XXIII, IV, and XIV Corps reached the railroad north of Jonesboro and south of Rough and Ready, whereupon they cut the telegraph wire to Atlanta. Thus, when Hood read Hardee's message, he realized that there was no possibility left of regaining control of the railroad and that the only choice left him was to evacuate Atlanta. This he ordered done as soon as it became dark on September 1. Meanwhile, Lee's corps, as previously directed, would return to Atlanta to guard against a Federal thrust from the south, and Hardee was to hold on at Jonesboro so as to cover the retreat of the rest of the Confederate army southward.

Sherman's orders for September 1 called for the IV Corps, followed by the XXIII Corps, to move down the railroad, destroying the track as it went, until it reached the Jonesboro area, where it was to join the XIV Corps in attacking Hardee's forces, which Sherman thought still included Lee's corps, despite having been notified to the contrary by Thomas. Not until the early afternoon of September 1 did Sherman realize that Thomas's information was correct and that only Hardee's corps faced him at Jonesboro. He then ordered Stanley's IV Corps to cease tearing up rails—long since an utterly pointless operation—and hasten to assist the XIV Corps in attacking what Sherman believed to be Hardee's exposed right flank north of Jonesboro. If Hardee could be crushed—and Sherman felt confident that he would be—then Hood either would have to abandon Atlanta or else stay there until starvation forced him to surrender the city and what remained of his army. Or so Sherman calculated. Evidently, it did not occur to him that with his sole supply line, the Macon Railroad, in Union possession, Hood's sole rational option was to do what he intended to do—leave Atlanta as soon as practicably possible.

Starting at 4 P.M., just as the van of the IV Corps came up, the XIV Corps launched a series of assaults on Hardee's right flank. By stripping his front facing Howard's forces, which Sherman had directed to "demonstrate" but who did not do even that, Hardee was able to reinforce his right sufficiently to repel the initial attacks. But then three XIV Corps brigades managed to carry a weak point on the Confederate line, swamping the Arkansas Brigade of Cleburne's division, most of whose men held their ground until killed or physically overpowered. It was the first and only successful frontal attack of the entire campaign. Yet Hardee, by bringing up still more troops from his center and left, sealed off the Union breakthrough and also prevented the IV Corps from getting into his rear until night put an end to combat. Hardee thereupon withdrew his forces from their trenches and headed south toward Lovejoy's Station, having conducted one of the finest defensive stands of the war—thanks in large part to Sherman, who botched an opportunity to demolish Hardee's corps and so wreck Hood's army, thereby removing it from the chessboard of the war.

While Hardee's men marched south, so too did the troops of Stewart's corps, Lee's corps, and the Georgia militia as they left Atlanta via the McDonough Road, the sole available safe southward exit from the city, something Sherman evidently failed to anticipate or else decided not to make an effort to prevent it. Before departing, the Confederates set fire to boxcars filled with ammunition, setting off explosions that leveled nearby buildings, among them the rolling mill, and which could be heard all the way to Jonesboro. Sherman, unsure as to what this meant, asked a local farmer (who presumably had become an expert on such matters during the past five some weeks) what this meant and was told that it sounded like a battle. Agreeing, Sherman concluded that Hood remained in Atlanta and probably was engaging Union forces south of the city—a curious conclusion since he had sent no troops to the south of Atlanta, even though the only practicable route in that direction from it was the McDonough road. But Sherman's prime purpose was to take Atlanta, not to destroy or force the surrender of the Army of Tennessee. Given the failure to accomplish this at the very outset of the campaign by way of Snake Creek Gap and during several subsequent occasions, this is understandable, perhaps even excusable. One may judge for oneself as to whether Sherman should be let off the hook for letting Hood escape. If raising this question seems unfair, consider the following: George McClellan has come under criticism by historians for celebrating as his greatest victories the occupation of empty cities, yet Sherman is hailed by many authors for accomplishing the same task. Let readers decide for themselves why this is.

Sherman also believed that Hardee still was at Jonesboro and that it would be impossible for him to slip away undetected. In the morning, on discovering that Hardee had done precisely that, Sherman gave belated pursuit. North of Lovejoy's Station he came upon Hardee's forces strongly entrenched—so strongly that he decided not to attack and instead await definite word as to the situation in and around Atlanta. Early on the morning of September 3, a dispatch arrived from Slocum that his troops had occupied the city the day before. Sherman at once scrawled a brief message to be telegraphed to Washington. It read: "Atlanta is ours, and fairly won."[9] Two days later, by which time all of Hood's army had reassembled at Lovejoy's, the Union troops left their trenches and began marching northward to Atlanta.

The news from Atlanta came at a most opportune time for Abraham Lincoln and the Republican Party; it offered equally bad news for the Democrats, who had hoped to unseat him in that fall's election. For on August 31, even as the Army of the Tennessee repulsed the Confederate attack at Jonesboro, the Democratic national convention, meeting in Chicago, had nominated General George B. McClellan for president on a platform that declared the war a failure and called for "cessation of hostilities, with a view to an ultimate convention of the States or other peaceable means, to the end that at the earliest practicable moment peace may be restored on the basis of the Federal Union of the States."[10] In short, the war was a failure. There was no chance for victory on the battlefield. It was time for a change.

Thus, as August turned into September, most Democrats and a large number of Republicans, including Lincoln himself, expected McClellan to become the next president. A war-weary North, despairing of victory, would install in the White House a man whose party was committed to restoring the Union by means of peace rather than force (although McClellan repudiated this platform plank and declared that he would continue the fight for reunion, although without the excesses of the Lincoln administration, including enforced emancipation). The same expectation prevailed in the South, where on August 20 the *Richmond Sentinel,* which reflected the views of Jefferson Davis, predicted that if the Confederate armies continued to hold Grant and Sherman at bay for six more weeks, "we are almost sure to be in a much better condition to treat for peace than we are now," for the North no longer would be willing and therefore able to go on with its futile war.[11]

Sherman's capture of Atlanta reversed the despondent mood of the North and the expectations of Lincoln, the Democrats, and the South. To the majority of Northerners, it meant that the war was being won and so should be continued until the Union was restored and slavery, the thing which had caused the war, was eradicated. Likewise, Lincoln's pessimism about his election prospects, which other Republican leaders shared, slowly turned to optimism, especially after the Republicans prevailed in a series of October state contests. In November he was reelected by a landslide majority of electoral votes: however, it is useful to recall that even in the aftermath of tremendous Union victories, McClellan still polled some 45 percent of the popular vote, meaning that a change in one out of every twenty votes cast from Lincoln to McClellan would have resulted in a dead heat in the popular vote. Nevertheless, the taking of Atlanta wrecked both the Democratic platform and McClellan's candidacy. And in the South it became clear to all except the most ignorant or fanatical that the North would go on with war so long as Lincoln remained in the White House, which now was scheduled to be for four more years.

But Sherman's capture of Atlanta was not the sole Union success as summer gave way to autumn in 1864. On August 5 Farragut, at the head of a squadron of armored gunboats and oak-reinforced frigates, steamed into Mobile Bay and sunk a supposedly unsinkable Rebel ironclad and then pulverized the remainder of the Rebel fleet, thereby closing Mobile, the main Confederate blockade-running port on the Gulf of Mexico. Next, starting in September in the Shenandoah Valley of Virginia, hitherto a graveyard of defeat for Federal generals, "Little Phil" Sheridan, as his admiring troops dubbed their undersized commander, achieved a series of spectacular victories, including one that transformed a seeming dismal defeat into a glorious triumph, a triumph that secured Northern control of the valley while at the same time reducing still more the Confederacy's ability to wage an already unwinnable war. We now turn to how that happened.

16

Sheridan in the Shenandoah

(August–October 1864)

To UNDERSTAND THE COURSE OF MILITARY operations in the Shenandoah Valley, it is a good idea first to orient oneself to the region's topography. The Shenandoah Valley derives its name from the Shenandoah River, which flows from southwest to northeast, emptying into the Potomac River at Harpers Ferry. For this reason, when an army in the Valley moved southward it *went up* the Valley, and when it headed northward it *marched down* it.

Second, but more important, because the Shenandoah Valley is separated from northeastern Virginia, otherwise known as the Tidewater, by a chain of high hills somewhat extravagantly titled the Blue Ridge Mountains, it provided, as we have had occasion to see, a covered way by which Lee's Army of Northern Virginia invaded Maryland and Pennsylvania in 1863. After both the Maryland Campaign of 1862 and the Gettysburg Campaign the following year, it was able to secure refuge by withdrawing into the Valley to recuperate before returning to northern Virginia to block any Union overland thrust toward Richmond.

Third, as the war went on and on, the Valley became ever more essential to Lee's lean legions. From its fertile fields and plenteous pastures they derived most of their already meager rations. Aware of this, Grant initially determined upon a two-pronged advance from both ends of the Valley to deprive the Confederates of its use for either movement or supply. To drive southward was the task assigned to Major General Franz Sigel, a onetime German army officer who in 1848 had, along with other idealistic Deutschlanders, risen in revolt to transform Germany, at least one hundred years prematurely, into a democracy. Following a probably inevitable failure and, in order to escape a firing squad, if not a hangman's noose, he fled to the United States. There, upon their becoming the divided states in 1861, he offered his military services to the Union army, had them accepted by Lincoln, and eventually obtained his high rank in spite of battlefield performances that can only be described as low, if not miserable, notably at Wilson's Creek near Springfield, Missouri, on August 10, 1861. Such setbacks did not deter Lincoln from appointing Sigel to command the Department of West Virginia in February 1864. After all, one might recall, it was an election year, and Sigel's presence in a command might be rewarded by voters at the polls.

Grant admitted that when it came to Sigel's advance, "I do not calculate on very great results." He was not to be disappointed, although what happened next suggests that even then he expected too much. For it took Sigel a mere week to stumble into disaster. On May 15 John C. Breckinridge, now heading an infantry division in the Army of Northern Virginia and having been sent to the Valley by Lee, attacked Sigel at New Market, midway between Winchester and Staunton, with about 5,000 troops, among them 225 cadets from the Virginia Military Institute. Thanks to his mostly veteran soldiers and superior tactics, he routed Sigel, inflicting on his force 831 casualties while suffering 577, among them 10 cadets killed and 47 wounded. Days later the southern prong of the thrust also fizzled.[1]

The news that Sigel had failed did not surprise Henry Halleck, who informed Grant of the defeat. "If you expect anything from him you will be mistaken," Halleck caustically commented. "He will do nothing but run. He never did anything else."[2] Grant immediately replaced the German with David Hunter. As Lee had summoned Breckinridge back to his army, Hunter faced little opposition as he commenced advancing south up the Valley. His men set fire to croplands, slaughtered livestock, and at Lexington on June 11 torched the Virginia Military Institute at Lexington. Hunter also would have burned nearby Washington College, today's Washington and Lee University, had not the officer placed in charge of this incendiary mission disobeyed orders. Ultimately, he exited from the Valley, his target Charlottesville, his objective the destruction of the Virginia Central Railroad, the sole remaining iron link between the Army of Northern Virginia and its prime agricultural supply base. To assist Hunter, Grant sent Sheridan with two divisions of cavalry westward. Learning of this, Lee in turn ordered Major General Wade Hampton's cavalry division to head him off. This Hampton did at Trevilian Station, in the process almost capturing a long-haired Yankee cavalryman named George Armstrong Custer.

At the same time, Lee also dispatched by rail to the Valley four crack infantry divisions totaling 20,000, all headed by Lieutenant General Jubal A. Early. They made their way to Lynchburg, where they checked the Union advance. Hunter fled into West Virginia, leaving the Valley wide open to Early, who promptly took advantage of the situation. He marched rapidly northward down the Valley, crossed the Potomac at Harpers Ferry into Maryland, and headed for Washington.[3]

Unlike 1862 and 1863, no strong garrison manned the capital's formidable fortifications. Owing to the heavy losses suffered during the Overland Campaign, Grant had stripped the District of Columbia of its defenders, which consisted of regiments called "heavies," because they had been serving as heavy artillery regiments manning the Washington fortifications. Each numbered nearly 1,200, a sum which rapidly dwindled once they engaged in combat. "Replacing" them were uniformed office clerks and "walking wounded" from the capital's hospitals, a makeshift garrison that was hardly a match for Early's veterans.

Fortunately for the Union cause, the Republicans, and Lincoln, Early was delayed for a day-plus on his way to Washington. On July 9, when he approached the Monocacy River, little more than a day's march from the capital, he encountered a contingent of 5,000 mostly fledgling Federal soldiers, headed by Lew Wallace—who at Shiloh had aroused Grant's wrath by taking what he had no way of knowing had become the wrong road to reinforce Sherman's surprised and beleaguered division. Wallace lacked the strength to repel Early's far more numerous veterans, but he delayed them a day, thereby providing just enough time for four divisions of the Army of the Potomac to reach Washington, having been sent there via water transport by Grant at the urgent urgings of Lincoln, Stanton, and Halleck.

On July 11 and 12 Early probed one of Washington's bulwarks due north of the city, correctly concluded that even if his soldiers managed to storm it their casualties would be catastrophic, and returned to the Valley content to have dimmed Lincoln's reelection prospects in what appeared to be a summer of stalemate for the Union cause. Union forces stumbled in pursuit, lacking a common head to give unified direction. Lincoln sought to solve that problem by giving Halleck command of the Washington defenses, which served only to remind everyone of Halleck's utter uselessness as a field commander (Charles Dana confided that Halleck was drinking heavily and his mind was "regularly muddled after dinner every day").

Several weeks later, Early moved northward once more, and one of his subordinates ordered the burning of Chambersburg, Pennsylvania, as retaliation for Hunter's incendiary behavior the previous month, the townspeople having proved unable to meet his original demand for ransom. The event took place on the same day as the Crater disaster, adding to the feeling among many northern voters that perhaps the war would never end and that it might be time to think about voting out the Lincoln administration.

Grant now resolved to eliminate once and for all the Shenandoah as a source of rations for the Army of Northern Virginia and a passageway for

Confederate forays into the North. At first he was willing to retain Hunter in department command while placing Sheridan "in command of all the troops in the field with instructions to put himself south of the enemy and follow him to the death." That idea pleased neither Stanton nor Halleck, who did what they could to get in the way, until Lincoln himself wired Grant that nothing was happening: "I repeat to you it will neither be done nor attempted unless you watch it every day, and hour, and force it." Tired of trying to motivate Halleck, who was far better at offering suggestions than following (or giving) orders, Grant traveled north to see personally what needed to be done. Realizing that he was in the way, Hunter gracefully bowed out, and Grant, seizing upon one of Halleck's suggestions, assigned Sheridan to the command of what was designated the Middle Military Division, consisting of what had been four separate departments. In so doing, Grant ignored objections from Stanton, who deemed Sheridan, thirty-three, to be too young. Moreover, Grant told Sheridan that he was to take orders only from the general in chief himself, a way to curtail interference from Washington.[4]

Grant believed that at last he had gotten his way when it came to the command situation at Washington. For several months he had floated suggestion after suggestion, from placing George G. Meade in charge (and thus detach the grumbling general from the Army of the Potomac) to handing command over to William B. Franklin, whose military abilities Grant continued to appreciate long after others had been disabused of his supposed skills—perhaps because Franklin had headed Grant's West Point class of 1843. There had even been discussion that perhaps McClellan himself would take charge of the Washington defenses, which would have been rich irony, indeed, given his previous troubles with the administration over the proper way to defend the capital. Sheridan's appointment would put an end to the confusion that had caused Grant to lose all patience with Stanton and Halleck. A few days later, Halleck suggested that in light of evidence of increased dissent in the North, with talk of secret societies, resistance to the draft, and various other plots, perhaps Grant should prepare to send troops northward to maintain order. Grant dismissed that idea out of hand: that same day he entertained the idea of sending Halleck to California in order to get him out of the way. Coming across Grant's dispatch rejecting the transfer of troops north, Lincoln approved, telling Grant: "Hold on with a bull-dog grip, and chew & choke, as much as possible." Grant smiled when he read Lincoln's telegram, remarking, "The President has more nerve than any of his advisers." As an aide put it, "Halleck has no control over troops except as Grant delegates it. He can give no orders and exercise no discretion. Grant now runs the whole machine independently of the Washington directory."[5]

If Grant ran the whole machine, he gave Sheridan total authority to operate it. Sheridan owed his elevation at such a high command at so low an age to his performance during the Overland Campaign. During it he transformed the Army of the Potomac's cavalry from what hitherto had been mainly picket service and escorting wagon trains into a highly mobile, hard-hitting combat force capable of holding its own and increasingly more than that when engaging Lee's cavaliers, thanks to repeating carbines and fighting as much, if not more, on foot rather than astride a saddle. Thus at Yellow Tavern on May 11, his first and, as it turned out, only encounter with Jeb Stuart, one of his dismounted troopers shot the South's *beau sabreur* from his saddle, mortally wounding him.

On August 7 Sheridan took command of what soon became the Army of the Shenandoah. It fielded 43,000 infantry, cavalry, and artillery, with most of its cavalry and one infantry corps detailed from the Army of the Potomac. Many thousands more Union soldiers, although officially commanded by Sheridan, guarded the Baltimore & Ohio Railroad and the borderlands of West Virginia, Maryland, and Pennsylvania, all subject to Rebel raiders, most notably John S. Mosby's fearsome partisans. Opposing Sheridan was Early, with 20,000 troops of all arms, most of them veterans of what had been Stonewall Jackson's corps, holding Winchester.[6]

Sheridan's mission was a simple one: defeat Early and deprive the Confederacy of the resources offered by the Shenandoah Valley. Grant was explicit on that score. "Do all the damage to railroads & crops you can," he instructed Sheridan. "Carry off stock of all descriptions and negroes, so as to prevent further planting. If the war is to last another year we want the Shenandoah Valley to remain a barren waste."[7]

In spite of his great numerical superiority, Sheridan made no attempt to engage Early for six weeks. This was not out of timidity. It was Sheridan's first time heading a large army, and he faced a foe that, although numerically outnumbered, was equal if not superior to his own forces in combat experience. Before engaging in the gamble of combat, Sheridan wanted to become better acquainted with the peculiar topography of the Valley, his new generals, and the intentions and potentialities of Early.

In the case of the last, he enjoyed a stroke of luck. During the night of September 14, a black man who peddled vegetables in the Valley town of Winchester came into Union lines and informed him that he knew there a young Quaker woman named Rebecca Wright, who was a Unionist and

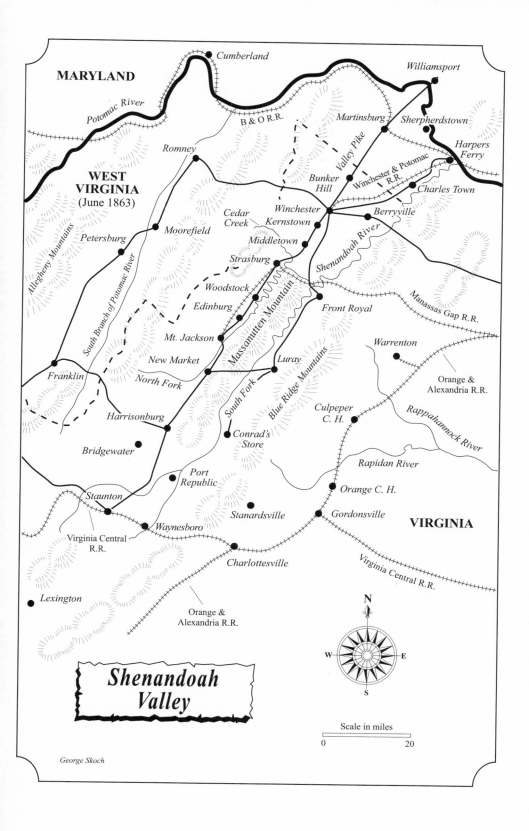

MARYLAND

Potomac River

Cumberland

Williamsport

B & O.R.R.

Martinsburg

Sherpherdstown

Harpers Ferry

Romney

WEST VIRGINIA
(June 1863)

Valley Pike

Bunker Hill

Winchester & Potomac R.R.

Charles Town

Allegheny Mountains

Petersburg

Moorefield

Cedar Creek

Winchester

Berryville

Kernstown

Shenandoah River

South Branch of Potomac River

Middletown

Strasburg

Woodstock

Edinburg

Massanutten Mountain

Front Royal

Manassas Gap R.R.

Warrenton

Mt. Jackson

New Market

Luray

Franklin

North Fork

South Fork

Blue Ridge Mountains

Orange & Alexandria R.R.

Culpeper C. H.

Rappahannock River

Harrisonburg

Bridgewater

Conrad's Store

Rapidan River

Port Republic

Orange C. H.

Staunton

Stanardsville

Gordonsville

VIRGINIA

Waynesboro

Virginia Central R.R.

Charlottesville

Virginia Central R.R.

Lexington

Orange & Alexandria R.R.

N

W   E

S

Shenandoah Valley

Scale in miles

0   20

George Skoch

who could provide him with useful information. He promptly sent the black to her with a written message enclosed in his mouth, where he could swallow it if apprehended by Confederates. She sent back word by the same courier that Kershaw's division of Early's army was on the way back to Lee with an artillery battery. Sheridan thereupon decided to engage Early and began making plans and preparations to that end.

It was well he did. His increasingly long failure to do so had produced mounting criticism in the Northern press and complaints from the politically influential president of the Baltimore & Ohio Railroad. This in turn induced Grant to travel by train to Charles Town in West Virginia, where on September 17 he met with Sheridan, in his overcoat pocket a plan he had written for defeating Early. But after Sheridan told him of Rebecca Wright's information and of his own intent to engage Early soon, Grant entrained back to the Army of the Potomac, his plan still in the pocket. Unfortunately for Sheridan, or, to be more precise, a large number of his soldiers, Early learned of Grant's visit from his spies and, correctly concluding that this portended offensive action by Sheridan, abandoned his intent to strike the Baltimore & Ohio, summoned Kershaw back to his army, and withdrew to a strong defensive position on the northern outskirts of Winchester.

On Monday, September 19, the day he had told Grant he would do it, Sheridan attacked Early. As almost always in battle, neither opponent succeeded in doing what he wanted to in the way he planned to do it. However, for a change, at least when it came to Civil War engagements, the attackers prevailed over the defenders, thanks mainly to Sheridan's cavalry being armed with Spencer and Henry repeating rifles, whereas Early's troopers, few if any of whom came from the Army of Northern Virginia, possessed single-shot, muzzle-loading Enfield muskets that were next to impossible to reload while on horseback and whose lack of sabers, except on the part of officers, rendered them vulnerable to the *arme blanche*, especially when charged by sword-wielding, mounted Yankee troopers, led by the likes of twenty-five-year-old Custer, who believed himself to be immortal (which he became in 1876 at a place in Montana called the Little Big Horn, albeit not in the way he presumably desired).

Sheridan's chief of staff telegraphed Washington, "We have just sent [Early's Confederates] whirling through Winchester." This struck the North's fancy, and Sheridan was promoted to brigadier general in the regular army. Meanwhile, "Little Phil" pursued Early and on September 22 struck him again at Fisher's Hill, this time in the left rear as well as the left flank. The outcome was another victory, an outcome that cost him a mere 528 casualties while inflicting more than twice that many on the Confederates, most of whom fled in utter rout.[8]

Grant honored Sheridan's new success with a hundred-gun "salute" on Lee's lines. At the same time, he endeavored to persuade, but refrained from ordering, him to march up the Valley to its southern terminus and then demolish the Virginia Central Railroad at and around Charlottesville. Sheridan demurred. His army, he protested, now was 104 miles from its supply base at Harpers Ferry. "I think the best policy," he contended, "will be to let the burning of the crops in the Valley be the end of this campaign, and let some of this army go elsewhere"—that is, back to the Richmond-Petersburg front.[9] Grant assented to this proposal, and Sheridan thereupon acted upon it, his troops transforming the verdant fields of the Shenandoah into scorched earth, over which no intelligent crow would deign flutter even with rations. Upon completing this fiery task, the question became: What next? Grant not having sent Sheridan new instructions, much less orders, Stanton and Halleck on October 13 summoned him to Washington. Just before he entrained for the capital, he received word that Federal signalmen had intercepted a Rebel telegram transmitted from Richmond to Early: "Be ready to move as soon as my forces join you and we will crush Sheridan. Longstreet."[10]

Was this valid? Or a ruse? Sheridan decided it was not. But he could not be sure. So he instructed Major General Horatio Wright, who would be in command during his absence, to "look well to your ground and be well prepared," then entrained from Winchester to Washington. There his meeting with Stanton and Halleck proved to be both brief and pointless. He returned to Winchester on the night of October 18 and went to bed.[11]

Shortly before dawn on October 19, Sheridan awakened to the rumble of artillery fire coming from the south in the vicinity of Cedar Creek. At first, he assumed it was only Wright conducting a reconnaissance. But after this sound not only continued but also grew louder, he set forth on his big black steed, Rienzi. As he rode farther, the roar of artillery grew ever louder. Then he met fleeing Federal soldiers, none armed, some wounded, all demoralized. They explained that Early had attacked the Yankee camps that morning and overrun them. Shocked, Sheridan spurred Rienzi into a gallop but slowed to a trot as the trickle of blue-clad refugees turned into a torrent.

At about 10:30 A.M. he reached what remained of his army (which was most of it), armed and (more or less) formed. It consisted of most of the infantry and artillery, and nearly all of the cavalry. Seeing one of his generals, he asked him what had happened. "Well," came the reply, "we did the best we could." "That is all right," said Sheridan. "My troops," added the general, "are prepared to cover the retreat." "Retreat!" roared Sheridan. "Retreat hell! We'll be back in our camps tonight!" He then asked what had happened and learned that the Rebels had made a surprise attack on the army's left wing, totally routing it and causing the rest of the Federals to fall back—or, to be more accurate, run for it until most of them, discovering that the Rebs were not pursuing, halted and began reforming.[12]

On hearing this, Sheridan decided to transform defeat into victory. Obtaining his personal banner, a red and white flag with the two stars of a major general emblazoned on it, he rode Rienzi along the lines of his cheering, now-ready-to-fight soldiers, shouting "Attack! Attack!" And attack they did, not only successfully but spectacularly, with the cavalry sweeping around and behind Early's left flank. Soon the Confederates were in total, unstoppable flight, leaving behind nearly 2,000 dead and wounded and at least if not more than 1,000 prisoners. Federal casualties came to about 3,000. Based on the success of the opening attack, Early had assumed that he had defeated Sheridan's army. This he did to the army but not to Sheridan—an understandable yet, as it turned out, unfortunate assumption both for him and the Confederacy.

Sheridan's transformation of a Federal defeat into a spectacular Federal victory at Cedar Creek led to Lee summoning all of Early's infantry, save a division, back to his army and to Grant having Sheridan elevated at the age of thirty-three to a major general in the regular army, thereby making him one of the youngest, if not the youngest, American ever to attain that rank at least prior to World War II. Another hundred-gun salute rained lead upon the heads of Lee's men. The dramatic victory also inspired a Northern poet to pen a poem titled "Sheridan's Ride," wherein Rienzi, as he carries Sheridan to Cedar Creek, speaks to him in galloping octameter verse, concluding with this couplet: "I have brought you Sheridan all the way / From Winchester down to save the day!"[13]

But from the historical standpoint, the prime importance of Sheridan transforming a shameful defeat into a spectacular victory at Cedar Creek was that, following as it did Foote's triumph in Mobile Bay and (much more) Sherman's seizure of Atlanta, it destroyed any chance, which obviously had seemed to Lincoln a certain one, of a war-weary North, in defeatist despair, choosing the "Young Napoleon" over the "Rail-Splitter." As it turned out, Lincoln defeated McClellan by a landslide electoral vote, whereupon the latter resigned his now-meaningless general's commission and voyaged with his wife and children to Europe, there to tell any who would listen that Lincoln prevented him from terminating the American

Civil War in a way that would have led to the Southern states returning voluntarily to the Union, with the status of slavery to be determined sometime in an undefined future.

Now only Grant and Sherman surpassed Sheridan in Northern prestige. But before resuming the tale of "Little Phil," we must pay a brief, but necessary, visit to the first two before narrating how Thomas, overcoming numerous obstructions and barely escaping unwarranted removal from the military stage, came to join them in standing on one of the top rungs of the ladder reserved for the victors in blue.

17

Sherman Marches to the Sea, Schofield Repulses Hood, and Thomas Vanquishes Hood at Nashville

(September–December 1864)

AFTER HE OCCUPIED ATLANTA, Sherman followed—pursued would be an exaggeration—Hood's army southward to Lovejoy's Station. There he found it so strongly positioned and barricaded that to attack it almost surely would be more costly than any success would be worth. Thus, he fell back to Atlanta, his primary target all along. Hood sidestepped westward to Palmetto, Georgia, a town situated on a rail line connecting it to Selma, Alabama, the warehouses and workshops of which became the prime source of his supplies. There he began rebuilding what remained of his badly battered army. Desertion and casualties to battle and illness had reduced the Army of Tennessee to little more than 20,000 effectives—all soldiers willing to fight and capable of fighting.

Sherman, having at long and bloody last attained Atlanta, promptly decreed that all of its civilian inhabitants evacuate the place but offered them a choice between seeking refuge in Rebel regions or traveling northward. Most, of course, chose the former, but a goodly number preferred the latter, and not a few remained in Atlanta, their disobedience ignored, they being either useful or harmless. Also, Sherman freed what remained of Daniel Govan's Arkansas Brigade, most of which had been captured in the final fighting at Jonesboro, in return for the release of George Stoneman from Andersonville. As to future operations, that remained to be determined by future events, political as well as military.

Should the reader assume that Hood, in the wake of his multiple defeats and heavy losses, was removed from command, he or she will be forgivably excused. But with whom could Jefferson Davis replace him? Johnston? To do that would be to admit making a mistake, and Davis rarely, if ever, admitted doing that. Hardee? He had been offered command following Chattanooga but had turned it down. Lee? Absurd; who could replace him in

Virginia? Longstreet? A good tactician, but his strategic ability was dubious, and in any case he was still recovering from his Wilderness wound. Beauregard? Here was a solution—or, rather, the appearance of one. Put him in titular command of a "Department of the West" but leave Hood as the actual head of the Army of Tennessee. Despite his failure to hold on to Atlanta, he fought Sherman, fought him hard, and could be counted on to continue doing so.

So Hood retained his post while Beauregard assumed his new responsibilities in early October. Hardee went to take charge of what was left of the Confederacy's Atlantic seaboard states south of Virginia, Benjamin Cheatham took over his corps, and Davis returned to Richmond. All that remained to be done was to restore the Army of Tennessee in number, health, and, above all, morale—morale defined as not merely a willingness to fight but as a *desire* to engage the enemy and not merely defeat him but crush him, in the process driving him from Georgia, then Tennessee, and finally Kentucky, with a view of liberating it from Northern dominance.

On September 27–28 Hood, his army restored to 30,000-some soldiers, with returnees from hospitals, recruits, reinforcements, and Wheeler's cavalry, crossed to the north side of the Chattahoochee and headed for Sherman's railroad lifeline from Chattanooga. Destroying it would force Sherman to withdraw all the way back to Tennessee in order to prevent his army from starving in Georgia. In theory, it was a superb plan; in practice, it proved to be a fizzle. Although Hood's soldiers tore up miles of track, Yankee work crews rapidly restored them. Hood's forces retook such places as Big Shanty, Acworth, and Dalton but suffered repulses at Allatoona and Resaca. Furthermore, never once did Hood attempt to engage Sherman's army in battle. Although no one would accuse him of lacking aggressiveness, he dared not do it, being so heavily outnumbered and outgunned. Hence, as October gave way to November, he withdrew westward into north Alabama.

Having taken Atlanta, Sherman soon realized that it was becoming an albatross around his neck. If Hood would not engage him, he could not track down the elusive Confederate. Within days of occupying Atlanta he was already thinking of something else to do—namely, picking up stakes and heading for the seacoast, living off the land, ripping up railroads, and destroying Confederate supplies. Just think of the terror he would inflict upon the psyche of civilians! He would prove to them that Jeff Davis could no longer defend them, and perhaps they would give up hope for the Confederacy altogether. "This may not be war, but rather statesmanship," he told Grant. Therefore, he proposed to Grant that after leaving with Thomas sufficient strength to deal with Hood that the bulk of his army march from Atlanta to Savannah, there to board ships that would transport it to Virginia, where it would join the Army of the Potomac in crushing Lee and winning the war. "I can make march and make Georgia howl," he declared.[1]

Initially, Grant rejected Sherman's proposal, contending that even if such a march proved practicable, it risked enabling Hood to sweep into Tennessee, seize Nashville, invade Kentucky, perhaps even raid Ohio, then join Lee. Moreover, Lincoln and Stanton were skittish about the idea. Once Grant gave his approval, he had to convince his boss that Sherman could do the job. That proved difficult to do. As October drew to an end, none other than Grant's chief of staff, John A. Rawlins, went to Washington to argue against the proposal once more—this time behind Grant's back. It would be some time before Grant learned of Rawlins's action: one may sense his reaction by noting that one of the few times Grant mentioned Rawlins in his memoirs was to report his subordinate's behavior. However, Grant prevailed on Sherman in one respect: the march was not to commence until after Election Day. No need to place at risk what by early November was now a sure reelection triumph for the incumbent.[2]

On November 16 Sherman set forth from Atlanta with 62,000 troops formed into two "armies," one consisting of the XV and XVI Corps of the Army of the Tennessee, the other of the XIV and the XX Corps of the Army of the Cumberland. His advance was covered by Kilpatrick's horsemen, with all troops authorized to "forage liberally." This they did, as did also Wheeler's cavalry, which, to use the term loosely, pursued Sherman.

If Hood considered also pursuing Sherman, he promptly dismissed the notion from his mind. Should he do so, his army would be unable to catch up with him and its troops soon would be starving. Instead, he decided to do what he had long desired to do—march into Tennessee and head for Nashville. This he did, but not until after being delayed by logistical difficulties. It was late November before his full army crossed the Tennessee River at Florence, Alabama, on its way to Middle Tennessee.[3]

Hood's advance came at a favorable time for him, but not for George H. Thomas. Like Sherman, Thomas had assumed that should Hood invade Tennessee, then A. J. Smith's XVII Corps and Wilson's cavalry corps would be available to provide ample strength, along with Stanley's and Schofield's soldiers, to repel, indeed crush, Hood. Such did not prove to be the case. Although Wilson's troopers were present near Nashville with a roster strength of 12,000, less than one-half of them possessed usable horses. As for Smith's corps, 9,200 strong, almost all of it still was on the way by steamboat from Missouri, it having been "borrowed" by Rosecrans to help repel an invasion by Sterling Price in another attempt by him to "liberate" his home state from Yankee thralldom—a move that angered Grant so much that he contemplated ordering Old Rosey's arrest. Thus Schofield found himself confronting Hood with little more than half Hood's strength.

Before proceeding with this narrative, let us become better acquainted with Schofield, who now possesses the opportunity, indeed the need, to defeat or at least frustrate a major enemy army and therefore become a victor in blue. Like Sheridan, Schofield was a mere thirty-three years of age, but he was a resident of Illinois instead of Ohio, that spawning place of Yankee generals, and a graduate of West Point. He was one of the least physically prepossessing generals in the Union army. Although not as short as Sheridan, he was far from tall, had a protruding belly, was, in spite of his youth, bald, and sported a rectangular beard that flowed down his chest like a hirsute waterfall. Yet he also possessed a powerful intellect, strong and steady nerves, immense physical stamina, enormous knowledge of military lore, and that gift deemed by Napoleon essential to success in war: *bonne chance.*[4]

To narrate in any fashion even approaching detail, the military waltz performed by Hood and Schofield during almost all of the final week of November would be as ineffectual as it would be tedious. Suffice to state that Hood endeavored again and again to trap and destroy Schofield's tiny army, only again and again to fail. Then on November 29, as evening surrendered to night (as it always does), it seemed to Hood that he had Schofield trapped near a Tennessee hamlet named Spring Hill. But again Hood was mistaken; Schofield already had taken measures to repel any likely enemy attack and was able to "escape" northward via a turnpike to a good defensive position situated between a loop in the Harpeth River and near the south outskirts of a small town called Franklin. Here he deployed and entrenched most of his army, while the rest planked a railroad bridge and a semiburned regular bridge so that his huge wagon train could cross the river and trundle on to Nashville and safety. Also, he and most of his troops took much-needed naps.

Toward midafternoon Hood's army began cresting the Winstead Hills overlooking the Federal entrenchments athwart the pike leading to Franklin and then Nashville. Forrest, beholding the Federal battle line, proposed to Hood that he cross the easily forded Harpeth River to the east with his cavalry and swing around the Yankee left flank. Hood agreed to let him send one of his three divisions across that stream but declared he intended to crush the Yankees with a frontal assault. Finally, at about 4:30 P.M., as the bright sun began descending, Hood's soldiers started advancing, with

Cheatham's division on the left and Stewart's on the right. At the same time, one of Forrest's divisions crossed the Harpeth.[5]

Federal artillery fire ripped the Rebel ranks, creating gaps, all of which were promptly refilled. Then Granbury's Texans became lucky—or so they thought. Owing to the stupendous stupidity of some general or staff officer who seems to have eluded historical detection, two Federal brigades had been posted athwart the pike without any fortification worthy of the name. Faced with the grim prospect of being literally overrun, the defenseless Federals took to their heels, thereby creating a human shield. Taking advantage of it, Brigadier General Hiram Granbury's veterans penetrated the Union center. They were then beat back by a Yankee counterattack made by a veteran brigade headed by Brigadier General Emerson Opdycke, who, upon emptying his revolver, employed it as a hammer to knock down at least one unlucky Texan.

Opdycke's counterattack, which he made on his own initiative, plugged the gap in Schofield's line, following which the battle turned into a one-sided slaughter, with the Confederates on the wrong side. Even so, they kept attacking, attacking, and attacking until pitch darkness terminated the carnage. Federal casualties came to a little over 3,000, with one-third of them being in the two unfortunate brigades stationed in what should have been no-man's-land. As for Hood's army, it lost 6,200 killed, wounded, or missing, with Cleburne and Granbury among the departed. As for the division of Forrest's cavalry allowed to turn the Yankee left, it forded the Harpeth without difficulty, but, on beholding Wilson's numerically superior troopers, reforded it.

On the morning of December 1 Schofield withdrew with his troops to the semicircle of fortifications protecting Nashville. After meeting with Thomas, who told him that he had done "well," he went to a hotel, secured a room, and then slept from noon of this day to noon of the ensuing day; evidently, he needed sleep. Meanwhile, Hood followed the Federals and entrenched along a line facing them. His plan, or, to be more accurate, his hope, was that he could repel an attack by the Yankees, then chase them, hard on their heels, beyond those fortifications and on into Nashville, there to accept their surrender and feast on their abundant rations. Also, he hoped, indeed more than hoped, that he would be reinforced by troops from the trans-Mississippi, unaware that those troops threatened to mutiny if told they were going to be transported across the Big River to quite possibly be killed while fighting to forestall some stranger's home from being looted and then burned.[6]

Although Thomas now had assembled nearly all of his army, on paper a 60,000-plus host, a major problem remained: most of Wilson's troopers lacked mounts capable of galloping or marching without floundering. Although they fought on foot—firing a repeater while mounted tended to waste ammunition—they required horses in order to be able to move about with more rapidity and flexibility than foot-slogging infantry. Well aware of this, Thomas authorized Wilson's troopers to acquire horses wherever and however they could be acquired. This they did, in the process securing some streetcar steeds in Nashville and an all-white circus horse.

At the same time, Thomas found himself countering doubts from Washington and City Point, Virginia, where Grant had established his headquarters, that he would pounce on Hood and crush him before Hood escaped northward. In part this was due to an impression that Schofield's victory at Franklin placed him in a position to follow up and finish the job; in part, there was a concern that Hood could still wreak havoc if he made his way to the Ohio River. From Washington came a dispatch to Grant from Stanton sharing Lincoln's concern at what appeared to be Thomas's reluctance to move. "The President feels solicitous about the disposition of Thomas to lay in fortifications for an indefinite period," Stanton telegraphed Grant, adding: "This looks like the McClellan & Rosecrans strategy of do nothing and let the Rebels raid the country. The president wishes you to consider the matter."[7]

Grant had been considering the matter. He believed Thomas was an extremely able commander on the defensive, but that he tended to wait until everything was in place before advancing. In a word, Thomas seemed slow, a far more damning noun than "deliberate." Now under pressure from Washington, he began to prod Thomas to strike sooner than later. Smarting under such reminders, Thomas described his situation and pledged to advance within a few days. Those days passed with no word from Thomas. Finally, Grant inquired of Thomas as to what was going on: Thomas said he needed a few more days to remount his cavalry. That news did not go over well with Stanton. "Thomas seems unwilling to attack because it is hazardous as if all war was anything but hazardous," the secretary declared. "If he waits for Wilson to get ready, Gabriel will be blowing his last horn." Grant once more urged Thomas to attack, warning him to do so before bad weather intervened. On December 9 Thomas promised to do so within a few days. Again Grant waited in vain to hear word of an attack. He finally prodded Thomas once more, only to hear that by the time Thomas was ready to move, the weather had turned bad—just as Grant had predicted.[8]

Thomas would have been wise to have kept Grant informed of the situation rather than await his hectoring telegrams. However, the two men simply lacked much in the way of chemistry, and what Larry Daniel has called the Rock of Chickamauga's "passive aggressiveness" (which may have been sheer stubbornness) made things worse. For his part, Grant never gave Thomas the slack he afforded Sherman and Sheridan, who were known to insist on their way of doing things. Neither Grant nor Thomas trusted each other. Thomas believed that Grant simply wasn't aware of the situation at Nashville and was being unreasonable. However, he seemed reluctant to inform Grant of the situation until asked about it by Grant. On the other hand, Grant was not willing to leave Thomas to his own devices. Given that he had once smarted at superiors telling him what to do, he might have shown more empathy. The relationship was proving as chilly as was the iced-over ground around Nashville, although both men were steamed.

By the time Grant received Thomas's weather report, he had already told Washington that he was willing to replace Thomas with someone else. At first, the candidate was Schofield. Halleck managed to sit on the order long enough for Thomas to report about weather delays. Stymied for the moment, Grant told Thomas that his patience was running thin: "I have as much confidence in your conducting a battle rightly as I have in any other officer. But it seems to me that you have been slow and I have had no explanation of affairs to convince me otherwise." For his part, Thomas said that he would submit to being relieved, if that was Grant's wish.[9]

And it was—almost. A day and a half later Grant ordered Thomas to attack at once. Probably with a shrug of his massive shoulders, Thomas instructed Wilson to assemble his troopers for an attack. Wilson endeavored to do so but with results that would have been comical had they not been so dismal. His troopers' steeds often staggered, slipped, and frequently fell, with in some cases broken bones being suffered by both humans and horses. Not until dusk did Wilson's cavalry reach its attack position, leaving Thomas with no rational alternative other than to cancel the attack.[10]

During the evening Thomas met with his corps commanders. Should an attack be delivered come morning, or should it be postponed until the ice thawed, he asked them. Unanimously, they chose the latter; to have done otherwise would have been folly. On the ensuing morning, Thomas telegraphed Halleck that he would attack as soon as the ice melted, adding that an attack now "would only result in a useless sacrifice of life." Halleck in turn transmitted Thomas's message to Grant. Now having what he considered a fully legitimate reason to relieve Thomas, Grant thereupon instructed "Black Jack" Logan, who had been given leave following the occupation of Atlanta to drum up votes in Illinois for Lincoln, to hasten to Nashville and relieve Thomas. But then, on December 14, he decided to do both of these himself. After all, while an excellent citizen soldier, Logan was not a West Point–certified professional. Perhaps Grant also realized that since Thomas and Logan were on poor personal terms, the former would be deeply insulted at being superseded by the latter. Or, just possibly, he wished personally to take over command from Thomas as he had with Rosecrans, another general he disliked.[11]

But on the morning of December 15, the ice having turned into mud, Thomas attacked, employing his infantry to tie down Hood in front while Wilson's troopers, advancing to combat on foot, assailed the Rebel left flank, which, in the form of a string of blockhouses, ran at a right angle to the front line. As almost always, the half-starved Confederates, many of whom were shoeless and in rags, fought valiantly and repelled most frontal attacks. But finding themselves in danger of being cut off by Wilson's turning movement, they fell back to entrench along a new line as dusk descended.[12]

The next day was, in essence, a repetition of the first, but with one big difference: this time the Confederates were routed, with many of them throwing down their arms and raising their hands. Most of them, though, simply fled, discarding their rifles as they did so. Had Wilson's cavalry been able to pursue quickly and rapidly, in all probability it could have overtaken and cut off most of what remained of Hood's army, leaving it with no choice other than to surrender. As it was, only a demoralized remnant of it managed to reach Tupelo, thanks mainly to superb rearguard action by Forrest's cavalry, which had been sent off by Hood in another attack of folly, or desperation, in what turned out to be a futile attempt to seize the strongly fortified supply base that Rosecrans had established at Murfreesboro following Stones River.

Logan, on learning at Louisville of Thomas's first-day success, aborted his trip to Nashville. Grant did likewise, but not without also telegraphing Thomas: "Push the enemy now, and give him no rest until he is completely destroyed." Lincoln also congratulated Thomas and had the Senate promote him to major general in the regular army. This, of course, pleased Thomas but did not remove his resentment at being treated "like a boy." "I earned this at Chickamauga," he declared—quite correctly.[13]

Thomas never conducted another battle. He did not need to. Nor would Grant allow him to. True, he accepted Thomas's victory at Nashville as good news, but within weeks it was evident that Thomas's pursuit of Hood had mixed results—enough to spark more complaints from Halleck, who excelled at being an armchair strategist. Grant began stripping units away from Thomas, authorizing Schofield to make his way east to reinforce Union offensives along the North Carolina coast. He explained to Sherman that Thomas's behavior after Nashville "indicated a sluggishness" that did not bode well for conducting offensive operations. "He is possessed of excellent judgment, great coolness and honesty, but he is not good on a pursuit."[14] Thomas might have replied that after Nashville there was not much left to pursue.

Thus, even in the wake of a smashing success, two of the Union's leading generals remained resentful rivals. Only a discerning observer would note that they had much in common, or that each of them bore some of the responsibility for their ragged relationship, as did Sherman, who was all too eager to feed Grant's reservations about Thomas. In years to come, comrades, historians, and biographers would engage in bitter disputes over the relative merits of Ulysses S. Grant and George H. Thomas, proving that some rivalries never die out.

The first two books describing Sherman's March to the Sea appeared early in 1865, each the product of a newspaper reporter who accompanied it. They were far from the last, and to repeat their accounts in detail would be needlessly repetitious. Suffice it to say that Sherman and his men waged war against the Confederate psyche with great success, to the point that the actual destruction wrought during the march has been greatly exaggerated in popular memory. The operation helped shred what remained of the rail network connecting the Confederate heartland with Virginia and North Carolina. Robert E. Lee ceased giving furloughs to Georgia troops, convinced that if they returned home, they would be lost to him forever. Nevertheless, Confederate strength continued to erode as soldiers deserted the ranks and headed back to the homes they had pledged to defend.[15]

Sherman's soldiers made their way across central Georgia toward Savannah in less than a month, facing very little organized opposition. Along the way, they stripped the land of produce and livestock, burning barns and twisting rails. Not all of the resulting chaos and destruction was due to their actions: some of Sherman's soldiers left the main columns and operated on their own as so-called bummers, while civilians reported that Joseph Wheeler's Confederate cavalry committed its share of depredations. Burning of houses occurred, but rarely, and there was but one case of raping a white woman, and even that is disputed, although recent studies suggest that black women were victims of rape. Perhaps the worst atrocity to take place happened when corps commander Jefferson C. Davis had a pontoon bridge pulled up, thereby leaving a large number of freedom-seeking slaves to the not-so-tender mercies of Wheeler's troopers, who also slew any bummer that fell into their hands and, of necessity, "lived off the country" themselves. Of course, they had no alternative, but it is doubtful that they enjoyed the gratitude of the farmers and planters who provided the living.

On reaching the outskirts of Savannah and capturing a fort that guarded ship access to the city's docks, Sherman appeared to have secured an excellent opportunity to force the surrender of Hardee's 10,000-man garrison. But Hardee, aware of this danger, slipped away via a makeshift pontoon bridge. Once more the foe had escaped Sherman's grasp, and once more he paid no mind to it. On December 22 he occupied the city and telegraphed Lincoln: "I beg to present you, as a Christmas gift, the city of Savannah, with 150 heavy guns and plenty of ammunition, and also about 25,000 bales of cotton." He did not add that he had passed up the chance to enlarge his gift by some 10,000 men.[16]

This message enhanced Sherman's status as a Northern hero, as, of course, did his "March to the Sea." His next military step should have been, indeed had planned to be, to load his troops aboard transport ships and go to Virginia to join with the Army of the Potomac in overwhelming Lee and concluding the war. Instead, Grant, stating that these ships were unavailable owing to another mission, notified Sherman that his army would have to foot it to the Old Dominion. Sherman did not protest. Neither did his soldiers. A tramp through South Carolina, the "Cradle of Secession," suited them just fine. In fact, they looked forward to it.

18

Death Blows

Grant, Sheridan, and Sherman Win the War, but the Union Generals Fight On

(March–May 1865)

ON THE EVENING OF MARCH 27, 1865, a steamer pulled up at one of the wharves at City Point, Virginia. William T. Sherman emerged, walked to the landing, and headed for a row of log cabins along a bluff overlooking the water. There waiting for him was Ulysses S. Grant. The two men had not seen each other for nearly a year, since they had met to outline operations for 1864. There would be time for reminiscing later: Grant told Sherman that the president was aboard his own steamer at the wharf. Perhaps they should pay the boss a visit.[1]

Sherman had not laid eyes upon Lincoln since he had left Virginia to take over for Robert Anderson in Kentucky in 1861. Now, in the wake of his marches through Georgia and the Carolinas, he did not need much prodding to share stories of his army's exploits with the president while Grant quietly listened. So much had happened over the last several months. Together, Grant and Sherman had set aside the idea of Sherman's command being transported from Savannah to Virginia to help close out Lee: better, they agreed, for Sherman to make his way north by land. In February, Sherman's columns struck northward from Savannah through South Carolina, destroying much of what they found in the cradle of secession. For years to come, people would argue as to the role of Sherman and his men in the fires that raged in Columbia, South Carolina, as the state capital was abandoned by its Confederate defenders and occupied by the invading Yankees. It mattered little, because Sherman believed the South Carolinians were simply reaping the whirlwind. One of George G. Meade's aides heard him declare: "Columbia!—pretty much all burned; and burned *good!*" Approaching North Carolina, Sherman looked to link up with another Union column in North Carolina coming from the coast: back in January Federal forces had landed on the North Carolina coast in mid-January, taken Fort Fisher, and then occupied Wilmington, the last major Confederate port, before being reinforced by John M. Schofield's forces (which had been taken from Thomas). That Union triumph was doubly sweet in Grant's eyes, because Benjamin F. Butler had botched a previous attempt to take Fort Fisher, opening the door for Grant to relieve him from field command, a measure now possible in the wake of Lincoln's reelection.[2]

The Confederate high command had proven helpless to check Sherman's advance through the Carolinas. Upon assuming overall command of Confederate forces at the end of February 1865, Robert E. Lee had placed Joseph Johnston in command of what remained of the Army of Tennessee plus William Hardee's corps and Wade Hampton's horsemen, with orders to do what he could to check the progress of the Yankee invader. For a moment, Johnston thought he had a chance to deliver a telling blow at Bentonville, North Carolina, by striking at one of Sherman's wings, but the resulting three days of battle (March 19–21) ended in a costly repulse. Following this encounter, Sherman resumed his northward march but neglected a splendid opportunity to trap and force the surrender of Johnston—an "oversight" he, in a unique confession, admitted in his *Memoirs*.

So Sherman had decided to pay Grant a visit to map out how to wrap things up. The generals met with the president, who seemed worried about how the conflict would end: he wanted to avoid if possible a final bloody battle and was in favor of a lenient peace. Then they returned to Grant's headquarters, where Phil Sheridan found them talking late into the night.

Upon hearing of Sherman's arrival, Sheridan had hurried back to City Point, worried that Grant might send him off to Sherman at the very moment when he wanted to be in at the kill in Virginia. He had taken advantage of bad weather a few weeks earlier to set aside any idea by Grant of his moving southward through central Virginia into North Carolina in favor of joining Grant at Petersburg. Yet the idea did not die, for Grant had brought it up again just a few days ago. Perhaps, said Grant, Sheridan should sweep south from Petersburg toward Danville before joining Sherman. Sheridan vigorously objected. Taking in the situation at a glance, Grant explained that the wording of the order was intended to allow Sheridan to break away if things did not go well outside Petersburg, because he did not want to hear the criticisms of the Peace Democrats if something went wrong. Sheridan did not question this reasoning, which was less than persuasive: all he wanted to know was that he would be part of the operations against Lee, Richmond, and Petersburg.[3]

Now, with Sherman at City Point, Sheridan wondered whether Grant would change his mind once more. Perhaps Sheridan did not reflect upon the fact that it had been Sherman who had provided him—unintentionally of course—with the opportunity to make the charge up Missionary Ridge that led to his winning Grant's favor and all that had stemmed from it. Perhaps he did not care.

No sooner had Sheridan joined Sherman and Grant than Sherman began setting forth his own idea of how to crush the Confederacy, which featured Sheridan in a supporting role in North Carolina. Once more Grant interjected that the orders were designed to mislead critics in case of a setback outside Petersburg, but Sherman was nothing if not persistent. Early the next morning, he barged into Sheridan's quarters to make his case for a Carolina junction one more time: once more Sheridan made it clear that he opposed the idea. Frustrated in this instance, Sherman decided to drop the matter, and headed with Grant to pay Lincoln a second visit before returning to his command.

Thus ended the only conference where Grant, Sherman, and Sheridan together discussed operational plans. One senses that Sheridan enjoyed his close relationship to Grant and saw Sherman as a threat to it. As for Sherman, he was so used to having his way with Grant in recent months that it must have come of something of a surprise that his friend did not second his own preferences. Fortunately for Grant, circumstances would soon take care of a situation where he might otherwise have had to mediate between his two trusted subordinates.

There was no time to waste. As March surrendered to April in 1865, Grant feared that Lee would take advantage of spring weather and dry roads to evacuate Richmond and Petersburg. Indeed, Lee had struck at Grant's lines near City Point on March 25 in an effort to force Grant to contract his lines in order to facilitate a Confederate evacuation. The assault had failed miserably, but Grant knew that the time was drawing near when Lee would move. He thus resolved to use Sheridan to sweep westward to sever Lee's last remaining rail links with what remained of the Confederate heartland. Such a move would force Lee to fight out in the open at a disadvantage or else be faced with a stark choice between capitulation or starvation. However, on March 29 heavy and incessant rain resumed, turning dirt roads into mud ones. Grant notified Sheridan to abandon his flanking move for the time being and instead wait for the rain to cease and the road to dry.

On receiving this, Sheridan headed for Grant's headquarters astride a horse named Breckinridge because, presumably, it had been captured from that general, who, to Bragg's displeasure, now was the Confederate secretary of war. On meeting with Grant, he declared: "I tell you, I'm ready to strike out tomorrow and go to smashing things." All he needed, he added, was some infantry support and he then would be able to slice Lee's rail supply lines, leaving him no alternative other than to abandon Richmond and Petersburg in an attempt to escape into North Carolina to link up with Johnston. Grant listened, agreed, and then authorized Sheridan to do as he proposed with the assistance of Gouverneur K. Warren's V Corps—the sole one available. Sheridan sulked, for he had wanted to use Horatio Wright's VI Corps, who were veterans of the victories in the Valley and responded to his touch. He had bad memories about Warren, stretching all the way back to that traffic jam between his horsemen and Warren's infantry columns that had enabled the Confederates to win the race to Spotsylvania Court House.[4]

The following day, Sheridan's cavalry, 13,000 strong, slogged its way to Dinwiddie Court House, where Sheridan and his staff put up at a ramshackle hotel and sang songs along with two Southern belles who also resided there. The ensuing day it made its way, slowly but surely, to the vicinity of Five Forks, so-named because five roads converged upon it. There it encountered the cavalry division of Brigadier General Fitzhugh Lee (a nephew of Robert E.) and five infantry brigades headed by George Pickett. Sheridan's troopers dealt successfully with the first and seemed to be on the verge of doing the same with the second until checked by its superior fire power coming from behind log barricades.

Night terminated the fighting, but it resumed with the advent of dawn on April 1. Again Pickett's foot-sloggers held Sheridan's dismounted horsemen at bay with their single-shot but longer range and more accurate rifles. Then, as a feeble sun verged on sinking out of sight, Warren's corps arrived and began deploying. But as it did so, one of its divisions headed in the wrong direction, threatening to create a dangerous gap in the Federal front. Sheridan, having been authorized by Grant, who also took a dim view of Warren's lack of aggressiveness, promptly relieved him of command and replaced him with one of the V Corps division commanders, who did what Warren already had set out to do—which was to get the straying divisions headed in the right direction. The outcome was the near total destruction of Fitzhugh Lee's and Pickett's forces, 5,000 to 6,000 of which became willing prisoners. Likewise, Pickett's and Fitzhugh Lee's military careers came to a dismal end, they having assumed that Sheridan no longer presented a danger and therefore gone off to enjoy with other high-ranking gray-clad officers a shad bake—from a culinary standpoint a forgivable mistake, but not from a military one.[5]

Warren's removal later became the subject of much controversy, and it would not be until the 1880s that the corps commander would get the hearing to which he was entitled. In due course, it appeared that Sheridan had acted hastily and unjustly with Warren: sadly, by the time the court of inquiry released its verdict, the savior of Little Round Top had passed away, and it would be left to his men and devoted followers to remember his best day of service in the war with a marvelous (and much-photographed) statue atop one of that height's boulders. Less evident was the fact that Warren's track record as a corps commander had justified his removal from command long before. Believing that Warren was not always willing to do what he was ordered to accomplish, Grant had paved the way for Sheridan's action by authorizing him to make a change. In so doing, the general in chief demonstrated that he had tired of appeasing the officer corps of the Army of the Potomac, and, now that the end was in sight, he would not put up with any more excuses or squabbles. Warren's removal was rough justice if his entire record was considered, although it was understandably seen as unjust if one restricted one's examination of events to Five Forks alone. The act continued to grind away at some of the officers present, notably Joshua Chamberlain, who turned much of his account of the final weeks of the war into a brief for Warren and the Army of the Potomac seasoned with snide comments about Grant and Sheridan. In retrospect, perhaps a change should have been made months before. But together Grant and Sheridan had sent out a signal: this time, commanders would pay for their mistakes on the spot. There would be no more putting up with the culture of the officer corps of the Army of the Potomac, especially when now it might cost Grant the opportunity to finish off Lee.[6]

Word of victory at Five Forks led to Grant ordering an assault along Lee's entire line of battle on the morning of April 2. As Union forces advanced against the Rebel entrenchments, achieving several breakthroughs, Lee issued orders to pull out. Evacuating Richmond and Petersburg on the night of April 2–3, he looked to retreat westward, make his way past the pursuing Yankees, and link up with Johnston's army in North Carolina. Perhaps together Lee and Johnston could defeat Sherman and then turn to face Grant in an attempt somehow to prolong the war until the North wearied of it.[7]

Grant wasted no time launching a pursuit. He knew that it was not enough to catch up with Lee's rear guard: the Union columns pushing westward would have to cut off the Confederate lines of retreat southward to North Carolina and westward to the Blue Ridge Mountains. It would also be, for the first time, Grant's army in Virginia. None of the four infantry corps commanders who had crossed the Rapidan and Rappahannock in May 1864 still held their commands. The Army of the James had been reorganized into two corps under new commanders and was now under the command of Edward O. C. Ord, one of Grant's old generals from the West.

Only Meade, as commander of the Army of the Potomac, and Sheridan, as commander of an expanded cavalry corps, still held their positions. While Geoffrey Weitzel's XXV Corps, composed of black regiments, marched into Richmond on April 3, Grant spent just enough time in Petersburg to meet with President Lincoln before moving out to head off Lee.

Sheridan spearheaded the pursuit. Aware that Lee anticipated being re-supplied at Amelia Court House, Little Phil pushed his men to Jetersville, effectively blocking the path to North Carolina. The cavalryman pressed to attack the Confederates once more, but Meade hesitated. It seemed the same old story all over again, and so Sheridan sent a message to Grant, asking that the commanding general make his way to the front and see the situation for himself. Grant arrived at Jetersville at midnight. Reviewing Meade's orders, he saw that they would simply follow up and hit Lee in the rear, leaving open a route to escape once more. Grant impressed upon Meade the need to cut off Lee's retreat: Meade countered that he desired the return of V Corps, now under the command of Charles Griffin. Sheridan was not sad to see the V Corps go: what he wanted most to do was to press ahead.

The morning of April 6 proved Sheridan right. Meade advanced his men, only to find that Lee was already gone. Sheridan swung around Lee's columns once more in an effort to intercept the retreating Rebels. He did so, isolating Richard Ewell's command at Sailor's Creek and shredding it with the help of Wright's VI Corps, Sheridan's preferred choice for infantry. Meade remained unaware of what had happened, and he did what he could to make sure that VI Corps remained under him, contradicting Grant's wish to have Wright under Sheridan's orders. It seemed as if the tug-of-war between those two generals would never end. At the same time, Andrew A. Humphreys directed his II Corps to take on John B. Gordon's men, while Ord and Gibbon traded shots with what was left of James Longstreet's corps.

Sheridan had scooped up a handful of Confederate generals and some eight thousand prisoners at Sailor's Creek, but he did not rest content with that result. As he told Grant, "If the thing is pressed I think Lee will surrender."[8]

Grant kept pressing. He could sense that the end was near. So could Lincoln, who upon reading Sheridan's message, directed Grant: "Let the *thing* be pressed." By the evening of April 7 the Union commander had reached Farmville, Virginia, where just hours before Lee's rearguard had struggled to fend off yet another attack by Humphreys. In moving as fast as he did, Grant had left Meade behind: he was anxious lest Lee evade capture once more and make his way to Lynchburg, where more supplies might await, and where he could deploy along the Blue Ridge Mountains. Sheridan informed him that he was advancing on Appomattox Station, where a cache of supplies awaited Lee. If the bluecoats got there first, Lee would find himself in a precarious position—so much so that Grant thought it only proper to contact his counterpart in gray. "The result of the last week must convince you of the hopelessness of further resistance on the part of the Army of Northern Virginia in this struggle." Perhaps it was time for Lee to surrender. By midnight Grant had his reply: not yet, although Lee did inquire about what terms Grant was willing to offer.[9]

April 8 saw Grant pursue Lee with a sword in one hand and an olive branch in the other. The sword was Sheridan, who during the day reached Appomattox Station and captured a freight train filled with supplies intended for Lee. The olive branch was yet another letter to Lee, this one declaring that "peace being my great desire, there is but one condition I would insist upon—namely, that the men and officers surrendered shall be disqualified for taking up arms against the Government of the United States until properly exchanged." There was nothing here about unconditional surrender, although Lee could rest assured that Grant would continue to move promptly against his army. During the day, Grant met up once more with Meade, and as the sun set, the generals could hear cannon fire to the west, where Sheridan had gone into action at Appomattox Station. Grant, suffering from a migraine headache, sought to get what sleep he could, a task complicated when several staff officers took turns playing the piano in the parlor of the house that served as headquarters for the evening. It did not help when he received Lee's rather defiant reply—"I do not think the emergency has arisen to call for the surrender of this army"—although Lee offered to meet Grant to discuss the situation.[10]

On the morning of April 9, 1865, Lee learned that the emergency had indeed arisen, in the form of Sheridan's horsemen astride Lee's path, with Griffin and Ord in support, and Humphreys and Wright hurrying forward to close the trap completely. It was time to meet Grant. That was easier said than done, because in the morning Grant had left behind an ailing Meade and ridden forward to see how things stood with Sheridan. As the commanding general and his staff made their way across to the front, a courier pulled up and handed Grant a message. It was from Lee, who was now ready to surrender. Grant's headache vanished completely. That afternoon, the two men met in Wilmer McLean's parlor near Appomattox Court House, and Robert E. Lee surrendered the Army of Northern Virginia to Ulysses S. Grant.[11]

The contrast between the two men was clear and iconic. There sat Lee, tall and resplendent in a new gray uniform—the sole one he had—while across the room Grant sat, wearing the only uniform available to him, a mud-splattered enlisted man's blouse with the sole indication of his rank being two shoulder bars, each with three stars on it. The terms of surrender were lenient, probably more so than in any previous or subsequent civil war. This was particularly true of a clause that Grant added on being told by Lee that in Confederate armies even enlisted men serving in the cavalry and artillery provided their own horses and mules. They would be needed, Grant remarked, for the spring plowing. Also present in the room was Philip H. Sheridan, whose drive and determination had proven so valuable to Grant; absent was George G. Meade, who had brought up the rear and who was under the weather this beautiful Palm Sunday in April.

In the end, Grant had simply overridden the command culture of the Army of the Potomac, a culture riddled with rivalries and backstabbing, to prevail over his rivals in blue as well as gray. Meade found himself less and less in charge of the Army of the Potomac, trailing at the rear while Grant sought to keep up with Sheridan. Indeed, by the time Meade was poised to attack on April 9, the negotiations preparatory to the surrender were already under way. Perhaps the lesson offered by Warren's removal had helped to encourage the others, for during its last week of combat, the Army of the Potomac marched and fought as it never had before, and now it never needed to do so again.

It would take days for the Confederates to stack their arms and sign their paroles. By the time that happened, Grant, Lee, and Meade all were on the way back whence they came, with Lee taking up residence in Richmond. Grant did not stop in the former Confederate capital; rather, he hurried to Washington, arriving on April 13. The next day he attended a cabinet meeting. The general should have been basking in the celebration of a job well done. Instead, the man who later enjoyed relating the stories Lincoln liked to tell was rankled by something the president said. Someone had asked Grant whether there was any news from Sherman. The general replied that he would doubtless hear from him before too long. The president agreed, adding that he knew that word would come soon because last night he had a dream about a vessel approaching "an indefinite shore." It was a recurring dream, and he had dreamt it before several major events, including several Union triumphs. Among them was Stones River. That got Grant's attention. Still harboring a deep distaste for Rosecrans, he remarked that Stones River "was certainly no victory, and he knew of no great results which followed from it." Lincoln, who had found news of a battlefield draw to be quite a relief in the wake of the defeats at Chickasaw Bayou and Fredericksburg, set aside his general's comment. Even in victory Grant still drew attention to his rivalry with the since-vanquished Rosecrans. The curt remark left a poor impression upon navy secretary Gideon Welles, who would make it his life's work to find fault with Grant in the years to come and doctor his diary accordingly.[12]

Lincoln would never hear anything more from Sherman. Perhaps the event of which he dreamt was of his assassination that evening by John Wilkes Booth while he attended a play at Ford's Theater. The president had intended to have Grant and his wife as the guests of the president and Mrs. Lincoln that evening, but both the Grants had experienced a very different sort of rivalry coming from Mary Lincoln, who resented the praise heaped upon the general and suspected his wife of harboring aspirations to be First Lady herself (a position Julia Dent Grant did not seem to want until she had a taste of it four years later, after which she proved reluctant to set it aside). The general excused himself due to his wife's wishes to see the children, and Lincoln, knowing full well the cost of defying one's spouse, acceded. It would be the last time the two men would see each other, thanks to an assassin's bullet.

A week later, in the aftermath of a state funeral, and with Lincoln's body on the way to Springfield, Illinois, Grant attended another cabinet meeting, this one under the leadership of the new president, Andrew Johnson. It was Grant, however, who had suggested to Secretary of War Stanton that the cabinet meet, so that it could consider a communication just received from Sherman.

The communication was Sherman's proposed draft of a peace settlement that he had reached with his opposite number, Joseph E. Johnston, in a farmhouse outside Durham, North Carolina. Never shy about his own abilities, Sherman had taken it upon himself to go far beyond his authority as a military commander to outline a grand peace settlement. Sherman would later say that he was acting on what he supposed to be Lincoln's wishes, and that he had been moved to act in such grand fashion by news of the assassination. In assaying to play the part of a politician, however, Sherman proved a flat failure, in part because no one was in the mood for such an outlandish, improvised, and unauthorized proposal, one which caused several excitable cabinet members to censure Sherman harshly. Stanton seemed particularly angry, making some wild accusations of his own touching on Sherman's loyalty.[13]

Grant listened as cabinet members raged. He knew that Sherman's terms were unacceptable: he had just finished warning his friend not to go beyond a military agreement based on the Appomattox terms. Indeed, Sherman had promised him that he would offer Johnston the same terms Grant had offered Lee "and be careful not to complicate any points of civil policy." Grant was well aware of how Sherman despised politicians and that he thought he was the smartest man in any room. Yet he also knew that Sherman's motives were as pure as his reasoning was muddled and his handiwork a disaster. He quietly volunteered to travel down to North Carolina to straighten things out.[14]

It would have been wise if Grant had been left to do just that, but Stanton could not restrain himself. No sooner had the general in chief departed Washington than the newspapers, long a target of Sherman's intense hatred, published the proposed agreement with Stanton's objections. Stanton freely pointed to a letter Lincoln had composed and he had signed on March 3, 1865, directing Grant not to confer with Lee "unless it be for the capitulation of Lee's army, or on solely minor and military matters," and that under no conditions was he "to decide, discuss, or confer upon any political questions." While Sherman had never seen this document, it was a good question as to whether those instructions had been superseded by what Lincoln had told Grant and Sherman aboard the *River Queen,* conversations to which Stanton had not been a party.[15]

In due time Sherman would learn all about this: he would also learn that on April 21, his old friend Henry Halleck, now in command at Richmond, was passing along to Stanton rumors that Jefferson Davis had taken the Confederacy's gold reserves in hopes of cutting a deal "with General Sherman or some other . . . commander" to permit their escape abroad. "Would it not be well to put Sherman and all other commanding generals on their guard?" Halleck asked. In his frenzied state of mind, Stanton overlooked the question, which implied that Sherman was ignorant of any such plot to facilitate Davis's escape. Misreading one of Sherman's orders, the war secretary concluded that the general's directives opened an escape route for Davis. Halleck, acting upon that supposition, informed Meade and Wright to "disregard any truce or orders from Sherman," which was taking matters a bit too far. So was Halleck's musing that once more there might be a "screw loose" in Sherman. Nor did Halleck rest content with that suspicion. Although Grant had simply told Halleck to order Sheridan southward should negotiations collapse, Halleck bluntly instructed Sheridan to ignore Sherman's truce and look out for the Confederate gold. Something was lost in the translation. This time Old Brains' ineptitude in recasting Grant's wishes into orders would cost him dearly.[16]

At first Sherman had taken with good grace the news that the terms had been rejected, largely because it was Grant who delivered the news with an explanation that made sense. A new agreement, based on the Appomattox terms, was drawn up and signed April 26. Two days later, however, Sherman laid eyes upon a newspaper carrying Stanton's accusations, and he exploded. Letter after letter went out justifying his position and attacking Stanton. Even more infuriating was news of what Halleck had done. Sherman thought these attacks were a sign of things to come: "I doubt not efforts will be made to sow dissension between Grant and myself . . . or after killing me off by libels, he will be the next to be assailed."[17]

When it came to carrying grudges, no one surpassed Sherman, and he prepared to wreak vengeance upon his enemies with an aggressiveness he had never shown in pursuing Confederates. He hungered for a confrontation with Stanton. When Halleck, who seemed genuinely clueless as to what he might have done to offend his confidant (and not for the first time, as his track record with Grant in 1862 suggested), invited Sherman to take advantage of his hospitality when Sherman's men approached Richmond, Sherman shot back that in light of what he had read, "I cannot have any friendly intercourse with you. . . . I prefer we should not meet."

Thus, just as Sherman should have been enjoying the end of hostilities, he was battling Stanton and Halleck. Gone was any recollection of how Halleck had rescued his career in 1861 and set him back on his feet in 1862. Forgotten was the fact that for some time Sherman had ranked Halleck ahead of Grant; set aside was the record of friendly correspondence between the two in which each had expressed disgust with politicians and reflected on how the war should go. Confiding to a friend, Halleck dismissed Sherman's complaints: "He is very easily excited, and on such occasions his mind loses its balance, and he has no self-control. I have seen him in this condition more than once."[18]

Sherman's men did not take kindly to the aspersions cast upon their leader's reputation. As it was, they resented the snobbishness they encountered when they came across veterans of the Army of the Potomac. Those effete Easterners had had their hands full with Bobby Lee until their old commander Grant had taken things in hand, while they had marched from Mississippi and Tennessee to the Carolinas, winning victory after victory under their beloved Cump. So it proved to be an angry army headed by a furious commander that made its way through Richmond, and tempers had not settled a week later when Sherman's men established their camp at Alexandria, across the Potomac from Washington. Finally, on May 24, the second day of the Grand Review of the armies down Pennsylvania Avenue toward the Treasury Building and the White House, Sherman, who headed the parade, dismounted at the reviewing stand and ignored Stanton's outstretched hand. As an observer recalled, "Sherman's face was scarlet and his red hair seemed to stand on end."[19]

Even on a day where the victors in blue could celebrate their triumph, they showed that they could still give vent to their personal rivalries. Nor would such rivalries disappear in the decades to come, as generals set down their recollections or battled each other politically. Winning the war was not enough: taking credit, casting blame, and pointing fingers remained the order of the day. To some extent, that tradition persists, with scholars taking up cudgels on behalf of their favorites, and thus it may always be. As to how one historian judges how the chips fell, the reader need only turn the page.

Epilogue

The Victors in Blue—Who and Why

FOREMOST AMONG THE VICTORS IN BLUE WAS, of course, Grant. Starting with Forts Henry and Donelson and culminating with Appomattox Court House, he gained most of the decisive Federal victories. He accomplished this with a combination of what Napoleon declared were the three requisites for victorious war: skill, superior numbers, and good luck. His reward was an eight-year residence in the White House. His greatest peacetime accomplishment was his *Memoirs,* written while he was dying a painful death from throat cancer, brought on by the cigars he smoked almost incessantly after being presented with hundreds of them following his victory at Fort Donelson. It is unlikely that any other Northern general, other than Rosecrans, could have overpowered Lee, the greatest general produced by the Civil War.

Sherman, of course, comes second among Northern generals in fame, rank, and historical status. This historian obviously disagrees with the last but bows to the persistent view of the vast majority of his historical peers. After all, Sherman did take Atlanta and thus reversed a tide of defeatism in the North that threatened to make McClellan the seventeenth president. His March to the Sea and excursion through the Carolinas, although they did little to achieve Confederate military defeat—that already had been accomplished in essence—did demonstrate to all except the hopelessly ignorant or the fanatically blind that the Confederacy was kaput. Sherman was rewarded for his loyalty to Grant by succeeding him as top general, and he too wrote a very readable memoir. (How truthful it was is another matter.) After succeeding Grant as top U.S. general, he probably could have done the same insofar as residing in the White House. But wisely he declared that he would not run if nominated or serve if elected. He died in 1891, having further immortalized himself with this profound statement made to a gathering of veterans in Columbus, Ohio: "War is hell." (Though for some, like George S. Patton and Douglas MacArthur, it is paradise.)

Sheridan, owing to the seniority in rank that he acquired as an award for his Shenandoah Valley victories, succeeded Sherman as the top American postwar general. Low in age for so high a post, he could have held it well into the 1890s. But excessive eating and inadequate exercise produced his death from heart failure in 1888 while still just fifty-seven. Only a few days before it he completed his *Memoirs,* a well-written work and as accurate and fair as any autobiography is likely to be. Last, but not necessarily least, he is the hero of Bruce Catton's superb *A Stillness at Appomattox,* from a literary standpoint one of the finest Civil War books ever published.

Upon Sheridan's premature death, and thanks to Grant having obtained for him a promotion to major general in the regular army, Schofield succeeded Sheridan as commander of the U.S. Army, all 16,000 soldiers of it. In that capacity, he presided (in Washington) over the final large-scale Indian outbreak, that at Wounded Knee, South Dakota, in 1890, and then in 1894 a bloody suppression of the Pullman Strike in Chicago. The ensuing year he retired from the army with the newly acquired rank of lieutenant general. Two years later, he published his memoirs, *Forty-Six Years in the Army.* Although a useful book, it tends at times to be tedious, devoting too many words to subjects of too little interest. In it he defends himself from a postwar allegation that he endeavored to supplant Thomas prior to the Battle of Nashville. I believe his defense is true. Grant seconded him on this, for when Grant did definitely decide to replace him he first instructed Logan to do so and then set out to do it himself, only to turn back on learning that Thomas was attacking. Probably only Sherman and Rosecrans could have surpassed him on an I.Q. exam had those conceit-inducing "tests" existed in the nineteenth century. Presumably he also was quite virile, for at the age of almost sixty he married his second wife, the first having died, a twenty-seven-year-old woman who had been his daughter's girlhood friend. Although his contributions to Union victory were limited, they were timely in terms of advancing his career after the conflict, for he found himself among Grant's favorites, and at war's end that was a good place to be.

And now we come to Thomas. But why not sooner, much sooner, many if not all readers will wonder? The answer lies in the title of this book, the lengthy portion following the colon: *How Union Generals Fought the Confederates, Battled Each Other, and Won the Civil War.* Thomas obviously did more to win the Civil War for the Union than did Schofield, but he remained a major general and a postwar department commander, first in Tennessee and then in the Division of the West, headquarters San Francisco. There, in March 1870, he read an article in the *New York Tribune* asserting that Schofield, not he, had won the Battle of Nashville. Concluding correctly that the article had been written at the behest of Schofield, on March 28 he took pen in hand to write a response. Halfway through it, he became ill, briefly rallied, but then died, like Sheridan a victim of a heart attack brought on by clogged arteries produced by overeating and underexercise.

There are several biographies, all favorable, some worshipful, written about him, with the best and perhaps most balanced being Christopher J. Einolf's *George Thomas: Virginian for the Union*.

Meade, of course, has been much written about, but mostly in connection with Gettysburg, about which books and articles verge on the innumerable. At Gettysburg, of course, he presided over what many believe to be *the* decisive Northern victory of the war. But much to the disappointment of Lincoln, he failed to annihilate Lee's badly battered army before it could escape back into Virginia. There he not only failed to gain an offensive victory against it, but also soon found himself so much on the defensive despite possessing superior numbers that Lee found it possible to send two crack divisions headed by Longstreet to reinforce Bragg and win a victory at Chickamauga. Then, starting in the spring of 1864, while he remained the titular commander of the Army of the Potomac, its actual chief was Grant, who more and more put him on the sideline, especially after the bloody fiasco of the Crater, during which his interference with the luckless Burnside turned what probably would have been a failure in any case into a debacle. And although he was with the Army of the Potomac at Appomattox Court House, he was so ill that he did not even appear at McLean's house to witness Lee's surrender. As the war ended, he belatedly became a major general in the regular army before taking on various postwar commands along the Atlantic coast. He died in 1872 but lives on in the libraries devoted to Gettysburg.

Next but not last is Halleck, who contributed to Union victory but whose shortcomings leave him far down the list. Also a regular army major general, "Old Brains," following his brief tenure as the occupation commander in Virginia, returned to California, where he briefly preceded Thomas as commander of the Division of the West before retiring. For some unknown and unfortunate reason, he, who had written so readily and readably about war prior to 1861, never penned his memoirs and died, far too early, in 1872. In the war's first two years, he saved Sherman from oblivion while nearly committing Grant to it; eventually, Halleck came to see Grant's talents as a subordinate commander in the West, especially when measured against his peers and possible replacements. While unsuited both physically and psychologically for field command, as witness his 100,000 man army digging its way to Corinth, Halleck as general in chief provided the Northern armies and Lincoln with a de facto chief of staff. He made errors, even blunders, in that capacity, as did George C. Marshall during World War II, but was far more than the "first-rate clerk" Lincoln dubbed him. However, when reduced to a de jure chief of staff in 1864, Halleck struggled with his new position, interfering with Grant's plans while carping about his former subordinate. Eventually, Grant bypassed him and would have been pleased to have been relieved of his services altogether.

Last, but far from least in what he contributed to Federal success in the Civil War, is Rosecrans. His first accomplishment in the war was his victory at Rich Mountain, the initial major Northern victory, one that resulted in western Virginia becoming West Virginia. Unfortunately, though, it also resulted in McClellan ("Young Napoleon"), whose fear of losing almost turned this engagement into a fiasco, becoming the top Yankee general, which resulted in the Civil War lasting much longer and costing far more lives than it should have. Next, following an interlude during which he repelled a Confederate effort led by Lee to regain western Virginia and then alienated the easily alienated Stanton, he conceived a plan by which he, in tandem with Grant, would remove Sterling Price's small but dangerous army from the chess board of the war by trapping it at Iuka, Mississippi, only to have it fail owing to an acoustic freak and Grant evidently assuming that the war was over because of an official but erroneous telegram asserting that Lee's army had been all but exterminated at Antietam. Price's escape led to him and Van Dorn joining to assault Corinth, where in a two-day battle Rosecrans achieved a great defensive victory, one that left the Rebel assailants badly shattered both in morale and numbers. Rosecrans, believing with good reason that pursuit of the fleeing Rebels would produce their virtual extermination and the seizure of Vicksburg, endeavored to do both, but was denied Grant's permission and needed reinforcements in spite of the approval of Halleck. Perhaps Grant was right, but probably he was wrong, given that Halleck was not exactly a reckless general. Furthermore, Price's and Van Dorn's troops were deserting, and as Grant subsequently discovered, it would have been quite possible for a large Federal army to have lived off the Mississippi countryside as it rapidly marched through.

Rosecrans found himself on the military sidelines with an "army," most of which had been sent off to reinforce the hapless Buell, but under the command of a general, Grant, who had come to distrust him as a general and dislike him as a person. But then his luck changed. Lincoln, as always eager to liberate predominantly Unionist East Tennessee from Rebel thralldom, assigned it to Rosecrans, the new head of what now was titled the Army of the Cumberland. And this he did, as well as it could be done, given that he had to operate in a region where food and forage was scanty, even for most of its sparse inhabitants and their animals. Thanks to his own determination and that of Sheridan, he turned imminent defeat into a defensive victory at Stones River. Next, having resisted the incessant demands of Stanton via Halleck to advance before accumulating sufficient provender for his soldiers and horses, he took two long leaps to flank Bragg out of Chattanooga and into Georgia.

He then should have halted, as Thomas had urged him to do. But eager for a total victory, one that would lead to the same for the war as a whole, he endeavored to overtake and destroy Bragg, unaware that Jefferson Davis was reinforcing his former comrade during the Mexican War with every available Confederate contingent, among them two crack divisions headed by Longstreet, while all that Stanton sent Rosecrans via Halleck were more telegrams urging pursuit.

Realizing, barely in time and thanks to Thomas, that he was trying to do too much with too little, Rosecrans turned about and headed back toward Chattanooga, believing and even expecting that he would be reinforced by Burnside, who had occupied Knoxville thanks to its garrison having gone to join Bragg. But before he could reach Chattanooga, he was overtaken by Bragg, who now heavily outnumbered him. Yet on the first day at Chickamauga it seemed he would be able to reach Chattanooga, his army having repelled all Rebel onslaughts. On the second day his luck turned bad owing to a poorly worded order written by an inexperienced staff scribe and then delivered to a disgruntled division commander who put petty pride ahead of military duty. As a consequence, what could have been a defensive success—albeit, as Wellington said of Waterloo, "a near-run thing"—turned into a bloody defeat that was saved from being a debacle owing to Thomas, whose sobriquet became ever after the "Rock of Chickamauga."

Rosecrans completed his Civil War career as commander of Federal forces in Missouri. This was, as was all of the Trans-Mississippi, a military backwater in Grant's eyes. Hence, from the very start he deprived Rosecrans of sufficient troops to cope successfully with the Confederate guerrillas that infested the state, in particular the bands of William Clarke Quantrill and William "Bloody Bill" Anderson. Also, in the late summer of 1864 Sterling Price made yet another attempt to "liberate" his home state from "Yankee thralldom" by invading Missouri from Arkansas at the head of 14,000 troops, his prime targets St. Louis, the state capital of Jefferson City, and Kansas City. Rosecrans annoyed, indeed outraged, Grant by "borrowing" A. J. Smith's corps, which happened to be in the Show Me State, to prevent Price from seizing any of these objectives and then harry the Confederates back southward into Arkansas, by which time they were reduced to a half-starved rabble, the vast majority of whom had thrown away their weapons because they were too inconvenient to carry. Grant rewarded Rosecrans for this victory by removing him from command in Missouri, whereupon he resigned from the army, his military career at an end.

It is tempting to write, albeit briefly, about Rosecrans's postwar career and his efforts to redeem his reputation. But I shall say no more than to state the wish, indeed the desire, that some other historian, one young, talented, and courageous, would produce a biography of Rosecrans that would supplant the sole full-fledged one known to me ever to be published, that of William M. Lamers, oft cited in this tome. It is an excellent book, both in style and content, but too long because too detailed; and, owing presumably to its publisher, the notes are crammed into almost unusable clusters, all concentrated at the end of the book and difficult to ascertain owing to them not being digitally indicated in the text.

Were I five years younger, or even three, I would undertake the production of a revisionist biography of Rosecrans. But I am not, and so I shall not.

AVE ATQUE VALE

NOTES

ABBREVIATIONS

B & L   Robert U. Johnson and Clarence C. Buel, eds., *Battles and Leaders of the Civil War* (New York: Century Co., 1884–1887).

OR   U.S. War Department, *The War of the Rebellion: A Compilation of the Official Records of the Union and Confederate Armies* (Washington, DC: Government Printing Office, 1880–1901).

PUSG   John Y. Simon, ed., *The Papers of Ulysses S. Grant,* 31 vols. (Carbondale: Southern Illinois University Press, 1967–2009).

PROLOGUE: ON JUDGING CIVIL WAR GENERALS

1. Quoted in Martin Van Creveld, *Command in War* (Cambridge, MA: Harvard University Press, 1985), xi.

2. James M. McPherson, *Battle Cry of Freedom: The Civil War Era* (New York: Oxford University Press, 1988), 858. Thomas J. "Stonewall" Jackson and Nathan Bedford Forrest, no doubt, possessed exceptional military talent amounting to genius. Douglass Southall Freeman, however, raises the question of whether Jackson's personal traits would have handicapped him as an independent commander of a major army in *Lee's Lieutenants: A Study in Command* (New York: Charles Scribner's Sons, 1943), 2:xxiii, and one must wonder how effective Forrest would have been heading a force larger than he could personally oversee and inspire.

3. Van Creveld, *Command in War,* 17–18.

4. In 1859 the military historian and theorist Antoine Jomini, who had served as a staff officer under Napoleon, drew up a plan for the French invasion of Austrian-held Italy that dealt with the existence of railroads by simply ignoring them. Lyn Montross, *War through the Ages* (New York: Harper & Brothers Publishers, 1944), 585.

5. Douglass Southall Freeman, *R. E. Lee: A Biography* (New York: Charles Scribner's Sons, 1935), 3:148; David Hamilton-Williams, *Waterloo: New Perspectives: The Great Battle Reappraised* (New York: John Wiley & Sons, 1994), 265–267.

6. For Grant's strength at the outset of the Overland Campaign, see Robert U. Johnson and Clarence C. Buel, eds., *Battles and Leaders of the Civil War* (New York: Century Co., 1887), 4:152. For Lee's numbers at the beginning of the Seven Days Battles and in the Gettysburg Campaign, see 2:317 and 3:440.

7. Albert Castel, "Mars and the Reverend Longstreet: Or, Attacking and Dying in the Civil War," *Civil War History: A Journal of the Middle Period* 33 (June 1987):103–114.

8. Technically, Union Major General James McPherson, killed at the Battle of Atlanta, July 22, 1864, was an army commander, but in practice his Army of the

Tennessee functioned as a corps, it being part of what today would be termed an army group headed by Sherman and consisting also of the Army of the Cumberland and the Army of the Ohio.

9. The German general staff began to emerge during the Napoleonic Wars, when the Prussian army discovered that, although its commander in chief had inherited Frederick the Great's throne, he had not inherited his military talent. It did not function, per se, though, until the 1866 war with Austria; and then Prussian victory owed as much, if not more, to the initiative of corps and division commanders, plus Austrian blunders. See Van Creveld, *Command in War,* 132–147.

10. The need for energy and endurance explains why most Civil War army commanders were young by modern standards. Thus, the average age of the six Union commanders described herein was forty when the war began. Meade, at forty-six, was the oldest, and Sheridan, at thirty, was the youngest. In contrast, Eisenhower was fifty-one, Patton fifty-six, and MacArthur sixty-one when the United States entered World War II in December 1941. Likewise, the most famous World War II German generals—Rommel, Guderian, Manstein—were in 1939 respectively forty-nine, fifty-one, and fifty-two, and Rundstedt had his sixty-fourth birthday that year. Napoleon said in 1815 that he was getting too old at forty-six to wage war successfully, and some would say that at Waterloo he demonstrated this to be true. Grant, who became thirty-nine soon after the Civil War began, considered Lee, who was in his mid-fifties during the war, over the hill—which, if true, perhaps was fortunate for both the Union cause and Grant.

11. Mahan's West Point course on "The Science of War" consisted of six lectures lasting a total of nine hours. James L. Morrison Jr., *"The Best School in the World": West Point, the Pre–Civil War Years, 1833–1861* (Kent, OH: Kent State University Press, 1985), 95–97.

12. Meade, who graduated from West Point in 1835, resigned from the army a year later but returned to it in 1842, remaining there until his death in 1872.

13. McClellan and Buell never again held commands, and both resigned from the army before the war ended. McDowell and Pope remained in the army, but the former ceased to serve against the Confederates following a poor performance at Second Bull Run (August 29–30, 1862). In 1864 he was assigned the Department of the Pacific, while the latter was sent after his defeat in the same battle to put down an Indian uprising in Minnesota and never again participated in the Civil War.

14. The best assessments of Halleck and his role during the Civil War, all of which go counter to the prevailing view of him among Civil War historians, are, in chronological order, the following: Kenneth P. Williams, *Lincoln Finds a General: A Military Study of the Civil War,* 5 vols. (New York: Macmillan, 1949–1959), 5:appendix; Stephen E. Ambrose, *Halleck: Lincoln's Chief of Staff* (Baton Rouge: Louisiana State University Press, 1962); Herman Hattaway and Archer Jones, *How the North Won: A Military History of the Civil War* (Urbana: University of Illinois Press, 1983); Curt Anders, *Henry Halleck's War: A Fresh Look at Lincoln's Controversial General-in-Chief* (Carmel: Guild Press of Indiana, 1999); and John F. Marszalek, *Commander of All Lincoln's Armies: A Life of General Henry W. Halleck* (Cambridge, MA: Harvard University Press, 2004).

1. ROSECRANS IN WEST VIRGINIA

1. Stephen W. Sears, ed., *The Civil War Papers of George B. McClellan: Selected Correspondence, 1860–1865* (New York: Ticknor & Fields, 1989), 44.

2. Stephen W. Sears, *George B. McClellan: The Young Napoleon* (New York: Ticknor & Fields, 1988), 3–75. The Department of the Ohio embraced Ohio, Indiana, Illinois, and, potentially, western Virginia and then-neutral Kentucky.

3. Ibid., 78–79.

4. Jacob D. Cox, "With McClellan in West Virginia," in *Battles and Leaders of the Civil War,* ed. Robert U. Johnson and Clarence C. Buel (New York: Century Co., 1884–1887), 1:126–130. Hereafter, *Battles and Leaders* will be cited as *B&L.*

5. U.S. War Department, *The War of the Rebellion: A Compilation of the Official Records of the Union and Confederate Armies* (Washington, DC: Government Printing Office, 1880–1901), ser. 1, 2:194–199. Hereafter, this source will be cited as *OR*, with all references being to series 1 unless otherwise indicated. Whenever a volume consists of two or more parts, the volume number will precede the *OR* and the part number will follow.

6. Jacob D. Cox, "War Preparations in the North," *B&L*, 1:89.

7. William M. Lamers, *The Edge of Glory: A Biography of General William S. Rosecrans, U.S.A.* (1961; paperback reprint, Baton Rouge: Louisiana State University Press, 1999), 8–26, 36.

8. Sears, *Civil War Papers of McClellan,* 46. McClellan wrote this to his wife on July 4, but it is obvious that it expresses his attitude from the very start of operations in western Virginia. Applying the axiom *ex pede Herculem* ("From the foot alone we may infer Hercules"), proof of McClellan's preference when it came to subordinates can be derived from a list of the officers he appointed to division command in the Army of the Potomac; with few exceptions they either were mediocrities or submediocrities such as Ambrose Burnside and George Stoneman.

9. *OR*, 2:212–213.

10. Sears, *Civil War Papers of McClellan,* 41.

11. Cox, "McClellan in West Virginia," 128–130; *OR*, 2:197.

12. *OR*, 2:198. It was Robert E. Lee, then a captain of engineers on Scott's staff, who discovered the route by which Scott outflanked the Mexican army at Cerro Gordo. See Douglas Southall Freeman, *R. E. Lee: A Biography* (New York: Charles Scribner's Sons, 1935), 1:238–241.

13. *OR*, 2:195, 198–201, 205.

14. Ibid., 205; Clayton R. Newell, *Lee vs. McClellan: The First Campaign* (Washington, DC: Regenery Publishing, 1996), 125.

15. *OR*, 2:205–206.

16. Ibid., 215–216; William S. Rosecrans, "A Sketch of His Campaigns, Article 1," 14–15 (MS in William S. Rosecrans Papers, University of California at Los Angeles, and written by Rosecrans long after the war and in the third person); Lamers, *Edge of Glory,* 28; Newell, *Lee vs. McClellan,* 125.

17. *OR*, 2:215–216; Rosecrans, "A Sketch of His Campaigns, Article 1," 16–18; Lamers, *Edge of Glory,* 28–32, 35–36; Newell, *Lee vs. McClellan,* 127–130, 132. Newell states, citing Martin K. Fleming, "The Northwestern Virginia Campaign

of 1861," *Blue and Gray Magazine,* August 1993, 50–51, as his source, that the courier carried a written order from McClellan to Rosecrans to abandon his turning move and rejoin the main army. Confederate sources (*OR,* 2:256, 260) make no mention of finding such an order on the courier, who had been shot and wounded, and whom they presumably searched, but merely state that the courier was "unable or unwilling" to tell from what direction Rosecrans was approaching the Hart farm, with the result that Pegram and De Lagnel assumed that most likely he would be coming from the same direction the courier came—the north. Finally, Union sources (as will be seen) demonstrate that when McClellan sent the courier, and for a long time afterward, he wanted and expected Rosecrans to attack the enemy force holding the entrance to Rich Mountain Pass in the rear prior to his attacking it in front, and hence would have had no reason to recall Rosecrans.

18. *OR,* 2:215–216; Rosecrans, "A Sketch of His Campaigns, Article 1," 16–18; Lamers, *Edge of Glory,* 35.

19. *OR,* 2:206; Cox, "McClellan in West Virginia," 132–133; John Beatty, *The Citizen-Soldier; or, Memoirs of a Volunteer* (Cincinnati: Wilstach & Baldwin & Co., 1879), 26.

20. *OR,* 2:206; 51 *OR,* 1:13–14. McClellan did not mention the speech and cheering among the Confederates in his July 14, 1861, report but waited until early 1864 to describe this alleged event in a *Report on the Organization and Campaigns of the Army of the Potomac: To Which Is Added an Account of the Campaign in Western Virginia,* a report published by a New York publisher and reprinted in Democratic newspapers throughout the North. At this time McClellan no longer was on active duty with the army but was the leading contender for the Democratic nomination for president, a nomination he received. Probably some officer did inform the Confederates holding the pass at Rich Mountain that the Yankees had been repulsed (as they were in their initial attack) at the Hart farm, eliciting thereby a cheer, but even so McClellan's 1864 account must be regarded as essentially an attempt to explain away his failure to attack on hearing the sound of Rosecrans's encounter.

21. *OR,* 2:216–217, 251–252, 264–265. According to the report of McClellan's chief of engineers, Orlando M. Poe, the Confederate defenses at the entrance to the pass were so poorly designed and constructed that an infantry assault could have easily driven the defenders from them or forced their surrender (51 *OR,* 1:14–15).

22. *OR,* 2:206–208, 210, 216, 219–223. Among the residents of Beverly was Stonewall Jackson's sister, Laura, the wife of the town's richest man, Jonathan Arnold. Unlike her soon-to-be-famous brother, she was a staunch Unionist who nursed Federal soldiers wounded in Rosecrans's fight at the Hart farm and who after the war was an honored guest at reunions of Union veterans from West Virginia and Ohio. For the full story of Laura Jackson Arnold, one that centers on her postwar divorce, see Albert Castel, "Arnold vs. Arnold: The Strange and Hitherto Untold Story of the Divorce of Stonewall Jackson's Sister," *Winning and Losing in the Civil War: Essays and Stories* (Columbia: University of South Carolina Press, 1996), 184–197. First published in *Blue and Gray Magazine,* October 1994.

23. *OR,* 2:206–207. According to Orlando Poe's report (52 *OR,* 1:14–15), one of the cavalrymen accompanying Rosecrans's column reported the flight of

the Confederates from Rich Mountain and the occupation of their camp by Rose-crans to McClellan on the morning of July 12. Obviously, McClellan assumed that the enemy remained in the pass and so made no attempt to ascertain whether they still held it and, if so, with what size of force. Had not the cavalryman, who presumably was sent by Rosecrans, informed him of the Confederate evacuation, McClellan's planned artillery bombardment would have fallen on Rosecrans's troops!

24. *OR*, 2:208, 211, 236; Sears, *Young Napoleon*, 92–93.

25. *OR*, 2:215; Whitelaw Reid, *Ohio in the War: Her Statesmen, Her Generals, and Soldiers* (Cincinnati: Moore, Wilstach & Baldwin, 1868), 1:316; Sears, *Young Napoleon*, 90–91.

26. Sears, *Young Napoleon*, 94.

27. Lamers, *Edge of Glory*, 37.

28. Freeman, *Lee*, 1:238–248, 431–447, 449–450, 491–540.

29. Rosecrans, "Sketch of His Campaigns, Article 2," 1–3; Lamers, *Edge of Glory*, 39–40.

30. *OR*, 5:128–132; Rosecrans, "Sketch of His Campaigns, Article 2," 4–5; Lamers, *Edge of Glory*, 45–50.

31. Freeman, *Lee*, 1, 560–576.

32. *OR*, 5:552; 51 *OR*, 2:211; Rosecrans, "Sketch of His Campaigns, Article 2," 5–7; Cox, "McClellan in West Virginia," 146–148; Freeman, *Lee*, 1:589–601; Cox, "McClellan in West Virginia," 147–148; Lamers, *Edge of Glory*, 52–53; Freeman, *Lee*, 1:589–601; A. L. Long, "Lee's West Virginia Campaign," *Annals of the Civil War* (1878; reprint, New York: Da Capo Press, 1994), 92–93.

33. Freeman, *Lee*, 1:577, 601–603; Newell, *Lee vs. McClellan*, 262–264. Other than the Northwestern Virginia Railroad, which ran from Parkersburg via Clarks-burg to Grafton, where it connected with the Baltimore & Ohio, there was not a single mile of track in all of western Virginia, and even small steamboats could not ascend the Kanawha much beyond Charleston. As for the Confederates, they had no river access whatsoever to western Virginia, and the Virginia Central railroad ended eleven miles east of Lewisburg. For a brief account of seesaw military operations in western Virginia during 1862, see Albert Castel, *Tom Taylor's Civil War* (Lawrence: University Press of Kansas, 2000), 32–46.

34. E. B. Long, *The Civil War Day by Day: An Almanac, 1861–1865* (Garden City, NY: Doubleday & Co., 1971), 131, 369. After the autumn of 1862 military ac-tivities in West Virginia consisted of, on the Union side, counterguerrilla operations and, by the Confederates, of occasional cavalry forays.

35. Sears, *Young Napoleon*, 122–125. McClellan tried to control Rosecrans's op-erations in western Virginia from Washington even though the Department of the Ohio did not come under his jurisdiction as commander of the Army of the Poto-mac. See *OR*, 5:555–556.

2. GRANT IN MISSOURI AND TENNESSEE

1. The preceding account of Grant's career up to July 1861 is based on Brooks D. Simpson, *Ulysses S. Grant: Triumph over Adversity, 1822–1865* (New York:

Houghton Mifflin Co., 2000), 1–87, but supplemented, as will be the case through-out this book when it deals with Grant, by knowledge and opinions acquired during sixty-some years of reading and sometimes writing about him.

2. Ulysses S. Grant, *Personal Memoirs of U.S. Grant*, 2 vols. (New York: Charles L. Webster & Co., 1885–1886), 1:249–250.

3. Simpson, *Grant*, 88–92; Thomas L. Connelly, *Army of the Heartland: The Army of Tennessee, 1861–1862* (Baton Rouge: Louisiana State University Press, 1967), 50–54; John Y. Simon, ed., *The Papers of Ulysses S. Grant*, 31 vols. (Carbon-dale: Southern Illinois University Press, 1967–2009), 2:190–192. This source herein after cited as *PUSG*.

4. Kenneth P. Williams, *Lincoln Finds a General*, 5 vols. (New York: Macmillan, 1949–1959), 3:59–67; Albert Castel, *General Sterling Price and the Civil War in the West* (Baton Rouge: Louisiana State University Press, 1968), 57–59.

5. The preceding account and analysis of the Belmont operation derives almost entirely from Nathaniel Cheairs Hughes Jr., *The Battle of Belmont: Grant Strikes South* (Chapel Hill: University of North Carolina Press, 1991). This is the definitive study of its subject, and any flaws in my account are solely my fault. Grant's report on Belmont (as presented in *OR*, 3:267–269) is not reliable or even authentic, for reasons presented in Hughes's book (51–53, 231–232, notes 5 and 8). Grant, *Memoirs*, 1:271–272, in essence merely repeats this report, which, although dated November 17, 1861, actually was written by Rawlins and other members of his staff in 1864. His actual reports, consisting of two short telegrams dated November 7 and 9, 1861, are in 53 *OR*, 5:506–507, which was not published until 1898.

6. Connelly, *Army of Heartland*, 55, 78–85.

7. Williams, *Lincoln Finds a General*, 3:104–105.

8. *OR*, 8:382.

9. Simpson, *Grant*, 103–108; Williams, *Lincoln Finds a General*, 3:112–129.

10. Williams, *Lincoln Finds a General*, 3:130–132, 144–145; Stephen D. Engle, *Don Carlos Buell: Most Promising of All* (Chapel Hill: University of North Carolina Press, 1999), 75–113.

11. Simpson, *Grant*, 108–109.

12. Ibid., 109–111.

13. The following account of the Fort Henry operation is based, unless otherwise indicated, on Simpson, *Grant*, 110–112; Connelly, *Army of Heartland*, 78–85, 106–108; and Benjamin Franklin Cooling, *Forts Henry and Donelson: The Key to the Confederate Heartland* (Knoxville: University of Tennessee Press, 1987), 89–107.

14. *PUSG*, 4:149.

15. Cooling, *Henry and Donelson*, 48–62, 82–88; Connelly, *Army of Heartland*, 78–85.

16. Firsthand accounts of the duel between Henry's cannons and Foote's iron-clads are provided by Henry Walke, "The Gun-Boats at Belmont and Fort Henry," in *Battles and Leaders of the Civil War*, ed. Robert U. Johnson and Clarence C. Buel (New York: Century Co., 1887), 1:362–367, and Jesse Taylor, "The Defense of Fort Henry," ibid., 369–372.

17. *PUSG*, 4:155, 157.

18. The ensuing description of Union operations leading to the capture of Fort Donelson is based mainly on Cooling, *Henry and Donelson*, 122–223, supplemented

by other sources that will be cited when used. Cooling's account is the most thorough and accurate ever published, and in the few instances that I differ with him it is solely because the available—and unavailable—primary sources pertaining to what happened and why at Donelson make it impossible for any two historians to fully agree about everything.

19. *OR*, 7:395.

20. *PUSG*, 4:211.

21. The foregoing account of Grant's activities during the morning and early afternoon of February 15, 1862, is based on his *Memoirs*, 1:304–308, which is supported in all essentials by a letter report he sent to Halleck's chief of staff the following day (*OR*, 7:159–160).

22. Simpson, *Grant*, 117; facsimile of Grant's reply to Buckner, found in Grant, *Memoirs*, 1:312, insert.

23. Simpson, *Grant*, 63.

24. For a variety of reasons it is impossible to arrive at a definite and precise figure as to the number of Confederates taken prisoner at Donelson. The best estimate appears in *PUSG*, 4:226n1, 230n1.

25. The best, because most balanced, portrayal of Pillow, the man and the soldier, is Nathaniel Cheairs Hughes Jr. and Roy P. Stonesifer Jr., *The Life and Wars of Gideon J. Pillow* (Chapel Hill: University of North Carolina Press, 1993).

26. *OR*, 7:386. In this same report, Forrest also asserted that if the Confederates had continued their attack during the afternoon of February 15, they not only could have escaped from Donelson to Nashville but also driven Grant's army all the way back to Fort Henry, thereby presumably making an evacuation unnecessary! However, in a subsequent report, dated November 7, 1862, and prepared for a Confederate congressional committee investigating Pillow's conduct at Donelson, Forrest stated that owing to a lack of needed preparations it would have been impracticable for the Confederates to have evacuated the fort on the afternoon of February 15; that because of the "scattered and exhausted condition of our troops" and the arrival of "a large, fresh force" of Federals the "pursuit of the enemy could not have been continued longer" that afternoon; and that an evacuation of Donelson by the route he took would have put the Confederates into a country that was excessively poor and broken, and at that time covered with snow and sleet, and [which] could not have furnished a half-day's ration for our force" (387). In other words, even had all or most of Donelson's defenders attempted on the night of February 15 to escape to Nashville by the route taken by Forrest, and even if they had not been intercepted by the Federals, large numbers of them, if not the majority, would have dropped by the wayside from hunger and exhaustion before reaching Nashville, something that it took Forrest's mounted men three days to do (386). It should be added that the reason Forrest did not meet or even see any Federals along the River Road is that the overflow of water from the creek emptying into the Cumberland prevented Grant from extending his right to that road (162).

27. Union losses in the fighting at Donelson came to 2,832 killed, wounded, and missing (*OR*, 7:169). Floyd, in his report (270), estimated Confederate casualties to be about 1,500 killed and wounded, but probably they were about the same as those of the Federals. Thus Forrest states in his February 1862 report (386) that his regiment alone lost "between 300 and 400 men" on February 15.

28. Simpson, *Grant*, 119.
29. *PUSG*, 4:229–230.

3. GRANT, HALLECK, AND A
FAILURE TO COMMUNICATE

1. *PUSG*, 4:272.
2. Ibid., 271.
3. Ibid., 245.
4. *OR*, 7:624–625, 627–637.
5. Ibid., 628, 633.
6. Ibid., 641.
7. Ibid., 645.
8. Ibid., 595, 614.
9. Ibid., 645, 655. Halleck's February 21 telegram to Stanton is misdated as February 23 in this source. Thomas A. Scott, investigating on behalf of Stanton the military situation in the West, had become a champion of Halleck's views on Union strategy there. See Kenneth P. Williams, *Lincoln Finds a General: A Military Study of the Civil War*, 5 vols. (New York: Macmillan, 1949–1959), 3:261–263.
10. *OR*, 7:652.
11. Ibid., 648.
12. Ibid., 650, 654, 656–657, 661.
13. Ibid., 653, 662–663.
14. Ulysses S. Grant, *Personal Memoirs of U.S. Grant*, 2 vols. (New York: Charles L. Webster & Co., 1885–1886), 1:318–320; *PUSG*, 4:284.
15. Grant, *Memoirs*, 1:320–321; *OR*, 7:670–671.
16. This sketch and appraisal of Buell is derived from Stephen D. Engle, *Don Carlos Buell: Most Promising of All* (Chapel Hill: University of North Carolina Press, 1999), the first full-fledged biography of Buell and the last that ever shall be needed owing to its excellent scholarship.
17. Grant, *Memoirs*, 1:321; Engle, *Buell*, 178–180; Thomas L. Connelly, *Army of the Heartland: The Army of Tennessee, 1861–1862* (Baton Rouge: Louisiana State University Press, 1967), 134–139.
18. *OR*, 7:674; 10 *OR*, 2:2; Grant, *Memoirs*, 1:326. Halleck's giving Smith the title of major general stemmed from Smith having been nominated, as was Buell, for promotion to that rank by Lincoln on March 3.
19. Grant to Halleck, March 5, 1862, 10 *OR*, 2:4–5.
20. Grant, *Memoirs*, 1:325; Cullum to Halleck, March 3, 4, 1862, *OR*, 7:435–437; Sherman to Halleck, February 25, 1862, *OR*, 7:665; Grant to Halleck, March 21, 1862, 10 *OR*, 2:56 (disloyal telegraph operator at Ft. Henry). The telegraph wire to Fort Henry was strung along the branches of trees, some of them dead, and either weakly attached or not attached at all, with the result that strong winds frequently blew them down. See report of officer in charge of maintaining this line (*PUSG*, 4:346–347).
21. Halleck to McClellan, February 24, 1862, ibid., 320, stating: "Wires down. Can get nothing south of the Ohio."
22. *OR*, 7:637.

23. Ibid., 679–680. Although dated March 3, the answering telegram from McClellan indicates that Halleck sent this telegram on March 2.

24. Ibid., 680.

25. Ibid., 682.

26. 10 *OR*, 2:15.

27. Ibid., 21.

28. Ibid., 19.

29. Ibid., 29.

30. Williams, *Lincoln Finds a General,* 3:287–307.

31. *OR*, 7:683.

32. 10 *OR*, 2:24–25.

33. Ibid., 27. Grant in fact did supply Washburne with copies of his correspondence with Halleck during the latter part of February and early March (Brooks D. Simpson, *Ulysses S. Grant: Triumph over Adversity, 1822–1865* [New York: Houghton Mifflin Co., 2000], 124). Whether Washburne showed Lincoln this correspondence or told him of it is unknown, but this would seem more likely than unlikely. Also, Halleck lied in claiming that he had sent daily requests to Grant for reports on the strength of his army, as copies of such requests do not exist in the headquarters files of either Halleck or Grant. *PUSG*, 4:320.

34. *PUSG*, 4:348–349.

35. Sears, *Civil War Papers of McClellan*, 206–207.

36. 10 *OR*, 2:28–29.

37. Sears, *Young Napoleon,* 149–167.

38. 10 *OR*, 2:13–14.

39. Ibid., 30. This source misdates Grant's telegram as March 11, 1862. The correct date comes from *PUSG*, 4:353.

40. 10 *OR*, 2:32. Like Halleck, Stanton dared not take any action against Grant without Lincoln's prior approval; that is why when Lincoln told him to do it he had Adjutant General Thomas ask Halleck to provide proof of his accusations against Grant.

41. Ibid., 36.

42. *OR*, 7:683–684; *PUSG*, 4:414.

43. *PUSG*, 4:414–415; Grant, *Memoirs,* 1:327–328; Simpson, *Grant,* 125.

44. *PUSG*, 4:375–376.

4. GRANT AT SHILOH

1. Except when otherwise indicated, this account of Grant at Shiloh is derived from the two most recent and detailed descriptions of the battle: Larry J. Daniel, *Shiloh: The Battle that Changed the Civil War* (New York: Simon & Schuster, 1997) and Wiley Sword, *Shiloh: Bloody April*, rev. ed. (Dayton, OH: Morningside House, 2001). I accept full responsibility for all analyses and interpretations.

2. Brooks D. Simpson, *Ulysses S. Grant: Triumph over Adversity, 1822–1865* (New York: Houghton Mifflin Co., 2000), 127–128.

3. *PUSG*, 4:443.

4. 10 *OR*, 2:50–51; *PUSG*, 1:27.

5. Ambrose Bierce, "What I Saw of Shiloh," in *Shadows of Blue and Gray: The*

Civil War Writings of Ambrose Bierce, ed. Brian M. Thompson (New York: A Forge Book, 2002), 204.

6. Richard L. Kiper, *Major General John Alexander McClernand: Politician in Uniform* (Kent, OH: Kent State University Press, 1999), 101–102.

7. Ibid.

8. Stephen D. Engle, *Don Carlos Buell: Most Promising of All* (Chapel Hill: University of North Carolina Press, 1999), 210–217. On March 19 Grant sent Buell, via two couriers, a short message stating that "I am massing troops at Pittsburg, Tenn.," a message Buell received on March 23 but, so he notified Halleck the same day, found it to contain "no information of importance" (10 *OR,* 2:47, 59)!

9. *PUSG,* 5:7.

10. The ensuing account of Sherman's career up to Shiloh derives from two articles of mine: (1) A three-part article that appeared in the July, August, and October 1979 issues of *Civil War Times Illustrated,* and which was republished, with substantial revisions in the third part, under the title of "The Fall and Rise of William Tecumseh Sherman" in a collection of my articles titled *Articles of War: Winners, Losers, and Some Who Were Both in the Civil War* (Mechanicsburg, PA: Stackpole Books, 2001), 195–232; and (2) "Liddell Hart's *Sherman: Propaganda as History,*" *Journal of Military History* 67 (April 2003): 405–426.

11. Neither Grant in his *Memoirs* nor any other source known to this author states which of his ankles was sprained, but since he seems to have been able to mount and dismount a horse without assistance, presumably it was the right one.

12. Don Carlos Buell, "Shiloh Reviewed," *B&L,* 1:519. Buell, writing twenty-three years afterward, did add to the quoted statement that "I would zealously have obeyed his [Grant's] orders." Other than McClellan's, and not even his when it came to East Tennessee, Buell never obeyed anyone's orders zealously.

13. 10 *OR,* 2:33–34.

14. Ibid., 1:89.

15. In addition to the sources cited in note 1, I consulted Thomas L. Connelly, *Army of the Heartland: The Army of Tennessee, 1861–1862* (Baton Rouge: Louisiana State University Press, 1967), 151–157, for the foregoing account of Confederate preparations and operations leading to Johnston's attack at Shiloh.

16. *PUSG,* 5:34–41; 10 *OR,* 1:323, 328, 331–332.

17. Lew Wallace's conduct or misconduct on April 6 during the Battle of Shiloh has been a source of controversy ever since and will ever be so. Two comments, however, are in order. One, Wallace was fully justified in thinking that Grant's order to "take position on the right of the army" meant linking up with Sherman in the vicinity of Shiloh Church. And, two, most of the testimony against Wallace comes from staff officers of Grant, in particular McPherson and Rawlins, and so is suspect. It might be added that even had Wallace marched directly by the River Road to the Union right, it is doubtful this would have made any basic difference in the course of the fighting on April 6, since most of the decisive part of that fighting took place on the Union left.

18. For the condition of the Confederates in general, and in particular the two brigades that delivered their final attack on April 6, see Connelly, *Army of the Heartland,* 167–169 and 10 *OR,* 1:550–551, 555. Regarding the role of the Thirty-sixth

Indiana in repelling the Confederate assault, suffice to say that its eight companies totaled only 400 men, 2 of whom were killed and 1 wounded (10 *OR*, 1:337).

19. Bierce, "What I Saw of Shiloh," 218.

20. According to Bierce in "What I Saw of Shiloh," "some regiments [of Nelson's division] had lost a third of their number from fatigue while marching [from Savannah] through country presenting nothing but interminable swamps" (205). Many of the troops in the other two divisions of Buell's army to see action on April 7 were in little, if any, better shape by the time Beauregard retreated.

21. Bruce Catton, *Grant Moves South* (Boston: Little, Brown & Co., 1960), 247; William Preston Johnston, "Albert Sidney Johnston at Shiloh," *B&L,* 1:567–568; William C. Davis, *Breckinridge: Statesman, Soldier, Symbol* (Baton Rouge: Louisiana State University Press, 1974), 310–311.

22. Connelly, *Army of the Heartland,* 168–170.

5. GRANT ADVANCES BY STAYING PUT

1. Curt Anders, *Henry Halleck's War: A Fresh Look at Lincoln's Controversial General-in-Chief* (Carmel: Guild Press of Indiana, 1999), 102–103; 10 *OR*, 1:114, 2:99.

2. Wiley Sword, *Shiloh: Bloody April,* rev. ed. (Dayton, OH: Morningside House, 2001), 430–435.

3. 10 *OR*, 2:94.

4. Ibid., 1:108–110. In his *Memoirs*, Grant states he "never made a full official report on Shiloh. In the sense of a long, very detailed report." This is true, but it also is true he had some good reasons not to write such a report. Ulysses S. Grant, *Personal Memoirs of U.S. Grant,* 2 vols. (New York: Charles L. Webster & Co., 1885–1886), 1:370.

5. Ibid., 1:248–250.

6. Ibid., 1:98.

7. Ibid., 102. Probably the low casualties in Lew Wallace's division resulted from Sherman having it advance on April 7 at right angles to his division and hence encountering little opposition, the Confederates having few troops on their left flank. Wallace's report, 10 *OR*, 2:170.

8. Brooks D. Simpson and Jean V. Berlin, eds., *Sherman's Civil War: Selected Correspondence of William T. Sherman, 1860–1865* (Chapel Hill: University of North Carolina Press, 1999), 203.

9. Bruce Catton, *Grant Moves South* (Boston: Little, Brown & Co., 1960), 252–256; 10 *OR*, 1:98–99.

10. 10 *OR*, 1:99.

11. Simpson and Berlin, *Sherman's Civil War,* 210.

12. 10 *OR*, 1:99.

13. Tuttle's report, 10 *OR*, 1:149. Although in the passage quoted Tuttle describes the experience of the brigade he commanded at the beginning of the battle and prior to W.H.L. Wallace being mortally wounded, what he describes applies to Wallace's division as a whole because it was camped to the rear of Prentiss's division. In *Grant Moves South,* Catton rightly states that while Reid exaggerated and even falsified

the degree of the surprise, Grant, Sherman, and, by implication, Halleck went too far in "saying there had been no surprise at all" (256).

14. 10 *OR*, 2:144–145.

15. Thomas B. Van Horne, *The Life of Major-General George H. Thomas* (New York: Charles Scribner's Sons, 1882), 1–64.

16. 10 *OR*, 2:144.

17. *PUSG*, 5:102–103.

18. Kenneth P. Williams, *Lincoln Finds a General: A Military Study of the Civil War*, 5 vols. (New York: Macmillan, 1949–1959), 3:411.

19. Stephen D. Engle, *Don Carlos Buell: Most Promising of All* (Chapel Hill: University of North Carolina Press, 1999), 234–239.

20. *PUSG*, 5:114–115.

21. 10 *OR*, 2:182–183.

22. *PUSG*, 5:115–119. In a rare mistake, Catton, *Grant Moves South*, asserts that Grant sent a letter to the *Cincinnati Commercial* defending his conduct at Shiloh (256–257). In fact, he wrote the letter to his father, who, without his permission or knowledge, sent a copy of it to the *Commercial*, which printed it in its May 2, 1862, issue, stating that it came from "a personal friend of Gen. Grant, in this city." On learning of what his father had done, Grant wrote Julia on May 11, 1862, declaring that "this should never have occurred" (*PUSG*, 5:78–79, 115–116).

23. For Sherman's post-Shiloh letters to family members, see Simpson and Berlin, *Sherman's Civil War*, 203–237.

24. Ibid., 217.

25. Richard L. Kiper, *Major General John Alexander McClernand: Politician in Uniform* (Kent, OH: Kent State University Press, 1999), 104–112. Kiper is a West Point graduate and retired lieutenant colonel who holds a PhD in history. He has also taught at West Point and the Command and General Staff College. See also McClernand's and Sherman's official reports (10 *OR*, 1:114–120, 248–252). Prentiss, like Sherman, was able to get his division in line of battle shortly (but not "hours") before being assailed by the Confederates in full force, but this was owing to the initiative of one of his regimental commanders, Colonel David Moore, and both of his flanks remained exposed, with the result that his troops soon were falling back in considerable confusion. Only their finding by sheer circumstance a strong defensive position in the "Hornet's Nest" enabled them, with the support of W.H.L. Wallace's and Hurlbut's divisions, to make the stand they made. This stand contributed far more to Grant's escape from disaster than anything Sherman's division did on April 6. See Prentiss's report (10 *OR*, 1:277–279) and Moore's report (10 *OR*, 1:282). Larry J. Daniel, *Shiloh: The Battle that Changed the Civil War* (New York: Simon & Schuster, 1997), concludes that "the valiant stand made at the Sunken Road [Hornet's Nest] probably saved the [Union] army, and clearly turned the tide in Grant's favor" (237).

26. Williams, *Lincoln Finds a General*, 3:415–423.

27. Simpson and Berlin, *Sherman's Civil War*, 213, 226.

28. *PUSG*, 5:134.

29. Ibid., 5:140–142. See also Catton, *Grant Moves South*, 274–275.

30. Engle, *Buell*, 252–258; Williams, *Lincoln Finds a General*, 428–429.

31. *PUSG*, 5:142.

32. Catton, *Grant Moves South,* 284.

33. *PUSG,* 5:206–207n.

34. Catton, *Grant Moves South,* 287–288. There is, of course, no way of knowing if Halleck was correct in telling Allen that he could have him promoted to senior major general in the West. However, a July 14 telegram from Lincoln to Halleck seems to indicate that Halleck at least had some reason to think he could do this, for in it Lincoln stated: "I am very anxious—almost impatient—to have you here [Washington]. Having due regard for what you leave behind [in the West], when can you reach here?" (16 *OR,* 2:143). Why Lincoln was "very anxious—almost impatient" for Halleck to take over as general in chief will be revealed in the next chapter.

6. NOBODY AT ANTIETAM

1. The following account of McClellan's Peninsula Campaign is based, unless otherwise indicated, on the pertinent portions of Stephen W. Sears, *George B. McClellan: The Young Napoleon* (New York: Ticknor & Fields, 1988). It is the definitive biography of McClellan.

2. Douglass Southall Freeman, *R. E. Lee: A Biography* (New York: Charles Scribner's Sons, 1935), 2:51–75, passim.

3. Stephen W. Sears, ed., *The Civil War Papers of George B. McClellan: Selected Correspondence, 1860–1865* (New York: Ticknor & Fields, 1989), 269–270.

4. Ibid., 244–245.

5. Daniel H. Hill, "Lee's Attacks North of the Chickahominy," *B&L,* 2:35–52.

6. Daniel H. Hill, "McClellan's Change of Base and Malvern Hill," *B&L,* 2:394.

7. Sears, *Civil War Papers of McClellan,* 323–324.

8. Ibid., 323n1.

9. Ibid., 357.

10. Ibid., 327.

11. Ibid., 327n1.

12. Ibid., 334.

13. Sears, *Young Napoleon,* 227, 436n5.

14. Sears, *Civil War Papers of McClellan,* 336–338.

15. Ibid., 344–345.

16. 17 *OR,* 2:90.

17. Quoted in Curt Anders, *Henry Halleck's War: A Fresh Look at Lincoln's Controversial Chief of Staff* (Carmel: Guild Press of Indiana, 1999), 146, 148.

18. 17 *OR,* 2:100.

19. Sears, *Civil War Papers of McClellan,* 369, 374.

20. Sears, *Young Napoleon,* 239–241.

21. Carl Sandburg, *Abraham Lincoln: The War Years,* 4 vols. (New York: Harcourt, Brace & Co., 1939), 1:498.

22. John F. Marszalek, *Commander of Lincoln's Armies: A Life of General Henry W. Halleck* (Cambridge: Belknap Press of Harvard University Press, 2004), 138.

23. William Marvel, *Burnside* (Chapel Hill: University of North Carolina Press, 1991), 98–100, 440n6; Sears, *Young Napoleon,* 58.

24. 12 *OR*, 3:524; 11 *OR*, 1:80–81; Marvel, *Burnside*, 100, 102.

25. 12 *OR*, 2:8–9; Sears, *Civil War Papers of McClellan*, 389.

26. The ensuing account of operations preceding the Battle of Second Bull Run and the battle itself are based, unless otherwise indicated, on the relevant portions of Peter Cozzens, *General John Pope: A Life for the Nation* (Urbana: University of Illinois Press, 2001). Also consulted for these events: Freeman, *Lee*, 2:259–339.

27. Quoted in Shelby Foote, *The Civil War: A Narrative*, 3 vols. (New York: Random House, 1954–1978), 1:529.

28. Sears, *Young Napoleon*, 250–258.

29. Sears, *Civil War Papers of McClellan*, 415.

30. Sears, *Young Napoleon*, 250–254; Tyler Dennett, ed., *Lincoln and the Civil War in the Diaries and Letters of John Hay* (Westport, CT: Negro University Press, 1972), 45.

31. Sears, *Young Napoleon*, 260.

32. Marszalek, *Life of Halleck*, 146–150, hypothesizes that early in September 1862 Halleck was dosing himself with opium and drinking heavily. The quantity and quality of his correspondence during this period indicates otherwise. See Williams, *Lincoln Finds a General*, 4:104.

33. My assessment of Halleck owes much to Kenneth P. Williams, *Lincoln Finds a General: A Military Study of the Civil War*, 5 vols. (New York: Macmillan Co., 1949–1959), 5:271–282; Stephen E. Ambrose, *Halleck: Lincoln's Chief of Staff* (Baton Rouge: Louisiana State University Press, 1962); Curt Anders, *Henry Halleck's War: A Fresh Look at Lincoln's Controversial General-in-Chief* (Carmel: Guild Press of Indiana, 1999); and especially Herman Hattaway and Archer Jones, *How the North Won the Civil War: A Military History of the Civil War* (Urbana: University of Illinois Press, 1983), especially chapter 10. My view of Halleck, however, derives mainly from a belated discovery that he was the first military leader of any country in all history to function as a modern chief of staff. During the spring of 1862, Robert E. Lee was chief of staff to Jefferson Davis, in which role he brought about Stonewall Jackson's Valley Campaign. However, after he took command of the Army of the Northern Virginia, Davis, who was a West Pointer and had distinguished himself as a regimental commander in the Mexican War, again became the Confederate commander in chief de facto as well as de jure.

34. 38 *OR*, 2:407–408.

35. Williams, *Lincoln Finds a General*, 5:277; Hattaway and Jones, *How the North Won*, 285–286. Von Moltke during the Franco-Prussian War (1870–1871) had a staff of 921 (235n45).

36. Freeman, *Lee*, 2:351, 353, 359–361.

37. Sears, *Young Napoleon*, 263–264; Sears, *Civil War Papers of McClellan*, 437.

38. Marvel, *Burnside*, 110–111.

39. Ibid., 111; Sears, *Young Napoleon*, 255; Sears, *Civil War Papers of McClellan*, 437. Lincoln and Halleck believed charges brought by Pope that Franklin should have come to his support on August 30, but in fact the real culprit was McClellan, who did not execute Halleck's repeated orders to hasten Franklin's corps to the battlefield.

40. Cozzens, *Pope*, 200–201.

41. Freeman, *Lee*, 2:375–386.

42. The best detailed account of the Battle of Antietam is Stephen W. Sears, *Landscape Turned Red: The Battle of Antietam* (New York: Ticknor & Fields, 1983).

43. Sears, *Civil War Papers of McClellan,* 469.

44. Ibid., 473–474.

45. Sears, *Young Napoleon,* 326.

46. Ibid., 324.

47. Ibid., 330.

48. Sears, *Civil War Papers of McClellan,* 488.

49. Sears, *Young Napoleon,* 331.

7. GRANT AND ROSECRANS AT IUKA AND CORINTH

1. Quoted in Curt Anders, *Henry Halleck's War: A Fresh Look at Lincoln's Controversial General-in-Chief* (Carmel: Guild Press of Indiana, 1999), 169.

2. Quoted in Brooks D. Simpson, *Ulysses S. Grant: Triumph over Adversity, 1822–1865* (New York: Houghton Mifflin Co., 2000), 253.

3. William M. Lamers, *The Edge of Glory: A Biography of General William S. Rosecrans, U.S.A.* (1961; paperback reprint, Baton Rouge: Louisiana State University Press, 1998), 64–82. The German immigrant was Brigadier General Ludwig Blenker, whose qualification for that rank consisted of having been an officer in the Bavarian army and participating in a failed 1848 attempt to establish a republic in Germany, following which he fled to the United States, where he settled in New York. His military background led to his becoming colonel of a volunteer regiment early in the Civil War. Because of seniority and political connections, he was promoted to brigadier general. To his credit, soon after making his way to West Virginia he resigned and returned to New York, where he died in 1863.

4. Ibid., 86–94.

5. Stephen D. Engle, *Don Carlos Buell: Most Promising of All* (Chapel Hill: University of North Carolina Press, 1999), 252–258; Kenneth P. Williams, *Lincoln Finds a General: A Military Study of the Civil War,* 5 vols. (New York: Macmillan, 1949–1959), 3:424–440.

6. Engle, *Buell,* 252–278; Lamers, *Edge of Glory,* 96–97.

7. Thomas L. Connelly, *Army of the Heartland: The Army of Tennessee, 1861–1862* (Baton Rouge: Louisiana State University Press, 1967), 177–208.

8. Engle, *Buell,* 277–278.

9. 16 *OR,* 2:278.

10. Ibid., 2:314–315.

11. Connelly, *Army of the Heartland,* 225; Engle, *Buell,* 282–284.

12. *PUSG,* 5:277–278.

13. Richard L. Kiper, *Major General John Alexander McClernand: Politician in Uniform* (Kent, OH: Kent State University Press, 1999), 128–132.

14. Lamers, *Edge of Glory,* 97–101.

15. The ensuing account of the Union and Confederate operations in Mississippi that preceded, included, and followed the Battle of Iuka, September 19–20, 1862, is based, unless otherwise indicated, on the following sources: William S. Rosecrans, "Article 2," William S. Rosecrans Papers, University of California, Los Angeles, 24–26; Lamers, *Edge of Glory,* 99–130; Albert Castel, *General Sterling Price and*

the Civil War in the West (Baton Rouge: Louisiana State University Press, 1968), 97–104; and Peter Cozzens, *The Darkest Days of the Civil War: The Battles of Iuka and Corinth* (Chapel Hill: University of North Carolina Press, 1997), 50–134. Grant's account of the Iuka operation in his *Memoirs* contains so many falsehoods as to make it worse than worthless. By the time he wrote the *Memoirs,* he, for reasons to be described, hated Rosecrans.

16. Dickey to Wife, September 21, 1862, *PUSG,* 6:177n8. Cozzens, *Iuka and Corinth,* 126, contends that Lagow and Dickey did not inform Rosecrans of Grant's order to Ord not to attack until after Rosecrans did, but this assertion is based on a source that not only is dubious but also, as presented in his notes and bibliography, mysterious.

17. 17 *OR,* 1:64.

18. Lamers, *Edge of Glory,* 174.

19. Bruce Catton, *Grant Moves South* (Boston: Little, Brown & Co., 1960), 320–321.

20. The following account of the Battle of Corinth is based, except when otherwise indicated, on Cozzens, *Iuka and Corinth,* 145–273, and Castel, *Price,* 108–119.

21. Cozzens, *Iuka and Corinth,* 273–300.

22. *PUSG,* 6:129.

23. Cozzens, *Iuka and Corinth,* 297–298, 301.

24. 17 *OR,* 1:163.

25. *PUSG,* 6:131.

26. Ibid., 132.

27. Ibid., 133.

28. 17 *OR,* 2:269.

29. *PUSG,* 6:130; Cozzens, *Iuka and Corinth,* 302–303.

30. William S. Rosecrans, "The Battle of Corinth," *B&L,* 2:755–756.

8. ROSECRANS AT STONES RIVER

1. Unless otherwise indicated, the ensuing account of Union and Confederate operations in Kentucky during September and October 1862 is based on Kenneth P. Williams, *Lincoln Finds a General,* 5 vols. (New York: Macmillan, 1949–1959), 4:107–143, and Thomas L. Connelly, *Army of the Heartland: The Army of Tennessee, 1861–1862* (Baton Rouge: Louisiana State University Press, 1967), 221–280.

2. Nathaniel C. Hughes Jr. and Gordon C. Whitney, *Jefferson Davis in Blue: The Life of Sherman's Relentless Warrior* (Baton Rouge: Louisiana State University Press, 2002), 104–126.

3. Stephen D. Engle, *Don Carlos Buell: Most Promising of All* (Chapel Hill: University of North Carolina Press, 1999), 298–302.

4. Ibid., 304–309.

5. Ibid., 312–318.

6. Sherman to Philemon B. Ewing, July 13, 1862, Brooks D. Simpson and Jean V. Berlin, eds., *Sherman's Civil War: Selected Correspondence of William T. Sherman, 1860–1865* (Chapel Hill: University of North Carolina Press, 1999), 253.

7. Stephen W. Sears, *George B. McClellan: The Young Napoleon* (New York: Ticknor & Fields, 1988), 330–336; Stephen W. Sears, ed., *The Civil War Papers of*

George B. McClellan: Selected Correspondence, 1860–1865 (New York: Ticknor & Fields, 1989), 515.

8. Williams, *Lincoln Finds a General*, 4:139–140.

9. *PUSG*, 6:164.

10. Ibid., 165, 180; Ulysses S. Grant, *Personal Memoirs of U.S. Grant*, 2 vols. (New York: Charles L. Webster & Co., 1885–1886), 1:420.

11. 16 *OR*, 2:640–641, 650; William M. Lamers, *The Edge of Glory: A Biography of General William S. Rosecrans, U.S.A.* (1961; paperback reprint, Baton Rouge: Louisiana State University Press, 1998), 181–182; Williams, *Lincoln Finds a General*, 4:144–146.

12. Ibid., 182–186.

13. 20 *OR*, 2:17; Larry J. Daniel, *Days of Glory: The Army of the Cumberland, 1861–1865* (Baton Rouge: Louisiana State University Press, 2004), 183; Lamers, *Edge of Glory*, 190–195.

14. Sears, *Young Napoleon*, 337–338, 340–341.

15. Sears, *Civil War Papers of McClellan*, 520.

16. Ibid., 481.

17. *PUSG*, 6:199–200.

18. Ibid., 210.

19. Ibid., 243.

20. Ibid.

21. Kiper, *McClernand*, 133–139.

22. Ibid., 140.

23. Ibid.

24. Ibid., 146–152.

25. Ibid., 156. Here Kiper states: "Unquestionably he [Halleck] knew of McClernand's order, having been directed by Stanton to meet with McClernand before the orders were issued." Since the order was confidential, Halleck withheld his knowledge of it from Grant until the order ceased officially to be confidential.

26. 17 *OR*, 2:307–308.

27. Kiper, *McClernand*, 142–143; *PUSG*, 6:288.

28. *PUSG*, 6:288.

29. Ibid., 304.

30. The ensuing account of Burnside's operations that culminated in the Battle of Fredericksburg is based, where not otherwise indicated, on Williams, *Lincoln Finds a General*, 2:482–536.

31. *B&L*, 2:145, 147.

32. Williams, *Lincoln Finds a General*, 4:154–186.

33. *PUSG*, 7:62.

34. Ibid., 61–63.

35. Kiper, *McClernand*, 148–155.

36. Williams, *Lincoln Finds a General*, 4:210–216; George W. Morgan, "The Assault on Chickasaw Bluffs," *B & L*, 3:463–470. Grant should not have ordered Sherman to break up the railroad from Monroe, Louisiana, for if Vicksburg fell to the Federals it would have ceased to be of any value to the Confederates.

37. Grant, *Memoirs*, 1:435. For Grant's orders to punish troops engaging in plundering and taking food from civilians, see *PUSG*, 6:266–267, 321–322, 399, 412,

and Grant, *Memoirs*, 7:18, 73. Not only did Halleck support Rosecrans's proposal to continue pursuing Van Dorn's army after its defeat at Corinth, on November 15, 1862, he also rejected a request from Grant for twelve additional locomotives to be used in supplying his army as it moved into Mississippi, stating that his operations "must be limited to rapid marches upon the enemy, feeding as far as possible on the country" (Grant, *Memoirs*, 6:305).

38. Lamers, *Edge of Glory*, 170; Williams, *Lincoln Finds a General*, 149–150.

39. Prior to the departure from his army—on orders from Jefferson Davis for Major General Carter L. Stevenson's division to reinforce Pemberton—Bragg far outnumbered Rosecrans in infantry, and the reason he did not have an overwhelming superiority in cavalry is because of Forrest's raid into west Tennessee in late December and a raid by Morgan's cavalry into Kentucky at the same time. See Peter Cozzens, *No Better Place to Die: The Battle of Stones River* (Urbana: University of Illinois Press, 1990), 38, 35. Unless otherwise indicated, the ensuing account of military operations leading to the Battle of Stones River is based on this book, but the battle should be named Stone's River, which is a more correct usage, that river being named after a man, not some rocks.

40. Cozzens, *No Better Place to Die*, 173–174, contends that since Rosecrans during this reconnaissance saw torch lights in the rear of his army he concluded that he could not retreat, not realizing that the torches had been lit by his own troops striving to stay warm. But since this interpretation is based on the subsequent testimony of McCook, hardly a reliable source given his typically incompetent performance at Stones River, probably Rosecrans's reconnaissance merely confirmed him in doing what he already had decided to do: stand and fight. Besides, this was the best thing he could have done, given the situation.

41. *B&L*, 3:611–612.

42. Herman Hattaway and Archer Jones, *How the North Won: A Military History of the Civil War* (Urbana: University of Illinois Press, 1983), 324–325; Williams, *Lincoln Finds a General*, 4:284–285; Cozzens, *No Better Place to Die*, 205.

43. Patricia L. Faust ed., *Historical Times Illustrated Encyclopedia of the Civil War* (New York: Harper & Row, 1986), 679.

44. Cozzens, *No Better Place to Die*, 205; Lamers, *Edge of Glory*, 246.

9. MEADE AT GETTYSBURG

1. The ensuing account of Burnside's final days as commander of the Army of the Potomac, his removal from command, and his replacement by Hooker is based on William Marvel, *Burnside* (Chapel Hill: University of North Carolina Press, 1991), 208–217, and Stephen R. Taaffe, *Commanding the Army of the Potomac* (Lawrence: University Press of Kansas, 2006), 73–81.

2. Quoted in Curt Anders, *Henry Halleck's War: A Fresh Look at Lincoln's Controversial General-in-Chief* (Carmel: Guild Press of Indiana, 1999), 363.

3. The ensuing account of Hooker's tenure as commander of the Army of the Potomac and of the Battle of Chancellorsville is based, unless otherwise indicated, on Kenneth P. Williams, *Lincoln Finds a General: A Military Study of the Civil War,* 5 vols. (New York: Macmillan, 1949–1959), 2:547–605.

4. Milo M. Quaife, ed., *From the Cannons Mouth: The Civil War Letters of*

General Alpheus S. Williams (Detroit: Wayne State University Press and the Detroit Historical Society, 1959), 198.

5. *B&L*, 3:237–238.

6. Taaffe, *Commanding the Army of the Potomac,* 99, citing a letter by Meade to his wife, May 8, 1863, in George Meade, *The Life and Letters of George Gordon Meade,* 2 vols. (New York: Charles Scribner's Sons, 1913), 1:372–373. (The editor, George Meade, was General Meade's son and an officer on his staff.)

7. John Bigelow Jr., *The Campaign of Chancellorsville: A Strategic and Tactical Study* (New Haven: Yale University Press, 1910), 478n.

8. The ensuing account of Hooker's final days as commander of the Army of the Potomac, of the beginning of the Gettysburg Campaign, and of Hooker's removal from command and his replacement by Meade is based, unless otherwise indicated, on Stephen W. Sears, *Gettysburg* (New York: Houghton Mifflin, 2003), 1–128, and Taaffe, *Commanding the Army of the Potomac,* 105–106.

9. Confederate brigades, divisions, and corps usually bore the name of their commander, although formally Longstreet's corps was designated First Corps, Ewell's Second Corps, and A. P. Hill's Third Corps.

10. The ensuing account of Meade's career prior to becoming commander of the Army of the Potomac and of events immediately preceding the Battle of Gettysburg is derived from Sears, *Gettysburg,* 125–160.

11. The ensuing account of the Battle of Gettysburg is based on Sears, *Gettysburg,* 154–458, 497–508, unless otherwise indicated.

12. At this stage of the war and well into 1864, Southern infantry regiments, brigades, and divisions often were larger than their Northern counterparts owing to the Confederate government replenishing existing regiments with new recruits or consolidating two such regiments into one; whereas the Union government continued to permit states to continue raising new regiments, with the result that many old regiments dwindled to only a few hundred men.

13. Freeman, *R. E. Lee,* 3:161.

14. Except when otherwise indicated, the ensuing account of Lee's retreat back into Virginia and Meade's pursuit of him is based on Sears, *Gettysburg,* 469–492, and Edwin B. Coddington, *The Gettysburg Campaign: A Study in Command* (1968; Dayton, OH: Press of the Morningside Bookshop, 1979), 534–573.

15. Both Sears and Coddington, whose studies of the Gettysburg Campaign are the best, take the same view. For a strong presentation of the negative view, see Williams, *Lincoln Finds a General,* 2:721–56. Most of the mammoth historical literature on Gettysburg approaches the subject from the standpoint of why Lee failed to win the battle. This is understandable. No one has ever contended that Meade per se was a better commander than Lee, for the very good reason that he was not.

10. GRANT VICTORIOUS AT VICKSBURG

1. *PUSG,* 7:171–172, 186, 197.
2. Ibid., 204–205.
3. Ibid., 208–209.
4. Ibid., 209–211.
5. Ibid., 217.

6. Ibid., 218–219. For Grant having false teeth, see Grant to Julia Grant, February 11, 1863, *PUSG*, 7:311.

7. *PUSG*, 7:219.

8. 17 *OR*, 2:566–567.

9. *PUSG*, 7:233–236; Richard L. Kiper, *Major General John Alexander McClernand: Politician in Uniform* (Kent, OH: Kent State University Press, 1999), 183–184; Brooks D. Simpson, *Ulysses S. Grant: Triumph over Adversity, 1822–1865* (New York: Houghton Mifflin Co., 2000), 169.

10. *PUSG*, 7:235.

11. Ibid., 233–235.

12. Ibid., 242; Kiper, *McClernand*, 182.

13. *PUSG*, 7:253.

14. Ibid., 264–265; Kiper, *McClernand*, 196–197.

15. Kiper, *McClernand*, 196–197.

16. The ensuing account of the Vicksburg Campaign (January–July 1863) is based, unless otherwise indicated, on Albert Castel, "The Road to Vicksburg: Grant's Masterpiece in the Mississippi Valley," *Strategy and Tactics* (September–October 1985): 14–19, which in turn is based on Ulysses S. Grant, *Personal Memoirs of U. S. Grant,* 2 vols. (New York: Charles L. Webster & Co., 1885–1886), 1:452–576; *B&L*, 3:472–550; Kenneth P. Williams, *Lincoln Finds a General: A Military Study of the Civil War,* 5 vols. (New York: Macmillan, 1949–1959), 4:306–425; Bruce Catton, *Grant Moves South* (Boston: Little, Brown & Co., 1960), 366–485.

17. Grant, *Memoirs,* 1:480–481.

18. Kiper, *McClernand,* 259–273.

19. 24 *OR*, 1:37.

20. Kiper, *McClernand,* 265–268.

21. Ibid., 268–278.

22. Quoted in Catton, *Grant Moves South,* 480.

23. What follows is derived mainly from Albert Castel, "Vicksburg: Myths and Realities," *North and South* (November 2003): 62–69. Other historians who have presented what might be termed heretical views on the effect of the fall of Vicksburg on the course and conduct of the Civil War are Thomas L. Connelly, "Vicksburg: Strategic Point or Propaganda Device?" *Military Affairs* 34 (April 1970): 49–53, and Herman Hattaway and Archer Jones, *How the North Won: A Military History of the Civil War* (Urbana: University of Illinois Press, 1983), 421–423. It should be added that during the Civil War the economic importance of the Mississippi for the farmers, manufacturers, and merchants in Northern states bordering that river and the Ohio was greatly exaggerated by the public and has continued to be so by most historians since then. See Robert R. Russel, *A History of the American Economic System* (New York: Appleton-Century-Crofts, 1964), 226–233.

11. ROSECRANS TAKES CHATTANOOGA AND GRANT TAKES A FALL

1. Unless otherwise indicated, this chapter's accounts of Union and Confederate military operations and preparations in Tennessee during January–September 1863 are based on Peter Cozzens, *This Terrible Sound: The Battle of Chickamauga*

(Urbana: University of Illinois Press, 1992), 6–55, and Larry J. Daniel, *Days of Glory: The Army of the Cumberland, 1861–1865* (Baton Rouge: Louisiana State University Press, 2004), 225–303.

2. William M. Lamers, *The Edge of Glory: A Biography of General William S. Rosecrans, U.S.A.* (1961; paperback reprint, Baton Rouge: Louisiana State University Press, 1999), 252.

3. The best-known account of Wilder's acquisition of the Spencers is Glenn W. Sunderland, *Wilder's Lightning Brigade—and Its Spencer Repeaters* (Washington, IL: Book Works, 1984), 28–69.

4. 23 *OR*, 2:95.

5. Ibid., 111.

6. Ibid., 297–298.

7. Ibid., 369.

8. Ibid.

9. Ibid., 873.

10. Ibid., 383.

11. *B&L*, 3:480, 550.

12. 24 *OR*, 3:376–377.

13. 23 *OR*, 2:402–415; Daniel, *Days of Glory,* 261.

14. 23 *OR*, 1:8.

15. Ibid.

16. Ibid., 9.

17. Alan Peskin, "Garfield, James Abram," in *Biographical Dictionary of the Union's Northern Leaders of the Civil War,* ed. John T. Hubbell and James Geary (Westport, CT: Greenwood Press, 1994), 193–194.

18. 23 *OR*, 2:420–424.

19. Cozzens, *This Terrible Sound,* 17.

20. 23 *OR*, 1:10.

21. Ibid.

22. Ibid., 425; Thomas L. Connelly, *Autumn of Glory: The Army of the Tennessee, 1862–1865* (Baton Rouge: Louisiana State University Press, 1971), 133–134.

23. 23 *OR*, 2:518.

24. Ibid.

25. 24 *OR*, 3:461, 555–556, 597, 601–602; Shelby Foote, *The Civil War: A Narrative,* 3 vols. (New York: Random House, 1954–1978), 2:646–647.

26. 23 *OR*, 2:592.

27. Ibid.

28. Ibid.

29. Ibid., 594.

30. Cozzens, *That Terrible Sound,* 25, citing a November 8, 1879, letter by Rosecrans to McCook, in the William S. Rosecrans Papers, UCLA.

31. Ibid., 25–26.

32. The ensuing account of what Grant did, both militarily and personally, is derived, unless indicated otherwise, from Bruce Catton, *Grant Takes Command* (Boston: Little, Brown & Co., 1968), 9–31.

33. Catton, *Grant Moves South,* 477.

34. 24 *OR*, 2:528.

35. Catton, *Grant Moves South,* 488–489.

36. 24 *OR,* 3:527–528.

37. Ibid., 542.

38. Ibid., 569.

39. Ibid.

40. Ibid., 584.

41. Ibid.

42. Catton, *Grant Takes Command,* 22–25.

43. Ulysses S. Grant, *Personal Memoirs of U.S. Grant,* 2 vols. (New York: Charles L. Webster & Co., 1885–1886), 1:581.

44. Ibid., 582; 30 *OR,* 1:161–162.

12. ROSECRANS AND THOMAS AT CHICKAMAUGA

1. Unless otherwise indicated, the following account of the Battle of Chickamauga is based on Peter Cozzens, *This Terrible Sound: The Battle of Chickamauga* (Urbana: University of Illinois Press, 1992). Although at times excessively detailed— it is the ultimate Civil War battle book—on the whole, it is the most accurate and perceptive description of its subject.

2. 30 *OR,* 3:483.

3. Ibid., 511.

4. Ibid.

5. Ibid., 564.

6. William Marvel, *Burnside* (Chapel Hill: University of North Carolina Press, 1991), 272, 280–288.

7. 30 *OR,* 1:36n.

8. Ibid., 625. This appears in Wood's report, wherein he, of course, endeavors to justify his creating a division-wide gap in the Union left wing. For Wood's subsequent attempts to defend his conduct, see pages 645–648. An article by William Glenn Robertson, "Chickamauga, Day 2, Sept. 20, 1863," *Blue and Gray* (Summer 2008): 27–28, contends that Wood removed his division from the Union line at the instruction, and even behest, of McCook. This may be true, but I have chosen to follow the standard version. If mistaken, I shall be in respectable company.

9. Ibid., 141.

10. Ibid., 140.

11. E. B. Long, *The Civil War Day by Day: An Almanac, 1861–1865* (Garden City, NY: Doubleday & Co., 1971), 412.

12. 30 *OR,* 1:142–143.

13. Ibid., 192–193.

14. Ibid., 144–145.

15. Ibid., 146.

16. Bruce Catton, *Grant Takes Command* (Boston: Little, Brown & Co., 1968), 30; William Tecumseh Sherman, *Memoirs of General W. T. Sherman,* ed. Charles Royster (New York: Library of America Edition, 1990), 375–376.

17. Thomas L. Connelly, *Autumn of Glory: The Army of the Tennessee, 1862–1865* (Baton Rouge: Louisiana State University Press, 1971), 226–241.

18. Catton, *Grant Takes Command,* 33.

19. Ibid., 33–34.

20. Cozzens, *This Terrible Sound,* 522–526; Daniel, *Days of Glory,* 352–353. Daniel, no doubt, is correct in stating that "the truth will never be known" about Garfield's role in Rosecrans's removal (353). Also, it would have occurred even had Garfield played no role in it.

21. 30 *OR,* 1:161, 4:57.

22. Ibid., 1:210.

23. Ibid., 59.

24. Ibid., 101–105.

25. Daniel, *Days of Glory,* 352.

26. Cozzens, *This Terrible Sound,* 523–527.

27. Catton, *Grant Takes Command,* 34–35.

28. 30 *OR,* 4:479.

29. Catton, *Grant Takes Command,* 35.

13. GRANT AT CHATTANOOGA

1. Unless otherwise indicated, this chapter is based on Peter Cozzens, *The Shipwreck of Their Hopes: The Battles for Chattanooga* (Urbana: University of Illinois Press, 1994), and Wiley Sword, *Mountains Touched by Fire: Chattanooga Besieged, 1863* (New York: St. Martin's Press, 1995).

2. Ulysses S. Grant, *Personal Memoirs of U. S. Grant,* 2 vols. (New York: Charles L. Webster & Co., 1885–1886), 2:228. For Rosecrans's case, which is a very persuasive one, that he made prior to his removal from command of the Army of the Cumberland the necessary preparations for establishing a better and more reliable supply route, read his "The Mistakes of Grant," *North American Review* (December 1885): 594–598. In a two-part piece published in *Battle and Leaders,* Smith claims to be the sole discoverer and implementer of the Brown's Ferry route, but his claim is politely, yet very effectively, demolished by Brigadier General Henry M. Cist (*B&L,* 317–318).

3. In addition to the reasons given in the text for why Rosecrans would have employed the Brown's Ferry crossing had he remained in command of the Army of the Cumberland and had "Baldy" Smith never existed, see William M. Lamers, *The Edge of Glory: A Biography of General William S. Rosecrans, U.S.A.* (1961; paperback reprint, Baton Rouge: Louisiana State University Press, 1999), 390–399, and the sources cited therein, in particular Philip H. Sheridan, *Personal Memoirs of P. H. Sheridan* (New York: Charles L. Webster & Co., 1888), 1:298–302. Sheridan, to put it mildly, did not possess an animus against Grant.

4. Larry J. Daniel, *Days of Glory: The Army of the Cumberland, 1861–1865* (Baton Rouge: Louisiana State University Press, 2004), 374, 384, states that Thomas had a "passive-aggressive" attitude toward Grant. Being unsure as to what this means, I think it better to state merely that Thomas disliked Grant for removing Rosecrans from command of the Army of the Cumberland and that Grant disliked and distrusted Thomas for having taken titular command of the Army of the Tennessee during Halleck's mile-a-day march to Corinth, and then for obviously resenting

Grant's removing Rosecrans from command of the Army of the Cumberland. More is presented about the less-than-friendly relationship between Grant and Thomas in chapter 17.

5. For a full account of the conflict between Bragg and his generals, see Thomas L. Connelly, *Autumn of Glory: The Army of the Tennessee, 1862–1865* (Baton Rouge: Louisiana State University Press, 1971), 235–257. Although Bragg still disliked Breckinridge for his alleged (by Bragg) failure to make a determined attack on the Federals during the second day of battle at Stones River, Breckinridge had not joined with most of the other generals of the Army of the Tennessee in calling for Bragg's removal. Besides, since Breckinridge, who had been vice president of the United States (1857–1861) and the Southern Democrat candidate for president of the United States in 1860, was the acknowledged leader of prosecessionist Kentuckians and on friendly terms with Jefferson Davis, it would have been impolitic for Bragg to do so. However, he blamed Breckinridge for the fiasco on Missionary Ridge and tried to have him relieved of command, only to be relieved himself.

6. 31 *OR*, 2:81–85, 88.

14. WHILE GRANT FAILS TO DEFEAT LEE, SHERMAN INVADES GEORGIA

1. 31 *OR*, 2:25.

2. *PUSG*, 9:477.

3. John F. Marszalek, *Commander of All Lincoln's Armies: A Life of General Henry W. Halleck* (Cambridge: Harvard University Press, 2004), 244–245.

4. 31 *OR*, 3:349–350; William Tecumseh Sherman, *Memoirs of General W. T. Sherman,* ed. Charles Royster (New York: Library of America Edition, 1990), 1:395. The turkeys for the banquet were taken from Knoxville civilians; also, Burnside and his staff were on short rations.

5. Brooks D. Simpson, *Ulysses S. Grant: Triumph over Adversity, 1822–1865* (New York: Houghton Mifflin Co., 2000), 245.

6. Ibid., 261–281.

7. Bruce Catton, *Grant Takes Command* (Boston: Little, Brown & Co., 1968), 89–90, 165.

8. Albert Castel, *Decision in the West: The Atlanta Campaign of 1864* (Lawrence: University Press of Kansas, 1992), 43–55. My brief account of Sherman's Meridian Campaign is fully documented in this work.

9. Richard B. Irwin, "The Red River Campaign," *B&L,* 4:345–446.

10. Catton, *Grant Takes Command,* 261–264.

11. Ulysses S. Grant, *Personal Memoirs of U. S. Grant,* 2 vols. (New York: Charles L. Webster & Co., 1885–1886), 2:117.

12. Simpson, *Grant,* 263–265; Irwin, "Red River Campaign," *B&L,* 4:352–362.

13. Simpson, *Grant,* 250–253, 267–270.

14. James M. McPherson, *Battle Cry of Freedom: The Civil War Era* (New York: Oxford University Press, 1988), 722–723.

15. For the Wilderness, the best account is Gordon C. Rhea, *The Battle of the Wilderness, May 5–6, 1864* (Baton Rouge: Louisiana State University Press, 1994).

16. Simpson, *Grant*, 297–298.

17. For Spotsylvania, see Gordon C. Rhea, *The Battles for Spotsylvania Court House and the Road to Yellow Tavern, May 7–12, 1864* (Baton Rouge: Louisiana State University Press, 1997).

18. Simpson, *Grant*, 313–315.

19. Ibid., 316–324.

20. E. B. Long with Barbara Long, *The Civil War Day by Day: An Almanac, 1861–1865* (Garden City, NY: Doubleday, 1971), 515; see Gordon C. Rhea, *Cold Harbor: Grant and Lee, May 26–June 3, 1864* (Baton Rouge: Louisiana State University Press, 2002).

21. Catton, *Grant Takes Command*, 223.

22. Unless otherwise indicated, the following account of the Atlanta Campaign is based on Castel, *Decision in the West*.

23. Ibid., 61.

24. Sherman to Ellen E. Sherman, May 22, 1864, Brooks D. Simpson and Jean V. Berlin, eds., *Sherman's Civil War: Selected Correspondence of William T. Sherman, 1860–1865* (Chapel Hill: University of North Carolina Press, 1999), 639.

25. Castel, *Decision in the West*, 275.

26. Sherman to Grant, June 18, 1864, *Sherman's Civil War*, 654–655; Castel, *Decision in the West*, 320.

27. Castel, *Decision in the West*, 317–319. By "abatised," Thomas was referring to the lines of sharpened wood stakes that by 1864 both armies routinely planted in front of their entrenchments or fortifications. They served the same purpose as today's barbwire.

15. GRANT REMAINS STYMIED, SHERMAN TAKES ATLANTA

1. Unless otherwise indicated, this chapter is based on Albert Castel, *Decision in the West: The Atlanta Campaign of 1864* (Lawrence: University Press of Kansas, 1992), 339–539.

2. Brooks D. Simpson, *Ulysses S. Grant: Triumph over Adversity, 1822–1865* (New York: Houghton Mifflin Co., 2000), 349–359. For William Smith's caustic postwar comments on Grant, see William M. Lamers, *The Edge of Glory: A Biography of General William S. Rosecrans, U.S.A.* (1961; paperback reprint, Baton Rouge: Louisiana State University Press, 1999), 399.

3. Simpson, *Grant*, 346–349, 359–360.

4. Ibid., 360–367, which covers the events leading up to the Crater.

5. Grant to Halleck, August 1, 1864, in John Y. Simon, ed., *The Papers of Ulysses S. Grant*, 31 vols. (Carbondale: Southern Illinois University Press, 1967–2009), 11:361–362.

6. Larry J. Daniel, *Days of Glory: The Army of the Cumberland, 1861–1865* (Baton Rouge: Louisiana State University Press, 2004), 414.

7. David Herbert Donald, *Lincoln* (New York: Simon & Schuster, 1995), 529.

8. I direct those readers curious enough or dedicated enough to learn the details to consult Castel, *Decision in the West*, 485–547.

9. Sherman to Halleck, September 3, 1864, Brooks D. Simpson and Jean V. Berlin, eds., *Sherman's Civil War: Selected Correspondence of William T. Sherman, 1860–1865* (Chapel Hill: University of North Carolina Press, 1999), 696.

10. Castel, *Decision in the West,* 508.

11. Ibid., 479.

16. SHERIDAN IN THE SHENANDOAH

1. Ulysses S. Grant, *Personal Memoirs of U. S. Grant,* 2 vols. (New York: Charles L. Webster & Co., 1885–1886), 2:132; John D. Imboden, "The Battle of New Market, Va., May 15th, 1864," *B&L,* 4:481–486; Franz Sigel, "Sigel in the Shenandoah Valley in 1864," *B&L,* 4:487–492.

2. Brooks D. Simpson, *Ulysses S. Grant: Triumph over Adversity, 1822–1865* (New York: Houghton Mifflin Co., 2000), 314.

3. For Hunter's campaign and Early's invasion, see Frank E. Vandiver, *Jubal's Raid: General Early's Famous Attack on Washington in 1864* (1960; reprint, Lincoln: University of Nebraska Press, 1988); Jubal A. Early, "March to Washington in 1864," *B&L,* 4:493–499.

4. Simpson, *Grant,* 367–369.

5. Ibid., 372–373.

6. What follows is based largely on Wesley Merritt, "Sheridan in the Shenandoah Valley," *B&L,* 4:522–532; Roy Morris Jr., *Sheridan: The Life and Wars of General Phil Sheridan* (New York: Crown Publishers, 1992), 149–221; and Philip H. Sheridan, *Personal Memoirs of P. H. Sheridan* (New York: Charles L. Webster & Co., 1888), 1:344–500.

7. Sheridan, *Memoirs,* 1:486.

8. *PUSG,* 12:178; John D. Stevenson to Stanton, September 20, 1864, quoting Sheridan to Stevenson, same date.

9. Ibid., 12:268–269; Sheridan to Grant, October 1, 1864.

10. Sheridan, *Memoirs,* 2:63.

11. Ibid., 2:64–68.

12. Morris, *Sheridan,* 213–214.

13. James F. Rusling, *Men and Things I Saw in Civil War Days* (New York: Eaton and Mains, 1899), 384.

17. SHERMAN MARCHES TO THE SEA, SCHOFIELD REPULSES HOOD, AND THOMAS VANQUISHES HOOD AT NASHVILLE

1. Sherman to Grant, November 6, 1864 (first quotation), October 9, 1864 (second quotation), Brooks D. Simpson and Jean V. Berlin, *Sherman's Civil War: Selected Correspondence of William T. Sherman, 1860–1865* (Chapel Hill: University of North Carolina Press, 1999), 751, 731.

2. Brooks D. Simpson, *Ulysses S. Grant: Triumph over Adversity, 1822–1865* (New York: Houghton Mifflin Co., 2000), 382–384, 390–391.

3. For the entire campaign, see Wiley Sword, *The Confederacy's Last Hurrah: Spring Hill, Franklin, and Nashville* (Lawrence: University Press of Kansas, 1993).

4. For Schofield, see James L. McDonough, *Schofield: Union General in the Civil War and Reconstruction* (Tallahassee: Florida State University Press, 1972), and Donald B. Connelly, *John M. Schofield and the Politics of Generalship* (Chapel Hill: University of North Carolina Press, 2006), as well as John M. Schofield, *Forty-Six Years in the Army* (New York: Century Co., 1897).

5. On Franklin, in addition to Sword, see James L. McDonough and Thomas L. Connelly, *Five Tragic Hours: The Battle for Franklin* (Knoxville: University of Tennessee Press, 1983).

6. Sword, *The Confederacy's Last Hurrah*, 273, 280–281.

7. Stanton to Grant, December 2, 1864, *PUSG*, 13:49–50.

8. Stanton to Grant, December 7, 1864, *PUSG*, 13:79; Christopher J. Einolf, *George Thomas: Virginian for the Union* (Norman: University of Oklahoma Press, 2007), 264–265.

9. Grant to Thomas, December 9, 1864, *PUSG*, 13:96; Einolf, *Thomas*, 265.

10. Einolf, *Thomas*, 266.

11. Ibid., 267; Simpson, *Grant*, 398–399.

12. For Nashville, in addition to Sword, see Stanley F. Horn, *The Decisive Battle of Nashville* (Baton Rouge: Louisiana State University Press, 1956).

13. Grant to Thomas, December 15, 1864, *PUSG*, 13:124; Einolf, *Thomas*, 267, 282.

14. Grant to Sherman, January 21, 1865, *PUSG*, 13:291.

15. As for Sherman's March to the Sea, I can do no better and, I hope, no worse, than to cite Albert Castel, *Decision in the West: The Atlanta Campaign of 1864* (Lawrence: University Press of Kansas, 1992), 533–555, and Albert Castel, "Liddell Hart's Sherman: Propaganda as History," *Journal of Military History* (April 2003): 420–425.

16. Sherman to Lincoln, December 2, 1865, Simpson and Berlin, *Sherman's Civil War*, 772.

18. DEATH BLOWS

1. Brooks D. Simpson, *Ulysses S. Grant: Triumph over Adversity, 1822–1865* (New York: Houghton Mifflin Co., 2000), 417–419, covers Sherman's visit to City Point and the meeting between Lincoln, Grant, and Sherman aboard the *River Queen*.

2. George R. Agassiz, ed., *Meade's Headquarters, 1863–1865: Letters of Colonel Theodore Lyman from the Wilderness to Appomattox* (Boston: Atlantic Monthly Press, 1922), 327.

3. Roy Morris Jr., *Sheridan: The Life and Wars of General Phil Sheridan* (New York: Crown Publishers, 1992), 241–242.

4. Ibid., 244.

5. Horace Porter, "Five Forks and the Pursuit of Lee," *B&L*, 4:708–714.

6. See Joshua L. Chamberlain, *The Passing of the Armies* (New York: G. P. Putnam, 1915); Bruce Catton, *A Stillness at Appomattox* (Garden City, NY: Doubleday, 1954), 346–358.

7. For the Appomattox Campaign, see Catton, *Stillness at Appomattox*, 363–380; Burke Davis, *To Appomattox: Nine April Days, 1865* (New York: Rinehart

& Co., 1959); Chris M. Calkins, *The Appomattox Campaign, March 29–April 9, 1865* (Conshohocken, PA: Combined Books, 1997); and William Marvel, *Lee's Last Retreat: The Flight to Appomattox* (Chapel Hill: University of North Carolina Press, 2002).

8. Morris, *Sheridan*, 254.

9. Ibid.; Simpson, *Grant*, 429–430.

10. Simpson, *Grant*, 430–431.

11. Ibid., 432–437, for the events of April 9.

12. David Herbert Donald, *Lincoln* (New York: Simon & Schuster, 1995), 592; John T. Morse, ed., *Diary of Gideon Welles*, 3 vols. (New York: Houghton Mifflin, 1911), 2:282–283. Howard K. Beale's edition of Welles's diary revealed the extent to which the navy secretary edited and altered his accounts.

13. See Brooks D. Simpson, *Let Us Have Peace: Ulysses S. Grant and the Politics of War and Reconstruction, 1861–1868* (Chapel Hill: University of North Carolina Press, 1991), 95–97.

14. Sherman to Grant, April 15, 1865, in Brooks D. Simpson and Jean V. Berlin, *Sherman's Civil War: Selected Correspondence of William T. Sherman, 1860–1865* (Chapel Hill: University of North Carolina Press, 1999), 862.

15. Stanton to Grant, March 3, 1865, *PUSG*, 14:91.

16. John F. Marszalek, *Commander of All Lincoln's Armies: A Life of General Henry W. Halleck* (Cambridge: Harvard University Press, 2004), 223.

17. Sherman to John A. Rawlins, April 29, 1865, Simpson and Berlin, *Sherman's Civil War*, 884–885.

18. Sherman to Halleck, May 7, 1865, Simpson and Berlin, *Sherman's Civil War*, 892; Marszalek, *Commander of All of Lincoln's Armies*, 225.

19. Lloyd Lewis, *Sherman: Fighting Prophet* (New York: Harcourt, Brace, 1932), 577.

INDEX